# COMMENTARIES

ON

# THE EPISTLES TO TIMOTHY, TITUS, AND PHILEMON

# COMMENTARIES

ON

## THE EPISTLES TO

## TIMOTHY, TITUS, AND PHILEMON

BY JOHN CALVIN

TRANSLATED FROM THE ORIGINAL LATIN,
BY THE REV. WILLIAM PRINGLE

**BAKER BOOK HOUSE**
Grand Rapids, Michigan

Wipf and Stock Publishers
199 W 8th Ave, Suite 3
Eugene, OR 97401

Commentaries on the Epistles to Timothy, Titus, and Philemon
By Calvin, John and Pringle, William
Softcover ISBN-13: 979-8-3852-1660-4
Hardcover ISBN-13: 979-8-3852-1661-1
eBook ISBN-13: 979-8-3852-1662-8
Publication date 2/13/2024
Previously published by Baker Book House, 2005

This edition is a scanned facsimile of the original edition published in 2005.

# CONTENTS.

| | PAGE |
|---|---|
| TRANSLATOR'S PREFACE, | vii |
| THE AUTHOR'S DEDICATION TO THE DUKE OF SOMERSET, | ix |
| THE ARGUMENT ON THE FIRST EPISTLE TO TIMOTHY, | 13 |
| COMMENTARIES ON THE FIRST EPISTLE TO TIMOTHY, | 19 |
| THE ARGUMENT ON THE SECOND EPISTLE TO TIMOTHY, | 179 |
| COMMENTARIES ON THE SECOND EPISTLE TO TIMOTHY, | 182 |
| DEDICATION TO WILLIAM FAREL AND PETER VIRET, | 275 |
| THE ARGUMENT ON THE EPISTLE TO TITUS, | 277 |
| COMMENTARIES ON THE EPISTLE TO TITUS, | 279 |
| COMMENTARIES ON THE EPISTLE TO PHILEMON, | 347 |
| TRANSLATION OF CALVIN'S VERSION OF THE EPISTLES TO TIMOTHY, TITUS, AND PHILEMON, | 363 |
| TABLE I. OF PASSAGES OF SCRIPTURE QUOTED AND ILLUSTRATED, | 385 |
| TABLE II. OF GREEK WORDS, | 389 |
| INDEX, | 391 |

# TRANSLATOR'S PREFACE.

It may be natural to inquire why the Epistles to Timothy and Titus have been less copiously illustrated by popular Commentaries than the other writings of the Apostle Paul. The reason probably is, that they are addressed chiefly to office-bearers, and not to private members of the Church; though they abound largely in those doctrinal statements and practical instructions which every Christian ought carefully to study.

While fewer expositors than might have been desired have devoted their labours to this portion of the word of God, the leading subject of it has been ably handled in a different form. Not to mention the early Fathers, it is sufficient to name "The Pastoral Care," "The Reformed Pastor," and other kindred works, which have taken their rank among the standard volumes of Christian Theology. Besides elaborate treatises, extending over the whole field of ministerial labour, detached parts of it have been sometimes selected for separate illustration. Of every collection of books fitted to make " the man of God perfect, thoroughly prepared for every good work,"[1] a goodly portion relates to the duties of the pastorate. It has been of unspeakable importance to the interests of religion, and ought to be recorded to the praise of divine grace, that the valuable instructions on this subject to which readers have access derive additional weight from the holy lives and devoted zeal of their authors, who have only inculcated on others what they had faithfully practised. To all whose views are directed to the sacred office, or who have already been invested with it, the perusal of such books must be exceedingly advantageous.

Yet here, as in everything else, let us appeal " to the law

[1] 2 Tim. iii. 17.

and to the testimony."[1] The foundation of every code of rules for guiding the ministers of Christ must be sought, not in the judgments of uninspired men, however able and judicious, but in the Holy Scriptures, and chiefly in the Epistles to Timothy and Titus, the accurate interpretation of which is therefore unspeakably valuable. CALVIN has examined them with his usual skill, and will be heard with profound attention. His candour appears to more than ordinary advantage. Never does he press the words of the Holy Spirit beyond what appears to him to be their natural meaning, or depart from the rigid discharge of his task as an expositor for the sake of giving undue prominence to his peculiar views. On this point it may be sufficient to refer to his remarks on the authority which some ministers of the gospel appear to have exercised over others, as a specimen of his unshaken determination to adhere to the sacred records, and of his utter indifference to any use that might be made of such statements by those whose views of church-government differed from his own. Nowhere is his sterling honesty more conspicuous.

The notes to the present volume are enriched by numerous extracts[2] from a rare work—the Author's Sermons on the two Epistles to Timothy.[3] But for the strong and general desire that posterity should listen to this great preacher, those Sermons would never have seen the light. They were written down, as they flowed from his lips, in the same manner as the extemporaneous Latin expositions of which some account has been given elsewhere.[4] While they are Expository Discourses, leaving no part of the two Epistles unexplored, they are addressed to the great body of the Christian people, and are distinguished by those homely and striking appeals, and that marvellous felicity of language, which even his biographer Audin reluctantly ascribes to him.

[1] Isa. viii. 20.     [2] Those Extracts are marked [*Fr. Scr.*]
[3] "Sermons de Jean Calvin sur les deux Epistres de Sainct Paul a Timothee, recueillis par l'escrivain ordinaire pour le bien et l'edification de l'Eglise du Seigneur."
[4] Commentary on the Twelve Minor Prophets, vol. i. p. xxiv. Com. on Isaiah, vol. i. p. vii.

TO THE MOST NOBLE AND TRULY CHRISTIAN PRINCE,

# EDWARD, DUKE OF SOMERSET,

EARL OF HERTFORD, &c., PROTECTOR OF ENGLAND AND IRELAND,

AND ROYAL TUTOR,

## JOHN CALVIN

OFFERS HIS SALUTATIONS.

THE brilliant reputation, most noble Prince, not only of your other virtues, altogether heroic, but especially of your distinguished piety,[1] produces so warm a love of you in the hearts of all good men, even of those to whom you are unknown by face, that you must unavoidably be regarded with extraordinary affection and reverence by all right-minded persons in the kingdom of England, on whom hath been bestowed the privilege, not only of beholding with their eyes those benefits which are admired by others who only hear of them, but likewise of reaping all the advantage which a most excellent governor can confer on the whole body of the people, and on every one of its members. Nor is there any reason why the praises bestowed on you should be suspected of falsehood, as if they proceeded from flatterers; for a clear proof of them is to be found in your actions.

When a pupil belongs to private life, and his wealth is moderate, the work of a tutor is attended by difficulty; but you hold the office of tutor, not of the King only, but of a very large kingdom, and you discharge that office with such wisdom and skill, that all are astonished at your success. That your virtue might not shine merely amidst the laws,

---

[1] " Et singulierement de ce desir Chrestien que vous avez d'avancer la vraye religion." " And especially of that Christian desire which you have to promote the true religion."

and in a peaceful state of the commonwealth, God has exhibited it to view in war also, which has hitherto been conducted by you with not less prosperity and valour.

Yet the great and numerous difficulties which every person readily perceived that you had experienced did not hinder you from making the restoration of religion your principal object. That consideration is certainly not less advantageous to the public benefit of the kingdom than it is worthy of a Prince; for then do kingdoms enjoy solid prosperity and faithful guardianship, when he, on whom they were founded, and by whom they are preserved—the Son of God himself—rules over them. Thus you could not have established more firmly the kingdom of England than by banishing idols and setting up there the pure worship of God; for the true doctrine of godliness, which had too long been crushed and buried[1] by the sacrilegious tyranny of the Roman Antichrist, cannot but be restored; and what is that but to place Christ on his throne? And this act, which in itself is excellent, is so much the more praiseworthy on account of the small number of rulers in the present day who own the subjection of their high rank to the spiritual sceptre of Christ.

It was therefore a high advantage to this illustrious King, that such a person, related to him by blood, was the guide of his youth; for, although the noble character of his mind is universally applauded, yet, in training him to habits of manly firmness, and in regulating the English Church, so long as his tender age does not permit him to discharge these duties, such an instructor was much needed. And I doubt not that even now he acknowledges that you were given to him by the peculiar kindness of God, in order that he might soon afterwards receive his affairs from your hands in excellent condition.

For my own part, neither the distance of place nor my humble rank could prevent me from congratulating you on your distinguished success in promoting the glory of Christ. And since it has pleased God to make me one of those by whose labours and exertions he has, in the present day, given

---

[1] "Opprimee et ensevelie."

to the world the doctrine of the gospel in greater purity than before, why should I not, however widely I am separated from you, express as strongly as I can my reverence for you, who have been appointed, through the extraordinary kindness of God, to be the defender and protector of that very doctrine? And since I had no other proof of it to give, I thought that, at least as an earnest of my regard, it was my duty to offer to you my Commentaries on two of Paul's Epistles. Nor have I selected at random the gift that I should offer, but, in the exercise of my judgment, have selected that which appeared to me to be the most suitable. Here Paul admonishes his beloved Timothy by what kind of doctrine he must edify the Church of God, what vices and enemies he must resist, and how many annoyances he must endure. He exhorts him to give way to no difficulties, to vanquish all dangers by courage, to restrain by authority the licentiousness of wicked men, and not to bestow gifts through eagerness to obtain their favour. In short, in these two Epistles we have the true government of the Church set before us in a lively picture.

Now, since in order to restore the English Church, which, along with almost every other part of Christendom, had been miserably corrupted by the shocking wickedness of Popery, you employ your strenuous efforts under the direction of your King, and for that purpose have many Timothys under your charge, neither they nor you can direct your holy transactions in a more profitable manner than by taking the rule here laid down by Paul for your pattern. For there is nothing in them that is not highly applicable to our times, and hardly anything that is necessary in the building of the Church that may not likewise be drawn from them. I trust that my labour will, at least, afford some assistance; but I choose that this should be known by experience rather than that I should boast of it in words. If you, most noble Prince, shall approve of it, I shall have abundant reason for congratulating myself; and your remarkable kindness does not permit me to doubt that you will take in good part that service which I now perform.

May the Lord, in whose hand are the ends of the earth,

long uphold the safety and prosperity of the kingdom of England, adorn its illustrious King with the royal spirit, bestow on him a large measure of all blessings, and grant to you grace to persevere happily in your noble course, that through you his renown may be more and more widely extended.

GENEVA, 25th *July* 1556.

# THE ARGUMENT

ON

# THE FIRST EPISTLE TO TIMOTHY.

THIS Epistle appears to me to have been written more for the sake of others than for the sake of Timothy, and that opinion will receive the assent of those who shall carefully consider the whole matter. I do not, indeed, deny that Paul intended also to teach and admonish him; but my view of the Epistle is, that it contains many things which it would have been superfluous to write, if he had had to deal with Timothy alone. He was a young man, not yet clothed with that authority which would have been sufficient for restraining the headstrong men that rose up against him. It is manifest, from the words used by Paul, that there were at that time some who were prodigiously inclined to ostentation, and for that reason would not willingly yield to any person, and who likewise burned with such ardent ambition, that they would never have ceased to disturb the Church, had not a greater than Timothy interposed. It is likewise manifest, that there were many things to be adjusted at Ephesus, and that needed the approbation of Paul, and the sanction of his name. Having therefore intended to give advice to Timothy on many subjects, he resolved at the same time to advise others under the name of Timothy.

In the *first* chapter, he attacks some ambitious persons who made their boast of discussing idle questions. It may readily be concluded that they were Jews, who, while they pretended to have zeal for the law, disregarded edification, and attended only to frivolous disputes. It is an intolerable profanation of the law of God, to draw out of it nothing that is profitable, but merely to pick up materials for talking, and to abuse the pretence of it for the purpose of burdening the Church with contemptible trifles.

Longer than enough have such corruptions prevailed in Popery; for what else was the scholastic theology than a huge chaos of empty and useless speculations? And in our own day there are many who, in order to display their acuteness in handling the word of God, allow themselves to sport with it in the same manner as if it were profane philosophy. Paul undertakes to support Timothy in the correction of this vice, and points out what is the principal instruction to be derived from the Law; that it may be evident that they who use the Law in a different manner are corrupters of it.

Next, that his authority may not be despised, after having acknowledged his unworthiness, he, at the same time, asserts in lofty terms what he became through the grace of God. At length he concludes the chapter by a solemn threatening, by means of which he both confirms Timothy in sound doctrine and a good conscience, and fills others with terror and alarm, by holding out to them the example of Hymenæus and Alexander.

In the *second* chapter, he enjoins that public prayers be offered to God for all men, and especially for princes and magistrates; and here, in passing, he likewise makes a remark on the advantage which the world derives from civil government. He then mentions the reason why we ought to pray for all men; namely, that God, by exhibiting to all the gospel and Christ the Mediator, shews that he wishes all men to be saved; and he likewise confirms this statement by his own apostleship, which was specially appointed to the Gentiles. Next, he invites all men, whatever may be their country or place of abode, to pray to God; and takes occasion for inculcating that modesty and subjection which females ought to maintain in the holy assembly.

In the *third* chapter, after having declared the excellence of the bishop's office, he delineates a true bishop, and enumerates the qualifications required in him. Next, he describes the qualifications of deacons, and of the wives both of deacons and of bishops. And in order that Timothy may be more diligent and conscientious in observing all things, he reminds him what it is to be employed in the government of " the Church, which is the house of God, and the pillar of truth." Finally, he mentions the chief and fundamental point of all heavenly doctrine—that which relates to the Son of God manifested in the flesh; in comparison of which all things else, to which he perceived that ambitious men were wholly devoted, should be reckoned of no value.

As to what follows, in the beginning of the *fourth* chapter, the false doctrines about forbidding marriage and various kinds of food, and the absurd fables which are at variance with this doctrine, are severely condemned by him. Next, he adds, that he and all good men, who hold this doctrine, have none for their adversaries but those who cannot endure that men shall place their trust in the living God. At the close of the chapter, he again fortifies Timothy by a new exhortation.

In the *fifth* chapter, after having recommended modesty and gentleness in reproofs, he reasons about widows, who at that time were admitted into the service of the Church. He enjoins that they shall not be received indiscriminately, but only those who, having been approved throughout their whole life, are arrived at sixty years of age, and have no domestic tie. Hence he passes on to the elders, and explains how they ought to conduct themselves, both in their manner of life and in the exercise of discipline. This doctrine the Apostle seals by a solemn oath, and again forbids him to admit any one heedlessly into the office of the eldership.[1] He exhorts him to drink wine, instead of water, for the preservation of his health. At the close of the chapter, he exhorts him to defer pronouncing judgment on concealed transgressions.

In the *sixth* chapter, he gives instruction concerning the duty of servants, and takes occasion to make a vehement attack on false teachers, who, by disputing about unprofitable speculations, are more eager for gain than for edification,

---

[1] " En l'estat de prestrise, c'est a dire du ministere." " Into the office of presbyters, that is, of the ministry."

and shews that covetousness is a most deadly plague. He then returns to a solemn charge similar to the former, that the exhortations which he now gives to Timothy may not be ineffectual. Lastly, after having taken a passing notice of riches, he again forbids Timothy to entangle himself with useless doctrines.

As to the ordinary Greek inscription, which states that this Epistle was written from Laodicea, I do not agree with it; for since Paul, writing to the Colossians while he was a prisoner, affirms that he had never seen the Laodiceans, those who hold the opinion, which I reject, are constrained to make two Laodiceas in Asia Minor, though only one is mentioned by historians. Besides, when Paul went into Macedonia, he left Timothy at Ephesus, as he expressly declares. He wrote this Epistle either on the road, before he arrived there, or after having returned from the journey. Now Laodicea is evidently at a greater distance from Macedonia than Ephesus is; and it is not probable that Paul, on his return, went to Laodicea, passing by Ephesus, especially since there were many reasons that urged him to visit it; and therefore I rather think that he wrote it from some other place. But this is not a matter of so much importance that I should wish to debate it with those who are of an opposite opinion. Let every person follow his own judgment. I only point out what—at least in my opinion—is more probable.

# COMMENTARIES

ON

# THE FIRST EPISTLE TO TIMOTHY.

# COMMENTARIES

ON

# THE FIRST EPISTLE TO TIMOTHY.

## CHAPTER I.

1. Paul, an apostle of Jesus Christ, by the commandment of God our Saviour, and Lord Jesus Christ, *which is* our hope;
2. Unto Timothy, *my* own son in the faith: Grace, mercy, *and* peace, from God our Father, and Jesus Christ our Lord.
3. As I besought thee to abide still at Ephesus, when I went into Macedonia, that thou mightest charge some that they teach no other doctrine;
4. Neither give heed to fables, and endless genealogies, which minister questions, rather than godly edifying, which is in faith; *so do.*

1. Paulus apostolus Iesu Christi secundum ordinationem Dei Salvatoris nostri, et Domini Iesu Christi spei nostræ:
2. Timotheo germano filio in fide, gratia, misericordia, pax a Deo Patre nostro, et Christo Iesu Domino nostro.
3. Quemadmodum rogavi te ut maneres Ephesi, quum proficiscerer in Macedoniam, volo denunties quibusdam, ne aliter doceant;
4. Neque attendant fabulis et genealogiis nunquam finiendis, quæ quæstiones præbent magis quam ædificationem Dei, quæ in fide consistit.

1. *Paul an apostle.* If he had written to Timothy alone, it would have been unnecessary to claim this designation, and to maintain it in the manner that he does. Timothy would undoubtedly have been satisfied with having merely the name; for he knew that Paul was an Apostle of Christ, and had no need of proof to convince him of it, being perfectly willing, and having been long accustomed, to acknowledge it. He has his eye, therefore, chiefly on others, who were not so ready to listen to him, or did not so easily believe his words. For the sake of such persons, that they may not treat lightly what he writes, he affirms that he is " an Apostle of Christ."

*According to the appointment of God our Saviour, and of the Lord Jesus Christ.* He confirms his apostleship by the *appointment* or command of God; for no man can make himself to be an apostle, but he whom God hath appointed is a true apostle, and worthy of the honour. Nor does he merely say, that he owes his apostleship to God the Father, but ascribes it to Christ also; and, indeed, in the government of the Church, the Father does nothing but through the Son, and therefore they both act together.

He calls God *the Saviour*, a title which he is more frequently accustomed to assign to the Son; but it belongs to the Father also, because it is he who gave the Son to us. Justly, therefore, is the glory of our salvation ascribed to him. For how comes it that we are saved? It is because the Father loved us in such a manner that he determined to redeem and save us through the Son. He calls Christ *our hope;* and this appellation is strictly applicable to him; for then do we begin to have good hope, when we look to Christ, since in him alone dwells all that on which our salvation rests.

2. *To Timothy my own son.* This commendation expresses no small praise. Paul means by it, that he owns Timothy to be a true and not a bastard son, and wishes that others should acknowledge him to be such; and he even applauds Timothy in the same manner as if he were another Paul. But how does this agree with the injunction given by Christ, (Matt. xxiii. 9,) "Call no man your father on the earth?" Or how does it agree with the declaration of the Apostle, "Though ye have many fathers according to the flesh, yet there is but One who is the Father of spirits." (1 Cor. iv. 15; Heb. xii. 9.)[1] I reply, while Paul claims for himself the appellation of father, he does it in such a manner as not to take away or diminish the smallest portion of the honour which is due to God. (Heb. xii. 9.) It is a common proverb, "That which is placed below another is not at variance with it." The name father, applied to Paul, with reference to God, belongs to this class. God alone is the

---

[1] Our author, quoting from memory, blends the two passages, not quite accurately, yet so as to convey the true meaning of both.—*Ed.*

Father of all in faith, because he regenerates us all by his word, and by the power of his Spirit, and because none but he bestows faith. But they whom he is graciously pleased to employ as his ministers for that purpose, are likewise allowed to share with him in his honour, while, at the same time, He parts with nothing that belongs to himself. Thus God, and God alone, strictly speaking, was Timothy's spiritual Father; but Paul, who was God's minister in begetting Timothy, lays claim to this title, by what may be called a subordinate right.

*Grace, mercy, peace.* So far as relates to the word *mercy*, he has departed from his ordinary custom in introducing it, moved, perhaps, by his extraordinary affection for Timothy. Besides, he does not observe the exact order; for he places first what ought to have been last, namely, the *grace* which flows from *mercy.* For the reason why God at first receives us into favour and why he loves us is, that he is merciful. But it is not unusual to mention the cause after the effect, for the sake of explanation. As to the words *grace* and *peace*, we have spoken on other occasions.

3. *As I besought thee.* Either the syntax is elliptical, or the particle ἵνα is redundant; and in both cases the meaning will be obvious.[1] First, he reminds Timothy why he was besought to remain at Ephesus. It was with great reluctance, and through hard necessity, that he parted with a companion so dearly beloved and so faithful, in order that he might laboriously hold the part of his deputy, which no other man would have been competent to fill; and, therefore, Timothy must have been powerfully excited by this consideration, not only not to throw away his time, but to conduct himself in an excellent and distinguished manner.

*I wish that thou shouldst forbid any.* Thus, by way of inference, he exhorts him to oppose the false teachers who corrupted pure doctrine. In the injunction given to Timothy, to occupy his place at Ephesus, we ought to observe the

---

[1] " The construction here is tortuous and elliptical. Πορευόμενος εἰς Μακεδονίαν must be construed between καθὼς and παρεκάλεσα, and the protasis at καθὼς is without its apodosis, οὕτως, which must be supplied. The simplest and most natural method is to understand οὕτω καὶ νῦν παρακαλῶ." —*Bloomfield.*

holy anxiety of the Apostle; for while he laboured so much to collect many churches, he did not leave the former churches destitute of a pastor. And, indeed, as an ancient writer remarks, " To keep what has been gained is not a smaller virtue than to make new acquisitions." The word *forbid* denotes power; for Paul wishes to arm him with power to restrain others.

*Not to teach differently.* The Greek word (ἑτεροδιδασκαλεῖν) which Paul employs, is a compound, and, therefore, may either be translated, " to teach differently," or after a new method, or, " to teach a different doctrine." The translation given by Erasmus, (*sectari*,) " to follow," does not satisfy me; because it might be understood to apply to the hearers. Now Paul means those who, for the sake of ambition, brought forward a new doctrine.

If we read it, " to teach differently," the meaning will be more extensive; for by this expression he will forbid Timothy to permit any new forms of teaching to be introduced, which do not agree with the true and pure doctrine which he had taught. Thus, in the Second Epistle, he recommends ὑποτύπωσις,[1] that is, a lively picture of his doctrine. (2 Tim. i. 13.) For, as the truth of God is one, so is there but one plain manner of teaching it, which is free from false ornament, and which partakes more of the majesty of the Spirit than of the parade of human eloquence. Whoever departs from that, disfigures and corrupts the doctrine itself; and, therefore, " to teach differently," must relate to the form.

If we read it, " to teach something different," it will relate to the matter. Yet it is worthy of observation, that we give the name of another doctrine not only to that which is openly at variance with the pure doctrine of the gospel, but to everything that either corrupts the pure gospel by new and borrowed inventions, or obscures it by ungodly speculations. For all the inventions of men are so many corrup-

---

[1] " Il ne recommande pas simplement a Timothee de retenir sa doctrine, mais il use d'un mot qui signifie le vray patron, ou vif portraict d'icelle." " He does not merely advise Timothy to hold by his doctrine, but employs a word which denotes the true pattern or lively portrait of it."

tions of the gospel; and they who make sport of the Scriptures, as ungodly people are accustomed to do, so as to turn Christianity into an act of display, darken the gospel. His manner of teaching, therefore, is entirely opposed to the word of God, and to that purity of doctrine in which Paul enjoins the Ephesians to continue.

4. *And not to give heed to fables.* He applies the term "fables," in my opinion, not only to contrived falsehoods, but to trifles or fooleries which have no solidity; for it is possible that something which is not false may yet be fabulous. In this sense, Suetonius speaks of fabulous history,[1] and Livy employs the word *fabulari*, "to relate fables," as denoting useless and foolish talk. And, undoubtedly, the word μῦθος, (which Paul here employs,) is equivalent to the Greek word φλυαρία, that is, "trifles." Moreover, by bringing forward one class by way of example, he has removed all doubt; for disputes about genealogies are enumerated by him amongst fables, not because everything that can be said about them is fictitious, but because it is useless and unprofitable.

This passage, therefore, may thus be explained:—"Let them not give heed to fables of that character and description to which genealogies belong." And that is actually the fabulous history of which Suetonius speaks, and which, even among grammarians, has always been justly ridiculed by persons of sound judgment; for it was impossible not to regard as ridiculous that curiosity which, neglecting useful knowledge, spent the whole life in examining the genealogy of Achilles and Ajax, and wasted its powers in reckoning up the sons of Priam. If this be not endured in childish knowledge, in which there is room for that which affords pleasure, how much more intolerable is it in heavenly wisdom?[2]

[1] "Et c'est en ceste signification que Suetone, en la vie de Tibère, dit que cest empereur là s'amusoit fort a l'histoire fabuleuse." "And it is in this sense that Suetonius, in his life of Tiberius, says that that emperor amused himself very much with fabulous history."

[2] "Here we see more clearly, that Paul did not merely condemn in this passage doctrines which are altogether false, and which contain some blasphemies, but likewise all those useless speculations which serve to turn aside believers from the pure simplicity of our Lord Jesus Christ. This is what Paul includes under the word "fables;" for he means not only deliberate

*And to genealogies that have no end.*[1] He calls them *endless*, because vain curiosity has no limit, but continually falls from labyrinth to labyrinth.

*Which produce questions.* He judges of doctrine by the fruit; for everything that does not edify ought to be rejected, although it has no other fault; and everything that is of no avail but for raising contentions, ought to be doubly condemned. And such are all the subtle questions on which ambitious men exercise their faculties. Let us, therefore, remember, that all doctrines must be tried by this rule, that those which contribute to edification may be approved, and that those which give ground for unprofitable disputes may be rejected as unworthy of the Church of God.

If this test had been applied during several centuries, although religion had been stained by many errors, at least that diabolical art of disputing, which has obtained the appellation of Scholastic Theology, would not have prevailed to so great an extent. For what does that theology contain but contentions or idle speculations, from which no advantage is derived? Accordingly, the more learned a man is in it, we ought to account him the more wretched. I am aware of the plausible excuses by which it is defended, but they will never make out that Paul has spoken falsely in condemning everything of the sort.

*Rather than the edification of God.*[2] Subtleties of this description edify in pride, and edify in vanity, but not in God. He calls it "the edification of God," either because God approves of it, or because it is agreeable to the nature of God.[3]

and manifest falsehoods, but likewise everything that is of no use; and this is implied in the word which he employs. What, then, does Paul set aside in this passage? All curious inquiries, all speculations which serve only to annoy and distress the mind, or in which there is nothing but a fair show and display, and which do not promote the salvation of those who hear them. This must be carefully remembered; for we shall afterwards see that the reason why Paul speaks of them in this manner is, that the word of God must be profitable. (2 Tim. iii. 16.) All who do not apply the word of God to good profit and advantage are despisers and falsifiers of good doctrine."—*Fr. Ser.*

[1] 'Απέραντος properly signifies interminable. Hence there is also an implicit sense of what is unprofitable. This, indeed, some, but I think injudiciously, make the principal one."—*Bloomfield.*

[2] " Rather than godly edifying."—*Eng. Tr.*

[3] " This word *edify* is sufficiently common in the Holy Scripture, but is

*Which consist in faith.* He next shews that this edification consists in faith; and by this term he does not exclude the love of our neighbour, or the fear of God, or repentance; for what are all these but fruits of "faith," which always produces the fear of God? Knowing that all the worship of God is founded on faith alone, he therefore reckoned it enough to mention "faith," on which all the rest depend.

5. Now, the end of the commandment is charity, out of a pure heart, and *of* a good conscience, and *of* faith unfeigned:
6. From which some having swerved, have turned aside unto vain jangling;
7. Desiring to be teachers of the law; understanding neither what they say, nor whereof they affirm.
8. But we know that the law *is* good, if a man use it lawfully;
9. Knowing this, that the law is not made for a righteous man, but for the lawless and disobedient, for the ungodly and for sinners, for unholy and profane, for murderers of fathers and murderers of mothers, for man-slayers,
10. For whoremongers, for them that defile themselves with man-

5. Porro finis præcepti est charitas, ex puro corde, et conscientia bona, et fide non simulata.
6. A quibus postquam nonnulli aberrarunt, deflexerunt ad vaniloquium,
7. Volentes esse legis doctores, non intelligentes quæ loquuntur, neque de quibus affirmant.
8. Scimus autem quòd lex bona sit, si quis ea legitimè utatur:
9. Sciens illud, quòd justo non sit lex posita, sed injustis et inobsequentibus, impiis et peccatoribus, irreligiosis et profanis, parricidis et matricidis, homicidis,

10. Scortatoribus, masculorum concubitoribus, plagiariis, mendaci-

not understood by all. In order to understand it aright, let us observe, that it is a comparison which is set before us; for we ought to be temples of God, because he wishes to dwell in us. Those who profit in a right manner, that is, in faith, in the fear of God, in holiness of life, are said to be edified; that is, God builds them to be his temples, and wishes to dwell in them; and also that we should unitedly form a temple of God; for each of us is a stone of that temple. Thus, when each of us shall be well instructed in his duty, and when we shall all be united in holy brotherhood, then shall we be edified in God. It is true, that men may sometimes be edified in pride: as we see that they who take delight in their vain imaginations, and who spread their wings, and swell themselves out like toads, think that they are well edified. Alas! what a poor building is this! But Paul expressly says, that we must be edified according to God. By which he shews, that when we shall be instructed to serve God, to render to him pure worship, to place all our confidence in him, this is the edification at which we must aim; and every doctrine that has that tendency is good and holy, and ought to be received; but all that is opposed to it must be rejected without farther dispute: it is unnecessary to make any longer inquiry. And why must this or that be rejected? Because it does not contribute to the edification of God."—*Fr. Ser.*

kind, for men-stealers, for liars, for perjured persons, and if there be any other thing that is contrary to sound doctrine ;

11. According to the glorious gospel of the blessed God, which was committed to my trust.

bus, perjuris, et si quid aliud est, quod sanæ doctrinæ adversatur;

11. Secundum Evangelium gloriæ beati Dei, quod concreditum est mihi.

Those unprincipled men with whom Timothy had to deal boasted of having the law on their side, in consequence of which Paul anticipates, and shews that the law not only gave them no support, but was even opposed to them, and that it agreed perfectly with the gospel which he had taught. The defence set up by them was not unlike that which is pleaded by those who, in the present day, subject the word of God to torture. They tell us that we aim at nothing else than to destroy sacred theology, as if they alone nourished it in their bosom. They spoke of the law in such a manner as to exhibit Paul in an odious light. And what is his reply? In order to scatter those clouds of smoke,[1] he comes frankly forward, by way of anticipation, and proves that his doctrine is in perfect harmony with the law, and that the law is utterly abused by those who employ it for any other purpose. In like manner, when we now define what is meant by true theology, it is clearly evident that we desire the restoration of that which had been wretchedly torn and disfigured by those triflers who, puffed up by the empty title of theologians, are acquainted with nothing but vapid and unmeaning trifles. *Commandment* is here put for the law, by taking a part for the whole.

*Love out of a pure heart.* If the law must be directed to this object, that we may be instructed in *love, which proceeds from faith and a good conscience,* it follows, on the other hand, that they who turn the teaching of it into curious questions are wicked expounders of the law. Besides, it is of no great importance whether the word *love* be regarded in this passage as relating to both tables of the law, or only to the second table. We are commanded to love God with our whole heart, and our neighbours as ourselves ; but when

[1] "Pour demesler tout ce qu'ils entassoyent pour esblouir les yeux des simples." "In order to sweep away all that they heaped up for the purpose of blinding the eyes of plain people."

love is spoken of in Scripture, it is more frequently limited to the second part. On the present occasion I should not hesitate to understand by it the love both of God and of our neighbour, if Paul had employed the word *love* alone ; but when he adds, "faith, and a good conscience, and a pure heart," the interpretation which I am now to give will not be at variance with his intention, and will agree well with the scope of the passage. The sum of the law is this, that we may worship God with true faith and a pure conscience, and that we may love one another. Whosoever turns aside from this corrupts the law of God by twisting it to a different purpose.

But here arises a doubt, that Paul appears to prefer "love" to "faith." I reply, they who are of that opinion reason in an excessively childish manner ; for, if love is first mentioned, it does not therefore hold the first rank of honour, since Paul shews also that it springs from faith. Now the cause undoubtedly goes before its effect. And if we carefully weigh the whole context, what Paul says is of the same import as if he had said, "The law was given to us for this purpose, that it might instruct us in faith, which is the mother of a good conscience and of love." Thus we must begin with faith, and not with love.

"A pure heart" and "a good conscience" do not greatly differ from each other. Both proceed from faith ; for, as to a pure heart, it is said that " God purifieth hearts by faith." (Acts xv. 9.) As to a good conscience, Peter declares that it is founded on the resurrection of Christ. (1 Pet. iii. 21.) From this passage we also learn that there is no true love where there is not fear of God and uprightness of conscience.

Nor is it unworthy of observation that to each of them he adds an epithet ;[1] for, as nothing is more common, so nothing is more easy, than to boast of faith and a good conscience. But how few are there who prove by their actions that they are free from all hypocrisy ! Especially it is proper to observe the epithet which he bestows on " faith," when he calls it *faith unfeigned ;* by which he means that

[1] " Il donne a chacune vertu son epithet. " He gives to each virtue its epithet."

the profession of it is insincere, when we do not perceive a good conscience, and when love is not manifested. Now since the salvation of men rests on faith, and since the perfect worship of God rests on faith and a good conscience and love, we need not wonder if Paul makes the sum of the law to consist of them.

6. *From which some having gone astray.* He continues to pursue the metaphor of an object or end; for the verb ἀστοχεῖν, the participle of which is here given, signifies to err or go aside from a mark.[1]

*Have turned aside to idle talking.* This is a remarkable passage, in which he condemns for "idle talking"[2] all the doctrines which do not aim at this single end, and at the same time points out that the views and thoughts of all who aim at any other object vanish away. It is, indeed, possible that useless trifles may be regarded by many persons with admiration; but the statement of Paul remains unshaken, that everything that does not edify in godliness is ματαιολογία,[3] "idle talking." We ought, therefore, to take the greatest possible care not to seek anything in the holy and sacred word of God but solid edification, lest otherwise he inflict on us severe punishment for abusing it.

7. *Wishing to be teachers of the law.* He does not reprove

---

[1] "Here he makes use of a metaphor taken from those who shoot with a bow; for they have their mark at which they aim, and do not shoot carelessly, or at random. Thus Paul shews that God, by giving us the law, has determined to give us a sure road, that we may not be liable to wander like vagabonds. And, indeed, it is not without reason that Moses exhorteth the people, 'This is the way, walk ye in it,' as if he had said that men do not know where they are, till God has declared to them his will; but then they have an infallible rule.—Let us carefully observe that God intends to address us in such a manner that it shall not be possible for us to go astray, provided that we take him for our guide, seeing that he is ready and willing to perform that office, when we do not refuse such a favour. This is what Paul meant by this metaphor; as we are told that all who have it not as their object to rely on the grace of God, in order that they may call on God as their Father, and may expect salvation from him, and who do not walk with a good conscience, and with a pure heart toward their neighbourhood, are like persons who have wandered and gone astray."—*Fr. Ser.*

[2] "De vanité et mesonge." "For vanity and falsehood."

[3] "Ματαιολογία has reference to the interminable and unprofitable ζητήσεις mentioned at verse 4, and called κενοφωνίας at vi. 20; this vain and empty talk being, by implication, opposed to the performance of substantial duties."—*Bloomfield.*

those who openly attack the instruction of the law, but those who boast of belonging to the rank of teachers of it. He affirms that such persons have no understanding, because they harass their faculties to no purpose by curious questions. And, at the same time, he rebukes their pride by adding,—

*Of what things they affirm;* for none will be found more bold in pronouncing rashly on matters unknown to them than the teachers of such fables. We see in the present day with what pride and haughtiness the schools of the Sorbonne pronounce their authoritative decisions. And on what subjects? On those which are altogether hidden from the minds of men—which no word of Scripture, and no revelation has ever made known to us. With greater boldness do they affirm their purgatory[1] than the resurrection of the dead. As to their contrivances about the intercession of the saints, if we do not hold them to be an undoubted oracle, they cry out that the whole of religion is overturned. What shall I say as to their vast labyrinths about the hierarchies of heaven, relationships, and similar contrivances? It is a matter that has no end. The Apostle declares that in all these is fulfilled what is said in a well-known ancient proverb, "Ignorance is rash;" as he says that, "puffed up by their carnal mind, they intrude into things which they know not." (Col. ii. 18.)

8. *Now we know that the law is good.* He again anticipates the calumny with which they loaded him; for, when-

---

[1] "And in Popery what are the articles that shall be held as most certain? What angel, or what devil, revealed to them that there is a purgatory? They have fabricated it out of their own brain; and, after having attempted to produce some passages of the Holy Scriptures, they have at length become bewildered, so that they have no defence of their purgatory, but its antiquity. 'There it is! It has been always held.' Such is the foundation of faith, according to the learned Papists. And then we must not call in question that we ought to apply to the departed saints as our advocates and intercessors. To go to God without having as our guide St. Michael, or the Virgin Mary, or some other saint whom the Pope shall have inserted in his calendar for the occasion, would be of no avail. And why? On what ground? Will they find in all the Holy Scriptures a single word, a single syllable, to shew that creatures, that is, deceased persons, intercede for us? For in this world we ought to pray for one another, and that is a mutual obligation; but as to deceased persons, not a word is said about them."—*Fr. Ser.*

ever he resisted their empty display, they seized on this shield for their defence: "What then? Do you wish to have the law buried, and blotted out of the remembrance of men?" In order to repel this calumny, Paul acknowledges that "the law is good," but contends that we are required to make a lawful use of it. Here he argues from the use of cognate terms; for the word *lawful* (legitimus) is derived from the word *law* (lex). But he goes still further, and shews that the law agrees excellently with the doctrine which it teaches; and he even directs it against them.

9. *That the law is not made for a righteous man.* The apostle did not intend to argue about the whole office of the law, but views it in reference to men. It frequently happens that they who wish to be regarded as the greatest zealots for the law, give evidence by their whole life that they are the greatest despisers of it. A remarkable and striking instance of this is found in those who maintain the righteousness of works and defend free-will. They have continually in their mouth these words, "Perfect holiness, merits, satisfactions;" but their whole life cries out against them, that they are outrageously wicked and ungodly, that they provoke in every possible way the wrath of God, and fearlessly set his judgment at nought. They extol in lofty terms the free choice of good and evil; but they openly shew, by their actions, that they are the slaves of Satan, and are most firmly held by him in the chains of slavery.

Having such adversaries, in order to restrain their haughty insolence, Paul remonstrates that the law is, as it were, the sword of God to slay them; and that neither he nor any like him have reason for viewing the law with dread or aversion; for it is not opposed to righteous persons, that is, to the godly and to those who willingly obey God. I am well aware that some learned men draw an ingenious sense out of these words; as if Paul were treating theologically about the nature of "the law." They argue that the law has nothing to do with the sons of God, who have been regenerated by the Spirit; because it was not given for righteous persons. But the connexion in which these words occur shuts me up to the necessity of giving a more simple interpretation to this statement. He takes for granted the well-known sentiment, that " from bad manners have sprung good laws," and maintains that the law of God was given in order to restrain the licentiousness of wicked men ; because they who are good of their own accord do not need the authoritative injunction of the law.

A question now arises, " Is there any mortal man who does not belong to this class ?" I reply, in this passage Paul gives the appellation " righteous" to those who are not absolutely perfect, (for no such person will be found,) but who, with the strongest desire of their heart, aim at what is good ; so that godly desire is to them a kind of voluntary law, without any motive or restraint from another quarter. He therefore wished to repress the impudence of adversaries, who armed themselves with the name of "the law" against godly men, whose whole life exhibits the actual rule of the law, since they had very great need of the law, and yet did not care much about it; which is more clearly expressed by the opposite clause. If there be any who refuse to admit that Paul brings an implied or indirect charge against his adversaries as guilty of those wicked acts which he enumerates, still it will be acknowledged to be a simple repelling of the slander ; and if they were animated by a sincere and unfeigned zeal for the law, they ought rather to have made use of their armour for carrying on war with offences and crimes, instead of employing it as a pretext for their own ambition and silly talking.

*For the unrighteous and disobedient.* Instead of " unrighteous," it would have been better if translators had made use of the word "lawless ;" for the Greek word is ἀνόμους, which does not differ much from the second word in the clause, " disobedient." By *sinners* he means wicked persons, or those who lead a base and immoral life.

*For the ungodly and profane.* These words might have been fitly rendered " profane and impure ;" but I did not wish to be fastidious in matters of little importance.

10. *For robbers.* The Latin word *plagium* was employed by ancient writers to denote the carrying off or enticing the slave of another man, or the false sale of a freeman. Those

who wish to obtain more full information on this subject may consult authors on the civil law, and especially on the Flavian Law.

Here Paul glances at several classes, which include briefly every kind of transgressions. The root is obstinacy and rebellion; which he describes by the first two words. *Ungodly and sinners* appear to denote transgressors of the first and second table. To these he adds the profane and impure, or those who lead a base and dissolute life. There being chiefly three ways in which men injure their neighbours, namely, violence, dishonesty, and lust, he reproves successively those three ways, as may be easily seen. First, he speaks of violence as manifested by man-slayers and murderers of parents; secondly, he describes shameful uncleanness; and thirdly, he comes down to dishonesty and other crimes.

*If there is anything else that is contrary to sound doctrine.* In this clause he maintains that his gospel is so far from being opposed to the law, that it is a powerful confirmation of it. He declares that by his preaching, he supports that very sentence which the Lord pronounced in his law, against "everything that is contrary to sound doctrine." Hence it follows, that they who depart from the gospel, do not adhere to the spirit of the law, but merely pursue its shadow.

*Sound doctrine* is contrasted with frivolous questions about which he says (1 Tim. vi. 3) that foolish teachers are in an unhealthy condition, and which, on account of the effect produced by them, are called diseased.[1]

---

[1] "All vices are contrary to sound doctrine. For what is the advantage to be derived from the Word of God? It is the pasture of our souls; and, next, it is a medicine. We have bread and various kinds of food for the nourishment of our body: the word of God is of the same use for our souls. But it is more advantageous in this respect, that, when we are diseased with our vices, when there are many corruptions and wicked desires, we must be purged of them; and the Word of God serves us for various purposes, for purging, for blood-letting, for drink, and for diet. In short, all that physicians can apply to the human body, for healing its diseases, is not a tenth part of what the Word of God accomplishes for the health of our souls.

On that account Paul speaks here of sound doctrine. For inquisitive and ambitious persons are always in a diseased state; they have no health in them; they are like those unhappy patients who have lost their appe-

11. *According to the gospel of glory.* By calling it "the gospel of glory," that is, "the glorious gospel," he sharply rebukes those who laboured to degrade the gospel, in which God displays his glory. He expressly says that it *hath been intrusted to him,* that all may know that there is no other gospel of God than that which he preaches; and consequently, that all the fables which he formerly rebuked are at variance both with the law and with the gospel of God.

| 12. And I thank Christ Jesus our Lord, who hath enabled me, for that he counted me faithful, putting me into the ministry; | 12. Et gratiam habeo, qui me potentem reddidit, Christo Iesu Domino nostro, quòd fidelem me judicavit, ponendo in ministerium, |
|---|---|
| 13. Who was before a blasphemer, and a persecutor, and injurious: but I obtained mercy, because I did it ignorantly in unbelief. | 13. Qui prius eram blasphemus et persequutor, et violentus, sed et misericordiam adeptus sum, quòd ignorans feci in incredulitate. |

12. *I give thanks.* Great is the dignity of the apostleship, which Paul has claimed for himself; and he could not, looking at his former life, be accounted at all worthy of so high an honour. Accordingly, that he may not be accused of presumption, he comes unavoidably to make mention of his own person, and at once frankly acknowledges his own unworthiness, but nevertheless affirms that he is an Apostle by the grace of God. But he goes further, and turns to his own advantage what appeared to lessen his authority, declaring that the grace of God shines in him so much the more brightly.

*To our Lord Jesus Christ.* When he gives thanks to Christ, he removes that dislike towards him which might have been entertained, and cuts off all ground for putting this question, "Does he deserve, or does he not deserve, so honourable an office?" for, although in himself he has no

tite, and who suck and lick, but cannot receive any nourishment. But when the Word of God is applied in a right manner, there must be a contest; there was a war against every vice; and the Word of God must condemn them in such a manner that the hearts of men shall be touched and pierced—shall be humbled and laid low with sincere repentance to groan before God; and, if there be nothing else, that they shall at least be convinced, that they shall have remorse within themselves, that there shall be a hot iron to sear them, and that God shall persecute them, that they may so be an example to all that are not altogether incorrigible. This is the way in which the Lord wishes that his word may be applied to a good use."—*Fr. Ser.*

excellence, yet it is enough that he was chosen by Christ. There are, indeed, many who, under the same form of words, make a show of humility, but are widely different from the uprightness of Paul, whose intention was, not only to boast courageously in the Lord, but to give up all the glory that was his own.[1]

*By putting me into the ministry.* Why does he give thanks? Because he has been placed in the ministry; for thence he concludes that *he hath been accounted faithful.* Christ does not receive any in the manner that is done by ambitious[2] people, but selects those only who are well qualified; and therefore all on whom he bestows honour are acknowledged by us to be worthy. Nor is it inconsistent with this, that Judas, according to the prediction, (Ps. cix. 8,) was elevated for a short time, that he might quickly fall. It was otherwise with Paul, who obtained the honour for a different purpose, and on a different condition, when Christ declared that he should be "a chosen vessel to him." (Acts ix. 15.)

But in this manner Paul seems to say that faithfulness, by which he had been previously distinguished, was the cause of his calling. If it were so, the thanksgiving would be hypocritical and contradictory; for he would owe his apostleship not only to God, but to his own merit. I deny, therefore, that the meaning is, that he was admitted to the rank of an apostle, because God had foreseen his faith; for Christ could not foresee in him anything good but what the Father had bestowed on him. Still, therefore, it continues to be true, "Ye have not chosen me, but I have chosen you." (John xv. 16.) On the contrary, he draws from it a proof of his fidelity, that Christ had made him an Apostle; for he declares that they whom Christ makes Apostles must be held to be pronounced faithful by his de-

---

[1] "Mais de se demettre de toute gloire, et recognoistre a bon escient son indignite." "But to part with all glory, and to acknowledge sincerely his own unworthiness."

[2] "Christ ne fait pas comme les hommes, lesquels par ambition mettent des gens en un estat, sans regarder quoy et comment." "Christ does not act like men, who, through ambition, put persons into an office, without considering what or how."

cree. In a word, this judicial act is not traced by him to foreknowledge, but rather denotes the testimony which is given to men; as if he had said, "I give thanks to Christ, who, by calling me into the ministry, has openly declared that he approves of my faithfulness."[1]

*Who hath made me powerful.* He now introduces the mention of another act of the kindness of Christ, that he strengthened him, or "made him powerful." By this expression he does not only mean that he was at first formed by the hand of God, so as to be well qualified for his office, but he likewise includes the continued bestowal of grace. For it would not have been enough that he was once declared to be faithful, if Christ had not strengthened him by the uninterrupted communication of aid. He acknowledges, therefore, that he is indebted to the grace of Christ on two accounts, because he was once elevated, and because he continues in his office.

13. *Who was formerly a blasphemer and persecutor;* a blasphemer against God, a persecutor and oppressor against the Church. We see how candidly he acknowledges that it might be brought against him as a reproach, and how far he is from extenuating his sins, and how, by willingly acknowledging his unworthiness, he magnifies the greatness of the grace of God. Not satisfied with having called himself a "persecutor," he intended to express more fully his rage and cruelty by an additional term, *an oppressor.*

[1] "Here is Paul, who was slandered by many people, as we see that there are always dogs that bark against God's servants, aiming at nothing but to bring them into contempt, or rather to make their doctrine be despised and abhorred. Wishing to shut the mouths of such people, Paul says that he is satisfied with having the authority and warrant of Christ. As if he had said, 'Men may reject me, but it is enough that I am declared to be faithful by him who has all authority in himself, and who, being the heavenly Judge, hath pronounced it. When he put me into that office, he declared that he reckoned me to be his servant, and that he intended to employ me in preaching his gospel. That is enough for me. Let men contrive and calumniate as much as they may, provided that I have Christ on my side, let men jeer at me, it will be of no avail; for the decision pronounced by the Lord Jesus Christ can never be recalled.' Thus we see what was Paul's intention, namely, that he does not here mean that Christ foresaw in him anything as the reason why he called him to so honourable an office, but only that, by putting him into it, he declared and made it evident to men, that he intended to make use of him."—*Fr. Ser.*

*Because I did it ignorantly in unbelief.* "I obtained pardon," said he, "for my unbelief; because it proceeded from ignorance;" for persecution and oppression were nothing else than the fruits of unbelief. But he appears to insinuate that there is no room for pardon, unless when ignorance can be pleaded in excuse. What then? Will God never pardon any one who has sinned knowingly? I reply, we must observe the word *unbelief;*[1] for this term limits Paul's statement to the first table of the law. Transgressions of the second table, although they are voluntary, are forgiven; but he who knowingly and willingly breaks the first table sins against the Holy Spirit, because he is in direct opposition to God. He does not err through weakness, but, by rushing wickedly against God, gives a sure proof of his reprobation.

And hence may be obtained a definition of the sin against the Holy Ghost; first, that it is open rebellion against God in the transgression of the first table; secondly, that it is a malicious rejection of the truth; for, when the truth of God is not rejected through deliberate malice, the Holy Spirit is not resisted. Lastly, *unbelief* is here employed as a general term; and malicious design, which is contrasted with ignorance, may be regarded as the point of difference.[2]

Accordingly, they are mistaken who make the sin against the Holy Ghost to consist in the transgression of the second table; and they are also mistaken, who pronounce blind and thoughtless violence to be a crime so heinous. For men commit the sin against the Holy Spirit, when they undertake a voluntary war against God, in order to extinguish that light of the Spirit which has been offered to them. This is shocking wickedness and monstrous hardihood. Nor is there room for doubting that, by an implied threatening,

---

[1] " Par incredulite, ou, n'ayant point la foy." "Through unbelief, or not having faith."

[2] En la definition du peche contre le S. Esprit, Incredulite est le terme general; et le Propos malicieux, qui est le contraire d'ignorance, est comme ce que les Dialecticiens appellent la difference, qui restraint ce qui estoit general." " In the definition of the sin against the Holy Spirit, Unbelief is the general term, and malicious intention, which is the opposite of ignorance, may be regarded as that which logicians call the difference, which limits what was general."

he intended to terrify all who had been once enlightened, not to stumble against truth which they knew; because such a fall is destructive and fatal; for if, on account of ignorance, God forgave Paul his blasphemies, they who knowingly and intentionally blaspheme ought not to expect any pardon.

But it may be thought that what he now says is to no purpose; for unbelief, which is always blind, can never be unaccompanied by ignorance. I reply, among unbelievers some are so blind that they are deceived by a false imagination of the truth; and in others, while they are blinded, yet malice prevails. Paul was not altogether free from a wicked disposition; but he was hurried along by thoughtless zeal, so as to think that what he did was right. Thus he was an adversary of Christ, not from deliberate intention, but through mistake and ignorance. The Pharisees, who through a bad conscience slandered Christ, were not entirely free from mistake and ignorance; but they were instigated by ambition, and a base hatred of sound doctrine, and even by furious rebellion against God, so that maliciously and intentionally, and not in ignorance, they set themselves in opposition to Christ.[1]

| | |
|---|---|
| 14. And the grace of our Lord was exceeding abundant with faith and love which is in Christ Jesus. | 14. Exuberavit autem supra modum gratia Domini nostri, cum fide et dilectione, quæ est in Christo Iesu. |
| 15. This *is* a faithful saying, and worthy of all acceptation, that Christ Jesus came into the world to save sinners; of whom I am chief. | 15. Fidelis sermo, et dignus omnino qui accipiatur, quòd Christus Iesus venit in mundum, ut peccatores salvos faceret, quorum primus sum ego. |
| 16. Howbeit for this cause I obtained mercy, that in me first Jesus Christ might shew forth all longsuffering, for a pattern to them which should hereafter believe on him to life everlasting. | 16. Verum ideo misericordiam sum adeptus, ut in me primo ostenderet Iesus Christus omnem clementiam, in exemplar iis, qui credituri essent in ipso in vitam æternam. |
| 17. Now, unto the King eternal | 17. Regi autem sæculorum im- |

---

[1] It may deserve consideration whether a large portion of this able argument might not have been avoided, by means of a different collocation of the passage. "Who was formerly a blasphemer, and a persecutor, and an oppressor, (for I did it ignorantly in unbelief,) but I obtained mercy; and the grace of our Lord was exceedingly abundant, with faith and love which is in Christ Jesus."—*Ed.*

| | |
|---|---|
| immortal, invisible, the only wise God, *be* honour and glory for ever and ever. Amen. | mortali, invisibili, soli sapienti Deo, honor et gloria in sæcula sæculorum. Amen. |

14. *And the grace of our Lord.* He again magnifies the grace of God towards himself, not only for the purpose of removing the dislike of it and testifying his gratitude, but also to employ it as a shield against the slanders of wicked men, whose whole design was to bring down his apostleship to a lower level. When he says that it *abounded,* and that, too, *beyond measure,* the statement implies that the remembrance of past transactions was effaced, and so completely swallowed up, that it was no disadvantage to him that God had formerly been gracious to good men.

*With faith and love.* Both may be viewed as referring to God, in this sense, that God showed himself to be true, and gave a manifestation of his love in Christ, when he bestowed his grace upon him. But I prefer a more simple interpretation, that " faith and love" are indications and proofs of that grace which he had mentioned, that it might not be supposed that he boasted needlessly or without good grounds. And, indeed, " faith," is contrasted with unbelief, and " love in Christ" is contrasted with the cruelty which he had exercised towards believers ; as if he had said, that God had so completely changed him, that he had become a totally different and new man. Thus from the signs and effects he celebrates in lofty terms the excellence of that grace which must obliterate the remembrance of his former life.

15. *It is a faithful saying.* After having defended his ministry from slander and unjust accusations, not satisfied with this, he turns to his own advantage what might have been brought against him by his adversaries as a reproach. He shews that it was profitable to the Church that he had been such a person as he actually was before he was called to the apostleship, because Christ, by giving him as a pledge, invited all sinners to the sure hope of obtaining pardon. For when he, who had been a fierce and savage beast, was changed into a Pastor, Christ gave a remarkable display of his grace, from which all might be led to entertain a firm belief that no sinner, how heinous and aggravated soever

might have been his transgressions, had the gate of salvation shut against him.

*That Christ Jesus came into the world to save sinners.* He first brings forward this general statement, and adorns it with a preface, as he is wont to do in matters of vast importance. In the doctrine of religion, indeed, the main point is, to come to Christ, that, being lost in ourselves, we may obtain salvation from him. Let this preface be to our ears like the sound of a trumpet to proclaim the praises of the grace of Christ, in order that we may believe it with a stronger faith. Let it be to us as a seal to impress on our hearts a firm belief of the forgiveness of sins, which otherwise with difficulty finds entrance into the hearts of men.

*A faithful saying.* What was the reason why Paul aroused attention by these words, but because men are always disputing with themselves[1] about their salvation? For, although God the Father a thousand times offer to us salvation, and although Christ himself preach about his own office, yet we do not on that account cease to tremble, or at least to debate with ourselves if it be actually so. Wherefore, whenever any doubt shall arise in our mind about the forgiveness of sins, let us learn to repel it courageously with this shield, that it is an undoubted truth, and deserves to be received without controversy.

*To save sinners.* The word *sinners* is emphatic; for they who acknowledge that it is the office of Christ to save, have difficulty in admitting this thought, that such a salvation belongs to "sinners." Our mind is always impelled to look at our worthiness; and as soon as our unworthiness is seen, our confidence sinks. Accordingly, the more any one is oppressed by his sins, let him the more courageously betake himself to Christ, relying on this doctrine, that he came to bring salvation not to the righteous, but to "sinners." It deserves attention, also, that Paul draws an argument from the general office of Christ, in order that what he had lately

[1] " Sinon d'autant que les hommes disputent tousjours, et sont en doute en eux-mesmes touchant leur salut." "But because men are always disputing, and are in doubt in themselves about their salvation."

testified about his own person might not appear to be absurd on account of its novelty.

*Of whom I am the first.* Beware of thinking that the Apostle, under a pretence of modesty, spoke falsely,[1] for he intended to make a confession not less true than humble, and drawn from the very bottom of his heart.

But some will ask, "Why does he, who only erred through ignorance of sound doctrine, and whose whole life, in every other respect, was blameless before men, pronounce himself to be the chief of sinners? I reply, these words inform us how heinous and dreadful a crime unbelief is before God, especially when it is attended by obstinacy and a rage for persecution. (Philip. iii. 6.) With men, indeed, it is easy to extenuate, under the pretence of heedless zeal, all that Paul has acknowledged about himself; but God values more highly the obedience of faith than to reckon unbelief, accompanied by obstinacy, to be a small crime.[2]

We ought carefully to observe this passage, which teaches us, that a man who, before the world, is not only innocent, but eminent for distinguished virtues, and most praiseworthy for his life, yet because he is opposed to the doctrine of the gospel, and on account of the obstinacy of his unbelief, is reckoned one of the most heinous sinners; for hence we may

---

[1] "Il se faut bien donner garde de cuider que l'Apostre ait ainsi parlé par une facon de modestie, et non pas qu'il se pensast en son cœur." "We must guard against thinking that the Apostle spoke thus under a pretence of modesty, and that he did not think so in his heart."

[2] "If we consider what is the chief service that God demands and accepts, we shall know what is meant by saying that humility is the greatest sacrifice that he approves. (1 Sam. xv. 22.) And that is the reason why it is said that faith may be regarded as the mother of all the virtues; it is the foundation and source of them; and, but for this, all the virtues that are visible, and that are highly valued by men, have no solid value; they are so many vices which God condemns. After we have loudly praised a man, and placed him in the rank of angels, he shall be rejected by God, with all his fine reputation, unless he have that obedience of faith. Thus it will be in vain for men to say, 'I did not intend it, that was my opinion;' for, notwithstanding their good intention and their reputation, they must be condemned before God as rebels. This would, at first sight, seem hard to digest. And why? For we see how men always endeavour to escape from the hand of God, and resort to many indirect means. And when can they find this palliation, 'I intended to do what was right, and why not accept my good intention?' When that can be alleged, we think that it is enough; but such palliations will be of no avail before God."— *Fr. Ser.*

easily conclude of what value before God are all the pompous displays of hypocrites, while they obstinately resist Christ.

16. *That in me the first Jesus Christ might shew.* When he calls himself *the first*, he alludes to what he had said a little before, that he was the first[1] among sinners; and, therefore, this word means " chiefly," or, " above all." The Apostle's meaning is, that, from the very beginning, God held out such a pattern as might be visible from a conspicuous and lofty platform, that no one might doubt that he would obtain pardon, provided that he approached to Christ by faith. And, indeed, the distrust entertained by all of us is counteracted, when we thus behold in Paul a visible model of that grace which we desire to see.

17. *Now to the King eternal.* His amazing vehemence at length breaks out into this exclamation ; because he could not find words to express his gratitude ; for those sudden bursts occur chiefly when we are constrained to break off the discourse, in consequence of being overpowered by the vastness of the subject. And is there anything more astonishing than Paul's conversion ? Yet, at the same time, by his example he reminds us all that we ought never to think of the grace manifested in God's calling[2] without being carried to lofty admiration.

*Eternal, invisible, only wise.* This sublime praise of the grace which God had bestowed on him[3] swallows up the remembrance of his former life. For how great a deep is the glory of God ! Those attributes which he ascribes to God, though they belong to him always, yet are admirably adapted to the present occasion. The Apostle calls him the *King eternal*, not liable to any change ; *Invisible,* because (1 Tim. vi. 16) he dwells in light that is inaccessible ; and, lastly, *the Only Wise,* because he renders foolish, and condemns as vanity, all the wisdom of men. The whole agrees with that conclusion at which he arrives : " O the depth of

---

[1] " Qu'il estoit le premier ou le principal de tous les pecheurs." " That he was the first, or the chief, of all sinners."

[2] " Nostre vocation, c'est a dire, la grace que Dieu nous a faite en nous appellant." " Our calling, that is, the grace which God has displayed in calling us."

[3] " De la grace de Dieu sur luy."

the riches both of the wisdom and knowledge of God! How incomprehensible are his designs! How unsearchable his ways!" (Rom. xi. 33.) He means that the infinite and incomprehensible wisdom of God should be beheld by us with such reverence that, if his works surpass our senses, still we may be restrained by admiration.

Yet as to the last epithet *Only,* it is doubtful whether he means to claim all glory for God alone, or calls him the only wise, or says that he only is God. The second of these meanings is that which I prefer; for it was in fine harmony with his present subject to say, that the understanding of men, whatever it may be, must bend to the secret purpose of God. And yet I do not deny that he affirms that God alone is worthy of all glory; for, while he scatters on his creatures, in every direction, the sparks of his glory, still all glory belongs truly and perfectly to him alone. But either of these meanings implies that there is no glory but that which belongs to God..

| | |
|---|---|
| 18. This charge I commit unto thee, son Timothy, according to the prophecies which went before on thee, that thou by them mightest war a good warfare; | 18. Hoc præceptum commendo tibi, fili Timothee, secundum præcedentes super te prophetias, ut milites in illis bonam militiam; |
| 19. Holding faith, and a good conscience; which some having put away, concerning faith have made shipwreck: | 19. Habens fidem et bonam conscientiam; a qua aversi quidam circa fidem naufragium fecerunt: |
| 20 Of whom is Hymeneus and Alexander; whom I have delivered unto Satan, that they may learn not to blaspheme. | 20. Ex quibus sunt Hymenæus et Alexander, quos tradidi Satanæ, ut discant non maledicere. |

18. *I recommend to thee this commandment.* All that he had introduced about his own person may be viewed as a digression from his subject. Having intended to arm Timothy with authority, it became necessary for himself to be clothed with the highest authority; and, therefore, he took an early opportunity of refuting an opinion which might have stood in his way. And now, after having proved that his apostleship ought not to be less esteemed by good men, because at one time he fought against the kingdom of Christ, this obstacle being removed, he returns to

the course of his exhortation. The *commandment,* therefore, is the same as he mentioned at the beginning.

*Son Timothy.* By calling him his *son,* he not only expresses his own warm regard towards him, but also recommends him to others under that name.

*According to the prophecies which went before concerning thee.* In order to encourage him still more, he reminds him what kind of testimony he had obtained from the Spirit of God; for it was no small excitement, that his ministry was approved by God, and that he had been called by divine revelation before he was called by the votes of men. " It is disgraceful not to come up to the expectations which men have been led to form; and how much more disgraceful will it be to make void, as far as lies in thy power, the judgment of God ?"

But we must first ascertain what are the *prophecies* of which he speaks. Some think that Paul was instructed by revelation to confer the office on Timothy. That I acknowledge to be true, but I add that others made revelations; for it was not without reason that Paul made use of the plural number. Accordingly, we conclude from these words that several prophecies were uttered concerning Timothy, in order to recommend him to the Church.[1] Being still a young man, he might have been despised on account of his age; and Paul might also have been exposed to calumnies, on account of having ordained youths, before the proper time, to the elder's office. Besides, God had appointed him to great and difficult undertakings; for he was not one of the ordinary rank of ministers, but approached very closely to that of the apostles, and frequently occupied the place of Paul during his absence. It was, therefore, necessary that he should receive an extraordinary testimony, in order to make it manifest that it was not conferred on him at random by men, but that he was chosen by God himself. To be adorned with the applauses of the prophets was not an ordinary occurrence, or one which was common to him along with many persons; but because there were some circum-

---

[1] " Pour le recommander a l'Eglise, et luy donner authorite." " In order to recommend him to the Church, and to give him authority."

stances peculiar to Timothy, it was the will of God that he should not be received by men until he had been previously approved by his own voice; it was the will of God that he should not enter into the exercise of his office until he had been called by the revelations of the prophets. The same thing happened to Paul and Barnabas, (Acts xiii. 2,) when they were ordained to be teachers of the Gentiles; for it was a new and uncommon occurrence, and they could not otherwise have escaped the charge of rashness.

It will now be objected by some, "If God had formerly declared, by his prophets, what kind of minister Timothy should be, what purpose did it serve to admonish him, to show that he was actually such a person? Could he falsify prophecies which had been uttered by divine revelation? I reply, it could not happen differently from what God had promised; but at the same time it was the duty of Timothy, not to give himself up to sloth and inactivity, but to render a cheerful compliance with the providence of God. It is therefore not without good reason, that Paul, wishing to stimulate him still more, mentions the "prophecies," by which God might be said to have pledged himself on behalf of Timothy; for he was thus reminded of the purpose for which he was called.

*That thou by them mayest war a good warfare.* By this he means that Timothy, relying on such approbation of God, ought to fight more courageously. What is there that either ought to give, or can give us greater cheerfulness than to know that God has appointed us to do what we are doing? These are our arms, these are our weapons of defence, by the aid of which we shall never fail.

By the word *warfare,* he states indirectly, that we must maintain a contest; and this applies universally to all believers, but especially to Christian teachers, who may be said to be standard-bearers and leaders. It is as if he had said, "O Timothy, if thou canst not fulfil thy office without a contest, remember that thou art armed by divine prophecies for cherishing assured hope of victory, and arouse thyself by calling them to remembrance. That warfare which we maintain, having God for our leader, is a good warfare; that is, it is glorious and successful."[1]

19. *Having faith and a good conscience.* I understand the word *faith* to be a general term, denoting sound doctrine. In the same sense he afterwards speaks of " the mystery of faith." (1 Tim. iii. 9.) And, indeed, the chief things demanded from a teacher are these two:—that he shall hold by the pure truth of the gospel; and next, that he shall administer it with a good conscience and honest zeal. Where these are found, all the others will follow of their own accord.

*From which some having turned aside concerning faith.* He shows how necessary it is that faith be accompanied by a good conscience; because, on the other hand, the punishment of a bad conscience is turning aside from the path of duty. They who do not serve God with a sincere and a perfect heart, but give a loose rein to wicked dispositions, even though at first they had a sound understanding, come to lose it altogether.

This passage ought to be carefully observed. We know that the treasure of sound doctrine is invaluable, and therefore there is nothing that we ought to dread more than to have it taken from us. But Paul here informs us, that there is only one way of keeping it safe; and that is, to secure it by the locks and bars of a good conscience. This is what we experience every day; for how comes it that there are so many who, laying aside the gospel, rush into wicked sects, or become involved in monstrous errors? It is because, by

[1] " When Paul speaks of 'warring,' he adds, by way of consolation, and in order to lessen the weariness we might have in this world, that ' this warfare is good;' as if he had said, that the result of it will be happy; for victory is promised, and we cannot fail to obtain it, as is said in Jeremiah, ' They shall fight against thee, but they shall not prevail against thee.' (Jer. i. 19.) This is what our Lord declared, that the world will always be so wicked as to resist his word, and distress those who carry it; but at last wicked men must be vanquished. When they have made all their efforts, God will not fail to triumph over them, and even that rebellion and that rage which they have exhibited, will add greater lustre to that power which our Lord gives to his word. Thus St. Paul here exhorts the ministers of the word of God not to be uneasy, and not to lose courage; because they shall be victorious, and, although the contests may be hard and severe, they must be fully persuaded, that God will stretch out his strong hand to them, and they shall never be vanquished by their enemies, but, at last, all who rose against them must perish."—*Fr. Ser.*

this kind of blindness, God punishes hypocrisy; as, on the other hand, a genuine fear of God gives strength for perseverance.

Hence we may learn two lessons. First, Teachers and ministers of the gospel, and, through them, all the churches are taught with what horror they ought to regard a hypocritical and deceitful profession of true doctrine, when they learn that it is so severely punished. Secondly, this passage removes the offence by which so many persons are greatly distressed, when they perceive that some, who formerly professed their attachment to Christ and to the gospel, not only fall back into their former superstitions, but (which is far worse) are bewildered and captivated by monstrous errors. For by such examples, God openly supports the majesty of the gospel, and openly shews that he cannot at all endure the profanation of it. And this is what experience has taught us in every age. All the errors that have existed in the Christian Church from the beginning, proceeded from this source, that in some persons, ambition, and in others, covetousness, extinguished the true fear of God. A bad conscience is, therefore, the mother of all heresies; and we see that a vast number of persons, who had not sincerely and honestly embraced the faith, are hurried along, like brute beasts, into the reveries of the Epicureans, so that their hypocrisy is exposed. And not only so, but contempt of God is universally prevalent, and the licentious and disgraceful lives of almost all ranks show that there is either none at all, or the smallest possible portion of integrity in the world; so that there is very great reason to fear lest the light which had been kindled may be speedily extinguished, and God may leave the pure understanding of the gospel to be possessed by very few.

*Have made shipwreck.* The metaphor taken from *shipwreck* is highly appropriate; for it suggests to us, that, if we wish to arrive safely at the harbour, our course must be guided by a good conscience, otherwise there is danger of " shipwreck;" that is, there is danger lest faith be sunk by a bad conscience, as by a whirlpool in a stormy sea.¹

¹ "What is human life, and what is the whole of its course? A naviga-

20. *Of whom are Hymenæus and Alexander.* The former will be again mentioned in the Second Epistle, in which the kind of "shipwreck" which he made is likewise described; for he said that the resurrection was past. (2 Tim. ii. 17, 18.) There is reason to believe that Alexander also was bewitched by an error so absurd. And shall we wonder at the present day, if any are deceived by the various enchantments of Satan, when we see that one of Paul's companions perished by so dreadful a fall?

He mentions both of them to Timothy as persons whom he knew. For my own part, I have no doubt that this is the same Alexander that is mentioned by Luke, and who attempted, but without success, to quell the commotion. Now he was an Ephesian, and we have said that this Epistle was chiefly written for the sake of the Ephesians. We now learn what was his end; and hearing it, let us keep possession of our faith by a good conscience, that we may hold it safe to the last.

*Whom I have delivered to Satan.* As I mentioned in the exposition of another passage, (1 Cor. v. 5,) there are some who interpret this to mean that extraordinary chastisement was inflicted on those persons; and they view this as referring to δυνάμεις, "the powers" mentioned by Paul in the same Epistle. (1 Cor. xii. 28.) For, as the apostles were endowed with the gift of healing, in order to testify the favour and kindness of God towards the godly, so against wicked and rebellious persons they were armed with power, either to deliver them to

tion. Not only are we travellers, as the Scripture tells us, (1 Pet. ii. 11,) but we have no solidity. They who travel by land, either on foot or on horseback, have still their sure and firm road; but in the world, instead of being on foot or on horseback, we must be, as it were, on a sea, and we have no solid footing. We are like people who are in a boat, and who are always within half a foot of their death; and the boat is a sort of grave, because they see the water all around, ready to swallow them up. Thus is it with us, while we live here below. For, on the one hand, there is the frailty that is in us, which is more fluid than water; and then all that surrounds us is like water, which flows on all sides, while at every minute winds, and storms, and tempests arise. Let us therefore learn that our life is but a kind of navigation, which we perform by water, and that we are, at the same time, exposed to many winds and storms. And if it be so, what shall become of us when we have not a good boat or a good pilot?"—*Fr. Ser.*

the devil to be tormented, or to inflict on them other chastisements. Of this "power," Peter gave a display in Ananias and Sapphira, (Acts v. 1,) and Paul in the magician Bar-jesus. (Acts xiii. 6.) But, for my own part, I choose rather to explain it as relating to excommunication; for the opinion that the incestuous Corinthian received any other chastisement than excommunication is not supported by any probable conjecture. And, if by excommunicating him, Paul delivered him to Satan, why should not the same mode of expression have a similar import in this passage? Besides, it explains very well the force of excommunication; for, since in the Church Christ holds the seat of his kingdom, out of the Church there is nothing but the dominion of Satan. Accordingly, he who is cast out of the Church must be placed, for a time, under the tyranny of Satan, until, being reconciled to the Church, he return to Christ. I make one exception, that, on account of the enormity of the offence, he might have pronounced a sentence of perpetual excommunication against them; but on that point I would not venture to make a positive assertion.

*That they may learn not to blaspheme.* What is the meaning of this last clause? For one who has been cast out of the Church takes upon himself greater freedom of acting, because, being freed from the yoke of ordinary discipline, he breaks out into louder insolence. I reply, to whatever extent they may indulge in their wickedness, yet the gate will be shut against them, so that they shall not contaminate the flock; for the greatest injury done by wicked men is, when they mingle with others under the pretence of holding the same faith. The power of doing injury is taken from them, when they are branded with public infamy, so that none are so simple as not to know that these are irreligious and detestable men, and therefore their society is shunned by all. Sometimes, too, it happens that—being struck down by this mark of disgrace which has been put upon them—they become less daring and obstinate; and therefore, although this remedy sometimes renders them more wicked, yet it is not always ineffectual for subduing their fierceness.

## CHAPTER II.

1. I exhort therefore, that, first of all, supplications, prayers, intercessions, *and* giving of thanks, be made for all men;
2. For kings, and *for* all that are in authority; that we may lead a quiet and peaceable life in all godliness and honesty.
3. For this *is* good and acceptable in the sight of God our Saviour;
4. Who will have all men to be saved, and to come unto the knowledge of the truth.

1. Adhortor igitur, ut ante omnia fiant deprecationes, obsecrationes, interpellationes, gratiarum actiones pro omnibus hominibus,
2. Pro regibus et omnibus in eminentia constitutis, ut placidam et quietam vitam degamus cum omni pietate et honestate.
3. Hoc enim bonum et acceptum coram Salvatore nostro Deo,
4. Qui omnes homines vult salvos fieri, et ad agnitionem veritatis venire.

1. *I exhort therefore.* These exercises of godliness maintain and even strengthen us in the sincere worship and fear of God, and cherish the good conscience of which he had spoken. Not inappropriately does he make use of the word *therefore*, to denote an inference; for those exhortations depend on the preceding commandment.

*That, above all, prayers be made.* First, he speaks of public prayers, which he enjoins to be offered, not only for believers, but for all mankind. Some might reason thus with themselves: " Why should we be anxious about the salvation of unbelievers, with whom we have no connexion? Is it not enough, if we, who are brethren, pray mutually for our brethren, and recommend to God the whole of his Church? for we have nothing to do with strangers." This perverse view Paul meets, and enjoins the Ephesians to include in their prayers all men, and not to limit them to the body of the Church.

What is the difference between three out of the four kinds which Paul enumerates, I own that I do not thoroughly understand. The view given by Augustine, who twists Paul's words so as to denote ceremonial observances customary at that time, is quite childish. A simpler exposition is given by those who think that " requests" are when we ask to be delivered from what is evil; "prayers," when we desire to obtain something profitable; and " supplications," when we deplore before God injuries which we have endured. Yet for my own part, I do not draw the difference so ingeniously; or, at least, I prefer another way of distinguishing them.

Προσευχαὶ is the Greek word for every kind of prayer; and δεήσεις denotes those forms of petitions in which something definite is asked. In this way the two words agree with each other, as genus and species. Ἐντεύξεις is the word commonly used by Paul to signify those prayers which we offer for one another. The word used for it in the Latin Translation is "intercessiones," *intercessions.* Yet Plato, in his second dialogue, styled Alcibiades, uses it in a different sense, to mean a definite petition offered by a person for himself; and in the very inscription of the book, and in many passages, he shews plainly, as I have said, that προσευχὴ is a general term.[1]

But not to dwell longer than is proper on a matter that is not essential, Paul, in my own opinion, simply enjoins that, whenever public prayers are offered, petitions and supplications should be made *for all men,* even for those who at present are not at all related to us. And yet this heaping up of words is not superfluous; but Paul appears to me purposely to join together three terms for the same purpose, in order to recommend more warmly, and urge more strongly, earnest and constant prayer. We know how sluggish we are in this religious duty; and therefore we need not wonder if, for the purpose of arousing us to it, the Holy Spirit, by the mouth of Paul, employs various excitements.

*And thanksgivings.* As to this term, there is no ob-

---

[1] "Δέησις, if we attend to its etymological import, is derived ἀπὸ τοῦ δεῖσθαι, 'from being in want,' and is a petition for that οὗ δεόμεθα, 'which we want.' It is very correctly defined by Gregory Nazianzen in his 15th Iambic Ode: Δέησιν οἴου τὴν αἴτησιν ἐνδεῶν, 'consider that when you are in want of anything, your petition is δέησις.' If we attend again to the customary usage of the word, it signifies 'a petition for a benefit.' My opinion is, that the various names express one and the same thing, viewed under various aspects. Our prayers are called δέησις, so far as by them we declare to God our *need;* for δεῖσθαι is 'to be in need.' They are προσευχαὶ, as they contain our wishes. They are αἰτήματα, as they express *petitions* and desires. They are ἐντεύξις, as we are permitted by God to approach Him, not with timidity, but in a familiar manner: for ἔντευξις is a familiar conversation and interview."—*Witsius on the Lord's Prayer.*

scurity; for, as he bids us make supplication to God for the salvation of unbelievers, so also to give thanks on account of their prosperity and success. That wonderful goodness which he shews every day, when "he maketh his sun to rise on the good and the bad," (Matt. v. 45,) is worthy of being praised; and our love of our neighbour ought also to extend to those who are unworthy of it.

2. *For kings.* He expressly mentions *kings* and other magistrates, because, more than all others, they might be hated by Christians. All the magistrates who existed at that time were so many sworn enemies of Christ; and therefore this thought might occur to them, that they ought not to pray for those who devoted all their power and all their wealth to fight against the kingdom of Christ, the extension of which is above all things desirable. The apostle meets this difficulty, and expressly enjoins Christians to pray for them also. And, indeed, the depravity of men is not a reason why God's ordinance should not be loved. Accordingly, seeing that God appointed magistrates and princes for the preservation of mankind, however much they fall short of the divine appointment, still we must not on that account cease to love what belongs to God, and to desire that it may remain in force. That is the reason why believers, in whatever country they live, must not only obey the laws and the government of magistrates, but likewise in their prayers supplicate God for their salvation. Jeremiah said to the Israelites, "Pray for the peace of Babylon, for in their peace ye shall have peace." (Jer. xxix. 7.) The universal doctrine is this, that we should desire the continuance and peaceful condition of those governments which have been appointed by God.

*That we may lead a peaceful and quiet life.* By exhibiting the advantage, he holds out an additional inducement; for he enumerates the fruits which are yielded to us by a well regulated government. The first is *a peaceful life;* for magistrates are armed with the sword, in order to keep us in peace. If they did not restrain the hardihood of wicked men, every place would be full of robberies and murders. The true way of maintaining peace, therefore, is, when every one obtains what is his own, and the violence of the more powerful is kept under restraint.

*With all godliness and decency.* The second fruit is the preservation of *godliness,* that is, when magistrates give themselves to promote religion, to maintain the worship of God, and to take care that sacred ordinances be observed with due reverence. The third fruit is the care of public *decency ;* for it is also the business of magistrates to prevent men from abandoning themselves to brutal filthiness or flagitious conduct, but, on the contrary, to promote decency and moderation. If these three things are taken away, what will be the condition of human life ? If, therefore, we are at all moved by solicitude about the peace of society, or godliness, or decency, let us remember that we ought also to be solicitous about those through whose agency we obtain such distinguished benefits.

Hence we conclude, that fanatics, who wish to have magistrates taken away, are destitute of all humanity, and breathe nothing but cruel barbarism. How different is it to say, that we ought to pray for kings, in order that justice and decency may prevail, and to say, that not only the name of kingly power, but all government, is opposed to religion ! We have the Spirit of God for the Author of the former sentiment, and therefore the latter must be from the Devil.

If any one ask, Ought we to pray for kings, from whom we obtain none of these advantages ? I answer, the object of our prayer is, that, guided by the Spirit of God, they may begin to impart to us those benefits of which they formerly deprived us. It is our duty, therefore, not only to pray for those who are already worthy, but we must pray to God that he may make bad men good. We must always hold by this principle, that magistrates were appointed by God for the protection of religion, as well as of the peace and decency of society, in exactly the same manner that the earth is appointed to produce food.[1] Accordingly, in like

---

[1] " Ne plus ne moins que la terre est destinee a produire ce qui est propre pour nostre nourriture." " Neither more nor less than the earth is appointed to produce what is adapted to our nourishment."

manner as, when we pray to God for our daily bread, we ask him to make the earth fertile by his blessing; so in those benefits of which we have already spoken, we ought to consider the ordinary means which he has appointed by his providence for bestowing them.

To this must be added, that, if we are deprived of those benefits the communication of which Paul assigns to magistrates, that is through our own fault. It is the wrath of God that renders magistrates useless to us, in the same manner that it renders the earth barren; and, therefore, we ought to pray for the removal of those chastisements which have been brought upon us by our sins.

On the other hand, princes, and all who hold the office of magistracy, are here reminded of their duty. It is not enough, if, by giving to every one what is due, they restrain all acts of violence, and maintain peace; but they must likewise endeavour to promote religion, and to regulate morals by wholesome discipline. The exhortation of David (Ps. ii. 12) to "kiss the Son," and the prophecy of Isaiah, that they shall be nursing-fathers of the Church, (Isa. xlix. 23,) are not without meaning; and, therefore, they have no right to flatter themselves, if they neglect to lend their assistance to maintain the worship of God.

3. *For this is good and acceptable before God.* After having taught that what he enjoined is useful, he now brings forward a stronger argument—that it pleases God; for when we know what is His will, this ought to have the force of all possible reasons. By *good* he means what is proper and lawful; and, since the will of God is the rule by which all our duties must be regulated, he proves that it is right because it pleases God.

This passage is highly worthy of observation; and, first, we draw from it the general doctrine, that the true rule for acting well and properly is to look to the will of God, and not to undertake anything but what he approves. Next, there is likewise laid down a rule for godly prayer, that we should follow God as our leader, and that all our prayers should be regulated by his will and command. If due force had been allowed to this argument, the prayers of Papists, in the present day, would not have abounded with so many corruptions. For how will they prove that they have the authority of God for having recourse to dead men as their intercessors, or for praying for the dead? In short, in all their form of prayer, what can they point out that is pleasing to God?

4. *Who wishes that all men may be saved.* Here follows a confirmation of the second argument; and what is more reasonable than that all our prayers should be in conformity with this decree of God?

*And may come to the acknowledgment of the truth.* Lastly, he demonstrates that God has at heart the salvation of all, because he invites all to the acknowledgment of his truth. This belongs to that kind of argument in which the cause is proved from the effect; for, if "the gospel is the power of God for salvation to every one that believeth," (Rom. i. 16,) it is certain that all those to whom the gospel is addressed are invited to the hope of eternal life. In short, as the calling is a proof of the secret election, so they whom God makes partakers of his gospel are admitted by him to possess salvation; because the gospel reveals to us the righteousness of God, which is a sure entrance into life.

Hence we see the childish folly of those who represent this passage to be opposed to predestination. "If God," say they, "wishes all men indiscriminately to be saved, it is false that some are predestinated by his eternal purpose to salvation, and others to perdition." They might have had some ground for saying this, if Paul were speaking here about individual men; although even then we should not have wanted the means of replying to their argument; for, although the will of God ought not to be judged from his secret decrees, when he reveals them to us by outward signs, yet it does not therefore follow that he has not determined with himself what he intends to do as to every individual man.

But I say nothing on that subject, because it has nothing to do with this passage; for the Apostle simply means, that there is no people and no rank in the world that is excluded from salvation; because God wishes that the gospel should be proclaimed to all without exception. Now the preaching of the gospel gives life ; and hence he justly concludes that God invites all equally to partake salvation. But the present discourse relates to classes of men, and not to individual persons ; for his sole object is, to include in this number princes and foreign nations. That God wishes the doctrine of salvation to be enjoyed by them as well as others, is evident from the passages already quoted, and from other passages of a similar nature. Not without good reason was it said, "Now, kings, understand," and again, in the same Psalm, "I will give thee the Gentiles for an inheritance, and the ends of the earth for a possession." (Ps. ii. 8, 10.)

In a word, Paul intended to shew that it is our duty to consider, not what kind of persons the princes at that time were, but what God wished them to be. Now the duty arising out of that love which we owe to our neighbour is, to be solicitous and to do our endeavour for the salvation of all whom God includes in his calling, and to testify this by godly prayers.

With the same view does he call *God our Saviour;* for whence do we obtain salvation but from the undeserved kindness of God ? Now the same God who has already made us partakers of salvation may sometime extend his grace to them also. He who hath already drawn us to him may draw them along with us. The Apostle takes for granted that God will do so, because it had been thus foretold by the predictions of the prophets, concerning all ranks and all nations.

| | |
|---|---|
| 5. For *there is* one God, and one mediator between God and men, the man Christ Jesus; | 5. Unus enim Deus, unus et Mediator Dei et hominum, homo Christus Iesus, |
| 6. Who gave himself a ransom for all, to be testified in due time. | 6. Qui dedit semetipsum pretium redemptionis pro omnibus, (ut esset) testimonium temporibus suis, |
| 7. Whereunto I am ordained a preacher, and an apostle, (I speak the truth in Christ, *and* lie not,) a teacher of the Gentiles in faith and verity. | 7. In quod positus sum præco et Apostolus: veritatem dico in Christo, non mentior, Doctor Gentium in fide et veritate. |

5. *For there is one God.* This argument might, at first sight, appear to be not very strong, that God wishes all men

to be saved, because he is one; if a transition had not been made from God to men. Chrysostom—and, after him, others—view it in this sense, that there are not many gods, as idolaters imagine. But I think that Paul's design was different, and that there is here an implied comparison of one God with the whole world and with various nations, out of which comparison arises a view of both, as they mutually regard each other. In like manner the Apostle says, "Is he the God of the Jews only? Is he not also of the Gentiles? Yea, it is one God who justifieth the circumcision by faith, and the uncircumcision through faith." (Rom. iii. 29.) Accordingly, whatever diversity might at that time exist among men, because many ranks and many nations were strangers to faith, Paul brings to the remembrance of believers the unity of God, that they may know that they are connected with all, because there is one God of all—that they may know that they who are under the power of the same God are not excluded for ever from the hope of salvation.

*And one Mediator between God and men.* This clause is of a similar import with the former; for, as there is one God, the Creator and Father of all, so he says that there is but one Mediator,[1] through whom we have access to the Father; and that this Mediator was given, not only to one nation, or to a small number of persons of some particular rank, but to all; because the fruit of the sacrifice, by which he made atonement for sins, extends to all. More especially because a large portion of the world was at that time alienated from

[1] "Christ is said to be the one Mediator in the same sense that God is said to be the one God. As there is but one Creator of man, so there is but one Mediator for men. As God is the God of all that died before Christ came, as well as of those that died after; so Christ is the Mediator of all that died before his coming, as well as of those that saw his day. They had Christ for their Mediator, or some other; some other they could not have, because there is but one. They might as well have had another Creator besides God, as another Mediator besides the man Christ Jesus. In regard of the antiquity of his mediation, from the foundation of the world, he is represented, when he walks as Mediator 'in the midst of the seven golden candlesticks,' with 'hair as white as wool,' a character of age (Rev. i. 14); as God is described so in regard of his eternity, (Dan. vii. 9.) There is but one God from eternity; but one Mediator, whose mediation hath the same date as the foundation of the world, and runs parallel with it."—*Charnock.*

God, he expressly mentions the Mediator, through whom they that were afar off now approach.

The universal term *all* must always be referred to classes of men, and not to persons; as if he had said, that not only Jews, but Gentiles also, not only persons of humble rank, but princes also, were redeemed by the death of Christ. Since, therefore, he wishes the benefit of his death to be common to all, an insult is offered to him by those who, by their opinion, shut out any person from the hope of salvation.

*The man Christ Jesus.* When he declares that he is " a man," the Apostle does not deny that the Mediator is God, but, intending to point out the bond of our union with God, he mentions the human nature rather than the divine. This ought to be carefully observed. From the beginning, men, by contriving for themselves this or that mediator, departed farther from God; and the reason was, that, being prejudiced in favour of this error, that God was at a great distance from them, they knew not to what hand to turn. Paul remedies this evil, when he represents God as present with us; for he has descended even to us, so that we do not need to seek him above the clouds. The same thing is said in Heb. iv. 15, " We have not a high priest who cannot sympathize with our infirmities, for in all things he was tempted."

And, indeed, if this were deeply impressed on the hearts of all, that the Son of God holds out to us the hand of a brother, and that we are united to him by the fellowship of our nature, in order that, out of our low condition, he may raise us to heaven; who would not choose to keep by this straight road, instead of wandering in uncertain and stormy paths! Accordingly, whenever we ought to pray to God, if we call to remembrance that exalted and inapproachable majesty, that we may not be driven back by the dread of it, let us, at the same time, remember " the man Christ," who gently invites us, and takes us, as it were, by the hand, in order that the Father, who had been the object of terror and alarm, may be reconciled by him and rendered friendly to us. This is the only key to open for us the gate of the heavenly kingdom, that we may appear in the presence of God with confidence.

Hence we see, that Satan has, in all ages, followed this course, for the purpose of leading men astray from the right path. I say nothing of the various devices by which, before the coming of Christ, he alienated the minds of men, to contrive methods of approaching to God. At the very commencement of the Christian Church, when Christ, with so excellent a pledge, was fresh in their remembrance, and while the earth was still ringing with that delightfully sweet word from his mouth, " Come to me, all ye that labour and are heavy laden, and I will give you rest," (Matt. xi. 28,) there were, nevertheless, some persons skilled in deception, who thrust angels into his room as mediators; which is evident from Col. ii. 18. But what Satan, at that time, contrived secretly, he carried to such a pitch, during the times of Popery, that scarcely one person in a thousand acknowledged Christ, even in words, to be the Mediator. And while the name was buried, still more was the reality unknown.

Now that God has raised up good and faithful teachers, who have laboured to restore and bring to the remembrance of men what ought to have been one of the best-known principles of our faith, the sophists of the Church of Rome have resorted to every contrivance for darkening a point so clear. First, the name is so hateful to them, that, if any one mentions Christ as Mediator, without taking notice of the saints, he instantly falls under a suspicion of heresy. But, because they do not venture to reject altogether what Paul teaches in this passage, they evade it by a foolish exposition, that he is called " one Mediator," not " the only Mediator." As if the Apostle had mentioned God as one out of a vast multitude of gods; for the two clauses are closely connected, that " there is one God and one Mediator;" and therefore they who make Christ one out of many mediators must apply the same interpretation in speaking of God. Would they rise to such a height of impudence, if they were not impelled by blind rage to crush the glory of Christ?

There are others who think themselves more acute, and

who lay down this distinction, that Christ is the only Mediator of redemption, while they pronounce the saints to be mediators of intercession. But the folly of these interpreters is reproved by the scope of the passage, in which the Apostle speaks expressly about prayer. The Holy Spirit commands us to pray for all, because our only Mediator admits all to come to him ; just as by his death he reconciled all to the Father. And yet they who thus, with daring sacrilege, strip Christ of his honour, wish to be regarded as Christians.

But it is objected that this has the appearance of contradiction ; for in this very passage Paul enjoins us to intercede for others, while, in the Epistle to the Romans, he declares that intercession belongs to Christ alone. (Rom. viii. 34.) I reply, the intercessions of the saints, by which they aid each other in their addresses to God, do not contradict the doctrine, that all have but one Intercessor ; for no man's prayers are heard either in behalf of himself, or in behalf of another, unless he rely on Christ as his advocate. When we intercede for one another, this is so far from setting aside the intercession of Christ, as belonging to him alone, that the chief reliance is given, and the chief reference made, to that very intercession.

Some person will perhaps think, that it will, therefore, be easy for us to come to an agreement with the Papists, if they place below the only intercession of Christ, all that they ascribe to the saints. This is not the case ; for the reason why they transfer to the saints the office of interceding is, that they imagine that otherwise we are destitute of an advocate. It is a common opinion among them, that we need intercessors, because in ourselves we are unworthy of appearing in the presence of God. By speaking in this manner, they deprive Christ of his honour. Besides, it is a shocking blasphemy, to ascribe to saints such excellence as would procure for us the favour of God : and all the prophets, and apostles, and martyrs, and even the angels themselves—are so far from making any pretension to this, that they too have need of the same intercession as ourselves.

Again, it is a mere dream, originating in their own brain, that the dead intercede for us ; and, therefore, to found our prayers on this is altogether to withdraw our trust from calling upon God. But Paul lays down, as the rule for calling on God in a proper manner, faith grounded on the word of God. (Rom. x. 17.) Justly, therefore, everything that men contrive, in the exercise of their own thoughts, without the authority of the word of God, is rejected by us.

But not to dwell on this subject longer than the exposition of the passage demands, let it be summed up in this manner; that they who have actually learned the office of Christ will be satisfied with having him alone, and that none will make mediators at their own pleasure but those who neither know God nor Christ. Hence I conclude, that the doctrine of the Papists—which darkens, and almost buries, the intercession of Christ, and introduces pretended intercessors without any support from Scripture—is full of wicked distrust, and also of wicked rashness.

6. *Who gave himself a ransom for all.*[1] The mention of redemption in this passage is not superfluous; for there is a necessary connexion between the two things, the sacrifice of the death of Christ, and his continual intercession. (Rom. viii. 34.) These are the two parts of his priesthood; for, when Christ is called our priest, it is in this sense, that he once made atonement for our sins by his death, that he might reconcile us to God; and now having entered into the sanctuary of heaven, he appears in presence of the Father, in order

---

[1] "He gave himself ἀντίλυτρον ὑπὲρ, 'a ransom for' all. If this does not imply the notion of Vicarious, I very much question whether language can express it. Λύτρον is a Ransom; which conveys a vicarious sense, in its most common and authorized acceptation. Ἀντὶ, which is equivalent to Instead, still more fully ascertains and strengthens the idea. (Ἀντὶ, Matt. ii. 22.) By this word the LXX. translated the word תחת, (*tăhhăth.*) And that תחת denotes the substitution of one instead of another, no student of the sacred language will venture to deny. (See Gen. xxii. 13; 2 Sam. xviii. 33; 2 Kings x. 24.) Ὑπὲρ, which is translated For, and denotes a substitution of one in the place of another; this, added to all, renders the expression as determinate and emphatical for the purpose as words can possibly be. Thus writes Clemens Romanus, Τὸ αἷμα αὐτοῦ ἔδωκεν ὑπὲρ ἡμῶν Ἰησοῦς Χριστὸς ὁ Κύριος ἡμῶν, καὶ τὴν σάρκα ὑπὲρ τῆς σάρκος ἡμῶν, καὶ τὴν ψυχὴν ὑπὲρ τῶν ψυχῶν ἡμῶν. "Jesus Christ our Lord gave his blood for us, and his flesh for our flesh, and his soul for our souls." (Ep. i. ad Corinth.) Exactly to the same purpose Justin the Martyr expresses himself: 'He gave his own Son a ransom (ὑπὲρ) for us, the holy for transgressors, the sinless for the sinful, the righteous for the unrighteous, the immortal for the mortal.' (Ep. ad Diogn.)"—Hervey's *Theron and Aspasio.*

to obtain grace for us, that we may be heard in his name. (Ps. cx. 4; Heb. vii. 17.) So much the more does he expose the wicked sacrilege of the Papists, who, by making dead saints to be companions of Christ in this affair, transfer to them likewise the glory of the priesthood. Read the fourth chapter of the Epistle to the Hebrews, towards the conclusion, and the beginning of the fifth chapter, and you will find what I maintain, that the intercession by which God is reconciled to us is founded on the sacrifice; which, indeed, is demonstrated by the whole system of the ancient priesthood. It follows, therefore, that it is impossible to take from Christ any part of the office of intercession, and bestow it on others, without stripping him of the title of priesthood.

Besides, when the Apostle calls him ἀντίλυτρον, "a ransom,"[1] he overthrows all other satisfactions. Yet I am not ignorant of the injurious devices of the Papists, who pretend that the price of redemption, which Christ paid by his death, is applied to us in baptism, so that original sin is effaced, and that afterwards we are reconciled to God by satisfactions. In this way they limit to a small period of time, and to a single class, that benefit which was universal and perpetual. But a full illustration of this subject will be found in the Institutes.

*That there might be a testimony in due time;* that is, in order that this grace might be revealed at the appointed time. The phrase, *for all*, which the Apostle had used, might have given rise to the question, "Why then had God chosen a peculiar people, if he revealed himself as a reconciled Father to all without distinction, and if the one redemption through Christ was common to all?" He cuts off all ground for that

---

[1] " Quand il l'appelle Rançon, ou, Pris de redemption." "When he calls him the Ransom or Price of our redemption."—" Christ came to give up his life as a λύτρον. Now λύτρον properly denotes the ransom paid, in order to deliver any one from death, or its equivalent, captivity, or from punishment in general. It has been satisfactorily proved that, among both the Jews and the Gentiles, peculiar victims were accepted as a ransom for the life of an offender, and to atone for his offence.—The ἀντίλυτρον of this passage is a stronger term than the λύτρον of Matt. xx. 28, and is well explained by Hesych., ἀντίδοτον, implying the substitution, in suffering punishment, of one person for another. See 1 Cor. xv. 3; 2 Cor. v. 21; Tit. ii 14; 1 Pet. i. 18."—*Bloomfield.*

question, by referring to the purpose of God the season¹ for revealing his grace. For if we are not astonished that, in winter, the trees are stripped of their foliage, the fields are covered with snow, and the meadows are stiff with frost, and that, by the genial warmth of spring, what appeared for a time to be dead, begins to revive, because God appointed the seasons to follow in succession; why should we not allow the same authority to his providence in other matters? Shall we accuse God of instability, because he brings forward, at the proper time, what he had always determined, and settled in his own mind?

Accordingly, although it came upon the world suddenly, and was altogether unexpected, that Christ was revealed as a Redeemer to Jews and Gentiles, without distinction; let us not think that it was sudden with respect to God, but, on the contrary, let us learn to subject all our sense to his wonderful providence. The consequence will be, that there will be nothing that comes from him which shall not appear to us to be highly seasonable. On that account this admonition frequently occurs in the writings of Paul, and especially when he treats of the calling of the Gentiles, by which, at that time, on account of its novelty, many persons were startled and almost confounded. They who are not satisfied with this solution, that God, by his hidden wisdom, arranged the succession of the seasons, will one day feel, that, at the time when they think that he was idle, he was framing a hell for inquisitive persons.

7. *For which I have been appointed.* That it may not be thought that he makes rash assertions—as many are wont to do—on a subject which he did not well understand, he affirms that God had appointed him for this purpose, that he might bring the Gentiles, who had formerly been alienated from the kingdom of God, to have a share in the gospel; for his apostleship was a sure foundation of the divine calling. And on this account he labours very hard in asserting it, as there are many who received it with no small difficulty.

*I speak the truth in Christ, I do not lie.* He employs an

¹ " Le temps propre et la droite saison." " The fit time and proper season."

oath, or protestation, as in a matter of extraordinary weight and importance, that he is *a teacher of the Gentiles*, and that in *faith and truth.* These two things denote a good conscience, but still it must rest on the certainty of the will of God. Thus he means, that he preaches the gospel to the Gentiles, not only with pure affection, but also with an upright and fearless conscience; because he does nothing but by the command of God.

| | |
|---|---|
| 8. I will therefore that men pray every where, lifting up holy hands, without wrath and doubting. | 8. Volo igitur orare viros in omni loco, sustollentes puras manus, absque ira et disceptatione. |
| 9. In like manner also, that women adorn themselves in modest apparel, with shamefacedness and sobriety; not with broidered hair, or gold, or pearls, or costly array; | 9. Consimiliter et mulieres in amictu decoro cum verecundia et temperantia ornare semetipsas, non tortis crinibus, aut auro, aut margaritis, aut vestitu sumptuoso; |
| 10. But (which becometh women professing godliness) with good works. | 10. Sed, quod decet mulieres profitentes pietatem, per bona opera. |

8. *I wish therefore that men may pray.* This inference depends on the preceding statement; for, as we saw in the Epistle to the Galatians, we must receive "the Spirit of adoption," in order that we may call on God in a proper manner. Thus, after having exhibited the grace of Christ to all, and after having mentioned that he was given to the Gentiles for the express purpose, that they might enjoy the same benefit of redemption in common with the Jews, he invites all in the same manner to pray; for faith leads to calling on God. Hence, at Rom. xv. 9, he proves the calling of the Gentiles by these passages. "Let the Gentiles rejoice with his people." (Ps. lxvii. 5.) Again, "All ye Gentiles, praise God." (Ps. cxvii. 1.) Again, "I will confess to thee among the Gentiles." (Ps. xviii. 49.) The material argument holds good, from faith to prayer, and from prayer to faith, whether we reason from the cause to the effect, or from the effect to the cause. This is worthy of observation, because it reminds us that God reveals himself to us in his word, that we may call upon him; and this is the chief exercise of faith.

*In every place.* This expression is of the same import as in the beginning of the First Epistle to the Corinthians, "with all that *in every place* call on the name of Jesus

Christ our Lord," (1 Cor. i. 2,) so that there is now no difference between Gentile and Jew, between Greek and barbarian, because all in common have God as their Father; and in Christ is now fulfilled what Malachi had foretold, that not only in Judea, but throughout the whole world, pure sacrifices are offered. (Mal. i. 11.)

*Lifting up pure hands.* As if he had said, "Provided that it be accompanied by a good conscience, there will be nothing to prevent all the nations from calling upon God everywhere. But he has employed the sign instead of the reality, for "pure hands" are the expressions of a pure heart; just as, on the contrary, Isaiah rebukes the Jews for lifting up "bloody hands," when he attacks their cruelty. (Isa. i. 15.) Besides, this attitude has been generally used in worship during all ages; for it is a feeling which nature has implanted in us, when we ask God, to look upwards, and has always been so strong, that even idolaters themselves, although in other respects they make a god of images of wood and stone, still retained the custom of lifting up their hands to heaven. Let us therefore learn that the attitude is in accordance with true godliness, provided that it be attended by the corresponding truth which is represented by it, namely, that, having been informed that we ought to seek God in heaven, first, we should form no conception of Him that is earthly or carnal; and, secondly, that we should lay aside carnal affections, so that nothing may prevent our hearts from rising above the world. But idolaters and hypocrites, when they lift up their hands in prayer, are apes; for while they profess, by the outward symbol, that their minds are raised upwards, the former are fixed on wood and stone, as if God were shut up in them, and the latter, wrapped up either in useless anxieties, or in wicked thoughts, cleave to the earth; and therefore, by a gesture of an opposite meaning,[1] they bear testimony against themselves.

*Without wrath.* Some explain this to mean a burst of indignation, when the conscience fights with itself, and, so to speak, quarrels with God, which usually happens when ad-

---

[1] " En monstrant une contenance contraire a ce qui est en le cœur. " By showing a countenance opposite to what is in their heart."

versity presses heavily upon us; for then we are displeased that God does not send us immediate assistance, and are agitated by impatience. Faith is also shaken by various assaults; for, in consequence of his assistance not being visible, we are seized with doubts, whether or not he cares about us, or wishes us to be saved, and things of that nature.

They who take this view think that the word *disputing* denotes that alarm which arises from doubt. Thus, according to them, the meaning would be, that we should pray with a peaceful conscience and assured confidence. Chrysostom and others think that the apostle here demands that our minds should be calm and free from all uneasy feelings both towards God and towards men; because there is nothing that tends more to hinder pure calling on God than quarrels and strife. On this account Christ enjoins, that if any man be at variance with his brother, he shall go and be reconciled to him before offering his gift on the altar.

For my part, I acknowledge that both of these views are just; but when I take into consideration the context of this passage, I have no doubt that Paul had his eye on the disputes which arose out of the indignation of the Jews at having the Gentiles made equal to themselves, in consequence of which they raised a controversy about the calling of the Gentiles, and went so far as to reject and exclude them from the participation of grace. Paul therefore wishes that debates of this nature should be put down, and that all the children of God of every nation and country should pray with one heart. Yet there is nothing to restrain us from drawing from this particular statement a general doctrine.

9. *In like manner also women.* As he enjoined men to lift up pure hands, so he now prescribes the manner in which women ought to prepare for praying aright. And there appears to be an implied contrast between those virtues which he recommends and the outward sanctification of the Jews; for he intimates that there is no profane place, nor any from which both men and women may not draw near to God, provided they are not excluded by their vices.

He intended to embrace the opportunity of correcting a

vice to which women are almost always prone, and which perhaps at Ephesus, being a city of vast wealth and extensive merchandise, especially abounded. That vice is—excessive eagerness and desire to be richly dressed. He wishes therefore that their dress should be regulated by modesty and sobriety; for luxury and immoderate expense arise from a desire to make a display either for the sake of pride or of departure from chastity. And hence we ought to derive the rule of moderation; for, since dress is an indifferent matter, (as all outward matters are,) it is difficult to assign a fixed limit, how far we ought to go. Magistrates may indeed make laws, by means of which a rage for superfluous expenditure shall be in some measure restrained; but godly teachers, whose business it is to guide the consciences, ought always to keep in view the end of lawful use. This at least will be settled beyond all controversy, that every thing in dress which is not in accordance with modesty and sobriety must be disapproved.

Yet we must always begin with the dispositions; for where debauchery reigns within, there will be no chastity; and where ambition reigns within, there will be no modesty in the outward dress. But because hypocrites commonly avail themselves of all the pretexts that they can find for concealing their wicked dispositions, we are under the necessity of pointing out what meets the eye. It would be great baseness to deny the appropriateness of modesty as the peculiar and constant ornament of virtuous and chaste women, or the duty of all to observe moderation. Whatever is opposed to these virtues it will be in vain to excuse. He expressly censures certain kinds of superfluity, such as curled hair, jewels, and golden rings; not that the use of gold or of jewels is expressly forbidden, but that, wherever they are prominently displayed, these things commonly draw along with them the other evils which I have mentioned, and arise from ambition or from want of chastity as their source.

10. *Which becometh women;* for undoubtedly the dress of a virtuous and godly woman must differ from that of a strumpet. What he has laid down are marks of distinction;

| | |
|---|---|
| 11. Let the woman learn in silence with all subjection. | 11. Mulier in quiete discat, cum omni subjectione. |
| 12. But I suffer not a woman to teach, nor to usurp authority over the man, but to be in silence. | 12. Docere autem mulieri non permitto, neque auctoritatem sibi sumere in virum, sed quietam esse. |
| 13. For Adam was first formed, then Eve. | 13. Adam enim creatus fuit prior, deinde Eva. |
| 14. And Adam was not deceived; but the woman, being deceived, was in the transgression. | 14. Et Adam non fuit deceptus; sed mulier decepta transgressionis rea fuit. |
| 15. Notwithstanding she shall be saved in child-bearing, if they continue in faith, and charity, and holiness, with sobriety. | 15. Servabitur autem per generationem, si manserit in fide, et caritate, et sanctificatione, cum temperantia. |

and if piety must be testified by works, this profession ought also to be visible in chaste and becoming dress.

11. *Let a woman learn in quietness.* After having spoken of dress, he now adds with what modesty women ought to conduct themselves in the holy assembly. And first he bids them learn quietly; for *quietness* means silence, that they may not take upon them to speak in public. This he immediately explains more clearly, by forbidding them to teach.

12. *But I suffer not a woman to teach.* Not that he takes from them the charge of instructing their family, but only excludes them from the office of teaching, which God has committed to men only. On this subject we have explained our views in the exposition of the First Epistle to the Corinthians.[1] If any one bring forward, by way of objection, Deborah (Judges iv. 4) and others of the same class, of whom we read that they were at one time appointed by the command of God to govern the people, the answer is easy. Extraordinary acts done by God do not overturn the ordinary rules of government, by which he intended that we should be bound. Accordingly, if women at one time held the office of prophets and teachers, and that too when they were supernaturally called to it by the Spirit of God, He who is above all law might do this; but, being a peculiar case,[2] this is not opposed to the constant and ordinary system of government.

---

[1] See Commentary on the Epistles of Paul to the Corinthians, vol. i. p. 467.

[2] "Pource que c'est un cas particulier et extraordinaire." "Because it is a peculiar and extraordinary case."

He adds—what is closely allied to the office of teaching—*and not to assume authority over the man;* for the very reason, why they are forbidden to teach, is, that it is not permitted by their condition. They are subject, and to teach implies the rank of power or authority. Yet it may be thought that there is no great force in this argument; because even prophets and teachers are subject to kings and to other magistrates. I reply, there is no absurdity in the same person commanding and likewise obeying, when viewed in different relations. But this does not apply to the case of woman, who by nature (that is, by the ordinary law of God) is formed to obey; for γυναικοκρατία (the government of women) has always been regarded by all wise persons as a monstrous thing; and, therefore, so to speak, it will be a mingling of heaven and earth, if women usurp the right to teach. Accordingly, he bids them be " quiet," that is, keep within their own rank.[1]

13. *For Adam was first created.* He assigns two reasons why women ought to be subject to men; because not only did God enact this law at the beginning, but he also inflicted it as a punishment on the woman. (Gen. iii. 16.) He accordingly shews that, although mankind had stood in their first and original uprightness, the true order of nature, which proceeded from the command of God, bears that women shall be subject. Nor is this inconsistent with the fact, that Adam, by falling from his first dignity, deprived himself of his authority; for in the ruins, which followed sin, there still linger some remains of the divine blessing, and it was not proper that woman, by her own fault, should make her condition better than before.[2]

Yet the reason which Paul assigns, that woman was second in the order of creation, appears not to be a very strong argument in favour of her subjection; for John the Baptist was before Christ in the order of time, and yet was greatly inferior in rank. But although Paul does not state

---

[1] " Il commande donc qu'elles demeurent en silence ; c'est a dire, qu'elles se contiennent dedans leurs limites, et la condition de leur sexe." " He therefore commands them to remain in silence; that is, to keep within their limits and the condition of their sex."

[2] " Que la femme par son peche amendast son condition."

all the circumstances which are related by Moses, yet he intended that his readers should take them into consideration. Now Moses shews that the woman was created afterwards, in order that she might be a kind of appendage to the man; and that she was joined to the man on the express condition, that she should be at hand to render obedience to him. (Gen. ii. 21.) Since, therefore, God did not create two chiefs of equal power, but added to the man an inferior aid, the Apostle justly reminds us of that order of creation in which the eternal and inviolable appointment of God is strikingly displayed.

14. *And Adam was not deceived.* He alludes to the punishment inflicted on the woman: "Because thou hast obeyed the voice of the serpent, thou shalt be subject to the authority of thy husband, and thy desire shall be to him."[1] (Gen. iii. 16.) Because she had given fatal advice, it was right that she should learn that she was under the power and will of another; and because she had drawn her husband aside from the command of God, it was right that she should be deprived of all liberty and placed under the yoke. Besides, the Apostle does not rest his argument entirely or absolutely on the cause of the transgression, but founds it on the sentence which was pronounced by God.

Yet it may be thought that these two statements are somewhat contradictory, that the subjection of the woman is the punishment of her transgression, and yet that it was imposed on her from the creation; for thence it will follow, that she was doomed to servitude before she sinned. I reply, there is nothing to hinder that the condition of obeying should be natural from the beginning, and that afterwards the accidental condition of serving should come into existence; so that the subjection was now less voluntary and agreeable than it had formerly been.

Again, this passage has given to some people an occasion for affirming that Adam did not fall by means of error, but that he was only overcome by the allurements of his wife. Accordingly, they think that the woman only was deceived

---

[1] "Et ta volonte sera sujete a la sienne." "And thy will shall be subject to his will."

by the wiles of the devil, to believe that she and her husband would be like the gods; but that Adam was not at all persuaded of this, but tasted the fruit in order to please his wife. But it is easy to refute this opinion; for, if Adam had not given credit to the falsehood of Satan, God would not have reproached him: "Behold, Adam is become like one of us." (Gen. iii. 22.) There are other reasons of which I say nothing; for there needs not a long refutation of an error which does not rest on any probable conjecture. By these words Paul does not mean that Adam was not entangled by the same deceitfulness of the devil,[1] but that the cause or source of the transgression proceeded from Eve.

15. *But she shall be saved.* The weakness of the sex renders women more suspicious and timid, and the preceding statement might greatly terrify and alarm the strongest minds. For these reasons he modifies what he had said by adding a consolation; for the Spirit of God does not accuse or reproach us, in order to triumph over us, when we are covered with shame, but, when we have been cast down, immediately raises us up. It might have the effect (as I have already said) of striking terror into the minds of women,[2] when they were informed that the destruction of the whole human race was attributed to them; for what will be this condemnation? especially when their subjection, as a testimony of the wrath of God, is constantly placed before their eyes. Accordingly, Paul, in order to comfort them and render their condition tolerable, informs them that they continue to enjoy the hope of salvation, though they suffer a temporal punishment. It is proper to observe that the good effect of this consolation is twofold. First, by the hope of salvation held out to them, they are prevented from falling into despair through alarm at the mention of their guilt. Secondly, they become accustomed to endure calmly and patiently the necessity of servitude, so as to submit willingly to their husbands, when they are informed that this kind of

---

[1] "Qu'il ne donna lieu a aucune persuasion du diable." "That he did not yield to any persuasion of the devil."

[2] "C'estoit une chose pour descourager les femmes, et les mettre en desespoir." "It was fitted to discourage women, and to reduce them to despair."

obedience is both profitable to themselves and acceptable to God. If this passage be tortured, as Papists are wont to do, to support the righteousness of works, the answer is easy. The Apostle does not argue here about the cause of salvation, and therefore we cannot and must not infer from these words what works deserve; but they only shew in what way God conducts us to salvation, to which he has appointed us through his grace.

*Through child-bearing.* To censorious men it might appear absurd, for an Apostle of Christ not only to exhort women to give attention to the birth of offspring, but to press this work as religious and holy to such an extent as to represent it in the light of the means of procuring salvation. Nay, we even see with what reproaches the conjugal bed has been slandered by hypocrites, who wished to be thought more holy than all other men. But there is no difficulty in replying to these sneers of the ungodly. First, here the Apostle does not speak merely about having children, but about enduring all the distresses, which are manifold and severe, both in the birth and in the rearing of children. Secondly, whatever hypocrites or wise men of the world may think of it, when a woman, considering to what she has been called, submits to the condition which God has assigned to her, and does not refuse to endure the pains, or rather the fearful anguish, of parturition, or anxiety about her offspring, or anything else that belongs to her duty, God values this obedience more highly than if, in some other manner, she made a great display of heroic virtues, while she refused to obey the calling of God. To this must be added, that no consolation could be more appropriate or more efficacious than to shew that the very means (so to speak) of procuring salvation are found in the punishment itself.

*If they continue in faith.* In consequence of the old translation having used the expression, "the birth of children," it has been commonly thought that this clause refers to the children. But the term used by Paul to denote "child-bearing" is a single word, τεκνογονία, and therefore it must refer to the women. As to the verb being plural, and the noun singular, this involves no difficulty; for an indefinite noun, at least when it denotes a multitude, has the force of a collective noun, and therefore easily admits a change from the singular to the plural number.

Besides, that he might not represent all the virtue of women as included in the duties of marriage, immediately afterwards he adds greater virtues, in which it is proper that godly women should excel, that they may differ from irreligious women. Even " child-bearing" is obedience acceptable to God, only so far as it proceeds from *faith and love*. To these two he adds *sanctification*, which includes all that purity of life which becomes Christian women. Lastly follows *sobriety*, which he formerly mentioned, while he was speaking about dress; but now he extends it more widely to the other parts of life.

## CHAPTER III.

1. This *is* a true saying, If a man desire the office of a bishop, he desireth a good work.
2. A bishop then must be blameless, the husband of one wife, vigilant, sober, of good behaviour, given to hospitality, apt to teach;
3. Not given to wine, no striker, not greedy of filthy lucre: but patient, not a brawler, not covetous;
4. One that ruleth well his own house, having his children in subjection with all gravity;
5. (For if a man know not how to rule his own house, how shall he take care of the church of God?)
6. Not a novice, lest, being lifted up with pride, he fall into the condemnation of the devil.
7. Moreover, he must have a good report of them which are without; lest he fall into reproach and the snare of the devil.

1. Certus sermo, si quis episcopatum appetit, præclarum opus desiderat.
2. Oportet ergo Episcopum irreprehensibilem esse, unius uxoris maritum, sobrium, temperantem, compositum, (*vel, honestum,*) hospitalem, aptum ad docendum.
3. Non vinolentum, (*vel, ferocem,*) non percussorem, non turpiter lucri cupidum, sed æquum, alienum a pugnis, alienum ab avaritia.
4. Qui domui suæ bene præsit, qui filios habeat in subjectione, cum omni reverentia.
5. Quodsi quis propriæ domui præesse non novit, ecclesiam Dei quomodo curabit?
6. Non novicium, ne inflatus in condemnationem incidat diaboli.
7. Oportet autem illum et bonum testimonium habere ab extraneis, ne in probrum incidat et laqueum diaboli.

1. *It is a true saying.* Chrysostom thinks, that this is the conclusion of the preceding doctrine. But I do not ap-

prove of the opinion; for Paul commonly makes use of this form of expression as a prelude to what he is about to introduce. Besides, in the former discourse there was no need of so strong an affirmation; but what he is now about to say, is somewhat more weighty. Let these words, therefore, be received as a preface intended to point out the importance of the subject; for Paul now begins a new discourse about ordaining pastors, and appointing the government of the Church.

*If any one desireth the office of a bishop.*[1] Having forbidden women to teach, he now takes occasion to speak of the office of a bishop. First, that it may be more clearly seen that it was not without reason that he refused to allow women to undertake so arduous a work; secondly, that it might not be thought that, by excluding women only, he admitted all men indiscriminately; and, thirdly, because it was highly proper that Timothy and others should be reminded what conscientious watchfulness ought to be used in the election of bishops. Thus the context, in my opinion, is as if Paul had said, that so far are women from being fit for undertaking so excellent an office, that not even men ought to be admitted into it without distinction.

*He desireth an excellent work.* The Apostle affirms that this is no inconsiderable work, such as any man might venture to undertake. When he says that it is καλόν, I have no doubt that he alludes to the ancient Greek proverb, often quoted by Plato, δύσκολα τὰ καλά, which means that "those things which are excellent, are also arduous and difficult;" and thus he unites difficulty with excellence, or rather he argues thus, that it does not belong to every person to discharge the office of a bishop, because it is a thing of great value.

I think that Paul's meaning is now sufficiently clear; though none of the commentators, so far as I perceive, have understood it. The general meaning is, that a selection ought to be made in admitting bishops, because it is a laborious and difficult charge; and that they who aim at it

[1] " Ou, Si aucun a affection d'estre evesque." " Or, If any one hath a desire to be a bishop."

should carefully consider with themselves, whether or not they were able to bear so heavy a burden. Ignorance is always rash; and a mature knowledge of things makes a man modest. How comes it that they who have neither ability nor wisdom often aspire so confidently to hold the reins of government, but because they rush forward with their eyes shut? On this subject Quintilian remarked, that the ignorant speak boldly, while the greatest orators tremble.

For the purpose of restraining such rashness in desiring the office of a bishop, Paul states, first, that this is not an indolent rank, but a *work;* and next, that it is not any kind of work, but *excellent,* and therefore toilsome and full of difficulty, as it actually is. It is no light matter to be a representative of the Son of God, in discharging an office of such magnitude, the object of which is to erect and extend the kingdom of God, to procure the salvation of souls which the Lord himself hath purchased with his own blood, and to govern the Church, which is God's inheritance. But it is not my intention at present to make a sermon, and Paul will again glance at this subject in the next chapter.

Here a question arises: "Is it lawful, in any way, to desire the office of a bishop?" On the one hand, it appears to be highly improper for any one to anticipate, by his wish, the calling of God, and yet Paul, while he censures a rash desire, seems to permit it to be desired with prudence and modesty. I reply, if ambition is condemned in other matters, much more severely ought it to be condemned in "the office of a bishop." But Paul speaks of a godly desire, by which holy men wish to employ that knowledge of doctrine which they possess for the edification of the Church. For, if it were altogether unlawful to desire the office of a teacher, why should they who spend all their youth in reading the Holy Scriptures prepare themselves by learning? What are the theological schools but nurseries of pastors?

Accordingly, they who have been thus instructed not only may lawfully devote themselves and their labours to God by a voluntary offering, but even ought to do so, and that too, before they have been admitted into the office; provided that, nevertheless, they do not thrust themselves forward, and do not, even by their own wish, make themselves bishops, but are only ready to discharge the office, if their labours shall be required. And if it turn out that, according to the lawful order, they are not called, let them know that such was the will of God, and let them not take it ill that others have been preferred to them. But they who, without any selfish motive, shall have no other wish than to serve God and the Church, will be affected in this manner, and, at the same time, will have such modesty that they will not be at all envious, if others be preferred to them as being more worthy.

If any one object, that the government of the Church is a matter of so great difficulty, that it ought rather to strike terror into the minds of persons of sound judgment than to excite them to desire it ; I reply, that the desire of great men does not rest on confidence of their own industry or virtue, but on the assistance of " God, from whom is our sufficiency," as Paul says elsewhere. (2 Cor. iii. 5.)

At the same time, it is necessary to observe what it is that Paul calls " the office of a bishop ;" and so much the more, because the ancients were led away, by the custom of their times, from the true meaning ; for, while Paul includes generally all pastors, they understand a bishop to be one who was elected out of each college to preside over his brethren. Let us remember, therefore, that this word is of the same import as if he had called them ministers, or pastors, or presbyters.[1]

[1] " Let us know that the Holy Spirit, speaking of those who are ordained ministers of the word of God, and who are elected to govern the Church, calls them Pastors. And why ? Because God wishes us to be a flock of sheep, to be guided by him, hearing his voice, following his guidance, and living peaceably. Since, therefore, the Church is compared to a flock, they who have the charge of guiding the Church by the word of God are called Pastors. And next, the word Pastor means Elder, not by age, but by office : as, at all times, they who govern have been called Elders, even among heathen nations Now the Holy Spirit has retained this metaphor, giving the name Elder to those who are chosen to proclaim the word of God. He likewise calls them Bishops, that is, persons who watch over the flock, to show that it is not a rank unaccompanied by active exertion. when a man is called to that office, and that he must not make an idol of it, but must know that he is sent to obtain the salvation of souls, and must be employed, and watch, and labour, for that purpose. We see then the reason of these words ; and since the Holy Spirit hath given them to us, we must

**2. *A bishop, therefore, must be blameless.*** The particle *therefore* confirms the exposition which I have given; for, on account of the dignity of the office, he concludes that it is requisite that he be a man endowed with rare gifts, and not any person taken out of the crowd.[1] If the expression used had been "a good work," as the ordinary translation has it, or "an honourable work," (*honestam,*) as Erasmus has translated it, the inference would not have been suitable.

He wishes a bishop to be *blameless,*[2] instead of which, in the Epistle to Titus, he has used (Tit. i. 7) the word ἀνέγκλητον, meaning by both words, that he must not be marked by any infamy that would lessen his authority. There will be no one found among men that is free from every vice; but it is one thing to be blemished with ordinary vices, which do not hurt the reputation, because they are found in men of the highest excellence, and another thing to have a disgraceful name, or to be stained with any baseness. In order, therefore, that a bishop may not be without authority, he enjoins that there shall be made a selection of one who has a good and honourable reputation, and not chargeable with any remarkable vice. Besides, he does not merely lay down a rule for Timothy what sort of person he must select, but likewise reminds every one of those who aspire to that rank, to institute a careful examination of himself and of his life.

*The husband of one wife.* It is a childish fancy to interpret this as meaning "the pastor of a single church." An-

retain them, provided that they be applied to a good and holy use."—*Fr. Ser.*

[1] "Et non pas le premier qui se pourroit presenter." "And not the first that might offer himself."

[2] Ἀνεπίληπτον—"This is properly an antagonistic term, signifying, 'one who gives his adversary no hold upon him;' but it is often (as here) applied metaphorically to one who gives others no cause justly to accuse him So Thucydides, v. 17, τοῖς ἐχθροῖς ἀνεπίληπτον εἶναι. 'Such (says a celebrated writer) is the perfect purity of our religion, such the innocence and virtue which it exacts, that he must be a very good man indeed who lives up to it.' And when we consider the still greater requirements in a teacher of religion, (who is to be an example to others,) and reflect on the injury done to religion through the side of false professors, how much reason will there appear that such a one should be, as the apostle says, *blameless.*"—*Bloomfield.*

other exposition has been more generally received, that the person set apart to that office must be one who has not been more than once married, that one wife being since dead, so that now he is not a married man. But both in this passage and in Titus i. 6, the words of the apostle are, "Who is," and not "Who hath been;" and in this very Epistle, where he treats of widows, (v. 10,) he expressly makes use of the participle of the past tense. Besides, in this way he would contradict himself; because elsewhere he declares that he has no wish to lay a snare on the consciences.

The only true exposition, therefore, is that of Chrysostom, that in a bishop he expressly condemns polygamy,[1] which at that time the Jews almost reckoned to be lawful. This corruption was borrowed by them partly from a sinful imitation of the Fathers, (for they who read that Abraham, Jacob, David, and others of the same class, were married to more wives than one at the same time, thought that it was lawful for them also to do the same) and partly from neighbouring nations; for the inhabitants of the East never observed that conscientiousness and fidelity in marriage which was proper. However that might be, polygamy was exceedingly prevalent among them;[2] and therefore with great propriety does Paul enjoin that a bishop should be free from this stain.

And yet I do not disapprove of the opinion of those who think that the Holy Spirit intended to guard against the diabolical superstition which afterwards arose; as if he had said, "So far is it from being right and proper that celibacy should be enforced on bishops, that marriage is a state highly becoming in all believers." In this way, he would not demand it as a thing necessary for them, but would only praise it as not inconsistent with the dignity of the office. Yet the view which I have already given is more simple and more solid, that Paul forbids polygamy in all who hold the office of a bishop, because it is a mark of an unchaste man, and of one who does not observe conjugal fidelity.

[1] "Qu'il condamne en l'Evesque d'avoir deux femmes ensemble vivantes." "That he condemns in a bishop the having two wives living at the same time."

[2] "La polygamie estoit une chose toute commune entre les Juifs." "Polygamy was a thing quite common among the Jews."

But here it might be objected, that what is sinful in all ought not to have been condemned or forbidden in bishops alone. The answer is easy. When it is expressly prohibited to bishops, it does not therefore follow that it is freely allowed to others. Beyond all doubt, Paul condemned universally what was contrary to an unrepealed law of God; for it is a settled enactment, "They shall be one flesh." (Gen. ii. 24.) But he might, to some extent, bear with that in others which, in a bishop, would have been excessively vile, and therefore not to be endured.

Nor is this a law laid down for the future, that no bishop, who already has one wife, shall marry a second or a third, while the first wife is still living; but Paul excludes from the office of a bishop any one who shall be guilty of such an enormity. Accordingly, what had been once done, and could not be corrected, he reluctantly endures, but only in the common people. For what was the remedy for those who, under Judaism, had fallen into the snare of polygamy? Should they have divorced their second and third wives? Such a divorce would not have been free from doing wrong. Since, therefore, the deed was done, and could not be undone, he left it untouched, but with this exception, that no bishop should be blemished by such a stain.

*Sober, temperate, modest.* The word which we have translated *sober*, Erasmus has translated (vigilantem) *watchful.* As the Greek word νηφάλεος[1] admits of either signification, the readers may make their own choice. I have preferred to translate σώφρονα, *temperate*, instead of *sober*, because σωφροσύνη has a more extensive meaning than sobriety. *Modest* means one who conducts himself with decency and propriety.

---

[1] " Νηφάλιον, 'vigilant or circumspect.' In which sense the word occurs in the later writers; as, for instance, Phavorinus. The force of the word is well expressed by the Pesch. Syr., 'mente sit vigilanti.' Instead of νηφάλιον, (the reading of many of the best MSS. and all the early editions,) νηφάλεον was introduced by Beza, but without any sufficient reason; and the former has been rightly restored by Wetstein, Griesbach, Matthæi, Tittmann, and Vater. Here, then, we have a quality suggested by the very term ἐπίσκοπος, which imports vigilant superintendence."
—*Bloomfield.*

*Hospitable.*[1] The "hospitality" here spoken of, is toward strangers, and this was very common among the ancients; for it would have been reckoned disgraceful for respectable persons, and especially for those who were well known, to lodge in taverns. In the present day, the state of matters is different; but this virtue is and always will be highly necessary in a bishop, for many reasons. Besides, during the cruel persecution of the godly, many persons must have been constrained frequently to change their habitation; and therefore it was necessary that the houses of bishops should be a retreat for the exiles. In those times hard necessity compelled the churches to afford mutual aid, so that they gave lodgings to one another. Now, if the bishops had not pointed out the path to others in this department of duty, the greater part, following their example, would have neglected the exercise of humanity, and thus the poor fugitives would have been greatly discouraged.[2]

*Able to teach.* In the epistle to Titus, doctrine is expressly mentioned; here he only speaks briefly about skill in communicating instruction. It is not enough to have profound learning, if it be not accompanied by talent for teaching. There are many who, either because their utterance is defective, or because they have not good mental abilities, or because they do not employ that familiar language which is adapted to the common people, keep within their own minds the knowledge which they possess. Such persons, as the phrase is, ought to sing to themselves and

---

[1] "Recueillant volontiers les estrangers." "Willingly entertaining strangers."
[2] "Let every one know that the virtues which are here required in all ministers of the word of God, are in order to give an example to the flock. It is highly proper for every one to know that, when it is said that ministers should be wise, temperate, and of good moral behaviour, it is in order that others may be conformed to their example; for it is not for three or four only, but for all in general, that these things are said. This is the way in which the example of men must be profitable to us, so far as they shall conduct themselves properly, according to the will of God. And if they depart from that will ever so little, we must not yield to them such authority as to follow them on that account; but we must attend to what Paul says, that we ought to follow men so far as they are entirely conformed to the pure word of God, and are imitators of Jesus Christ, to lead us in the right way."—*Fr. Ser.*

to the muses.¹ They who have the charge of governing the people, ought to be qualified for teaching. And here he does not demand volubility of tongue, for we see many persons whose fluent talk is not fitted for edification; but he rather commends wisdom in applying the word of God judiciously to the advantage of the people.

It is worth while to consider how the Papists hold that the injunctions which the apostle gives do not at all belong to them. I shall not enter into a minute explanation of all the details; but on this one point what sort of diligence do they observe? And, indeed, that gift would be superfluous; for they banish from themselves the ministry of teaching as low and grovelling, although this belonged especially to a bishop. But everybody knows how far it is from observing Paul's rule, to assume the title of bishop, and boast proudly of enacting a character without speaking, provided only that they make their appearance in a theatrical dress. As if a horned mitre, a ring richly set in jewels, or a silver cross, and other trifles, accompanied by idle display, constituted the spiritual government of a church, which can no more be separated from doctrine than any one of us can be separated from his own soul.

3. *Not addicted to wine.* By the word πάροινον,² which is here used, the Greeks denote not merely drunkenness, but any intemperance in guzzling wine. And, indeed, to drink wine excessively is not only very unbecoming in a pastor, but commonly draws along with it many things still worse; such as quarrels, foolish attitudes, unchaste conduct, and other things which it is not necessary to describe. But the contrast which is added shortly afterwards, shews that Paul goes farther than this.

¹ " Il faut que tels s'employent a autre chose." " Such persons ought to be employed in something else."

² " Some expositors, ancient and modern, take this to be equivalent to ὑβριστὴν or αὐθάδη; which is, indeed, much countenanced by three *vices* in this clause, standing opposed to the three *virtues* in the next. But considering that we have at verse 8 the expression μὴ οἴνῳ προσέχοντας used of the deacons, here at least the physical sense must be included; and, according to every principle of correct exegesis, it must stand first. In the word πάροινος, the παρὰ means beyond, denoting excess. So the expression in Hab. ii. 5, 'he transgresseth by wine.'"—*Bloomfield.*

*Not a striker, not wickedly desirous of gain.*[1] As he contrasts with "a striker" one who is not quarrelsome, and with him who is covetous of dishonest gain (ἀφιλάργυρον) one who is not covetous, so with τῷ παροίνῳ, him who is addicted to wine, he contrasts one who is gentle or kind. The true interpretation is that which is given by Chrysostom, that men of a drunken and fierce disposition ought to be excluded from the office of a bishop. As to the opinion given by Chrysostom, that "a striker" means one who wounds with the tongue, (that is, who is guilty of slander or of outrageous reproaches,) I do not admit it. Nor am I moved by his argument, that it will be no great matter, if the bishop do not strike with the hand; for I think that here he reproves generally that fierceness which is often found in the military profession, and which is utterly unbecoming in the servants of Christ. It is well known to what ridicule they expose themselves, who are more ready to strike a blow with the fist, and—we might even say— to draw the sword, than to settle the disputes of others by their own sedate behaviour. *Strikers* is therefore the term which he applies to those who deal much in threatenings, and are of a warlike temperament.

All covetous persons are *wickedly desirous of gain;* for, wherever covetousness is, there will also be that baseness of which the apostle speaks. "He who wishes to become rich wishes also to become rich soon."[2] The consequence is, that all covetous persons, even though this is not openly manifest, apply their minds to dishonest and unlawful gains. Accordingly, he contrasts with this vice the contempt of money; as there is no other remedy by which it can be corrected. He who will not patiently and mildly endure poverty will never escape the disease of mean and sordid covetousness.

*Mild and not quarrelsome.* He contrasts with "the striker" the man who is "not quarrelsome." *Mild*—which,

---

[1] " Ne convoiteux de gain deshonneste." "Not covetous of dishonourable gain."

[2] " Dives fieri qui vult,
Et cito vult fieri."—*Juvenal.*

we have said, is contrasted with being "addicted to wine"—is the term applied to him who knows how to bear injuries with a gentle and moderate disposition, who forgives much, who passes by insults, who neither makes himself be dreaded through harsh severity, nor exacts with full rigour. *Not quarrelsome,* one who avoids disputes and quarrels; for, as he elsewhere writes, "the servant of the Lord must not be quarrelsome." (2 Tim. ii. 24.)

4. *Who ruleth well his own house.* Hence it is evident, that Paul does not demand that a bishop shall be unacquainted with human life,[1] but that he shall be a good and praiseworthy master of a household; for, whatever may be the admiration commonly entertained for celibacy and a philosophical life altogether removed from ordinary custom, yet wise and thoughtful men are convinced by experience, that they who are not ignorant of ordinary life, but are practised in the duties of human intercourse, are better trained and adapted for governing the Church. And, therefore, we ought to observe the reason which is added, (ver. 5,) that he who does not know how to rule his family, will not be qualified for governing the Church. Now, this is the case with very many persons, and indeed with almost all who have been drawn out of an idle and solitary life,[2] as out of dens and caverns; for they are a sort of savages and destitute of humanity.

*Who hath his children in subjection with all reverence.* The apostle does not recommend a clever man, and deeply skilled in domestic matters, but one who has learned to govern a family by wholesome discipline. He speaks chiefly of *children,* who may be expected to possess the natural disposition of their father; and therefore it will be a great disgrace to a bishop, if he has children who lead a wicked and scandalous life. As to wives, he will speak of them afterwards; but at present, as I have said, he glances at the most important part of a house.

In the Epistle to Titus, (i. 6,) he shows what is here

---

[1] "Que l'Evesque ne sache que c'est de vivre au monde." "That the bishop shall not know what it is to live in the world."

[2] "C'est a dire, de la moinerie." "That is, from monkhood."

meant by the word *reverence;* for, after having said that the children of a bishop must not be unruly and disobedient, he likewise adds, " nor liable to the reproach of profligacy or of intemperance." He therefore means, in a word, that their morals shall be regulated by all chastity, modesty, and gravity.

5. *And if any one know not how to rule his own house.*[1] This argument, drawn from the less to the greater, is in itself manifest, that he who is unfit for governing a family will be altogether unable to govern a people. Besides that it is evident that he is destitute of the virtues necessary for that purpose, what authority will he have over the people, seeing that his own house makes him contemptible?

6. *Not a novice.* There being many men of distinguished ability and learning who at that time were brought to the faith, Paul forbids that such persons shall be admitted to the office of a bishop, as soon as they have made profession of Christianity. And he shews how great would be the danger; for it is evident that they are commonly vain, and full of ostentation, and, in consequence of this, haughtiness and ambition will drive them headlong. What Paul says we experience; for "novices" have not only impetuous fervour and bold daring, but are also puffed up with foolish

---

[1] " The house of a believer ought to be like a little church. Heathens, who did not know what a church is, said that a house is but an image and figure of any public government. A poor man, living with his wife and children and servants, ought to be in his house like a public governor. But Christians ought to go beyond this. Every father of a family should know that God has appointed him to that place, that he may know how to govern his wife and children and servants; so that God shall be honoured in the midst of them, and all shall do Him homage. Paul speaks of children; and why? Because he who wishes to discharge his duty as pastor of a church must be like a father to all believers. Now, let us suppose that a man cannot govern two or three children which he has in the house. They are his own children, and yet he cannot keep them in subjection; they are deaf to all that he says to them. How then shall he be able to govern those who are at a distance, and who may be said to be unknown to him, who even refuse to become wiser, and think that they have no need of being instructed? How shall he be able to keep men in dread, when his own wife is not subject to him? Let us not, therefore, think it strange if it is required in all pastors, that they be good fathers of a family, and know what it is to govern their own children well. It is not enough to condemn the children, but we must condemn the fathers, when they permit their children to be worse than others."—*Fr. Ser.*

confidence, as if they could fly beyond the clouds. Consequently, it is not without reason that they are excluded from the honour of a bishopric, till, in process of time, their proud temper shall be subdued.

*Lest he fall into the condemnation of the devil.* The *judgment* or *condemnation of the devil* may be interpreted in three ways; for some take Διαβόλου (of the devil) to mean Satan; and others, to mean slanderers. I give the preference to the former view; because it rarely happens that "judgment" means slander. But again, "the judgment of Satan" may be taken either actively or passively. This latter sense is adopted by Chrysostom, with whom I willingly agree. There is an elegant contrast, which heightens the enormity of the case, "If he who is placed over the Church of God fall, by his pride, into the same condemnation with the devil." Yet I do not reject the active signification, namely, that he will give the devil occasion for accusing him. But the opinion of Chrysostom is more correct.¹

7. *A good report from those who are without.* This appears to be very difficult, that a religious man should have, as witnesses of his integrity, infidels themselves, who are furiously mad to tell lies against us. But the apostle means, that, so far as relates to external behaviour, even unbelievers themselves shall be constrained to acknowledge him to be a good man; for, although they groundlessly slander all the children of God, yet they cannot pronounce him to be a wicked man, who leads a good and inoffensive life amongst them. Such is that acknowledgment of uprightness which Paul here describes. The reason is added,—

*Lest he fall into reproach and the snare of the devil;* which

---

¹ "The words εἰς κρῖμα ἐμπέσῃ τοῦ Διαβόλου are, by most expositors, ancient and modern, understood of falling into the same condemnation and punishment that the devil fell into through pride, which is supported by the authority of the Pesch. Syr. Several eminent expositors, from Luther and Erasmus downwards, take τοῦ Διαβόλου to mean the "calumniator," or slanderous enemy of the gospel, the noun being, they say, used generically of those who seek an occasion to calumniate the Christians; but, as Calvin observes, 'it rarely happens that "judgment" means slander.' Moreover, the expression Διάβολος would thus have to be taken of *just* condemnation."—*Bloomfield.*

I explain in this manner: "lest, being subject to reproach, he begin to be hardened, and abandon himself the more freely to all iniquity, which is to entangle himself in the snares of the devil." For what hope is left for him who sins without any shame?

8. Likewise *must* the deacons be grave, not double tongued, not given to much wine, not greedy of filthy lucre;
9. Holding the mystery of the faith in a pure conscience.
10. And let these also first be proved; then let them use the office of a deacon, being *found* blameless.
11. Even so *must their* wives be grave, not slanderers, sober, faithful in all things.
12. Let the deacons be the husbands of one wife, ruling their children and their own houses well.
13. For they that have used the office of a deacon well purchase to themselves a good degree, and great boldness in the faith which is in Christ Jesus.

8. Diaconos similiter graves, non bilingues, non multo vino deditos, non turpiter lucri cupidos:
9. Habentes mysterium fidei in pura conscientia.
10. Et hi probentur primum; deinde ministrent ubi irreprehensibiles comperti fuerint.
11. Uxores similiter graves, non calumniatrices, sobrias, fideles in omnibus.
12. Diaconi sint unius uxoris mariti, qui honeste præsint liberis et domibus suis.
13. Nam qui bene ministraverint gradum sibi bonum (*vel, honestum*) acquirunt, et multam libertatem in fide, quæ est in Christo Iesu.

8. *Likewise the deacons.* There is no reason why the diversity of interpretations should lead us to entertain any doubt. It is certain that the Apostle speaks of those who hold a public office in the Church; and this refutes the opinion of those who think that domestic servants are here meant. As to the view given by others, that it denotes presbyters who are inferior to the bishop, that is without foundation; for it is manifest from other passages, that the term bishop belongs alike to all presbyters.[1] All are constrained to acknowledge this; and more especially a passage in the first chapter of the Epistle to Titus proves clearly that this is the meaning. (Tit. i. 7.) It remains to be stated that we understand "the deacons" to be those who are mentioned by Luke, (Acts vi. 3,) and who had the charge of the

---

[1] " Que le nom d'Evesque estoit commun a tous prestres, et qu'entre prestre et evesque il n'y a nulle difference." "That the term bishop was common to all presbyters, and that there is no difference between presbyter and bishop."

poor. But those who wish to have a more full account of the duties of deacons may consult the Institutes.¹

*Grave, not double-tongued.* The first four virtues, with which he wishes them to be endowed, are of themselves sufficiently well known. Yet it ought to be carefully observed that he advises them not to be *double-tongued;* because it is a vice which it is difficult to avoid in the discharge of that office, and yet ought, more than anything else, to be kept at a distance from it.

9. *Holding the mystery of faith.* As if he had said, "Holding the pure doctrine of religion, and that from the heart, with a sincere fear of God;" or, "Being well instructed in the faith, so as not to be ignorant of anything which it is necessary for Christians to know." He gives to the sum of Christian doctrine the honourable appellation of a *mystery;* as indeed God, through the gospel, reveals to men on earth a wisdom which angels in heaven behold with admiration; and, therefore, we need not wonder if it exceed human capacity.

Let us therefore remember that it ought to be embraced with the deepest reverence; and because we could never, by our own strength, ascend to such a height, let us humbly entreat God to impart it to us by the Spirit of revelation. On the other hand, when we see wicked men either ridicule those doctrines or have no relish for them, let us acknowledge that it is owing to the grace of God that those things which have been hidden from others are in our hearts, and before our eyes, as Moses says, (Deut. xxx. 11.)

Thus he wishes that deacons should be well instructed in "the mystery of faith;" because, although they do not hold the office of teaching, yet it would be exceedingly absurd to hold a public office in the Church, while they were ill-informed in the Christian faith, more especially since they must frequently be laid under the necessity of administering advice and consolation, if they do not choose to neglect their duties. It is added, *in a pure conscience*, which extends to the whole life, but chiefly that they may know how to obey God.

¹ See Calvin's Inst. of the Christian Religion, vol. iii. p. 65.

10. *And let those be first tried.* He wishes that they who are chosen should not be unknown, but that their integrity should be ascertained, like that of the bishops. And hence it is evident, that they are called *blameless* who are not stained by any marked vice. Besides, this trial is not for a single hour, but consists in long experience. In a word, when deacons are to be ordained, the choice must not fall at random, and without selection, on any that come to hand; but those men are to be chosen who are approved by their past life in such a manner that, after what may be called full inquiry, they are ascertained to be well qualified.

11. *Likewise the wives.* He means the wives both of deacons and of bishops, for they must be aids to their husbands in their office; which cannot be, unless their behaviour excel that of others.

*Let the deacons be.* Since he mentioned wives, he lays down the same injunction about deacons as he had formerly laid down about bishops; namely, that each of them—satisfied with having but one wife—shall set an example of a chaste and honourable father of a family, and shall keep his *children* and his whole house under holy discipline. And this refutes the error of those who understand this passage as referring to domestic servants.[1]

13. *For they who have served well.* Owing to a practice which came into use one or two centuries after the death of the apostles, of choosing presbyters from the order of deacons, this passage has been commonly interpreted as describing elevation to a higher rank, as if the Apostle called to the honour of being presbyters those who had faithfully discharged the office of a deacon. For my own part, though I do not deny that the order of deacons might sometimes be the nursery out of which presbyters were taken, yet I take Paul's words as meaning, more simply, that they who have discharged this ministry in a proper manner are worthy of no small honour; because it is not a mean employment, but a highly honourable office. Now by this expression he intimates how much it is for the advantage of the Church to

---

[1] "Des serviteurs domestiques, et non pas des diacres de l'Eglise." "To domestic servants, and not to the deacons of the Church."

have this office discharged by choice men; because the holy discharge of it procures esteem and reverence.

How absurd is it for Papists to maintain that, in making deacons, they do what Paul enjoins! First, why do they make deacons but to carry the cup in a procession, and to feed the eyes of the ignorant with I know not what ridiculous exhibitions? Besides, they do not even observe this; for not a single deacon has been made, during the last five hundred years, except that, after taking this step, he may immediately rise to the priesthood. What impudence is it, to boast of elevating to a higher rank those who have ministered well, when they confer their priesthood on none but those who have never touched a single part of the former office!

*And much liberty in the faith.* With good reason does he add this; for there is nothing that tends so much to produce liberty as a good conscience and a life free from crime and reproach; as, on the contrary, timidity must be the lot of those who have a bad conscience. And if they sometimes make a valiant boast of liberty, yet it is not uniform and constant, nor has it any weight. For this reason he describes also the kind of liberty. "In the faith," says he, *which is in Christ;* that is, that they may serve Christ with greater boldness; as, on the other hand, they who have acted basely in the discharge of their office may be said to have their mouth shut and their hands tied, and are unfit for doing good; because no reliance—no authority is given to them.

14. These things write I unto thee, hoping to come unto thee shortly.
15. But if I tarry long, that thou mayest know how thou oughtest to behave thyself in the house of God, which is the church of the living God, the pillar and ground of the truth.
16. And, without controversy, great is the mystery of godliness: God was manifest in the flesh, justified in the Spirit, seen of angels, preached unto the Gentiles, believed on in the world, received up into glory.

14. Hæc tibi scribo, sperans brevi ad te venire.
15. Quodsi tardavero, ut videas quomodo oporteat in domo Dei versari, quæ est Ecclesia Dei viventis, columna et firmamentum veritatis.
16. Et sine controversia magnum est pietatis mysterium; Deus manifestatus est in carne. justificatus in Spiritu, visus Angelis, prædicatus, Gentibus, fidem obtinuit in mundo receptus est in gloria.

14. *These things I write to thee.* He holds out to Timothy the hope of his coming, partly in order to encourage him, and partly in order to repress the insolence of those who grew more haughty on account of his absence. And yet he does not make any feigned promise to Timothy, or terrify others through false pretence; for he fully expected that he would come, as it is probable that he came, if he wrote this epistle at the time when he passed through Phrygia, as is related by Luke. (Acts xviii. 23.) Let us look on this as a proof how great was his anxiety for the churches, when he could not endure to delay for a short time a remedy for a present evil. Yet immediately afterwards he adds, that he wrote this epistle for the purpose of informing Timothy, if it should happen that he were delayed longer than he thought.

15. *How thou oughtest to conduct thyself.* By this mode of expression he commends the weight and dignity of the office; because pastors[1] may be regarded as stewards, to whom God has committed the charge of governing his house. If any person has the superintendence of a large house, he labours night and day with earnest solicitude, that nothing may go wrong through his neglect, or ignorance, or carelessness. If only for men this is done, how much more should it be done for God?

*In the house of God.* There are good reasons why God bestows this name on his Church; for not only has he received us to be his children by the grace of adoption, but he also dwelleth in the midst of us.

*The pillar and foundation of truth.* No ordinary enhancement is derived from this appellation. Could it have been described in loftier language? Is anything more venerable, or more holy, than that everlasting *truth* which embraces both the glory of God and the salvation of men? Were all the praises of heathen philosophy, with which it has been adorned by its followers, collected into one heap, what is this in comparison of the dignity of this wisdom, which alone deserves to be called light and truth, and the instruction of

---

[1] "Les Evesques, c'est a dire, pasteurs de l'Eglise." "Bishops, that is, pastors of the Church."

life, and the way, and the kingdom of God? Now it is preserved on earth by the ministry of the Church alone. What a weight, therefore, rests on the pastors, who have been intrusted with the charge of so inestimable a treasure! With what impudent trifling do Papists argue from the words of Paul that all their absurdities ought to be held as oracles of God, because they are "the pillar of truth," and therefore cannot err!

First, we ought to see why Paul adorns the Church with so magnificent a title. By holding out to pastors the greatness of the office, he undoubtedly intended to remind them with what fidelity, and industry, and reverence they ought to discharge it. How dreadful is the vengeance that awaits them, if, through their fault, that truth which is the image of the Divine glory, the light of the world, and the salvation of men, shall be allowed to fall! This consideration ought undoubtedly to lead pastors to tremble continually, not to deprive them of all energy, but to excite them to greater vigilance.

Hence we may easily conclude in what sense Paul uses these words. The reason why the Church is called the " pillar of truth" is, that she defends and spreads it by her agency. God does not himself come down from heaven to us, nor does he daily send angels to make known his truth; but he employs pastors, whom he has appointed for that purpose. To express it in a more homely manner, is not the Church the mother of all believers? Does she not regenerate them by the word of God, educate and nourish them through their whole life, strengthen, and bring them at length to absolute perfection? For the same reason, also, she is called "the pillar of truth;" because the office of administering doctrine, which God hath placed in her hands, is the only instrument of preserving the truth, that it may not perish from the remembrance of men.

Consequently this commendation relates to the ministry of the word; for if that be removed, the truth of God will fall to the ground. Not that it is less strong, if it be not supported by the shoulders of men, as the same Papists idly talk; for it is a shocking blasphemy to say, that the word of

God is uncertain, till it obtain from men what may be called a borrowed certainty. Paul simply means what he states elsewhere in other words, that since our " faith is by hearing," there will be no faith, unless there be preaching. (Rom. x. 17.) Accordingly in reference to men, the Church maintains the truth, because by preaching the Church proclaims it, because she keeps it pure and entire, because she transmits it to posterity. And if the instruction of the gospel be not proclaimed, if there are no godly ministers who, by their preaching, rescue truth from darkness and forgetfulness, instantly falsehoods, errors, impostures, superstitions, and every kind of corruption, will reign. In short, silence in the Church is the banishment and crushing of the truth. Is there anything at all forced in this exposition?

Having ascertained Paul's meaning, let us return to the Papists. First, by applying this eulogium to themselves, they act wickedly ; because they deck themselves with borrowed feathers. For, granting that the Church were elevated above the third heaven, I maintain that it has nothing to do with them in any manner. Nay, I even turn the whole passage against them ; for, if the Church " is the pillar of truth," it follows that the Church is not with them, when the truth not only lies buried, but is shockingly torn, and thrown down, and trampled under foot. Is this either a riddle or a quibble ? Paul does not wish that any society, in which the truth of God does not hold a lofty and conspicuous place, shall be acknowledged to be a Church ; now there is nothing of all this in Popery, but only ruin and desolation ; and, therefore, the true mark of a Church is not found in it. But the mistake arises from this, that they do not consider, what was of the greatest importance, that the truth of God is maintained by the pure preaching of the gospel ; and that the support of it does not depend on the faculties or understandings of men, but rests on what is far higher, that is, if it does not depart from the simple word of God.

16. *Great is the mystery of godliness.* Again, here is another enhancement. That the truth of God might not, through the ingratitude of men, be less esteemed than it ought, he extols its value, by stating that " great is the

secret of godliness;" that is, because it does not treat of mean subjects, but of the revelation of the Son of God, " in whom are hidden all the treasures of wisdom." (Col. ii. 3.) From the greatness and importance of such matters, pastors ought to judge of their office, that they may devote themselves to the discharge of it with greater conscientiousness and deeper reverence.

*God manifested in the flesh.* The Vulgate translator, by leaving out the name of *God*, refers what follows to "the mystery," but altogether unskilfully and inappropriately, as will clearly be seen on a bare perusal, though he has Erasmus on his side, who, however, destroys the authority of his own views, so that it is unnecessary for me to refute it. All the Greek copies undoubtedly agree in this rendering, " God manifested in the flesh." But granting that Paul did not express the name of God, still any one who shall carefully examine the whole matter, will acknowledge that the name of Christ ought to be supplied. For my own part, I have no hesitation in following the reading which has been adopted in the Greek copies. In calling the manifestation of Christ, such as he afterwards describes it, a " great mystery," the reason is obvious; for this is " the height, depth, and breadth of wisdom," which he has elsewhere mentioned, (Eph. iii. 18,) by which all our senses must unavoidably be overwhelmed.

Let us now examine the various clauses in their order. He could not have spoken more appropriately about the person of Christ than in these words, " God manifested in the flesh." First, we have here an express testimony of both natures; for he declares at the same time that Christ is true God and true man. Secondly, he points out the distinction between the two natures, when, on the one hand, he calls him God, and, on the other, expresses his " manifestation in the flesh." Thirdly, he asserts the unity of the person, when he declares, that it is one and the same who was God, and who has been manifested in the flesh.

Thus, by this single passage, the true and orthodox faith is powerfully defended against Arius, Marcion, Nestorius, and Eutyches. There is also great emphasis in the contrast of the two words, *God in flesh.* How wide is the difference between God and man! And yet in Christ we behold the infinite glory of God united to our polluted flesh in such a manner that they become one.[1]

*Justified in the Spirit.* As the Son of God "emptied himself," (Philip. ii. 7,) by taking upon him our flesh, so there was displayed in him a spiritual power which testified that he is God. This passage has received various interpretations; but, for my own part, satisfied with having explained the Apostle's real meaning, as far as I understand it, I shall add nothing more. First, *justification* here denotes an acknowledgment of divine power; as in Ps. xix. 9, where it is said, that "the judgments of God are justified," that is, are wonderfully and absolutely perfect;[2] and in Ps. li. 5, that "God is justified," meaning that the praise

---

[1] "By the word *flesh* Paul declares that Christ was true man, and that he was clothed with our nature; but, at the same time, by the word *manifested*, he shows that there were two natures. We must not imagine a Jesus Christ who is God, and another Jesus Christ who is man; but we must know that he alone is both God and man. Let us distinguish his two natures, so as to know that this is the Son of God who is our brother. Now I have said that God permits the ancient heresies, with which the church was troubled, to be revived in our time, in order to excite us to greater activity. But, on the other hand, let us observe, that the devil is constrained to do his utmost to overthrow this article of faith, because he sees clearly that it is the foundation of our salvation. For if we have not that mystery of which Paul speaks, what will become of us? We are all children of Adam, and therefore we are accursed; we are in the pit of death; in short, we are deadly enemies of God, and thus there is nothing in us but condemnation and death, till we know that God came to seek us, and that, because we could not rise to him, he came down to us. Till we have known this, are we not more than wretched? For this reason the Devil wished, as far as he could, to destroy that knowledge, or rather to mix it with his lies, so as to be perverted. On the other hand, when we see that there is such majesty in God, how shall we dare to approach unto Him, seeing that we are full of misery? We must therefore come to this union of the majesty of God with human nature. And thus, in every respect, till we have known the divine majesty that is in Jesus Christ, and our human weakness which he hath taken upon him, it is impossible for us to have any hope, or to be capable of having recourse to the goodness of God, or of having the boldness to call upon him, and return to him. In a word, we are entirely shut out from the heavenly kingdom, the gate is shut against us, and we cannot approach to it in any way whatever."—*Fr. Ser.*

[2] "When he says, 'They are justified together,' the meaning is, They are all righteous from the greatest to the least, without a single exception. By this commendation he distinguishes the law of God from the doctrines of men; for no blemish or fault can be found in it, but it is in all points absolutely perfect."—*Calvin's Com. on the Book of Psalms*, vol. i. p. 323.

of his justice is illustriously displayed. So also, (Matt. xi. 19, and Luke vii. 35,) when Christ says, that " Wisdom hath been justified by her children," he means that they have given honour unto her; and when Luke (vii. 29) relates that the publicans " justified God," he means that they acknowledged, with due reverence and gratitude, the grace of God which they beheld in Christ. What we read here has, therefore, the same meaning as if Paul had said, that he who appeared clothed with human flesh was, at the same time, declared to be the Son of God, so that the weakness of the flesh made no diminution of his glory.

Under the word *Spirit,* he includes everything in Christ that was divine and superior to man; and he does so for two reasons: First, because he had been humbled in " the flesh," the Apostle now, by exhibiting the illustration of his glory, contrasts " the Spirit" with " the flesh." Secondly, that glory, worthy of the only-begotten Son of God, which John affirms to have been seen in Christ, (John i. 14,) did not consist in outward display, or in earthly splendour, but was almost wholly spiritual. The same form of expression is used by him, (Rom. i. 3, 4,) " Who was made of the seed of David according to the flesh, and declared by the power of the Spirit to be the Son of God;" but with this difference, that in that passage he mentions one kind of manifestation, namely, the resurrection.

*Seen by angels, preached to the Gentiles.* All these statements are wonderful and astonishing; that God deigned to bestow on the Gentiles, who had hitherto wandered in the blindness of their minds, a revelation of his Son, which had been unknown even to the angels in heaven. When the Apostle says, that he was " seen by angels," he means that the sight was such as drew the attention of angels, both by its novelty and by its excellence. How uncommon and extraordinary the calling of the Gentiles was, we have stated in the exposition of the second chapter of the Epistle to the Ephesians.[1] Nor is it wonderful that it was a new spectacle to angels, who, though they knew about the redemption of mankind, yet did not at first understand the means by

---

[1] Calvin's Com. on the Ep. to the Galatians and Ephesians, p. 226.

which it should be accomplished, and from whom it must have been concealed, in order that this remarkable display of the goodness of God might be beheld by them with greater admiration.

*Obtained belief in the world.* It was above all things astonishing that God made the Gentiles, who were heathens, and the angels, who held uninterrupted possession of his kingdom, to be equally partakers of the same revelation. But this great efficacy of the preached gospel was no ordinary miracle, when Christ, overcoming all obstacles, subdued to the obedience of faith those who seemed to be altogether incapable of being tamed. Certainly nothing appeared to be less probable—so completely was every entrance closed and shut up. Yet faith vanquished, but by an incredible kind of victory.

Lastly, he says that he was *received into glory;* that is, from this mortal and wretched life. Accordingly, as in the world, so far as related to the obedience of faith, so also in the person of Christ, the change was wonderful, when, from the mean condition of a servant, he was exalted to the right hand of the Father, that every knee may bow to him.

## CHAPTER IV.

1. Now the Spirit speaketh expressly, that in the latter times some shall depart from the faith, giving heed to seducing spirits, and doctrines of devils;

2. Speaking lies in hypocrisy; having their conscience seared with a hot iron;

3. Forbidding to marry, *and commanding* to abstain from meats, which God hath created to be received with thanksgiving of them which believe and know the truth.

4. For every creature of God *is* good, and nothing to be refused, if it be received with thanksgiving:

5. For it is sanctified by the word of God and prayer.

1. Spiritus autem clarè dicit, quòd in posterioribus temporibus desciscent quidam a fide, attendentes spiritibus impostoribus, et doctrinis dæmoniorum;

2. In hypocrisi falsiloquorum, cauterio notatam habentium conscientiam;

3. Prohibentium matrimonia contrahere, jubentium abstinere a cibis, quos Deus creavit ad percipiendum cum gratiarum actione fidelibus, et qui cognoverunt veritatem.

4. Quòd omnis creatura Dei bona, et nihil rejiciendum quod cum gratiarum actione sumatur:

5. Sanctificatur enim per sermonem Dei et precationem.

1. *Now the Spirit plainly saith.* He had industriously

admonished Timothy about many things; and now he shews the necessity, because it is proper to provide against the danger which the Holy Spirit forewarns to be fast approaching, namely, that false teachers will come, who shall hold out trifles as the doctrine of faith, and who, placing all holiness in outward exercises, shall throw into the shade the spiritual worship of God, which alone is lawful. And, indeed, the servants of God have always had to contend against such persons as Paul here describes. Men being by nature inclined to hypocrisy, Satan easily persuades them that God is worshipped aright by ceremonies and outward discipline; and, indeed, without a teacher, almost all have this conviction deeply rooted in their hearts. Next is added the craftiness of Satan to confirm the error. The consequence is, that, in all ages, there have been impostors, who recommended false worship, by which true godliness was buried. Again, this plague produces another, namely, that, in matters indifferent, men are laid under restraint; for the world easily permits itself to be hindered from doing that which God had declared to be lawful, in order that they may have it in their power to transgress with impunity the laws of God.

Here Paul, therefore, in the person of Timothy, forewarns not only the Ephesians, but all the churches throughout the world, about hypocritical teachers, who, by setting up false worship, and by ensnaring consciences with new laws, adulterate the true worship of God, and corrupt the pure doctrine of faith. This is the real object of the passage, which it is especially necessary to remark.

Besides, in order that all may hear with more earnest attention what he is going to say, he opens with a preface, that this is an undoubted and very clear prophecy of the Holy Spirit. There is, indeed, no reason to doubt that he drew all the rest from the same Spirit; but, although we ought always to listen to him as communicating the will of Christ, yet in a matter of vast importance he wished especially to testify that he said nothing but by the Spirit of prophecy. By a solemn announcement, therefore, he recommends to us this prophecy; and, not satisfied with doing this, he adds that it is plain, and free from all ambiguity.

*In the latter times.* At that time certainly it could not have been expected that, amidst so clear light of the gospel, any would have revolted. But this is what Peter says, that, as false teachers formerly gave annoyance to the people of Israel, so they will never cease to disturb the Christian Church. (2 Pet. iii. 3.) The meaning is the same as if he had said, "The doctrine of the gospel is now in a flourishing state, but Satan will not long refrain from labouring to choke the pure seed by tares."[1] (Matt. xiii. 25, 38.)

This warning was advantageous in the age of the Apostle Paul, that both pastors and others might give earnest attention to pure doctrine, and not suffer themselves to be deceived. To us in the present day it is not less useful, when we perceive that nothing has happened which was not foretold by an express prophecy of the Spirit. Besides, we may here remark how great care God exercises about his Church, when he gives so early warning of dangers. Satan has, indeed, manifold arts for leading us into error, and attacks us by astonishing stratagems; but, on the other hand, fortifies us sufficiently, if we did not of our own accord choose to be deceived. There is therefore no reason to complain that darkness is more powerful than light, or that truth is vanquished by falsehood; but, on the contrary, we suffer the punishment of our carelessness and indolence, when we are led aside from the right way of salvation.

But they who flatter themselves in their errors object, that it is hardly possible to distinguish whom or what kind of persons Paul describes. As if it were for nothing that the Spirit uttered this prophecy, and published it so long before; for, if there were no certain mark, the whole of the present warning would be superfluous, and consequently absurd. But far be it from us to think that the Spirit of God gives us unnecessary alarm, or does not accompany the threatening of danger by shewing how we should guard against it! And that slander is sufficiently refuted by the

[1] "A force d'yvroye et mauvaises herbes." "By means of darnel and pernicious herbs."

words of Paul; for he points out, as with the finger, that evil which he warns us to avoid. He does not speak, in general terms, about false prophets, but plainly describes the kind of false doctrine; namely, that which, by linking godliness with outward elements, perverts and profanes, as I have already said, the spiritual worship of God.

*Some will revolt from the faith.* It is uncertain whether he speaks of teachers or of hearers; but I am more disposed to refer it to the latter; for he afterwards calls teachers " spirits that are impostors." And this is (ἐμφατικώτερον) more emphatic, that not only will there be those who sow wicked doctrines, and corrupt the purity of faith, but that they can never want disciples whom they can draw into their sect; and when a lie thus gains prevalence, there arises from it greater trouble.

Besides, it is no slight vice which he describes, but a very heinous crime—apostasy *from the faith;* although, at first sight, in the doctrine which he briefly notices there does not appear to be so much evil. What is the case? Is faith completely overturned on account of the prohibition of marriage, or of certain kinds of food? But we must take into view a higher reason, that men pervert and invent at their pleasure the worship of God, that they assume dominion over the consciences, and that they dare to forbid that use of good things which the Lord has permitted. As soon as the purity of the worship of God is impaired, there no longer remains anything perfect or sound, and faith itself is utterly ruined.

Accordingly, although Papists laugh at us, when we censure their tyrannical laws about outward observances, yet we know that we are pleading a cause of the greatest weight and importance; because the doctrine of faith is destroyed, as soon as the worship of God is infected by such corruptions. The controversy is not about flesh or fish, or about a black or ashy colour, or about Friday or Wednesday, but about the mad superstitions of men, who wish to appease God by such trifles, and, by contriving a carnal worship of him, contrive for themselves an idol instead of God. Who will deny that this is revolting from the faith?

*To deceiving spirits.* He means prophets or teachers, to whom he gives this designation, because they boast of the Spirit, and, under this title, insinuate themselves into the favour of the people. This, indeed, is true at all times, that men, whatever they are, speak under the excitement of the spirit. But it is not the same spirit that excites them all; for sometimes Satan is a lying spirit in the mouth of the false prophets, in order to deceive unbelievers, who deserve to be deceived. (1 Kings xxii. 21-23.) On the other hand, every one that renders due honour to Christ speaks by the Spirit of God, as Paul testifies. (1 Cor. xii. 3.)

Now that mode of expression, of which we are now speaking, originated at first from this circumstance, that the servants of God professed to have from the revelation of the Spirit, everything that they uttered in public. This was actually true; and hence they received the name of the Spirit, whose organs they were. But the ministers of Satan, by a false emulation, like apes, began afterwards to make the same boast, and likewise falsely assumed the name. On the same grounds John says, " Try the spirits, whether they are of God." (1 John iv. 1.)

Moreover, Paul explains his meaning by adding, *to doctrines of devils;* which is as if he had said, " Attending to false prophets, and to their devilish doctrines." Again observe, that it is not an error of small importance, or one that ought to be concealed, when consciences are bound by the contrivances of men, and at the same time the worship of God is corrupted.

2. *Speaking lies in hypocrisy.* If these words refer to " demons," then this word will mean men deceiving through the instigation of the devil. But we may also supply the words, " of men speaking." He now descends to a particular instance, when he says that they " speak lies in hypocrisy," and *have their conscience seared with a hot iron.* And, indeed, it ought to be known that these two are so closely joined together that the former springs from the latter; for consciences, that are bad and seared with the hot iron of their crimes, always flee to hypocrisy as a ready refuge; that is, they contrive hypocritical pretences, in order to dazzle

the eyes of God; and what else is done by those who endeavour to appease God by the mask of outward observances?

The word *hypocrisy* must therefore be explained agreeably to the passage in which it now occurs; for, first, it must relate to doctrine, and, next, it denotes that kind of doctrine which adulterates the spiritual worship of God by exchanging its genuine purity for bodily exercises; and thus it includes all methods contrived by men for appeasing God or obtaining his favour. The meaning may be thus summed up; first, that all who assume a pretended sanctimoniousness are led by the instigation of the devil; because God is never worshipped aright by outward ceremonies; for true worshippers "worship him in spirit and truth," (John iv. 24;) and, secondly, that this is a useless medicine, by which hypocrites mitigate their pains, or rather a plaster by which bad consciences conceal their wounds, without any advantage, and to their utter destruction.

3. *Forbidding to marry.* Having described the class, he next mentions two instances,[1] namely, the prohibition of marriage and of some kinds of food. They arise from that hypocrisy which, having forsaken true holiness, seeks something else for the purpose of concealment and disguise; for they who do not keep from ambition, covetousness, hatred, cruelty, and such like, endeavour to obtain a righteousness by abstaining from those things which God has left at large. Why are consciences burdened by those laws, but because perfection is sought in something different from the law of God? This is not done but by hypocrites, who, in order that they may with impunity transgress that righteousness of the heart which the law requires, endeavour to conceal their inward wickedness by those outward observances as veils with which they cover themselves.

This was a distinct threatening of danger, so that it was not difficult for men to guard against it, at least if they had lent their ears to the Holy Spirit, when he gave so express

---

[1] "Apres avoir mis le terme general, a scavoir Doctrines des diables, et puis une espece, a scavoir hypocrisie; maintenant il met deux poincts particuliers de ceste hypocrisie." "After having employed the general term, namely, Doctrines of devils, and next mentioned one class, namely, hypocrisy, he mentions two individual instances of that hypocrisy."

a warning. Yet we see that the darkness of Satan generally prevailed, so that the clear light of this striking and memorable prediction was of no avail. Not long after the death of the apostle, arose Encratites, (who took their name from continence,) Tatianists,[1] Catharists, Montanus with his sect, and at length Manichæans, who had extreme aversion to marriage and the eating of flesh, and condemned them as profane things. Although they were disowned by the Church, on account of their haughtiness, in wishing to subject others to their opinions, yet it is evident that those who opposed them yielded to their error more than was proper. It was not intended by those of whom I am now speaking to impose a law on Christians; but yet they attached greater weight than they ought to have done to superstitious observances, such as abstaining from marriage, and not tasting flesh.

Such is the disposition of the world, always dreaming that God ought to be worshipped in a carnal manner, as if God were carnal. Matters becoming gradually worse, this tyranny was established, that it should not be lawful for priests or monks to enter into the married state, and that no person should dare to taste flesh on certain days. Not unjustly, therefore, do we now maintain that this prediction was uttered against the Papists, since celibacy and abstinence from certain kinds of food are enjoined by them more strictly than any commandment of God. They think that they escape by an ingenious artifice, when they torture Paul's words to direct them against Tatianists or Manichæans, or such like; as if the Tatianists had not the same means of escape open to them by throwing back the censure of Paul on the Cataphrygians, and on Montanus the

[1] " Tatian, by birth an Assyrian, and a disciple of Justin Martyr, had a great number of followers, who were, after him, called Tatianists, but were nevertheless more frequently distinguished from other sects by names relative to the austerity of their manners. For, as they rejected with a sort of horror all the comforts and conveniences of life, and abstained from wine with such a rigorous obstinacy as to use nothing but water even at the celebration of the Lord's Supper; as they macerated their bodies by continual fastings, and lived a severe life of celibacy and abstinence; so they were called Encratites, (temperate,) Hydroparastates, (drinkers of water,) and Apotactites, (renouncers.)"—*Mosheim's* Eccl. History.

author of that sect ; or as if the Cataphrygians had it not in their power to bring forward the Encratites, in their room, as the guilty parties. But Paul does not here speak of persons, but of the thing itself ; and, therefore, although a hundred different sects be brought forward, all of which are charged with the same hypocrisy in forbidding some kinds of food, they shall all incur the same condemnation.

Hence it follows, that to no purpose do the Papists point to the ancient heretics, as if they alone were censured ; we must always see if they are not guilty in the same manner. They object, that they do not resemble the Encratites and Manichæans, because they do not absolutely forbid the use of marriage and of flesh, but only on certain days constrain to abstinence from flesh, and make the vow of celibacy compulsory on none but monks and priests and nuns. But this excuse also is excessively frivolous ; for, first, they nevertheless make holiness to consist in these things ; next, they set up a false and spurious worship of God ; and lastly, they bind consciences by a necessity from which they ought to have been free.

In the fifth book of Eusebius,[1] there is a fragment taken out of the writings of Apollonius, in which, among other things, he reproaches Montanus with being the first that dissolved marriage, and laid down laws for fasting. He does not say, that Montanus absolutely prohibited marriage or certain kinds of food. It is enough if he lay a religious obligation on the consciences, and command men to worship God by observing those things ; for the prohibition of things

---

[1] "The heresy of the Phrygians, as it is called, still continuing to prevail in Phrygia, Apollonius undertook to refute it in a particular work which he wrote ; on the one hand, correcting their false predictions in reference to what they said, and on the other describing the life that those led who were its founders. Hear him in his own words respecting Montanus: 'But who,' says he, 'is this new teacher? His works and his doctrines sufficiently shew it. This is he that taught the dissolutions of marriage ; he that imposed laws of fasting : that called Pepuza and Tymium, little places in Phrygia, a Jerusalem, in order to collect men from every quarter thither ; who established exactors of money, and, under the name of offerings, devised the artifice to procure presents ; who provided salaries for those that preached his doctrine, that it might grow strong by gormandizing and gluttony.' Thus far concerning Montanus."—*Clare's Trans. of Eusebius*, Eccl. Hist., Book v., ch. xviii.

that are indifferent, whether it be general or special, is always a diabolical tyranny. That this is true in regard to certain kinds of food will appear more clearly from the next clause.

*Which God hath created.* It is proper to observe the reason, that, in the use of various kinds of food, we ought to be satisfied with the liberty which God has granted to us; because He created them for this purpose. It yields inconceivable joy to all the godly, when they know that all the kinds of food which they eat are put into their hands by the Lord, so that the use of them is pure and lawful. What insolence is it in men to take away what God bestows! Did they create food? Can they make void the creation of God? Let it always be remembered by us, that he who created the food, gave us also the free use of it, which it is vain for men to attempt to hinder.

*To be received with thanksgiving.* God created food *to be received;* that is, that we may enjoy it. This end can never be set aside by human authority. He adds, *with thanksgiving;* because we can never render to God any recompense for his kindness but a testimony of gratitude. And thus he holds up to greater abhorrence those wicked lawgivers who, by new and hasty enactments, hinder the sacrifice of praise which God especially requires us to offer to him. Now, there can be no thanksgiving without sobriety and temperance; for the kindness of God is not truly acknowledged by him who wickedly abuses it.

*By believers.* What then? Does not God make his sun to rise daily on the good and the bad? (Matt. v. 45.) Does not the earth, by his command, yield bread to the wicked? Are not the very worst of men fed by his blessing? When David says, " He causeth the herb to grow for the service of men, that he may bring forth food out of the earth," (Ps. civ. 14,) the kindness which he describes is universal. I reply, Paul speaks here of the lawful use, of which we are assured before God. Wicked men are in no degree partakers of it, on account of their impure conscience, which, as is said, (Tit. i. 15,) " defileth all things." And indeed, properly speaking, God has appointed to his children alone the whole world and all that is in the world. For this reason, they are also called the heirs of the world; for at the beginning Adam was appointed to be lord of all, on this condition, that he should continue in obedience to God. Accordingly, his rebellion against God deprived of the right, which had been bestowed on him, not only himself but his posterity. And since all things are subject to Christ, we are fully restored by His mediation, and that through faith; and therefore all that unbelievers enjoy may be regarded as the property of others, which they rob or steal.

*And by those that know the truth.* In this clause he defines who they are whom he calls "believers," namely, those that have a knowledge of sound doctrine; for there is no faith but from the word of God; in order that we may not falsely think, as the Papists imagine, that faith is a confused opinion.

4. *For every creature of God is good.* The use of food must be judged, partly from its substance, and partly from the person of him who eats it. The Apostle therefore avails himself of both arguments. So far as relates to food, he asserts that it is pure, because God has created it; and that the use of it is consecrated to us by faith and prayer. The goodness of the creatures, which he mentions, has relation to men, and that not with regard to the body or to health, but to the consciences. I make this remark, that none may enter into curious speculations unconnected with the scope of the passage; for, in a single word, Paul means, that those things which come from the hand of God, and are intended for our use, are not unclean or polluted before God, but that we may freely eat them with regard to conscience.

If it be objected, that many animals were formerly pronounced to be unclean under the Law, and that fruit, which was yielded by the tree of knowledge of good and evil, was destructive to man; the answer is, that creatures are not called pure, merely because they are the works of God, but because, through his kindness, they have been given to us; for we must always look at the appointment of God, both what he commands and what he forbids.

5. *For it is sanctified by the word of God and prayer.*

This is the confirmation of the preceding clause, *if it be received with thanksgiving.* And it is an argument drawn from contrast; for "holy" and "profane" are things contrary to each other. Let us now see what is the sanctification of all good things, which belong to the sustenance of the present life. Paul testifies that it consists of "the word of God and prayer." But it ought to be observed, that this *word* must be embraced by faith, in order that it may be advantageous; for, although God himself sanctifies all things by the Spirit of his mouth, yet we do not obtain that benefit but by faith. To this is added "prayer;" for, on the one hand, we ask from God our daily bread, according to the commandment of Christ, (Matt. vi. 11;) and, on the other hand we offer thanksgiving to Him for His goodness.

Now Paul's doctrine proceeds on this principle, that there is no good thing, the possession of which is lawful, unless conscience testify that it is lawfully our own. And which of us would venture to claim for himself a single grain of wheat, if he were not taught by the word of God that he is the heir of the world? Common sense, indeed, pronounces, that the wealth of the world is naturally intended for our use; but, since dominion over the world was taken from us in Adam, everything that we touch of the gifts of God is defiled by our pollution; and, on the other hand, it is unclean to us, till God graciously come to our aid, and, by ingrafting us into his Son, constitutes us anew to be lords of the world, that we may lawfully use as our own all the wealth with which he supplies us.

Justly, therefore, does Paul connect lawful enjoyment with "the word," by which alone we regain what was lost in Adam; for we must acknowledge God as our Father, that we may be his heirs, and Christ as our Head, that those things which are his may become ours. Hence it ought to be inferred that the use of all the gifts of God is unclean, unless it be accompanied by true knowledge and calling on the name of God; and that it is a beastly way of eating, when we sit down at table without any prayer, and, when we have eaten to the full, depart in utter forgetfulness of God.

And if such sanctification is demanded in regard to common food, which, together with the belly, is subject to corruption, what must we think about spiritual sacraments? If "the word," and calling on God through faith, be not there, what remains that is not profane? Here we must attend to the distinction between the blessing of the sacramental table and the blessing of a common table; for, as to the food which we eat for the nourishment of our body, we bless it for this purpose, that we may receive it in a pure and lawful manner; but we consecrate, in a more solemn manner, the bread and wine in the Lord's Supper, that they may be pledges to us of the body and blood of Christ.

| | |
|---|---|
| 6. If thou put the brethren in remembrance of these things, thou shalt be a good minister of Jesus Christ, nourished up in the words of faith and of good doctrine, whereunto thou hast attained. | 6. Hæc suggerens fratribus, bonus eris Iesu Christi minister, innutritus sermonibus fidei, et bonæ doctrinæ quam sequutus es. |
| 7. But refuse profane and old wives' fables, and exercise thyself *rather* unto godliness. | 7. Profanas autem et aniles fabulas devita; quin potius exerce te ipsum ad pietatem. |
| 8. For bodily exercise profiteth little; but godliness is profitable unto all things, having promise of the life that now is, and of that which is to come. | 8. Nam corporalis exercitatio paululum habet utilitatis; at pietas ad omnia utilis est, ut quæ promissiones habeat vitæ præsentis et futuræ. |
| 9. This *is* a faithful saying, and worthy of all acceptation. | 9. Fidelis sermo, dignusque qui modis omnibus approbetur. |
| 10. For therefore we both labour and suffer reproach, because we trust in the living God, who is the Saviour of all men, specially of those that believe. | 10. Nam in hoc et laboramus, et probris afficimur, quod spem fixam habemus in Deo vivente, qui servator est omnium hominum, maximè fidelium. |

6. *Exhibiting these things to the brethren.* By this expression he exhorts Timothy to mention those things frequently; and he afterwards repeats this a second and a third time; for they are things of such a nature as it is proper to call frequently to remembrance. And we ought to make the contrast which is implied; for the doctrine which he commends is here contrasted by him not with false or wicked doctrines, but with useless trifles which do not edify. He wishes that those trifles may be entirely buried in forgetfulness, when he enjoins Timothy to be earnest in exhibiting other things.

*Thou shalt be a good minister.* Men frequently aim at

something else than to approve themselves to Christ; and consequently many are desirous of being applauded for genius, eloquence, and profound knowledge. And that is the very reason why they pay less attention to necessary things, which do not tend to procure the admiration of the common people. But Paul enjoins Timothy to be satisfied with this alone, to be a faithful minister of Christ. And certainly we ought to look on this as a far more honourable title than to be a thousand times called seraphic and subtle doctors. Let us, therefore, remember, that as it is the highest honour of a godly pastor to be reckoned a good servant of Christ, so he ought to aim at nothing else during his whole ministry; for whoever has any other object in view, will have it in his power to obtain applause from men, but will not please God. Accordingly, that we may not be deprived of so great a blessing, let us learn to seek nothing else, and to account nothing so valuable, and to treat everything as worthless in comparison of this single object.

*Nourished.* The Greek word ἐντρεφόμενος being a participle in the Middle Voice, might also have been translated in an active signification, *nourishing;* but as there is no noun governed by the verb, I think that this would be rather a forced construction; and, therefore, I prefer to take it in a passive sense, as confirming the preceding exhortation by the education of Timothy. As if he had said, "As thou hast been, from thy infancy, properly instructed in the faith, and, so to speak, hast sucked along with the milk sound doctrine, and hast made continual progress in it hitherto, endeavour, by faithful ministration, to prove that thou art such." This meaning agrees also with the composition of the word ἐντρεφόμενος.

*In the words of faith and of good doctrine. Faith* is here taken for the sum of Christian doctrine; and what he immediately adds, about *good doctrine,* is for the sake of explanation;[1] for he means, that all other doctrines, how plausible soever they may be, are not at all profitable.

*Which thou hast followed.* This clause denotes persever-

---

[1] "C'est pour mieux exposer et declarer le mot precedent." "It is for the purpose of explaining more clearly and fully the preceding word."

ance; for many who, from their childhood, had purely learned Christ, afterwards degenerate in process of time; and the Apostle says, that Timothy was very unlike these persons.

7. *Exercise thyself to godliness.*[1] After having instructed him as to doctrine, what it ought to be, he now also admonishes him what kind of example he ought to give to others. He says, that he ought to be employed in "godliness;" for, when he says, *Exercise thyself,* he means that this is his proper occupation, his labour, his chief care. As if he had said, "There is no reason why you should weary yourself to no purpose about other matters; you will do that which is of the highest importance, if you devote yourself, with all your zeal, and with all your ability, to godliness alone." By the word *godliness,* he means the spiritual worship of God, which consists in purity of conscience; which is still more evident from what follows, when it is contrasted with bodily exercise.

8. *For bodily exercise is of little profit.* By the exercise " of the body," he does not mean that which lies in hunting, or in the race-course, or in wrestling, or in digging, or in the mechanical occupations; but he gives that name to all the

---

[1] "He who wishes to be faithfully employed in the service of God must not only avoid, as Paul says, the lies and superstitions that tend to poison souls; but he must avoid *profane fables,* that is, subtleties that cannot edify, and that contain no instruction which is good for the salvation of souls. Here is a passage that well deserves to be considered; for we see that it was a part of the corruptions which came into the world, and which, even at the present day, prevail in Popery. True, there will be doctrines in the highest degree absurd, and errors most foolish and debasing. We know that idolatry is as gross and flagrant among them as it ever was among the heathens, that the whole worship of God is corrupted, and, in short, that there is nothing which is not spurious. Such errors ought to be held in abhorrence by us; but there is an evil which is still more concealed, and which is unknown to the common people. For although the doctrine of the Papists were not false as it really is, though it were not perverse; yet it is " profane," as Paul calls it here. And why? They have questions which they debate, about things in which there is no profit. Were a man to know all the questions that are debated in the schools of theology of Popery, there would be nothing but wind. Yet they give themselves the greatest trouble about these matters, and can never succeed; for they put forward questions that cannot be answered but by divination; and though a man should wish to search out the secrets of God, about which nothing is said in the Holy Scripture, does he not plunge into an abyss? Now the Papists have had that pride and audacity, to wish to inquire into those matters which ought to be unknown to us. And thus it was that God withdrew his truth, when the world so corrupted it."—*Fr. Ser.*

outward actions that are undertaken, for the sake of religion, such as watchings, long fasts, lying on the earth, and such like. Yet he does not here censure the superstitious observance of those things; otherwise he would totally condemn them, as he does in the Epistle to the Colossians, (ii. 21,) but at present he only speaks slightingly of them, and says that they are of little advantage. So, then, though the heart be altogether upright, and the object proper, yet, in outward actions, Paul finds nothing that he can value highly.

This is a very necessary warning; for the world will always lean to the side of wishing to worship God by outward services; which is an exceedingly dangerous imagination. But—to say nothing about the wicked opinion of merit—our nature always disposes us strongly to attribute more than we ought to austerity of life; as if it were no ordinary portion of Christian holiness. A clearer view of this cannot be adduced, than the fact, that, shortly after the publication of this command, the whole world was ravished with immoderate admiration of the empty form of bodily exercises. Hence arose the order of monks and nuns, and nearly all the most excellent discipline of the ancient Church, or, at least, that part of it which was most highly esteemed by the common people. If the ancient monks had not dreamed that there was some indescribably divine or angelical perfection in their austere manner of living, they would never have pursued it with so much ardour. In like manner, if pastors had not attached undue value to the ceremonies which were then observed for the mortification of the flesh, they would never have been so rigid in exacting them. And what does Paul say on the other hand? That, when any one shall have laboured much and long in those exercises, the profit will be small and inconsiderable; for they are nothing but the rudiments of childish discipline.

*But godliness is profitable for all things.* That is, " he who has godliness wants nothing, though he has not those little aids; for godliness alone is able to conduct a man to complete perfection. It is the beginning, the middle, and the end, of Christian life; and, therefore, where that is entire, nothing is imperfect. Christ did not lead so austere a manner of life as John the Baptist; was he, therefore, any whit inferior? Let the meaning be thus summed up. " We ought to apply ourselves altogether to piety alone; because, when we have once attained it, God asks nothing more from us; and we ought to give attention to bodily exercises in such a manner as not to hinder or retard the practice of godliness."

*Which hath the promises.* It is a very great consolation, that God does not wish the godly to be in want of anything; for, having made our perfection to consist in godliness, he now makes it the perfection of all happiness. As it is the beginning of happiness in this life, so he likewise extends to it the promise of divine grace, which alone makes us happy, and without which we are very miserable; for God testifies that, even in this life, he will be our Father.

But let us remember to distinguish between the good things of the present and of the future life; for God bestows kindness on us in this world, in order that he may give us only a taste of his goodness, and by such a taste may allure us to the desire of heavenly benefits, that in them we may find satisfaction. The consequence is, that the good things of the present life are not only mingled with very many afflictions, but, we may almost say, overwhelmed by them; for it is not expedient for us to have abundance in this world, lest we should indulge in luxury. Again, lest any one should found on this passage the merits of works, we ought to keep in mind what we have already said, that godliness includes not only a good conscience toward men, and the fear of God, but likewise faith and calling upon him.

9. *This is a faithful saying.* He now sets down, at the conclusion of the argument, what he stated twice at the beginning of it; and he appears to do so expressly, because he will immediately subjoin the contrary objection. Yet it is not without good reason that he employs so strong an assertion; for it is a paradox strongly at variance with the feeling of the flesh, that God supplies his people, in this world, with everything that is necessary for a happy and joyful life; since they are often destitute of all good things, and, on that account, appear to be forsaken by God. Accordingly, not

satisfied with the simple doctrine, he wards off all opposing temptations by this shield, and in this manner instructs believers to open the door to the grace of God, which our unbelief shuts out ; for, undoubtedly if we were willing to receive God's benefits,[1] he would use greater liberality toward us.

10. *For in this we both labour and suffer reproaches.* This is an anticipation by which he solves that question, " Are not believers the most miserable of all men, because they are oppressed by tribulations of every kind ?" In order to show, therefore, that their condition must not be judged from outward appearance, he distinguishes them from others, first in the cause, and next in the result. Hence it follows, that they lose nothing of the promises which he has mentioned, when they are tried by adversity. The sum is, that believers are not miserable in afflictions, because a good conscience supports them, and a blessed and joyful end awaits them.

Now, since the happiness of the present life consists chiefly of two parts, honour and conveniences, he contrasts them with two evils, *toils* and *reproach*, meaning by the former words, inconveniences and annoyances of every kind, such as poverty, cold, nakedness, hunger, banishments, spoliations, imprisonments, scourgings, and other persecutions.

*We have hope fixed on the living God.* This consolation refers to the cause ; for so far are we from being miserable, when we suffer on account of righteousness, that it is rather a just ground of thanksgiving. Besides, our afflictions are accompanied by hope in the living God, and, what is more, hope may be regarded as the foundation ; but it never maketh ashamed, (Rom. v. 5,) and therefore everything that happens to the godly ought to be reckoned a gain.

*Who is the Saviour.*[2] This is the second consolation,

---

[1] " Si les benefices de Dieu trouvoyent entree a nous, et que nous fussion disposez a les recevoir." " If God's benefits found admission to us, and if we were disposed to receive them."

[2] " The word *Saviour* is not here taken in what we call its proper and strict meaning, in regard to the eternal salvation which God promises to his elect, but it is taken for one who delivers and protects. Thus we see

though it depends on the former; for the deliverance of which he speaks may be viewed as the fruit of hope. To make this more clear, it ought to be understood that this is an argument drawn from the less to the greater; for the word σωτὴρ[1] is here a general term, and denotes one who defends and preserves. He means that the kindness of God extends to all men. And if there is no man who does not feel the goodness of God towards him, and who is not a partaker of it, how much more shall it be experienced by the godly, who hope in him? Will he not take peculiar care in them? Will he not more freely pour out his bounty on them? In a word, will he not, in every respect, keep them safe to the end?

| | |
|---|---|
| 11. These things command and teach. | 11. Præcipe hæc et doce. |
| 12. Let no man despise thy youth: but be thou an example of the believers, in word, in conversation, in charity, in spirit, in faith, in purity. | 12. Nemo tuam juventutem despiciat; sed esto exemplar fidelium, in sermone, in conversatione, in caritate, in spiritu, in fide, in castitate. |
| 13. Till I come, give attendance to reading, to exhortation, to doctrine. | 13. Donec venio, attende lectioni, exhortationi, doctrinæ. |

that even unbelievers are protected by God, as it is said (Matt. v. 45) that "he maketh his sun to shine on the good and the bad;" and we see that all are fed by his goodness, that all are delivered from many dangers. In this sense he is called "the Saviour of all men;" not in regard to the spiritual salvation of their souls, but because he supports all his creatures. In this way, therefore, our Lord is the Saviour of all men; that is, his goodness extends to the most wicked, who are estranged from him, and who do not deserve to have any intercourse with him, who ought to have been struck off from the number of the creatures of God and destroyed; and yet we see how God hitherto extends his grace to them; for the life which he gives to them is a testimony of his goodness. Since, therefore, God shows such favour towards those who are strangers to him, how shall it be with us who are members of his household? Not that we are better or more excellent than those whom we see to be cast off by him, but the whole proceeds from his mercy and free grace, that he is reconciled to us through our Lord Jesus Christ, since he hath called us to the knowledge of the gospel, and then confirms us, and seals his bounty toward us, so that we ought to be convinced that he reckons us to be his children. Since, therefore, we see that he nourishes those who are estranged from him, let us go and hide ourselves under his wings; for, having taken us under his protection, he has declared that he will show himself to be a Father toward us."—*Fr. Ser.*

[1] "Le mot Grec que nous traduisons *Sauveur.*" "The Greek word which we translate Saviour."

| 14. Neglect not the gift that is in thee, which was given thee by prophecy, with the laying on of the hands of the presbytery. | 14. Ne donum, quod in te est, negligas, quod tibi datum est per prophetiam cum impositione manuum presbyterii. |
| 15. Meditate upon these things; give thyself wholly to them, that thy profiting may appear to all. | 15. Hæc cura, in his esto; ut profectus tuus in omnibus manifestus fiat. |
| 16. Take heed unto thyself, and unto the doctrine; continue in them: for in doing this thou shalt both save thyself, and them that hear thee. | 16. Attende tibi ipsi et doctrinæ, permane in his; hoc enim si feceris, et te ipsum servabis, et eos qui te audiunt. |

11. *Instruct and teach these things.* He means that the doctrine is of such a kind, that men ought not to be weary of it, though they heard it every day. There are, no doubt, other things to be taught; but there is emphasis in the demonstrative *these;* for it means that they are not things of small importance, of which it is enough to take a passing and brief notice; but, on the contrary, that they deserve to be repeated every day, because they cannot be too much inculcated. A prudent pastor ought, therefore, to consider what things are chiefly necessary, that he may dwell on them. Nor is there reason to dread that it shall become wearisome; for whosoever is of God will gladly hear frequently those things which need to be so often uttered.

12. *Let no man despise thy youth.* He says this, both in regard to others, and to Timothy himself. As to others, he does not wish that the age of Timothy should prevent him from obtaining that reverence which he deserves, provided that, in other respects, he conduct himself as becomes a minister of Christ. And, at the same time, he instructs Timothy to supply by gravity of demeanour what is wanting in his age. As if he had said, " Take care that, by gravity of demeanour, thou procure for thyself so great reverence, that thy youthful age, which, in other respects lays one open to contempt, may take nothing from thy authority." Hence we learn that Timothy was still young, though he held a place of distinguished excellence among many pastors; and that it is a grievous mistake to estimate by the number of years how much is due to a person.

*But be an example of the believers.*[1] He next informs him

[1] " Be very careful to lead a holy and blameless life. Let it be your care to set a good example to those who are to be taught by you, of so-

what are the true ornaments; not external marks, such as the crozier, the ring, the cloak, and such like trifles, or children's rattles; but soundness of doctrine and holiness of life. When he says, by *speech* and *conversation*, the meaning is the same as if he had said, "by words and actions," and therefore by the whole life.

Those which follow are parts of a godly conversation—*charity, spirit, faith, chastity.* By the word *spirit*, I understand ardour of zeal for God, if it be not thought better to interpret it more generally, to which I have no objection. *Chastity* is not merely contrasted with uncleanness, but denotes purity of the whole life. Hence we learn, that they act a foolish and absurd part, who complain that no honour is paid to them, while they have nothing about them that is worthy of applause, but, on the contrary, expose themselves to contempt, both by their ignorance, and by a detestable example of life, or by levity or other abominations. The only way of procuring reverence is, by excellent virtues, to guard ourselves against contempt.

13. *Attend to reading.* He knew Timothy's diligence, and yet he recommends to him diligent reading of the Scriptures. How shall pastors teach others if they be not eager to learn? And if so great a man is advised to study to make progress from day to day, how much more do we need such an advice? Woe then to the slothfulness of those who do not peruse the oracles of the Holy Spirit by day and night,[1] in order to learn from them how to discharge their office!

*Till I come.* This reference to the time gives additional briety, temperance, justice, and a due government of the tongue. Let it not be said that you preach what you will not practise; for you may be sure, that perverse sinners who will not hear good advice will endeavour to countenance themselves in sin by a bad example. Examples sometimes do good, where precepts are of very little force. He is a wise and happy instructor, who can say with sincerity, in some degree, after the Apostle, when he addresses himself in a solemn way to his hearers: 'those things which you have learned, and received, and heard, and seen in me, do.' Such serious religion is what every one that dispenses the bread of life must practise." —*Abraham Taylor.*

[1] Our author may have had in his eye the advice of the poet:—
"Vos exemplaria Græca
Nocturna versate manu, versate diurna."
"Peruse the Grecian models night and day."
It has always been a prominent feature in the character of a good man,

weight to the exhortation; for, while Paul hoped that he would come soon, yet he was unwilling, meanwhile, that Timothy should remain unemployed even for a short time; how much more ought we to look forward diligently to our whole life!

*To exhortation, to doctrine.* Lest it should be thought that careless reading was enough, he, at the same time, shews that it must be explained with a view to usefulness, when he enjoins him to give earnest attention "to doctrine and exhortation;" as if he enjoined him to learn in order to communicate to others. It is proper, also, to attend to this order, that he places *reading* before *doctrine* and *exhortation;* for, undoubtedly, the Scripture is the fountain of all wisdom, from which pastors must draw all that they place before their flock.

14. *Neglect not the gift that is in thee.* The Apostle exhorts Timothy to employ, for the edification of the Church, that grace with which he was endued. God does not wish that talents—which he has bestowed on any one, that they may bring gain—should either be lost, or be hidden in the earth without advantage. (Matt. xxv. 18, 25.) To *neglect* a gift is carelessly to keep it unemployed through slothfulness, so that, having contracted rust, it is worn away without yielding any profit. Let each of us, therefore, consider what gift he possesses, that he may diligently apply it to use.

He says that grace was *given* to him *by prophecy.* How was this? It was because, as we have already said, the Holy Spirit marked out Timothy by revelation, that he might be admitted into the rank of pastors; for he had not only been chosen by the judgment of men, in the ordinary way, but had previously been named by the Spirit.

*With the laying on of the hands of the presbytery.* He says that it was conferred "with the laying on of hands;" by which he means, that, along with the ministry, he was also adorned with the necessary gifts. It was the custom

---

that "his delight is in the law of the Lord, and in his law doth he meditate day and night."—(Ps. i. 2.) How much more may we reasonably expect that the servant of Christ, who speaks to the people in the name of his Master, and whose office it is to "shew them that which is written in the Scripture of truth," (Dan. x. 21,) shall devoutly and laboriously read the oracles of God!—*Ed.*

and ordinary practice of the Apostles to ordain ministers "by the laying on of hands." As to this ceremony, and its origin and meaning, I have formerly given a brief explanation of them, and the rest may be learned from the Institutes. (Book iv. chap. iii.)

They who think that *presbytery* is here used as a collective noun, for "the college of presbyters or elders,"[1] are, I think, correct in their opinion; although, after weighing the whole matter, I acknowledge that a different meaning is not inapplicable, that is, that *presbytery* or *eldership*—is the name of an office. He put the ceremony for the very act of ordination; and therefore the meaning is, that Timothy—having been called to the ministry by the voice of the prophets, and having afterwards been solemnly ordained—was, at the same time, endued with the grace of the Holy Spirit for the discharge of his office. Hence we infer that it was not a useless ceremony, because God, by his Spirit, accomplished that consecration which men expressed symbolically "by the laying on of hands."

15. *Take heed to these things.*[2] The greater the difficulty in faithfully discharging the ministry of the Church, so much the more ought a pastor to apply himself earnestly, and with his whole might; and that not only for a short time, but with unfailing perseverance.[3] Paul therefore reminds Timothy that this work leaves no room for indolence, or for slackening his labours, but demands the utmost industry and constant application.

*That thy profiting may be manifest.* By adding these words, he means, that he ought to labour to this purpose, that by his agency the edification of the Church may be more and more advanced, and that corresponding results may be visible; for it is not the work of a single day, and

---

[1] "Pour l'assemblee des prestres, c'est a dire, des pasteurs et anciens de l'Eglise."—"For the assembly of presbyters, that is, of the pastors and elders of the Church."

[2] "Ταῦτα μελίτα, meaning, 'Exercise thyself in these things, make them thy perpetual care and study;' both this and the next phrase, (ἐν τούτοις ἴσθι,) being, in the best writers, used of diligent attention."—*Bloomfield.*

[3] "Mais perseverant jusqu'au bout."—"But persevering till the end."

therefore he should strive to make daily progress. Some refer this to Timothy, that he may profit more and more; but I choose rather to interpret it as referring to the effect of his ministry.

The Greek words, $\dot{\epsilon}\nu$ $\pi\hat{a}\sigma\iota\nu$, may either be translated, *to all men,* or, *in all things.* There will thus be a twofold meaning; either, "that all may see the progress which springs from his labours," or, "that in all respects, or in every possible way, (which is the same thing,) they may be visible." I prefer the latter view.

16. *Give heed to thyself, and to the doctrine.* There are two things of which a good pastor should be careful; to be diligent in teaching, and to keep himself pure.[1] It is not enough if he frame his life to all that is good and commendable, and guard against giving a bad example, if he do not likewise add to a holy life continual diligence in teaching; and, on the other hand, doctrine will be of little avail, if there be not a corresponding goodness and holiness of life. With good reason, therefore, does Paul urge Timothy to "give heed," both to himself personally, and to doctrine, for the general advantage of the Church. On the other hand, he commends his constancy, that he may never grow weary; for there are many things that frequently happen, which may lead us aside from the right course, if we do not set our foot firmly to resist.

*If thou shalt do these things, thou shalt both save thyself and them that hear thee.* It is no ordinary spur to excite the thoughtfulness of pastors, when they learn that their own salvation, as well as that of the people, depends on the industry and perseverance with which they devote themselves to their office. And as doctrine, which solidly edifies, is commonly attended by little display, Paul says that he ought to consider what is profitable. As if he had said, " Let men who are desirous of glory be fed by their ambition, let them applaud themselves for their ingenuity; to you, let it be enough to devote yourself to your own salvation and that of the people."

[1] "Et de se garder pur de tous vices."—"And to keep himself pure from all vices."

Now, this exhortation applies to the whole body of the Church, that they may not take offence at the simplicity which both quickens souls and preserves them in health. Nor ought they to think it strange that Paul ascribes to Timothy the work of saving the Church; for, certainly, all that is gained to God is saved, and it is by the preaching of the gospel that we are gathered to Christ. And as the unfaithfulness or carelessness of the pastor is ruinous to the Church, so the cause of salvation is justly ascribed to his faithfulness and diligence. True, it is God alone that saves; and not even the smallest portion of his glory can lawfully be bestowed on men. But God parts with no portion of his glory when he employs the agency of men for bestowing salvation.

Our salvation is, therefore, the gift of God alone, because from him alone it proceeds, and by his power alone it is performed; and therefore, to him alone, as the author, it must be ascribed. But the ministry of men is not on that account excluded, nor does all this interfere with the salutary tendency of that government on which, as Paul shews, the prosperity of the Church depends. (Eph. iv. 11.) Moreover, this is altogether the work of God, because it is he who forms good pastors, and guides them by his Spirit, and blesses their labour, that it may not be ineffectual.

If thus a good pastor is the salvation of his hearers, let bad and careless men know that their destruction must be ascribed to those who have the charge of them; for, as the salvation of the flock is the crown of the pastor, so from careless pastors all that perishes will be required. Again, a pastor is said to *save* himself, when, by faithfully discharging the office committed to him, he serves his calling; not only because he avoids that terrible vengeance which the Lord threatens by Ezekiel,—"His blood will I require at thy hand," (Ezek. xxxiii. 8,) but because it is customary to speak of believers as performing their salvation when they walk and persevere[1] in the course of their salvation. Of this mode of expression we have spoken in our exposition of the Epistle to the Philippians, (ii. 12.)

[1] "Quand ils cheminent et perseverent."

## CHAPTER V.

1. Rebuke not an elder, but entreat *him* as a father; *and* the younger men as brethren;
2. The elder women as mothers; the younger as sisters, with all purity.
3. Honour widows that are widows indeed.
4. But if any widow have children or nephews, let them learn first to shew piety at home, and to requite their parents: for that is good and acceptable before God.

1. Seniorem ne asperè objurges sed hortare ut patrem, juniores ut fratres;
2. Mulieres natu grandiores, ut matres; juniores, ut sorores, cum omni castitate.
3. Viduas honora, quæ verè sunt viduæ.
4. Porro si qua vidua liberos aut nepotes habet, discunt primum erga propriam domum pietatem colere, et mutuum rependere progenitoribus; hoc enim bonum et acceptum est coram Deo.

1. *Do not harshly rebuke an elder.* He now recommends to Timothy gentleness and moderation in correcting faults. Correction is a medicine, which has always some bitterness, and consequently is disagreeable. Besides, Timothy being a young man, his severity would have been less tolerable, if it had not been somewhat moderated.

*But exhort him as a father.* The Apostle enjoins him to reprove elder persons as parents; and he even employs the milder term, *exhort.* It is impossible not to be moved with reverence, when we place before our eyes our father or our mother; in consequence of which, instead of harsher vehemence, we are immediately influenced by modesty. Yet it ought to be observed, that he does not wish old men to be spared or indulged in such a manner as to sin with impunity and without correction; he only wishes that some respect should be paid to their age, that they may more patiently bear to be admonished.

*The younger as brethren.* Even towards younger persons he wishes moderation to be used, though not in an equal degree; for the vinegar must always be mingled with oil, but with this difference, that reverence should always be shewn to older persons, and equals should be treated with brotherly gentleness. Hence pastors are taught, that they must not only take into account their office, but must also see particularly what is due to the age of individuals; for the same things are not applicable to all. Let it therefore be remembered, that, if dramatic performers attend to decorum on the stage, it ought not to be neglected by pastors, who occupy so lofty a station.

2. *The younger as sisters, with all chastity.* The phrase, **with all chastity,** relates to younger women; for at that age they ought always to dread every kind of suspicion. Yet Paul does not forbid Timothy to have any criminal or immodest conduct towards young women, (for there was no need of such a prohibition,) but only enjoins him to beware of giving to wicked men any handle for laughter. For this purpose, he demands a chaste gravity, which shall shine throughout all their intercourse and conversation; so that he may more freely converse with young persons, without any unfavourable reports.

3. *Honour widows that are really widows.* By the word *honour* he does not mean any expression of respect, but that special care of them which bishops[1] took in the ancient Church; for widows were taken under the protection of the Church, that they might be supported out of the common funds. The meaning of this mode of expression is as if he had said, "For selecting widows that are to be taken under your care and that of the deacons, you ought to consider who they are *that are really widows.*[2] What was their con-

---

[1] "Les Pasteurs et Evesques." "Pastors and bishops."
[2] "From what the Fathers and Greek commentators tell us, it appears that those persons were maintained from the funds of the Church; and from what follows, it is clear that they filled an office; the name χήραι being as much one of office as διάκονος, though the exact nature of its duties has not been determined. That the persons who held it instructed the younger females in the principles of the Christian faith, is pretty certain; but whether they were, as some say, 'the same as the deaconesses,' is yet a disputed point. It would seem that they were not necessarily the same; but that, having once been such, during the life of their husbands, they were not removed from that office. Otherwise, it would seem their duties were different from those of the deaconesses; and if we were to call them by such a name as would designate their chief duties, we might call them 'Female Catechists.' That these differed from the deaconesses is certain from the positive testimony of Epiphanius. Yet they might occasionally *assist* them in their duty of visiting the sick. Be that as it may, the existence of such an order as the χήραι requires no very strong testimony from ecclesiastical history; since, from the extremely retired life of the women in Greece and other parts of the East, and their almost total separation from the other sex, they would much *need* the

dition, we shall afterwards explain more fully. But we must here attend to the reason why Paul does not admit any but those who are absolutely widows, and, at the same time, widows without children; for, in that condition, they dedicated themselves to the Church, that they might withdraw from all the private concerns of a family, and might lay aside every hindrance. Justly, therefore, does Paul forbid to receive the mothers of families, who are already bound by a charge of a different kind. When he calls them "really widows," he alludes to the Greek word χήρα, which is derived ἀπὸ τοῦ χηροῦσθαι, from a verb which signifies to be "deprived" or "destitute."

4. *If any widow.* There are various ways of explaining this passage; and the ambiguity arises from this circumstance, that the latter clause may refer either to widows or to their children. Nor is this consistent with the verb (*let them learn*) being plural, while Paul spoke of a *widow* in the singular number; for a change of number is very customary in a general discourse, that is, when the writer speaks of a whole class, and not of an individual. They who think that it relates to widows, are of opinion that the meaning is, "Let them learn, by the pious government of their family, to repay to their successors the education which they received from their ancestors." This is the explanation given by Chrysostom and some others. But others think that it is more natural to interpret it as relating to children and grandchildren. Accordingly, in their opinion, the Apostle teaches that the mother or grandmother is the person towards whom they should exercise their piety; for nothing is more natural than (ἀντιπελαργία) the return of filial for parental affection; and it is very unreasonable that it should be excluded from the Church. Before the Church is burdened with them, let them do their duty.

Hitherto I have related the opinions of others. But I wish my readers to consider if it would not agree better with the context in this manner: "Let them learn to conduct

assistance of such persons, who might either convert them to the Christian faith, or farther instruct them in its doctrines and duties."—*Bloomfield.*

themselves in a godly manner at home." As if he had said, that it would be valuable as a preparatory instruction, that they should train themselves to the worship of God, by performing godly offices at home towards their relatives; for nature commands us to love our parents next to God; so that this secondary piety leads to the highest piety. And as Paul saw that the very rights of nature were violated under the pretence of religion,[1] in order to correct this fault, he commanded that widows should be trained by a domestic apprenticeship to the worship of God.

*To shew piety towards their own house.* Almost all the commentators take the verb εὐσεβεῖν in an active sense, because it is followed by an accusative; but that is not a conclusive argument, for it is customary with the Greek authors to have a preposition understood. And this exposition agrees well with the context, that, by cultivating human piety, they should train themselves in the worship of God; lest a foolish and silly devotion should divest them of human feelings. Again, let widows learn to repay what they owe to their ancestors by educating their own offspring.

*For this is good and acceptable before God.* Not to shew gratitude to our ancestors is universally acknowledged to be monstrous; for that is a lesson taught us by natural reason. And not only is this conviction natural to all, that affection towards our parents is the second degree of piety; but the very storks teach us gratitude by their example; and that is the etymology of the word ἀντιπελαργία.[2] But Paul, not satisfied with this, declares that God hath sanctioned it; as

---

[1] " C'est a dire, qu'on oublivit l'amour que nature enseigne." "That is, that they forgot the love which nature teaches."

[2] "This word is compounded of ἀντὶ, ('instead of,' or, 'in return for,') and πελαργὸς, 'a stork.' The stork is a bird of passage, and is mentioned, along with the crane and the swallow, as knowing the appointed time. (Jer. viii. 7.) Its name, in the Hebrew, means Mercy, or Piety; and its English name, taken (indirectly at least) from the Greek στοργὴ, signifying natural affection. This accords with our knowledge of its character, which is remarkable for tenderness, especially in the young towards the old birds. It is not uncommon to see several of the old birds, which are tired and feeble with the long flight, supported at times on the backs of the young; and the peasants (of Jutland) speak of it as well known, that such are carefully laid in their old nests, and cherished by the young

if he had said, "There is no reason why any one should think that it has its origin in the opinion of men; but God hath so ordained."

| | |
|---|---|
| 5. Now she that is a widow indeed, and desolate, trusteth in God, and continueth in supplications and prayers night and day. | 5. Porro quæ verè vidua est ac desolata, sperat in Deo, et perseverat in orationibus et obsecrationibus noctu et die. |
| 6. But she that liveth in pleasure is dead while she liveth. | 6. Quæ autem in deliciis versatur, vivens mortua est. |
| 7. And these things give in charge, that they may be blameless. | 7. Et hæc præcipe, ut irreprehensibiles sint. |
| 8. But if any provide not for his own, and specially for those of his own house, he hath denied the faith, and is worse than an infidel. | 8. Quod si quis suis et maximè familiaribus non providet, fidem abnegavit, et est infideli deterior. |

5. *She who is really a widow.* He expresses his meaning more clearly than before; for he shews that they are really widows who are solitary and have no children. He says that such persons *hope in God.* Not that this is done by all, or by them alone; for we may see many widows that are childless, and that have no relatives whatever, who nevertheless are haughty and insolent, and altogether ungodly both in heart and in life. On the other hand, then, are those who have many children, and who are not prevented from having their hope placed in God; such as Job and Jacob and David. But for this, (πολυτεκνία) a multitude of children would be a curse, whereas Scripture always reckons it among the remarkable blessings of God. But Paul says here that widows "hope in God," in the same manner as he elsewhere writes, that the unmarried study only to please God, because their affections are not divided like those of married persons. (1 Cor. vii. 32.) The meaning therefore is, that they have nothing to disturb their thoughts from looking to God alone; because they find nothing in the world on which they can rely. By this argument he commends them; for, when human aid and every refuge fails them, it

ones whom they reared the spring before. The stork has long been a peculiar emblem of filial duty."—*Eadie's Cyclopædia.*

"The stork's an emblem of true piety;
Because when age has seized and made its dame
Unfit for flight, the grateful young one takes
His mother on his back, provides her food,
Repaying thus her tender care of him
Ere he was fit to fly."—*Beaumont.*

is the duty of the Church to stretch forth her hand to render assistance; and thus the condition of the widow, who is childless and desolate, implores the aid of the pastor.

*Continueth in prayers.* This is the second ground of commendation, that they continually devote themselves to prayer. Hence it follows, that they ought to be relieved and supported at the expense of the Church. At the same time, by these two marks he distinguishes between the worthy and the unworthy; for these words are of the same import as if he enjoined that they only shall be received who look for no aid from men, but rely on God alone, and, laying aside other cares and employments, are earnestly devoted to prayer; and that others are ill qualified and of no advantage to the Church. Again, this constancy in prayer demands freedom from other cares; for they who are occupied with the government of a family have less freedom and leisure. We are all, indeed, commanded to pray continually; but it ought to be considered what is demanded by every person's condition, when, in order to prayer, retirement and exemption from all other cares are demanded.

What Paul praises in widows, Luke (ii. 36) asserts as to Anna, the daughter of Phanuel; but the same thing would not apply to all, on account of the diversity in their manner of life. There will be foolish women—apes, and not imitators, of Anna—who will run from altar to altar, and will do nothing but sigh and mutter till noon. On this pretence, they will rid themselves of all domestic affairs; and, having returned home, if they do not find everything arranged to their wish, they will disturb the whole family by outrageous cries, and will sometimes proceed to blows. Let us therefore remember that there are good reasons why it is the peculiar privilege of those who are widows and childless, to have leisure for praying by night and by day; because they are free from lawful hindrances, which would not permit those who govern a family to do the same.

And yet this passage lends no countenance to monks or nuns, who sell their mutterings or their loud noises for the sake of leading an easy and idle life. Such were anciently the Euchites or Psallians; for monks and Popish priests differ in no respect, except that the former, by continually praying, thought that none but themselves were pious and holy, while the latter, with inferior industry, imagine that they sanctify both themselves and others. Paul had no thought of anything of this sort, but only intended to shew how much more freely they may have leisure for prayer who have nothing else to disturb them.

6. *She who is in luxury.* After having described the marks by which real widows may be known, he now contrasts them with others that ought not to be received. The Greek participle which he employs, $\sigma\pi\alpha\tau\alpha\lambda\hat{\omega}\sigma\alpha$, means one who allows herself every indulgence, and leads an easy and luxurious life. Accordingly, Paul (in my opinion) censures those who abuse their widowhood for this purpose, that, being loosed from the marriage yoke, and freed from every annoyance, they may lead a life of pleasant idleness; for we see many who seek their own freedom and convenience, and give themselves up to excessive mirth.

*Is dead while she liveth.* When Paul says that such persons "are dead while they live," this is supposed by some to mean that they are unbelievers; an opinion with which I do not at all agree. I think it more natural to say that a woman "is dead," when she is useless, and does no good; for to what purpose do we live, if it be not that our actions may yield some advantage? And what if we should say that the emphasis lies in the word *liveth?* For they who covet an indolent life, that they may live more at their ease, have constantly in their mouth the proverbial saying:—

"For life is not to live, but to be well."[1]

The meaning would therefore be: "If they reckon themselves happy, when they have everything to their heart's wish, and if they think that nothing but repose and luxury can be called life, for my part, I declare that they are dead." But as this meaning might seem liable to the charge of excessive ingenuity, I wished merely to give a passing glimpse of it, without making any positive assertion. This at least

[1] Non est vivere, sed valere vita.

is certain, that Paul here condemns indolence, when he calls those women dead who are of no use.

7. *And command these things.* He means, that not only does he prescribe to Timothy the course which he ought to follow, but the women also must be carefully taught not to be stained with such vices. It is the duty of the pastor not only to oppose the wicked practices or ambition of those who act an unreasonable part, but to guard against every danger, as far as lies in his power, by instruction and constant warnings.

*That they may be blameless.* It was the natural result of prudence and steadfastness not to admit widows, unless they were worthy; but yet it was proper to assign a reason why they were not admitted; and it was even necessary to forewarn the Church that unworthy persons should not be brought forward, or should not offer themselves. Again, Paul commends this part of instruction on the ground of utility; as if he had said, that it must by no means be despised, because it is common, since it aims at the chief part of a good and perfect life. Now there is nothing that ought to be more diligently learned in God's school than the study of a holy and upright life. In a word, moral instruction is compared with ingenious speculations, which are of no visible advantage, agreeably to that saying, "All Scripture is profitable, that the man of God may become perfect," &c. (2 Tim. iii. 16.)

8. *And if any person do not provide for his own.* Erasmus has translated it, "If any woman do not provide for her own," making it apply exclusively to females. But I prefer to view it as a general statement; for it is customary with Paul, even when he is treating of some particular subject, to deduce arguments from general principles, and, on the other hand, to draw from particular statements a universal doctrine. And certainly it will have greater weight, if it apply both to men and to women.

*He hath denied the faith.*[1] He says that they who do not care about any of their relatives, and especially about their own house, have "denied the faith." And justly; for there

---

[1] "Ou, il a renoncé a la foy." "Or, he hath renounced the faith."

is no piety towards God, when a person can thus lay aside the feelings of humanity. Would faith, which makes us the sons of God, render us worse than brute beasts? Such inhumanity, therefore, is open contempt of God, and denying of the faith.

Not content with this, Paul heightens the criminality of their conduct, by saying, that he who forgets his own *is worse than an infidel.* This is true for two reasons. First, the further advanced any one is in the knowledge of God, the less is he excused; and therefore, they who shut their eyes against the clear light of God are worse than infidels. Secondly, this is a kind of duty which nature itself teaches; for they are (στοργαὶ φυσικαί) natural affections. And if, by the mere guidance of nature, infidels are so prone to love their own, what must we think of those who are not moved by any such feeling? Do they not go even beyond the ungodly in brutality? If it be objected, that, among unbelievers, there are also many parents that are cruel and savage; the explanation is easy, that Paul is not speaking of any parents but those who, by the guidance and instruction of nature, take care of their own offspring; for, if any one have degenerated from that which is so perfectly natural, he ought to be regarded as a monster.

It is asked, Why does the Apostle prefer the members of the household to the children? I answer, when he speaks of *his own and especially those of his household,* by both expressions he denotes the children and grandchildren. For, although children may have been transferred, or may have passed into a different family by marriage, or in any way may have left the house of the parents; yet the right of nature is not altogether extinguished, so as to destroy the obligation of the older to govern the younger as committed to them by God, or at least to take care of them as far as they can. Towards domestics, the obligation is more strict; for they ought to take care of them for two reasons, both because they are their own blood, and because they are a part of the family which they govern.

9. Let not a widow be taken into the number under threescore years old, having been the wife of one man,

9. Vidua deligatur non minor annis sexaginta, quæ fuerit unius viri uxor.

10. Well reported of for good works; if she have brought up children, if she have lodged strangers, if she have washed the saints' feet, if she have relieved the afflicted, if she have diligently followed every good work.

11. But the younger widows refuse: for when they have begun to wax wanton against Christ, they will marry;

12. Having damnation, because they have cast off their first faith.

13. And withal they learn *to be* idle, wandering about from house to house; and not only idle, but tattlers also, and busybodies, speaking things which they ought not.

10. In operibus bonis habens testimonium, si liberos educavit, si fuit hospitalis, si sanctorum pedes lavit, si afflictis subministravit, si in omni bono opere fuit assidua.

11. Porro juniores viduas rejice; quum enim lascivire cœperint adversus Christum, nubere volunt;

12. Habentes condemnationem, quòd primam fidem rejecerint.

13. Simul autem et otiosæ discunt circuire domos; nec solum otiosæ, verum etiam garrulæ et curiosæ, loquentes quæ non oportet.

9. *Let a widow be chosen.* He again points out what kind of widows should be taken under the care of the Church;[1] and more clearly than he had formerly done.

*Not under sixty years of age.* First, he describes the age, *sixty years;* for, being supported at the public expense, it was proper that they should have already reached old age. Besides, there was another and stronger reason; for they consecrated themselves to the ministry of the Church, which would have been altogether intolerable, if there were still a likelihood of their being married. They were received on the condition that the Church should relieve their poverty, and that, on their part, they should be employed in ministering to the poor, as far as the state of their health allowed. Thus there was a mutual obligation between them and the Church. It was unreasonable that those who were under that age, and who were still in the vigour of life, should be a burden to others. Besides, there was reason to fear that they would change their mind and think of being married again. These are two reasons why he does not wish any to be admitted "under sixty years of age."

*Who hath been the wife of one man.* As to the desire of marrying, that danger had been sufficiently guarded against, when a woman was more than sixty years old; especially

[1] "Quelles vefues on doit recevoir a estre entretenues aux depens de l'Eglise." "What widows ought to be received, to be supported at the expense of the Church."

if, during her whole life, she had not been married to more than one husband. It may be regarded as a sort of pledge of continence and chastity, when a woman has arrived at that age, satisfied with having had but one husband. Not that he disapproves of a second marriage, or affixes a mark of ignominy to those who have been twice married; (for, on the contrary, he advises younger widows to marry;) but because he wished carefully to guard against laying any females under a necessity of remaining unmarried, who felt it to be necessary to have husbands. On this subject we shall afterwards speak more fully.

10. *For good works.* Those qualifications which are next enumerated relate partly to honour, and partly to labour. There can be no doubt that the assemblies of widows were honourable, and highly respectable; and, therefore, Paul does not wish that any should be admitted into them, but those who had excellent attestations of the whole of their past life. Besides, they were not appointed in order to lazy and indolent inactivity, but to minister to the poor and the sick, until, being completely worn out, they should be allowed honourably to retire. Accordingly, that they may be better prepared for the discharge of their office, he wishes them to have had long practice and experience in all the duties which belong to it; such as—labour and diligence in bringing up children, hospitality, ministering to the poor, and other charitable works.

If it be now asked, Shall all that are barren be rejected, because they have never borne any children? We must reply, that Paul does not here condemn barrenness, but the daintiness of mothers, who, by refusing to endure the weariness of bringing up their children, sufficiently shew that they will be very unkind to strangers. And at the same time he holds out this as an honourable reward to godly matrons, who have not spared themselves, that they, in their turn, shall be received into the bosom of the Church in their old age.

By a figure of speech, in which a part is taken for the whole, he means by *the washing of the feet* all the services which are commonly rendered to the saints; for at that time it was customary to "wash the feet."[1] An employment of this nature might have the appearance of being mean and almost servile; and therefore he makes use of this mark for describing females who were industrious, and far from being fastidious or dainty. What next follows relates to liberality; and, lastly, he expresses the same thing in general terms, when he says, *if she hath been diligent in every good work;* for here he speaks of acts of kindness.

11. *Refuse younger widows.* He does not enjoin that they be excommunicated from the Church, or have any mark of disgrace put upon them; but he only asserts that they must not be rewarded by obtaining that honour which he has already mentioned. And if the Spirit of God, by the mouth of Paul, declares that no woman under sixty years of age deserves to be admitted into that order, because at that age the unmarried state was dangerous; what effrontery was it, afterwards, to lay down a law of celibacy for young women in all the warmth of youthful years? Paul, I say, does not allow of abstaining from marriage till they are in extreme old age, and altogether beyond the danger of incontinence. They afterwards came to forty years as the age for putting the veil on virgins, and next to thirty; and at length they began to put the veil—indiscriminately, and without exception—on females of any age. They allege, that continence is much easier for virgins, who have never had a husband, than it is for widows. But they will never succeed in proving, that there is no reason to dread that danger against which Paul guards and commands others to guard. Accordingly, it is rash, and even cruel, to lay a snare for those who still are young girls, and who would have been fitter for the married state.

*For when they have begun to be wanton against Christ.* He says that they are "wanton against Christ," who, forgetting the condition to which they were called, indulge in unbecoming mirth; for they ought to have kept themselves under

---

[1] This observance was usually administered by, or under the superintendence of, the mistress of the house; and, being in the East particularly grateful, is meant to designate, generally, kind attention to the guests." —*Bloomfield.*

the yoke of modesty, as becomes grave and respectable females. Accordingly, a more luxurious and abandoned course of life is a sort of wantonness against Christ, to whom they had pledged their fidelity. As Paul had seen many instances of this kind, he meets it by a general remedy, that none should be admitted who were of an age that could ever induce them to desire to be married.

How many monsters of crimes are produced every day in Popery by that compulsory celibacy of nuns! What barriers does it not deliberately break through! And therefore, although this course had at first appeared to be commendable, yet, taught by experiments so many and so terrible, they ought to have somewhat complied with the counsel of Paul. But they are so far from doing this, that they provoke the wrath of God more and more, from day to day, by their obstinacy. Nor do I speak of nuns only, but priests and monks are also compelled by them to observe perpetual celibacy. Yet disgraceful lusts rage amongst them, so that hardly one in ten lives chastely; and in monasteries, the least of the evils is ordinary fornication. If they would incline their heart to hear God speaking by the mouth of Paul, they would instantly have recourse to this remedy which he prescribes; but so great is their pride, that they furiously persecute all who remind them of it.

Some read the words thus:—" When they become wanton, they will marry in opposition to Christ." Although this makes little difference as to Paul's meaning, the former view is preferable.

12. *Having condemnation, because they have renounced their first faith.* "To have condemnation," is interpreted by some as signifying "to deserve reproof." But I take it to be a statement of greater severity, that Paul terrifies them by the damnation of eternal death; as if he reproved them by saying that that excellent order, which ought rather to have united them to Christ, was the very ground of their condemnation. And the reason is added, that they entirely "revolt from the faith" of baptism and from Christianity. I am aware that there are some who interpret it differently; that is, that they break the pledge which they gave to

the Church by marrying, having formerly promised that they would live unmarried till death. This is exceedingly absurd. Besides, why should he call it their *first faith?*

Accordingly, Paul rises to greater vehemence against them, and magnifies the enormity of the offence, by saying that not only would they bring disgrace on Christ and his Church by departing from the condition to which they had agreed, but they likewise broke their "first faith" by wicked revolt. Thus it usually happens, that he who has once transgressed the bounds of modesty gives himself up to all impudence. It grieved him that the levity of those women was a reproach to the godly, and that their lustfulness was reproved, or, at least, was liable to reproof. This led them to proceed to greater and greater degrees of licentiousness, till they renounced Christianity. That amplification is exceedingly appropriate; for is there anything more absurd than that they should, through a wish to promote the advantage of persons, open the door to the denial of Christ?

The attempt of the Papists to support, by means of this passage, a vow of perpetual celibacy, is absurd. Granting that it was customary to exact from the widows an engagement in express terms, still they would gain nothing by this admission. First, we must consider the end. The reason why widows formerly promised to remain unmarried, was not that they might lead a holier life than in a state of marriage, but because they could not, at the same time, be devoted to husbands and to the Church; but in Popery, they make a vow of continence, as if it were a virtue acceptable to God on its own account. Secondly, in that age they renounced the liberty of marrying at the time when they ceased to be marriageable; for they must have been, at least, sixty years old, and, by being satisfied with being once married, must have already given a proof of their chastity. But now, vows are made among the Papists to renounce marriage, either before the time, or in the midst of the ardour of youthful years.

Now we disapprove of the tyrannical law about celibacy, chiefly for two reasons. First, they pretend that it is meritorious worship before God; and secondly, by rashness in vowing, they plunge souls into destruction. Neither of these was to be found in the ancient institution. They did not make a direct vow of continence, as if the married life were less acceptable to God, but only, so far as it was rendered necessary by the office to which they were elected, they promised to keep from the tie of marriage for their whole life; nor did they deprive themselves of the liberty of marrying, till the time when, though they had been ever so free, it was foolish and unreasonable for them to marry. In short, those widows differed as much from the nuns, as Anna the prophetess from Clauda the Vestal.[1]

13. *And not only so, but they grow idle.* Nothing is more becoming in women than keeping the house; and hence, among the ancients, a tortoise [2] was the image of a good and respectable mother of a family. But there are many who are diseased with the opposite vice. Nothing delights them more than the liberty of running from one place to another, and especially when, being freed from the burden of a family, they have nothing to do at home.

*Tattlers and busybodies.* Besides, those widows, under the pretence of the respect due to the public character which they sustained, had more easy access to many persons. This opportunity, obtained through the kindness of the Church, they abused for purposes of "idleness;" and next, as usually happens, from slothfulness sprung curiosity, which is also the mother of talkativeness. Most true is the saying of Horace: "Shun an inquisitive person, for he is always a tattler."[3] "No trust should be placed," as Plutarch says, "in inquisitive persons, for, as soon as they have heard anything, they are never at rest till they have blabbed it out." This is especially the case with women, who, by nature, are prone to talkativeness, and cannot keep a secret. With good

---

[1] "A Rome on appeloit Vestales les vierges consacrees a une deesse nommee Vesta (comme qui diroit aujourd'huy les nonnains de saincte Claire) et ceste Claude en estoit une qui a este fort renommee."—"At Rome they gave the name of Vestals to virgins consecrated to a goddess called Vesta, (as if we should say, at the present day, the nuns of St. Claire) and that Clauda was one of them that was highly celebrated."

[2] "Une tortue ou limace."—"A tortoise or a snail."

[3] "Percunctatorem fugito; nam garrulus idem est."—*Hor.*

reason, therefore, has Paul joined together these three things, sloth, inquisitiveness, and tattling.

| | |
|---|---|
| 14. I will therefore that the younger women marry, bear children, guide the house, give none occasion to the adversary to speak reproachfully. | 14. Volo igitur juniores nubere, liberos gignere, domum administrare, nullam occasionem dare adversario, ut habeat maledicendi causam. |
| 15. For some are already turned aside after Satan. | 15. Nonnullæ enim jam deflexerunt post Satanam. |
| 16. If any man or woman that believeth have widows, let them relieve them, and let not the church be charged; that it may relieve them that are widows indeed. | 16. Quodsi quis fidelis, aut si qua fidelis habet viduas, suppeditet illis, et non oneretur Ecclesia, ut iis, quæ verè viduæ sunt, suppetat. |

14. *I wish the younger* (widows) *to marry.* Censorious men laugh at this injunction of the Apostle. "As if," say they, "it had been necessary to stimulate their excessively strong desire; for who does not know that almost all widows have naturally a wish to be married?" Superstitious men, on the other hand, would reckon that this doctrine concerning marriage is highly unsuitable to an Apostle of Christ. But, after a careful examination of the whole matter, men of sound judgment will acknowledge that Paul teaches nothing here but what is necessary and highly useful. For, on the one hand, there are many to whom widowhood gives the opportunity of greater licentiousness; and, on the other hand, there are always arising spirits speaking lies in hypocrisy, who make holiness to consist in celibacy, as if it were angelical perfection, and either totally condemn marriage, or despise it as if it savoured of the pollution of the flesh. There are few either of men or women that consider their calling. How rarely do you find a man who willingly bears the burden of governing a wife! The reason is, that it is attended by innumerable vexations. How reluctantly does a woman submit to the yoke!

Consequently, when Paul bids the younger widows marry, he does not invite them to nuptial delights; and, when he bids them bear children, he does not exhort them to indulge lust; but, taking into account the weakness of the sex, and the slipperiness of the age, he exhorts them to chaste marriage, and, at the same time, to the endurance of those burdens which belong to holy marriage. And he does this, especially, in order that he may not be thought to have acted contemptuously in excluding them from the rank of widows; for he means, that their life will be not less acceptable to God than if they remained in widowhood. And, indeed, God pays no regard to the superstitious opinions of men, but values this obedience more highly than all things else, when we comply with our calling, instead of permitting ourselves to be carried along by the wish of our own heart.

Having heard that consolation, they have no reason to complain that injury is done to them, or to take it ill that they are excluded from one kind of honour; for they learn that, in the married state, they are not less acceptable to God, because they obey his calling. When he speaks of *bearing children,* he includes, under a single word, all the annoyances that must be endured in bringing up children; in the same manner as, under *the government of the house,* he includes all that belongs to household management.

*To give no occasion to the adversary.* For, as the husband may be said to be the covering of the wife, so widowhood is liable to many unfavourable suspicions. And what purpose does it serve, to arm the enemies of the gospel with calumnies, without any necessity? But it is very difficult for a widow, in the flower of her age, to act with such caution that wicked men shall not find some pretext for slandering her; and, therefore, if they sincerely desire edification, let them, in order to shut the mouth of evil speakers, choose a way of life that is less liable to suspicion. Here, I suppose, the common *adversaries* of the gospel to be meant, rather than the private adversaries of any woman; for Paul speaks indefinitely.[1]

---

[1] "Let us ponder well this doctrine of Paul; for, although he treats here of widows in particular, yet we are all admonished, that, in order to perform our duty towards God, it is not enough that our conscience be pure and clean, and that we walk without any bad disposition; but we ought likewise to add such prudence that enemies shall have their mouth shut when they wish to slander us, that their impudence may be known, and that we may always be ready to give an account of what we have done, and that they may have no pretence for blaspheming against the name of God and his word, because there will be no appearance of evil in us. True, we cannot avoid being slandered; but let us always

15. *For some have already turned aside.* It is certain, that there is no ordinance so holy that some evil may not arise out of it through the wickedness of men. Yet those things which are necessary ought to remain unmoved, whatever may happen to them, although the sky should fall. But when we are at liberty to choose either way, and when this or that has been found by experience to be advantageous, it is a matter of prudence to lay aside what was formerly approved, as in the present case. It was not at all necessary that women, who were still young, should be admitted into the rank of widows; experience shewed that it was dangerous and hurtful; and, therefore, Paul justly advises to take care for the future that nothing of this kind may happen.

If the revolt of some women was regarded by him as a sufficiently strong argument for seeking a universal remedy, how many arguments would the Papists have for abolishing their filthy celibacy, if they had any regard to edification! But they choose rather to strangle millions of souls by the cruel cords of a wicked and diabolical law than to loose a single knot; and this makes it evident how widely their cruelty differs from the holy zeal of Paul.

*After Satan.* The expression is worthy of notice; because no one can turn aside from Christ, in the smallest degree, without following Satan; for he has dominion over all who do not belong to Christ. We learn from this how destructive is turning aside from the right course, since, from being children of God, it makes us slaves of Satan, and, by withdrawing us from the government of Christ, places Satan over us as our guide.[1]

attend to this, that no occasion may be given on our part, or by our imprudence." —*Fr. Ser.*

[1] "Since the gospel is preached to us, it is Jesus Christ who holds out his sceptre, and shews us that he wishes to be our king, and to take us for his people. When we have thus made profession of the gospel, if we do not persevere till the end, if it happen that we debauch ourselves in any way, not only do we refuse to be in obedience to the Son of God, but we give to Satan all mastery over us, and he will seize it, and we must be in his service in spite of our teeth. If this is dreadful and absolutely shocking, ought we not to be better advised than we have been to conceal ourselves under the wings of our God, and to suffer ourselves to be governed by him, till he renew us by his Holy Spirit in such a manner that we shall

16. *If any believer.* It being customary for every one willingly to throw his own burdens on the whole Church, on this account he expressly enjoins that it be guarded against. He speaks of believers who ought to support their widows; for, as to those widows who renounced a wicked relationship, it was proper that they should be received by the Church. And if they act a sinful part, who, by sparing themselves, allow the Church to be burdened with expense, let us learn from this in what aggravated sacrilege they are involved, who, by fraud or robbery, profane what was once dedicated to the Church.

17. Let the elders that rule well be counted worthy of double honour, especially they who labour in the word and doctrine.
18. For the scripture saith, Thou shalt not muzzle the ox that treadeth out the corn. And, The labourer *is* worthy of his reward.
19. Against an elder receive not an accusation, but before two or three witnesses.
20. Them that sin rebuke before all, that others also may fear.
21. I charge *thee* before God, and the Lord Jesus Christ, and the elect angels, that thou observe these things, without preferring one before another, doing nothing by partiality.

17. Presbyteri, qui bene præsunt, duplici honore digni habeantur; maximè qui laborant in verbo et doctrina.
18. Dicit enim scriptura: Non obligabis os bovi trituranti, (Deut. xxv. 4,) et, Dignus est operarius mercede sua, (Matt. x. 10.)
19. Adversus presbyterum accusationem ne admittas, nisi sub duobus aut tribus testibus.
20. Peccantes coram omnibus argue, ut et cæteri timorem habeant.
21. Contestor coram Deo, et Domino Iesu Christo, et electis angelis, ut hæc custodias absque præcipitatione judicii, nihil faciens, alteram in partem declinando.

17. *Elders.*[1] For preserving the good order of the Church, it is likewise highly necessary that elders should not be neglected, but that due regard should be paid to them; for what could be more unfeeling than to have no care about those who have the care of the whole Church? Here πρεσ-βύτερος (*elder*) is not a name of age, but of office.

*Accounted worthy of double honour.* Chrysostom interprets "double honour" as meaning " support and reverence."

not be so giddy and foolish as we have been? For that purpose, let us consider that we must have our Lord Jesus Christ for our guide; for if we wish to be truly the people of God, the saying of the Prophet must be fulfilled in us, that the people shall walk, and David their king shall go before them. Let us always have his doctrine before our eyes, and let us follow him step by step, hearing his voice as that of our good Shepherd, (John x. 4)."—*Fr. Ser.*

[1] "Les prestres ou anciens." "Presbyters or elders."

I do not oppose his opinion; let it be adopted by any one that chooses. But for my own part, I think it is more probable that a comparison is here drawn between widows and elders. Paul had formerly enjoined that honour should be paid to widows; but elders are more worthy of being honoured than widows, and, with respect to them, ought therefore to receive double honour.

But in order to shew that he does not recommend masks, he adds, *who rule well;* that is, who faithfully and laboriously discharge their office. For, granting that a person should a hundred times obtain a place, and though he should boast of his title; yet, if he do not also perform his duty, he will have no right to demand that he shall be supported at the expense of the Church. In short, he means that honour is not due to the title, but to the work performed by those who are appointed to the office.

Yet he prefers *those who labour in word and doctrine,* that is, those who are diligent in teaching the word; for those two terms, *word* and *doctrine,* signify the same thing, namely, the preaching of the word. But lest any one should suppose him to mean by the *word* an indolent, and, as it is called, a speculative study of it, he adds *doctrine.*[1]

We may learn from this, that there were at that time two kinds of elders; for all were not ordained to teach. The words plainly mean, that there were some who "ruled well" and honourably, but who did not hold the office of teachers. And, indeed, there were chosen from among the people men of worth and of good character, who, united with the pastors

---

[1] "He shews that we might do many other things, and might allege that we had no leisure; but yet we must consider chiefly what it is to which God calls us. They who would wish to be reckoned pastors ought to devote themselves especially to that word. And how? In order to study it secretly in their closet? Not at all; but for the general instruction of the Church. That is the reason why Paul chose to add the term *doctrine.* It was quite enough to have said, *word;* but he shews that we must not privately speculate what we shall think fit; but that, when we have studied, it is that others may profit along with us, and that the instruction may be common to the whole Church.—This is the true mark for distinguishing properly between the pastors whom God approves and wishes to be supported in his Church, and those who claim that title and honour, and yet are excluded and rejected by him and by the Holy Spirit."—*Fr. Ser.*

in a common council and authority, administered the discipline of the Church, and were a kind of censors for the correction of morals. Ambrose complains that this custom had gone into disuse, through the carelessness, or rather through the pride, of the doctors, who wish to possess undivided power.

To return to Paul, he enjoins that support shall be provided chiefly for pastors, who are employed in teaching. Such is the ingratitude of the world, that very little care is taken about supporting the ministers of the word; and Satan, by this trick, endeavours to deprive the Church of instruction, by terrifying many, through the dread of poverty and hunger, from bearing that burden.[1]

18. *Thou shalt not muzzle the ox.* This is a political precept, which recommends to us equity and humanity[2] in general; as we have said in expounding the First Epistle to the Corinthians;[3] for, if he forbids us to be unkind to brute animals, how much greater humanity does he demand towards men! The meaning of this statement, therefore, is the same as if it had been said in general terms, that they must not make a wrong use of the labour of others. At the present day, the custom of treading out the corn is unknown in many parts of France, where they thresh the corn with flails. None but the inhabitants of Provence know what is meant by " treading it out." But this has nothing to do with the meaning; for the same thing may be said about ploughing.

[1] " In this passage Paul did not look to himself, but spoke by the authority of God, in order that the Church might not be destitute of persons who should teach faithfully. For the devil, from the beginning, had the trick of attempting to hunger good pastors, that they might cease to labour, and that there might be very few who were employed in preaching the word of God. Let us not view the recommendation here contained as coming from a mortal man, but let us hear God speaking, and let us know that there is no accepting of persons, but that, knowing what was profitable to the whole Church, and perceiving that many were cold and indifferent on this subject, he has laid down a rule, that they whose duty it is to preach the gospel shall be supported; as we see that Paul speaks of it in other passages, and treats of it very fully in the First Epistle to the Corinthians, though he likewise mentions it in the Epistle to the Galatians."—*Fr. Ser.*
[2] " Equité et humanité."
[3] See Commentary on the Corinthians, vol. i. p. 294.

*The labourer is worthy of his hire.* He does not quote this as a passage of Scripture, but as a proverbial saying, which common sense teaches to all. In like manner, when Christ said the same thing to the Apostles, (Matt. x. 10,) he brought forward nothing else than a statement approved by universal consent. It follows that they are cruel, and have forgotten the claims of equity, who permit cattle to suffer hunger; and incomparably worse are they that act the same part towards men, whose sweat they suck out for their own accommodation. And how intolerable is the ingratitude of those who refuse support to their pastors, to whom they cannot pay an adequate salary!

19. *Against an elder receive not an accusation.* After having commanded that salaries should be paid to pastors, he likewise instructs Timothy not to allow them to be assailed by calumnies, or loaded with any accusation but what is supported by sufficient proof. But it may be thought strange, that he represents, as peculiar to elders, a law which is common to all. God lays down, authoritatively, this law as applicable to all cases, that they shall be decided "by the mouth of two or three witnesses." (Deut. xvii. 6; Matt. xviii. 16.) Why then does the Apostle protect elders alone by this privilege, as if it were peculiar to them, that their innocence shall be defended against false accusations?

I reply, this is a necessary remedy against the malice of men; for none are more liable to slanders and calumnies than godly teachers.[1] Not only does it arise from the difficulty of their office, that sometimes they either sink under it, or stagger, or halt, or blunder, in consequence of which wicked men seize many occasions for finding fault with them; but there is this additional vexation, that, although they perform their duty correctly, so as not to commit any error whatever, they never escape a thousand censures. And this is the craftiness of Satan, to draw away the hearts of men from ministers, that instruction may gradually fall into contempt. Thus not only is wrong done to innocent persons, in having their reputation unjustly wounded, (which is ex-

---

[1] "Que les docteurs ou pasteurs fideles." "Than faithful teachers or pastors."

ceedingly base in regard to those who hold so honourable a rank,) but the authority of the sacred doctrine of God is diminished.

And this is what Satan, as I have said, chiefly labours to accomplish; for not only is the saying of Plato true in this instance, that "the multitude are malicious, and envy those who are above them," but the more earnestly any pastor strives to advance the kingdom of Christ, so much the more is he loaded with envy, and so much the fiercer are the assaults made on him. Not only so, but as soon as any charge against the ministers of the word has gone abroad, it is believed as fully as if they were already convicted. This is not merely owing to the higher degree of moral excellence which is demanded from them, but because almost all are tempted by Satan to excessive credulity, so that, without making any inquiry, they eagerly condemn their pastors, whose good name they ought rather to have defended.

On good grounds, therefore, Paul opposes so heinous iniquity, and forbids that elders shall be subjected to the slanders of wicked men till they have been convicted by sufficient proof. We need not wonder, therefore, if they whose duty it is to reprove the faults of all, to oppose the wicked desires of all, and to restrain by their severity every person whom they see going astray, have many enemies. What, then, will be the consequence, if we shall listen indiscriminately to all the slanders that are spread abroad concerning them?

20. *Those that sin rebuke before all.*[1] Whenever any measure is taken for the protection of good men, it is immediately seized by bad men to prevent them from being condemned. Accordingly, what Paul had said about repelling unjust accusations he modifies by this statement, so that none may, on this pretence, escape the punishment due to sin. And, indeed, we see how great and diversified are the privileges by which Popery surrounds its clergy; so that, although their life be ever so wicked,[2] still they are exempted from all reproof. Certainly, if regard be had to the cautions

---

[1] "Repren publiquement." "Rebuke publicly."
[2] "Combien que la vie de leurs moines et prestres soit la plus meschante

which are collected by Gratian,[1] (Caus. ii. Quest. 4 and Quest. 7,) there will be no danger of their being ever compelled to give an account of their life. Where will they find the seventy-two witnesses for condemning a bishop, which are demanded by the disgusting bull issued by Pope Sylvester? Moreover, seeing that the whole order of laymen is debarred from accusing, and as the inferior orders, even of the clergy, are forbidden to give any annoyance to the higher classes of them, what shall hinder them from fearlessly mocking at all decisions?

It is therefore proper carefully to observe this moderation, that insolent tongues shall be restrained from defaming elders by false accusations, and yet that every one of them who conducts himself badly shall be severely corrected; for I understand this injunction to relate to elders, that they who live a dissolute life shall be openly reproved.

*That others also may fear.* Wherefore? That others, warned by such an example, may fear the more, when they perceive that not even those who are placed above them in rank and honour are spared; for as elders ought to lead the way to others by the example of a holy life, so, if they commit crime, it is proper to exercise severity of discipline toward them, that it may serve as an example to others. And why should greater forbearance be used toward those whose offences are much more hurtful than those of others? Let it be understood that Paul speaks of crimes or glaring transgressions, which are attended by public scandal; for, if any of the elders shall have committed a fault, not of a public nature, it is certain that he ought to be privately admonished and not openly reproved.

21. *I adjure thee before God.* Paul introduced this solemn appeal, not only on account of the very great importance of

et desbordee qu'on scauroit dire."—" Although the life of their monks and priests be the most wicked and dissolute that can be described."

[1] "Gratian, a Benedictine of the 12th century, was a native of Chiusi, and was the author of a famous work, entitled "Decretal," or "Concordantia Discordantium Canonum," in which he endeavoured to reconcile those canons that seem to contradict each other. He was, however, guilty of some errors, which Anthony Augustine endeavoured to correct in his work entitled "De emendatione Gratiani." Gratian's "Decretal" forms one of the principal parts of the canon law."—*Gorton's Biog. Dict.*

the subject, but likewise on account of its extreme difficulty. Nothing is more difficult than to discharge the office of a public judge with so great impartiality as never to be moved by favour for any one, or to give rise to suspicions, or to be influenced by unfavourable reports, or to use excessive severity, and in every cause to look at nothing but the cause itself; for only when we shut our eyes to persons[1] do we pronounce an equitable judgment.

Let us remember that, in the person of Timothy, all pastors are admonished, and that Timothy is armed, as with a shield, against wicked desires, which not unfrequently occasion much trouble even to some excellent persons. He therefore places God before the eyes of Timothy, that he may know that he ought to execute his office not less conscientiously than if he were in the presence of God and of his angels.

*And the Lord Jesus Christ.* After having named *God*, he next mentions *Christ;* for he it is to whom the Father hath given all power to judge, (John v. 22,) and before whose tribunal we shall one day appear.

*And the elect angels.* To " Christ " he adds " angels," not as judges, but as the future witnesses of our carelessness, or rashness, or ambition, or unfaithfulness. They are present as spectators, because they have been commanded to take care of the Church. And, indeed, he must be worse than stupid, and must have a heart of stone, whose indolence and carelessness are not shaken off by this single consideration, that the government of the Church is under the eye of God and the angels; and when that solemn appeal is added, our fear and anxiety must be redoubled. He calls them "*elect angels*,"[2] not only to distinguish them from the reprobate

---

[1] " Et qu'on regarde seulement le faict." " And when we look at nothing but the fact."

[2] " Let us remark that he wishes to distinguish them from those who rebelled. For the devils were not created wicked and malicious as they now are, enemies of all that is good, and false and cursed in their nature. They were angels of God, but they were not elected to persevere, and so they fell. Thus God reserved what he chose among the angels. And so we have already a mirror of God's election of us to heaven, by free grace, before we came into the world. Now, if we see the grace of God displayed

angels, but on account of their excellence, in order that their testimony may awaken deeper reverence.

*Without hastiness of judgment.*¹ The Greek word προκρίμα, to translate it literally, answers to the Latin word *præjudicium,* " a judgment beforehand." But it rather denotes excessive haste,² as when we pronounce a decision at random, without having fully examined the matter; or it denotes immoderate favour, when we render to persons more than is proper, or prefer some persons as being more excellent than others; which, in the decisions of a judge, is always unjust. Paul, therefore, condemns here either levity or acceptance of persons.

To the same purpose is that which immediately follows, that there must be no *turning to this side or that;* for it is almost impossible to tell how difficult it is, for those who hold the office of a judge, to keep themselves unmoved, amidst assaults so numerous and so diversified. Instead of κατὰ πρόσκλισιν,³ some copies have κατὰ πρόσκλησιν. But the former reading is preferable.

| | |
|---|---|
| 22. Lay hands suddenly on no man, neither be partaker of other men's sins: keep thyself pure. | 22. Manus citò ne cui imponas; neque communices peccatis alienis; temetipsum purum custodi. |
| 23. Drink no longer water, but use a little wine for thy stomach's sake, and thine often infirmities. | 23. Ne posthac bibas aquam; sed paululo vino utere propter stomachum tuum, et crebras tuas infirmitates. |
| 24. Some men's sins are open beforehand, going before to judg- | 24. Quorundam hominum peccata antè manifestata sunt, festi- |

even to angels, what shall become of us? For all mankind were lost and ruined in Adam, and we are all accursed, and, as the Scripture tells us, are born " children of wrath." (Eph. ii. 3.) What must we become if God do not choose us by pure goodness, since from our mother's womb (Ps. li. 6) we are corrupted, and are alienated from him? This gracious election must prevail, in order to separate us from the reprobate, who remain in their perdition. We ought, therefore, carefully to remark this passage, that Paul, when speaking of the angels, shews that their high rank proceeds from their having been chosen and elected by God. And so, by a still stronger reason, we are separated from all other visible creatures, only because God separates us by his mercy."—*Fr. Ser.*

¹ " Sans jugement precipité, ou, sans preferer l'un a l'autre." " Without hasty judgment, or, without preferring one before another."
² " Une trop soudaine hastivete." " A too sudden haste."
³ " Κατὰ πρόσκλισιν, ' through partiality,' or undue favour. So Clemens, in his Epistle to the Corinthians, has κατὰ προσκλίσεις (through partialities.) The word properly signifies a leaning towards, or upon.—*Bloomfield.*

ment; and some *men* they follow after.

25. Likewise also the good works *of some* are manifest beforehand; and they that are otherwise cannot be hid.

nantia ad judicium; in quibusdam verò etiam subsequuntur.

25. Similiter et bona opera antè manifesta sunt; et quæ secus habent latere nequeunt.

22. *Lay not hands suddenly on any man.* There can be no doubt that he intended to guard Timothy against ill-will, and to obviate many complaints, which are continually arising against the godly servants of Christ, who refuse to comply with the ambitious requests of any. For some accuse them of sternness, others of envy; and some exclaim that they are cruel, because they do not at once receive those who boast of having some recommendatory qualities. This is what we abundantly experience in the present day. Paul therefore exhorts Timothy not to lay aside judicious caution, and not to suffer himself to be overpowered by improper feelings; not that Timothy needed such an admonition, but to restrain, by his authority, those who otherwise might have given annoyance to Timothy,

First, the " laying on of hands" means Ordination;[1] that is, the sign is put for the thing signified; for he forbids him to receive too easily any one that has not been fully tried. There are some who, through a desire of novelty, would wish to receive into the ministerial office, some person hardly at all known, as soon as he has given one or two exhibitions that are reckoned good. It is the duty of a wise and thoughtful bishop, to resist this troublesome feeling, in the same manner as Paul here bids Timothy do.

*Neither partake of other men's sins.* He means that he who consents to an unlawful act of ordination is involved in the same guilt as the chief actors in it. Yet some explain it thus: " If he admit unworthy persons, whatever faults they may afterwards commit, to him will be imputed the blame or a part of the blame." But I think that this is a more simple view of it: " Though others rush forth to such rashness, do not make thyself a partaker with them, lest thou share in their guilt." Even where our judgment is otherwise

---

[1] " Laquelle on appelle Ordination ou Consecration." " What is called Ordination or Consecration."

sound, it often happens that we are carried away by the folly and levity of others.¹

*Keep thyself pure.* I consider this also to have the same reference as the preceding clause. As if he had said, " If others do anything that is wrong, beware lest any contagion reach you, either by consent or by approbation. If you cannot hinder them from polluting themselves, it is at least your duty to have your counsels at all times separated from theirs, so that you may keep yourself pure." If any prefer to view it as a general statement, let him enjoy his opinion; but, for my own part, I reckon it to be more suitable to limit it to the present context.

23. *No longer drink water.* There are some who conjecture that this sentence, which breaks off the train of thought, was not written by Paul. But we see that Paul was not so anxious about keeping up the close connexion of a discourse, and that it was very customary with him to intermingle a variety of statements without any arrangement. Besides, it is possible that what had been formerly written in the margin of the Epistle afterwards found its way into this passage through the mistake of the transcribers. Yet there is no necessity for giving ourselves much trouble on that point, if we consider Paul's custom, which I have mentioned, of sometimes mingling various subjects.

What is said amounts to this, that Timothy should accustom himself to drink a little wine, for the sake of preserving

---

¹ " To whom does the Apostle speak? Is it only to ministers who preach the doctrine of the gospel? Is it only to magistrates, and to those who have the sword and the administration of civil government? No, but to all Christians, great and small. It is then said, that we must not partake of the sins of others. And in what manner? By reproving them. (Eph. v. 11.) And so he who intends to flatter his neighbour, and who shuts his eyes when he sees that God is offended, and especially he who consents to it will be still more blamable. Let us seriously think, that we shall have a hard account to render to God, if we have walked amidst the corruptions of the world, so as to make it appear that we approved of them. And so much the more ought we to meditate on this doctrine, when we see that there is such boldness in sinning, that custom appears to have become the law. Let a man be convinced that he is doing wrong, yet provided that he has many companions, he thinks that he is excused. ' Among wolves we must howl,' it will be said. Now we see that the sins of others will not excuse us before God; and though the whole world sin along with us, we shall not fail to be involved in the same condemnation. Let us think of that."—*Fr. Ser.*

his health; for he does not absolutely forbid him to "drink water," but to use it as his ordinary beverage; and that is the meaning of the Greek word ὑδροποτεῖν.

But why does he not simply advise him to *drink wine?* For when he adds, *a little*, he appears to guard against intemperance, which there was no reason to dread in Timothy. I reply, this was rather expressed, in order to meet the slanders of wicked men, who would otherwise have been ready to mock at his advice, on this or some such pretext: "What sort of philosophy is this, which encourages to drink wine? Is that the road by which we rise to heaven?" In order to meet jeers of this kind, he declares that he provides only for a case of necessity; and at the same time he recommends moderation.

Now it is evident that Timothy was not only frugal, but even austere, in his mode of living; so much so as even not to take care of his health; and it is certain that this was done, neither through ambition nor through superstition. Hence we infer, that not only was he very far from indulging in luxury and superfluities, but that, in order that he might be better prepared for doing the work of the Lord, he retrenched a portion even of his ordinary food; for it was not by natural disposition, but through a desire of temperance, that he was abstemious.

How few are there at the present day, who need to be forbidden the use of water; or rather how many are there that need to be limited to drink wine soberly! It is also evident how necessary it is for us, even when we are desirous to act right, to ask from the Lord the spirit of prudence, that he may teach us moderation. Timothy was, indeed, upright in his aims; but, because he is reproved by the Spirit of God, we learn that excess of severity of living was faulty in him. At the same time a general rule is laid down, that, while we ought to be temperate in eating and drinking, every person should attend to his own health, not for the sake of prolonging life, but that, as long as he lives, he may serve God, and be of use to his neighbours.

And if excessive abstinence is blamed, when it brings on or promotes diseases, how much more should superstition be avoided? What judgment shall we form as to the obstinacy of the Carthusians,[1] who would sooner have died than taste the smallest morsel of flesh in extreme necessity? And if those who live sparingly and soberly are commanded not to injure their health by excessive parsimony, no slight punishment awaits the intemperate, who, by cramming their belly, waste their strength. Such persons need not only to be advised, but to be kept back from their fodder like brute beasts.

24. *The sins of some men are visible beforehand.* As there is nothing that distresses more the faithful ministers of the Church, than to see no way of correcting evils, and to be compelled to endure hypocrites, of whose wickedness they are aware, and to be unable to banish from the Church many who are destructive plagues, or even to hinder them from spreading their venom by secret arts;[2] Paul supports Timothy by this consolation, that, when it shall please God, they will one day be brought to public view. Thus he strengthens him for the exercise of patience; because he ought calmly to await the fit time which God in his wisdom has appointed.

There is another kind of base conduct that sorely distresses good and holy pastors. When they have most conscientiously discharged their duty, they are provoked by many unfair statements, are loaded with much ill-will, and

[1] "In the year 1084, was instituted the famous order of the Carthusians, so called from Chartreux, a dismal and wild spot of ground near Grenoble in Dauphiné, surrounded with barren mountains and craggy rocks. The founder of this monastic society, which surpassed all the rest in the extravagant austerity of their manners and discipline, was Bruno, a native of Cologne, and canon of the cathedral of Rheims in France. This zealous ecclesiastic, who had neither power to reform, nor patience to bear, the dissolute manners of his Archbishop Manasse, retired from his church, with six of his companions, and, having obtained the permission of Hugh, bishop of Grenoble, fixed his residence in the miserable desert already mentioned. He adopted at first the rule of St. Benedict, to which he added a considerable number of severe and rigorous precepts. His successors, however, went still farther, and imposed upon the Carthusians new laws, much more intolerable than those of their founder,—laws which inculcated the highest degrees of austerity that the most gloomy imagination could invent."—*Mosheim's Eccl. Hist.*

[2] "Par moyens secrets, et comme par dessous terre." "By secret and underground arts."

perceive that those actions which deserved praise are turned into blame. Paul meets this case also, by informing Timothy, that there are some good works which are reserved for being brought to light at a future period; and consequently that, if their praise is, as it were, buried under ground by the ingratitude of men, that also ought to be patiently endured, till the time of revelation have arrived.

Yet not only does he provide a remedy for these evils, but, because it often happens that we are mistaken in choosing ministers, unworthy persons insinuating themselves cunningly, and the good being unknown to us; and even though we do not go wrong in judging, but still cannot bring others to approve of our judgment, the most excellent being rejected, notwithstanding all our efforts to the contrary, while bad men either insinuate or force themselves forward; it is impossible that our condition and that of the Church should not occasion great anguish. Accordingly, Paul strenuously endeavours to remove, or at least to alleviate, this cause of uneasiness. The meaning may be thus summed up. "We must bear what cannot be immediately corrected; we must sigh and groan, while the time for the remedy is not fully come; and we must not apply force to diseases, till they are either ripened or laid open. On the other hand, when virtue does not receive the honour which it deserves, we must wait for the full time of revelation, and endure the stupidity of the world, and wait quietly in darkness till the day dawn."

*Hastening to judgment.* I now come to the words, after having given a brief illustration of the subject. When he says that *the sins of some men are visible beforehand*, he means that they are discovered early, and come to the knowledge of men, as it were, before the time. He expresses the same thing by another comparison, that they run, as it were, and "hasten to their judgment;" for we see that many run headlong, and, of their own accord, bring damnation on themselves, though the whole world is desirous to save them. Whenever this happens, let us remember that the reprobate are prompted by an unseen movement of Providence, to throw out their foam.

*In some they follow after.* The rendering given by Erasmus, "Some they follow after," I do not approve. Although it seems to be more in accordance with the Greek construction, yet the sense requires that the preposition ἐν be understood; for the change of case does not destroy the contrast. As he had said that the sins of some men hasten rapidly to their judgment; so now, on the other hand, he adds, that the sins of some men (or, of others) come slowly to be known. But instead of the genitive "of some," he uses the dative "in some," (or "in others.") He means that, although the sins of some men may be concealed longer than we would wish, and are slowly brought to light, yet they shall not always be concealed; for they too shall have their own time. And if the version of Erasmus be preferred, still the meaning must be the same, that, although the vengeance of God does not hasten, yet it follows slowly behind them.

25. *In like manner also the good works.* He means, that sometimes piety and other virtues obtain early and speedily their applause among men; so that great men are held in estimation; and that, if it happen otherwise, the Lord will not suffer innocence and uprightness to be always oppressed; for it is often obscured by calumnies, or by clouds, but at length shall be fulfilled the prediction, (Dan. xii. 3; Matt. xiii. 43,) that God will cause them to shine forth like the dawn of the day. But we have need of a calm spirit to endure; and therefore we must always consider what is the limit of our knowledge, that we may not go beyond it; for that would be to assume to ourselves the prerogative of God.

## CHAPTER VI.

1. Let as many servants as are under the yoke count their own masters worthy of all honour, that the name of God and *his* doctrine be not blasphemed.

2. And they that have believing masters, let them not despise *them,* because they are brethren; but ra-

1. Quicunque sub jugo sunt servi, suos dominos omni honore dignos existiment; ut ne Dei nomen et doctrina blasphemetur.

2. Qui autem fideles habent dominos, ne despiciant eò quòd fratres sunt; sed magis serviant, quòd fide-

ther do *them* service, because they are faithful and beloved, partakers of the benefit. These things teach and exhort.

les sint et dilecti, et beneficentiæ participes. Hæc doce, et exhortare.

It appears that, at the beginning of the gospel, slaves cheered their hearts, as if the signal had been given for their emancipation ; for Paul labours hard, in all his writings, to repress that desire ; and indeed the condition of slavery was so hard that we need not wonder that it was exceedingly hateful. Now, it is customary to seize, for the advantage of the flesh, everything that has the slightest appearance of being in our favour. Thus when they were told that we are all brethren, they instantly concluded that it was unreasonable that they should be the slaves of brethren. But although nothing of all this had come into their mind, still wretched men are always in need of consolation, that may allay the bitterness of their afflictions. Besides, they could not without difficulty be persuaded to bend their necks, willingly and cheerfully, to so harsh a yoke. Such, then, is the object of the present doctrine.

1. *They who are slaves under the yoke.* Owing to the false opinion of his own excellence which every person entertains, there is no one who patiently endures that others should rule over him. They who cannot avoid the necessity do, indeed, reluctantly obey those who are above them ; but inwardly they fret and rage, because they think that they suffer wrong. The Apostle cuts off, by a single word, all disputes of this kind, by demanding that all who live " under the yoke" shall submit to it willingly. He means that they must not inquire whether they deserve that lot or a better one ; for it is enough that they are bound to this condition.

When he enjoins them *to esteem worthy of all honour the masters* whom they serve, he requires them not only to be faithful and diligent in performing their duties, but to regard and sincerely respect them as persons placed in a higher rank than themselves. No man renders either to a prince or to a master what he owes to them, unless, looking at the eminence to which God has raised them, he honours them, because he is subject to them ; for, however unworthy of it they may often be, still that very authority which God bestows on them always entitles them to honour. Besides, no one willingly renders service or obedience to his master, unless he is convinced that he is bound to do so. Hence it follows, that subjection begins with that honour of which Paul wishes that they who rule should be accounted worthy.

*That the name and doctrine of God may not be blasphemed.* We are always too ingenious in our behalf. Thus slaves, who have unbelieving masters, are ready enough with the objection, that it is unreasonable that they who serve the devil should have dominion over the children of God. But Paul throws back the argument to the opposite side, that they ought to obey unbelieving masters, in order that the name of God and the gospel may not be evil spoken of; as if God, whom we worship, incited us to rebellion, and as if the gospel rendered obstinate and disobedient those who ought to be subject to others.

2. *Who have believing masters.* The name of *brother* may be thought to constitute equality, and consequently to take away dominion. Paul argues, on the contrary, that slaves ought the more willingly to subject themselves to believing masters, because they acknowledge them to be children of God, and are bound to them by brotherly love, and are partakers of the same grace.[1] It is no small honour, that God has made them equal to earthly lords, in that which is of the highest importance; for they have the same adoption in common with them; and therefore this ought to be no slight inducement to bear slavery with patience.

*They are believers and beloved.* It is an additional argu-

[1] "Let us learn to honour the graces of God when they shall be placed before our eyes; and when we shall see a man who has some token of the fear of God and of faith, let us value him so much the more, that we may seek to cherish the closest friendship with him, that we may bear with him as far as we are able, and that we may desire to be on good terms with him. And let every one consider what is said here, that, since God has thus brought us together, it is that we may know that it is in order that he may make us all his heirs, that we have one Spirit to guide us, one faith, one Redeemer, one baptism; for all this is included in the word *Benefit*. Since therefore we have that, let us learn to esteem the graces of God, in order that they may lead us to all mutual kindness, and that we may act in accordance with the lesson which Paul teaches us in another passage, (Eph. iv. 2,) namely, that we owe to each other brotherly love; for that is 'a bond' which ought to be reckoned sufficient for uniting us." —*Fr. Ser.*

ment, that slavery is much more easily endured under mild lords, who love us, and whom we love in return. There is also the bond of faith which binds very closely together those who are of different conditions.

*These things teach and exhort.* He means that these are matters on the teaching of which he ought to dwell largely, and wishes that doctrine should be accompanied by exhortations. It is as if he had said, that this kind of instruction ought to be daily repeated, and that men need not only to be taught, but likewise to be roused and urged by frequent exhortations.

| | |
|---|---|
| 3. If any man teach otherwise, and consent not to wholesome words, *even* the words of our Lord Jesus Christ, and to the doctrine which is according to godliness; | 3. Si quis aliter (*vel, alia*) docet, nec acquiescit sanis sermonibus Domini nostri Iesu Christi, et ei quæ secundum pietatem est doctrinæ, |
| 4. He is proud, knowing nothing, but doting about questions and strifes of words, whereof cometh envy, strife, railings, evil surmisings, | 4. Inflatus est, nihil sciens, sed languens circa quæstiones et pugnas verborum, ex quibus oritur invidia, contentio, maledicentiæ, suspiciones malæ, |
| 5. Perverse disputings of men of corrupt minds, and destitute of the truth, supposing that gain is godliness: from such withdraw thyself. | 5. Supervacuæ conflictationes hominum mente corruptorum, et qui veritate privati sunt, existimantium quæstum esse pietatem; sejunge te a talibus. |

3. *If any one teacheth differently.* The word ἑτεροδιδασκαλεῖ, being a compound, may also, not improperly, be translated, *teacheth other things.* Yet there is no ambiguity as to the meaning; for he condemns all those who do not agree with this manner of teaching, although they do not openly and avowedly oppose sound doctrine. It is possible that he who does not profess any wicked or open error may yet, by endeavouring to insinuate himself by means of silly babbling, corrupt the doctrine of godliness; for, when there is no progress, and no edification in the doctrine itself, there is already a departure from the ordinance of Christ. Now although Paul does not speak of the avowed supporters of wicked doctrines, but of vain and irreligious teachers, who, by their ambition or covetousness, disfigure the plain and simple doctrine of godliness, yet we see with what sharpness and severity he attacks them. Nor need we wonder at

this; for it is almost impossible to tell how much injury is done by preaching that is hypocritical and altogether framed for the purposes of ostentation and of idle display. But who they are that are blamed by him, appears more clearly from what immediately follows—

*And consenteth not to sound words.* This clause is intended to explain the former. It frequently happens that such men as are here described, carried away by foolish curiosity, despise everything that is useful and solid, and thus indulge in wanton freaks, like unruly horses. And what is this but to reject *the sound words of Christ?* for they are called "sound" or "healthful," because they give health to us, or are fitted to promote it.

*And to the doctrine which is according to godliness.* This has the same meaning with the former clause; for the "doctrine" will not be consistent with "godliness," if it do not instruct us in the fear and worship of God, if it do not edify our faith, if it do not train us to patience, humility, and all the duties of that love which we owe to our fellow-men. Whoever, therefore, does not strive to teach usefully, does not teach as he ought to do; and not only so, but that doctrine is neither godly nor sound, whatever may be the brilliancy of its display, that does not tend to the profit of the hearers.

4. *He is puffed up, knowing nothing.* Such persons Paul first charges with pride, foolish and empty pride. Next, because no punishment can be imagined that is better adapted to chastise ambitious persons than to declare that all that they delight in proves their ignorance, Paul pronounces that they *know nothing*, though they are swelled with many subtleties; for they have nothing that is solid, but mere wind. At the same time, he instructs all believers not to be carried away by that windy ostentation, but to remain steadfast in the simplicity of the gospel.

*But languishing after questions and debates of words.* There is an indirect contrast between "the soundness of the doctrine of Christ," and that "languishing;" for, when they have wearied themselves much and long with ingenious questions, what advantage do they reap from their labour, but that the disease continually grows? Thus not only do they consume their strength to no purpose, but their foolish curiosity begets this languishing; and hence it follows, that they are very far from profiting aright, as the disciples of Christ ought to do.

Not without reason does the Apostle connect "questions and disputes of words;" for by the former term he does not mean every kind of questions, which either arise from a sober and moderate desire to learn, or contribute to clear explanation of useful things, but to such questions as are agitated, in the present day, in the schools of the Sorbonne, for displaying acuteness of intellect. There one question gives rise to another; for there is no limit to them, when every person, desiring to know more than is proper, indulges his vanity; and hence, there afterwards arise innumerable quarrels. As the thick clouds, during hot weather, are not dispelled without thunder, so those thorny questions must burst into disputes.

He gives the name λογομαχίας (logomachies, or disputes about words) to contentious disputes about words rather than things, or, as it is commonly expressed, without substance or foundation; for if any person carefully inquire what sort of contentions are burning among the sophists, he will perceive that they do not arise from realities, but are framed out of nothing. In a word, Paul intended to condemn all questions which sharpen us for disputes that are of no value.

*From which arises envy.* He demonstrates from the effects how much an ambitious desire of knowledge ought to be avoided; for ambition is the mother of envy. Where envy reigns, there also rage brawlings, contentions, and other evils, which are here enumerated by Paul.

5. *Of men corrupt in understanding, and that are destitute of the truth.* It is certain that here he censures the sophists, who, neglecting edification, turn the word of God into trivial distinctions, and an art of ingenious discussion. If the Apostle only shewed that the doctrine of salvation is thus rendered useless, even that would be an intolerable profanation; but far heavier and fiercer is that reproof, when he

says that evils so pernicious, and plagues so hurtful, spring from it. From this passage, therefore, let us learn to detest (σοφιστικὴν) sophistry as a thing more destructive to the Church of God than can easily be believed.

*That godliness is gain.* The meaning is, that godliness is a gainful art; that is, because they measure the whole of Christianity by gain. Just as if the oracles of the Holy Spirit had been recorded with no other design than to serve the purposes of their covetousness, they traffic in it as merchandise exposed to sale.

*Withdraw thyself from such.* Paul forbids the servants of Christ to have any intercourse with such persons. He not only warns Timothy not to resemble them, but exhorts him to avoid them as dangerous plagues; for, although they do not openly resist the gospel, but, on the contrary, make a false profession of adhering to it, yet their society is infectious. Besides, if the multitude see that we are on familiar terms with those men, the danger is, lest they insinuate themselves under the guise of our friendship.[1] We should, therefore, labour to the utmost, that all may know, that so far are we from being agreed with them, that they have no communication with us.[2]

6. But godliness with contentment is great gain.
7. For we brought nothing into

6. Est autem quæstus magnus pietas cum sufficientia.
7. Nihil enim intulimus in mun-

[1] "Il y a danger que nostre amitie ne leur serve d'une couverture pour avoir entree a abuser les gens." "There is danger lest our friendship serve as a disguise for obtaining access to deceive people."

[2] "When we hear that they who thus misrepresent the word of God make merchandise of our souls, as the Apostle Peter says, (2 Pet. ii. 3,) and that they make traffic of us and of our salvation, without any conscience, and that they make no scruple of plunging us into hell, and even to set aside the price which was paid for our redemption, it is certain that they ruin souls, and also mock at the blood of our Lord Jesus Christ. When we hear all this, ought we not to hold such teachers in abhorrence? Besides, experience shews us that we have good reason for attending to this warning of the Apostle Paul. For to what a pitch has religion arrived! Has it not been made like a public fair? What has it become in Popery? The Sacraments are exposed to sale, and everything else belonging to our religion has a fixed price put upon it. Not more did Judas sell the Son of God in his own person than the Pope and all that filth of his clergy have sold the graces of the Holy Spirit, and all that belonged to his office and to our salvation. When we see this, have we not good reason for being on our guard?"—*Fr. Ser.*

| | |
|---|---|
| *this* world, and *it is* certain we can carry nothing out. | dum; certum quòd neque efferre quicquam possumus. |
| 8. And having food and raiment, let us be therewith content. | 8. Habentes autem alimenta et tegmina, his contenti erimus. |
| 9. But they that will be rich fall into temptation, and a snare, and *into* many foolish and hurtful lusts, which drown men in destruction and perdition. | 9. Nam qui volunt ditescere incidunt in tentationem et laqueum, et stupiditates multas et noxias, quæ demergunt homines in exitium et interitum. |
| 10. For the love of money is the root of all evil; which while some coveted after, they have erred from the faith, and pierced themselves through with many sorrows. | 10. Radix enim omnium malorum est avaritia; cui addicti quidam aberrarunt a fide, et se ipsos implicuerunt doloribus multis. |

6. *But godliness with sufficiency is great gain.* In an elegant manner, and with an ironical correction, he instantly throws back those very words in an opposite meaning, as if he had said—" They do wrong and wickedly, who make merchandise of the doctrine of Christ, as if 'godliness were gain ;' though, undoubtedly, if we form a correct estimate of it, godliness is a great and abundant gain." And he so calls it, because it brings to us full and perfect blessedness. Those men, therefore, are guilty of sacrilege, who, being bent on acquiring money, make godliness contribute to their gain.[1] But for our part, godliness is a very great gain to us, because, by means of it, we obtain the benefit, not only of being heirs of the world, but likewise of enjoying Christ and all his riches.

*With sufficiency.*[2] This may refer either to the disposition of the heart, or to the thing itself. If it be understood as referring to the heart, the meaning will be, that " godly persons, when they desire nothing, but are satisfied with their humble condition, have obtained very great gain." If we understand it to be " sufficiency" of wealth, (and, for my own part, I like this view quite as well as the other,) it will be a promise, like that in the book of Psalms, " The lions wander about hungry and famished; but they that seek the

---

[1] " Qui estans addonnez au gain de la bourse, font servir la piete et la doctrine de vraye religion a leur gain." " Who, being devoted to the gain of the purse, make piety and the doctrine of true religion contribute to their gain.
[2] " Avec suffisance, ou, contentement." " With sufficiency, or, with contentment."

Lord shall not be in want of any good thing." (Ps. xxxiv. 10.) The Lord is always present with his people, and, as far as is sufficient for their necessity, out of his fulness he bestows on each his portion. Thus true happiness consists in piety; and this sufficiency may be regarded as an increase of gain.

7. *For we brought nothing into the world.* He adds this for the purpose of setting a limit to the sufficiency. Our covetousness is an insatiable gulf, if it be not restrained; and the best bridle is, when we desire nothing more than the necessity of this life demands; for the reason why we transgress the bounds, is, that our anxiety extends to a thousand lives which we falsely imagine. Nothing is more common, and indeed nothing is more generally acknowledged, than this statement of Paul; but as soon as all have acknowledged it, (as we see every day with our eyes,) every man swallows up with his wishes his vast possessions, in the same manner as if he had a belly able to contain half of the world. And this is what is said, that, "although the folly of the fathers appears in hoping that they will dwell here for ever, nevertheless their posterity approve of their way."[1] (Ps. xlix. 13.) In order, therefore, that we may be satisfied with a sufficiency, let us learn to have our heart so regulated, as to desire nothing but what is necessary for supporting life.

8. *Having food and raiment.* When he mentions *food and raiment,* he excludes luxuries and overflowing abundance; for nature is content with a little,[2] and all that goes beyond the natural use is superfluous. Not that to use them more largely ought to be condemned on its own account, but lusting after them is always sinful.

9. *They who wish to be rich.* After having exhorted him to be content, and to despise riches, he now explains how dangerous is the desire of having them, and especially in the ministers of the Church, of whom he expressly speaks in this passage. Now the cause of the evils, which the Apostle here enumerates, is not riches, but an eager desire of them, even

---

[1] "Toutesfois les successeurs ne laissent pas de suyvre le mesme train." "Yet their successors do not cease to follow the same course."

[2] "Man wants but little; nor that little long."—*Young's Night Thoughts.*

though the person should be poor. And here Paul shews not only what generally happens, but what must always happen; for every man that has resolved to become rich gives himself up as a captive to the devil. Most true is that saying of the heathen poet,—" He who is desirous of becoming rich is also desirous of acquiring riches soon."[1] Hence it follows, that all who are violently desirous of acquiring wealth rush headlong.

Hence also those *foolish*, or rather, mad *desires, which* at length *plunge them into perdition.* This is, indeed, a universal evil; but in the pastors of the Church it is more easily seen; for they are so maddened by avarice, that they stick at nothing, however foolish, whenever the glitter of gold or silver dazzles their eyes.

10. *For the root of all evils is avarice.*[2] There is no necessity for being too scrupulous in comparing other vices with this. It is certain that ambition and pride often produce worse fruits than covetousness does; and yet ambition does not proceed from covetousness. The same thing may be said of the sins forbidden by the seventh commandment. But Paul's intention was not to include under covetousness every kind of vices that can be named. What then? He simply meant, that innumerable evils arise from it; just as we are in the habit of saying, when we speak of discord, or gluttony, or drunkenness, or any other vice of that kind, that there is no evil which it does not produce. And, indeed, we may most truly affirm, as to the base desire of gain, that there is no kind of evils that is not copiously produced by it every day; such as innumerable frauds, falsehoods, perjury, cheating, robbery, cruelty, corruption in judicature, quarrels, hatred, poisonings, murders; and, in short, almost every sort of crime.

Statements of this nature occur everywhere in heathen writers; and, therefore, it is improper that those persons who would applaud Horace or Ovid, when speaking in that

---

[1] " Dives fieri qui vult,
Et cito vult fieri."—*Juvenal.*
[2] " C'est avarice, ou, convoitise des richesses." "Is avarice, or, an eager desire of riches."

manner, should complain of Paul as having used extravagant language. I wish it were not proved by daily experience, that this is a plain description of facts as they really are. But let us remember that the same crimes which spring from avarice, may also arise, as they undoubtedly do arise, either from ambition, or from envy, or from other sinful dispositions.

*Which some eagerly desiring.* The Greek word ὀρεγόμενοι is overstrained, when the Apostle says that avarice is "eagerly desired;" but it does not obscure the sense. He affirms that the most aggravated of all evils springs from avarice—revolting from the faith; for they who are diseased with this disease are found to degenerate gradually, till they entirely renounce the faith. Hence those *sorrows*, which he mentions; by which term I understand frightful torments of conscience, which are wont to befall men past all hope; though God has other methods of trying covetous men, by making them their own tormentors.

11. But thou, O man of God, flee these things; and follow after righteousness, godliness, faith, love, patience, meekness.

12. Fight the good fight of faith, lay hold on eternal life, whereunto thou art also called, and hast professed a good profession before many witnesses.

13. I give thee charge in the sight of God, who quickeneth all things, and *before* Christ Jesus, who before Pontius Pilate witnessed a good confession,

14. That thou keep *this* commandment without spot, unrebukeable, until the appearing of our Lord Jesus Christ:

15. Which in his times he shall shew, *who is* the blessed and only Potentate, the King of kings, and Lord of lords;

16. Who only hath immortality, dwelling in the light which no man can approach unto; whom no man hath seen, nor can see: to whom *be* honour and power everlasting. Amen.

11. Tu vero, o homo Dei, hæc fuge; sectare vero justitiam, pietatem, fidem, caritatem, patientiam, mansuetudinem.

12. Certa bonum certamen fidei; apprehende vitam æternam, ad quam etiam vocatus es, et confessus bonam confessionem coram multis testibus.

13. Denuntio (*vel, præcipio*) tibi coram Deo qui vivificat omnia, et Christo Iesu, qui testificatus est bonam confessionem coram Pontio Pilato,

14. Ut serves mandatum immaculatus et irreprehensibilis, usque ad revelationem Domini nostri Iesu Christi;

15. Quam suis temporibus manifestabit beatus et solus princeps, Rex regnantium et Dominus dominantium,

16. Qui solus habet immortalitatem, qui lumen habitat inaccessum, quem vidit nullus hominum, nec videre potest, cui honor et potentia æterna (*vel, imperium æternum.*) Amen.

11. *But thou, O man of God, flee these things.* By calling

him *man of God* he adds weight to the exhortation. If it be thought proper to limit to the preceding verse the injunction which he gives to *follow righteousness, piety, faith, patience,* this is an instruction which he gives, by contrast, for correcting avarice, by informing him what kind of riches he ought to desire, namely, spiritual riches. Yet this injunction may also be extended to other clauses, that Timothy, withdrawing himself from all vanity, may avoid that (περιεργίαν) *vain curiosity* which he condemned a little before; for he who is earnestly employed about necessary employments will easily abstain from those which are superfluous. He names, by way of example, some kinds of virtues, under which we may suppose others to be included. Consequently, every person who shall be devoted to the pursuit of "righteousness," and who shall aim at "piety, faith, charity," and shall follow patience and gentleness, cannot but abhor avarice and its fruits.[1]

12. *Fight the good fight of faith.* In the next epistle he says, "He who hath become a soldier doth not entangle himself with matters inconsistent with his calling." (2 Tim. ii. 4.) In like manner, in order to withdraw Timothy from excessive solicitude about earthly things, he reminds him that he must "fight;" for carelessness and self-indulgence arise from this cause, that the greater part wish to serve Christ at ease, and as if it were pastime, whereas Christ calls all his servants to warfare.

For the purpose of encouraging him to fight such a fight courageously, he calls it *good;* that is, successful, and there-

[1] "And thus we see that not without reason does Paul add this word *piety*, which means religion and the fear of God, and that he connects it with faith, saying that, when we have put our confidence in God, and when we expect from him the means of our support, we must also attend to this, not to live in this world as if it were our end, and not to fix our heart upon it, but to look upwards to the heavenly kingdom. Having said this, he next leads us onwards to the love of our fellow-men and to meekness, as we are also bound to walk in all good friendship with our neighbours; otherwise we shall not shew that we have the righteousness which he has mentioned. And thus let us see that, by all these words, he means nothing more than to confirm the exhortation which he had given, to follow righteousness and sincerity. And how shall we follow it? First, by placing our confidence in God; secondly, by raising our thoughts to the heavenly kingdom; and thirdly, by living in good friendship with each other."—*Fr. Ser.*

fore not to be shunned; for, if earthly soldiers do not hesitate to fight, when the result is doubtful, and when there is a risk of being killed,[1] how much more bravely ought we to do battle under the guidance and banner of Christ, when we are certain of victory? More especially, since a reward awaits us, not such as other generals are wont to give to their soldiers, but a glorious immortality and heavenly blessedness; it would certainly be disgraceful that we, who have such a hope held out to us, should grow weary or give way. And that is what he immediately afterwards adds,—

*Lay hold on eternal life.* As if he had said, " God calls thee to eternal life, and therefore, despising the world, strive to obtain it." When he commands them to "lay hold on it," he forbids them to pause or slacken in the middle of their course; as if he had said, that " nothing has been done,[2] till we have obtained the life to come, to which God invites us." In like manner, he affirms that he strives to make progress, because he has not yet laid hold. (Philip. iii. 12.)

*To which also thou hast been called.* Because men would run at random, and to no purpose, if they had not God as the director of their course, for the purpose of promoting their cheerful activity, he mentions also the *calling;* for there is nothing that ought to animate us with greater courage than to learn that we have been "called" by God; for we conclude from this, that our labour, which God directs,

---

[1] "We see princes whose ambition leads them to risk all that they have, and to place themselves in danger of being stript of all their power. We see soldiers, who, instead of earning wages by labouring in vineyards or in the fields, go and expose their life at a venture. And what leads them to this? A doubtful hope, nothing certain. And though they have gained, and have obtained a victory over their enemies, what advantage do they reap from it? But when God calls us to fight, and wishes us to be soldiers under his banner, it is on no such condition, but we are made certain that the war will be good and successful. And thus Paul intended to comfort believers while he exhorted them, as God also condescends to us by shewing to us what is our duty, and, at the same time, declaring that, when we shall do what he commands us, all will turn to our profit and salvation."—*Fr. Ser.*

[2] "Nihil actum esse." The expression reminds us of the beautiful encomium pronounced by the poet Lucan on the unwearied activity of Julius Cæsar, that he " thought nothing done, while aught remained to do."

"Nil actum reputans, dum quid superesset agendum."—*Ed.*

and in which he stretches out his hand to us, will not be fruitless. Besides, to have rejected the calling of God would be a disgraceful reproach ; and, therefore, this ought to be a very powerful excitement : " God calls thee to eternal life ; beware of being drawn aside to anything else, or of falling short in any way, before thou hast attained it."

*And hast confessed a good confession.* By mentioning his former life, the Apostle excites him still more to persevere ; for to give way, after having begun well, is more disgraceful than never to have begun. To Timothy, who had hitherto acted valiantly, and had obtained applause, he addresses this powerful argument, that the latter end should correspond to the beginning. By the word *confession* I understand not that which is expressed in words, but rather what is actually performed ; and that not in a single instance merely, but throughout his whole ministry. The meaning therefore is : " Thou hast many witnesses of thy illustrious confession, both at Ephesus and in other countries, who have beheld thee acting faithfully and sincerely in the profession of the gospel ; and, therefore, having given such a proof of fidelity, thou canst not, without the greatest shame and disgrace, shew thyself to be anything else than a distinguished soldier of Christ." By this passage we are taught in general, that the more any of us excels, the less excusable is he if he fail, and the stronger are his obligations to God to persevere in the right course.

13. *I charge thee.* The great vehemence of solemn appeal, which Paul employs, is a proof how rare and hard a virtue it is, to persevere in the ministry, in a proper manner, till the end ; for, although he exhorts others, in the person of Timothy, yet he addresses him also.

*Before God, who quickeneth all things.* What he affirms concerning Christ and concerning God, has an immediate relation to the present subject ; for, when he ascribes this to God, that he *quickeneth all things*, he wishes to meet the offence of the cross, which presents to us nothing but the appearance of death. He therefore means, that we should shut our eyes, when ungodly men hold out and threaten death ; or rather, that we should fix our eyes on God alone, because it is he who restoreth the dead to life. The amount of the whole is, that, turning away our gaze from the world, we should learn to look at God alone.

*And Christ Jesus, who testified a good confession before Pontius Pilate.* What he now adds about *Christ* contains a remarkable confirmation; for we are taught, that we are not in the school of Plato, to learn philosophy from him, and to hear him discoursing in the shade about idle disputes; but that the doctrine which Timothy professes was ratified by the death of the Son of God. Christ made his confession before Pilate, not in a multitude of words, but in reality; that is, by undergoing a voluntary death; for, although Christ chose to be silent before Pilate, rather than speak in his own defence, because he had come thither—devoted already to a certain condemnation; yet in his silence there was a defence of his doctrine not less magnificent than if he had defended himself with a loud voice. He ratified it by his blood, and by the sacrifice of his death, better than he could have ratified it by his voice.[1]

This confession the Apostle calls *good.* For Socrates also died; and yet his death was not a satisfactory proof of the doctrine which he held. But when we hear that the blood of the Son of God was shed, that is an authentic seal which removes all our doubt. Accordingly, whenever our hearts waver, let us remember that we should always go to the death of Christ for confirmation. What cowardice would there be in deserting such a leader going before us to show us the way!

14. *That thou keep the commandment.* By the word *commandment* he means all that he hath hitherto said about the office of Timothy, the sum of which was, that he should show

---

[1] "By his silence he confirmed the truth of God his Father, and the death which he underwent was intended to give authority to the gospel; so that, when the doctrine of salvation is preached at the present day, in order that we may be confirmed in the faith of it, we must direct our view to the blood of the Lamb without spot, which was shed. As anciently, under the Law, the book was sprinkled with the blood of the sacrifice, so now, whenever we are spoken to in the name of God, the blood of Christ must be brought to our remembrance, and we must know that the gospel is sprinkled with it, and that our faith rests upon it in such a manner, that the utmost efforts of Satan cannot shake it."—*Fr. Ser.*

himself to be a faithful minister to Christ and to the Church. What is the use of extending this to the whole law? But perhaps it will be thought preferable to view it as denoting the office which he had received by divine authority; for we are appointed to be ministers of the Church on no other condition than this, that God enjoins upon us whatever he wishes us to do. Thus to "keep the commandment" would be nothing else than to discharge honestly the office committed to him. I certainly view it as referring altogether to the ministry of Timothy.

*Spotless and unblameable.*[1] Whether we consider the case or the termination[2] of the two Greek adjectives which are thus translated, they may apply either to the commandment given, or to the person of Timothy; but the meaning which I have assigned is much more appropriate.[3] Paul informs Timothy, that he must be careful to maintain holiness of life and purity of morals, if he wish to discharge his office in a proper manner.

*Till the revelation of our Lord Jesus Christ.* It is impossible to tell how necessary it was to all the godly, at that time, to have their mind entirely fixed on the day of Christ; because innumerable offences existed everywhere in the world. They were assailed on every hand, were universally hated and abhorred, were exposed to the mockeries of all, were oppressed every day with new calamities; and yet they saw no fruit of so many toils and annoyances. What then remained, but that in thought they should fly away to that blessed day of our redemption?

Yet the same reason is in force with regard to us in the present day, and indeed applies equally to almost every age. How many things does Satan constantly present to our eyes, which, but for this, would a thousand times draw us aside from the right course! I say nothing about fires, and

[1] "Sans macule et sans reprehension." "Without spot and without censure."

[2] That is, they may be either in the accusative case masculine, agreeing with Τιμόθιον, or in the accusative case feminine, agreeing with ἐντολήν.—*Ed.*

[3] "Nonobstant il est beaucoup plus propre de les rapporter a sa personne." "Nevertheless it is much more suitable to view them as relating to his person."

swords, and banishments, and all the furious attacks of enemies. I say nothing about slanders and other vexations. How many things are within, that are far worse! Ambitious men openly attack us, Epicureans and Lucianists jeer at us, impudent men provoke us, hypocrites murmur at us, they who are wise after the flesh secretly bite us, we are harassed by various methods in every direction. In short, it is a great miracle that any man perseveres steadfastly in an office so difficult and so dangerous. The only remedy for all these difficulties is, to cast our eyes towards the appearing of Christ, and to keep them fixed on it continually.[1]

15. *Which in his seasons he will show.* We are commonly hasty in our wishes, and not far from prescribing a day and hour to God, as if we should say, that he must not delay to perform anything that he has promised; and for that reason the Apostle takes an early opportunity of restraining excessive haste, by expecting the coming of Christ. For that is the meaning of the words, " Which in his seasons he will show." When men know that the proper time for anything is not fully come, they wait for it more patiently. How comes it that we are so patient in bearing with the order of nature, but because we are restrained by this consideration, that we shall act unreasonably, if we struggle against it with our desires? Thus we know, that the revelation of Christ has its appointed time, for which we must wait patiently.

*The blessed and only Prince.* Those splendid titles are

---

[1] "Believers might, indeed, be weakened in their faith, when they looked at present things. For, as to the great people in this world, what would they wish but to rise above the Church, and trample God under their feet? We see that they sport with religion as with a ball. We even see that they are deadly enemies of it, and that they persecute it with such rage that everybody is terrified at them. We see these things. Yet what shall be said of the children of God? They are pointed at with the finger, they are thought to be fools, so that what is said by the Prophet Isaiah is to-day fulfilled in us, that unbelievers reckon us to be monsters. (Isa. viii. 18.) 'What? These poor fools? What are they thinking about? What do they mean? We must live with the living, and howl with the wolves. They wish to be always in a state of perplexity. They speak of nothing but eternal life, and have no leisure for enjoyment.' Thus it is that we are accounted fools and madmen by unbelievers. And Peter says, (2 Pet. iii. 2-4,) that this must be fulfilled in us; as the Prophet Isaiah had made the complaint in his time; Christians must experience the like in the present day."—*Fr. Ser.*

here employed in exalting the princely authority of God, in order that the brilliancy of the princes of this world may not dazzle our eyes. And such instruction was, at that time, especially necessary; for by how much all kingdoms were then great and powerful, by so much were the majesty and glory of God thrown into the shade. For all that governed the kingdoms of the world not only were deadly enemies of the kingdom of God, but proudly mocked at God, and trampled his sacred name under their feet; and the greater the haughtiness with which they despised true religion, the more happy did they imagine themselves to be. From such an aspect of things who would not have concluded that God was miserably vanquished and oppressed? We see to what a pitch of insolence Cicero rises against the Jews on account of their humbled condition, in his oration for Flaccus.

When good men see that the wicked are puffed up with prosperity, they are sometimes cast down; and therefore Paul, for the purpose of withdrawing the eyes of the godly from that transitory splendour, ascribes to God alone " blessedness, principality, and kingly power." When he calls God *the only prince,* he does not overthrow civil government, as if there ought to be no magistrates or kings in the world, but means that it is He alone who reigns from himself and from his own power. This is evident from what follows, which he adds by way of exposition,—

*King of kings, and Lord of lords.* The sum of it is, that all the governments of the world are subject to his dominion, depend upon him, and stand or fall at his bidding; but that the authority of God is beyond all comparison, because all the rest are nothing as compared with his glory, and while they fade and quickly perish, his authority will endure for ever.

16. *Who alone hath immortality.* Paul labours to demonstrate that there is no happiness, no dignity or excellence, no life, out of God. Accordingly, he now says that God alone is immortal, in order to inform us, that we and all the creatures do not, strictly speaking, live, but only borrow life from Him. Hence it follows that, when we look up to God as the fountain of immortal life, we should reckon this present life as of no value.

But it is objected, that the human soul and angels have their immortality, and therefore this cannot be truly affirmed of God alone. I reply, when it is said, that God alone possesses immortality, it is not here denied that he bestows it, as he pleases, on any of his creatures. The meaning is the same as if Paul had said, that God alone not only is immortal from himself and from his own nature, but has immortality in his power; so that it does not belong to creatures, except so far as he imparts to them power and vigour; for if you take away the power of God which is communicated to the soul of man, it will instantly fade away; and the same thing may be said about angels. Strictly speaking, therefore, immortality does not subsist in the nature of souls or of angels, but comes from another source, namely, from the secret inspiration of God, agreeably to that saying, "In him we live, and move, and are." (Acts xvii. 28.) If any one wish to have a larger and more acute discussion of this subject, let him consult the twelfth book of Augustine "On the City of God."

*Who inhabiteth unapproachable light.* He means two things, that God is concealed from us, and yet that the cause of obscurity is not in himself, as if he were hidden in darkness, but in ourselves, who, on account of the weak vision, or rather the dulness of our understanding, cannot approach to his light. We must understand that the *light* of God is *unapproachable,* if any one endeavour to approach to it in his own strength; for, if God did not open up the entrance to us by his grace, the prophet would not say: "They who draw near to him are enlightened." (Ps. xxxiv. 5.) Yet it is true that, while we are surrounded by this mortal flesh, we never penetrate so far into the deepest secrets of God as to have nothing hidden from us; for "we know in part, and we see as by a mirror, and in a riddle." (1 Cor. xiii. 9-12.) By faith, therefore, we enter into the light of God, but only in part. Still it is true, that it is a "light unapproachable" by man.

*Whom no man hath seen or can see.* This is added for the sake of additional explanation, that men may learn to look by faith to him, whom they cannot see with the bodily eyes, or even with the powers of their understanding; for I view this as referring not only to the bodily eyes, but also to the faculties of the soul. We must always consider what is the Apostle's design. It is difficult for us to overlook and disregard all those things of which we have immediate vision, that we may endeavour to come to God, who is nowhere to be seen. For this thought always comes into our mind: " How knowest thou if there is a God, seeing that thou only hearest that he is, and dost not see him?" The Apostle fortifies us against this danger, by affirming that it ought not to be judged according to our senses, because it exceeds our capacity; for the reason why we do not see is, that our sight is not so keen as to ascend to so great a height.

There is a long dispute in Augustine on this point, because it appears to contradict what is said, in the first Epistle, " Then shall we see him as he is, because we shall be like him." (1 John iii. 2.) While he reasons on this subject in many passages, there appears to me to be none in which he explains it more clearly than in the letter which he writes to the widow Paulina.

So far as relates to the meaning of the present passage, the answer is easy, that we cannot see God in this nature, as it is said elsewhere, " Flesh and blood shall not possess the kingdom of God." (1 Cor. xv. 50.) We must be renewed, that we may be like God, before it be granted to us to see him. And that our curiosity may not be beyond measure, let us always remember, that the manner of living is of more importance in this inquiry than the manner of speaking. At the same time, let us remember the judicious caution which Augustine gives us, to be on our guard lest, while we are keenly disputing how God can be seen, we lose both peace and sanctification, without which no man can ever see God.

| | |
|---|---|
| 17. Charge them that are rich in this world, that they be not highminded, nor trust in uncertain riches, but in the living God, who giveth us richly all things to enjoy; | 17. Iis, qui divites sunt in hoc sæculo, præcipe (*vel, denuntia*) ne efferantur, neve sperent in divitiarum incertitudine, sed in Deo vivo, qui abundè suppeditat omnia ad fruendum; |

| | |
|---|---|
| 18. That they do good, that they be rich in good works, ready to distribute, willing to communicate; | 18. Ut benefaciant, ut divites sint in operibus bonis, faciles ad largiendum (*vel, ad communicationem,*) libenter communicantes, |
| 19. Laying up in store for themselves a good foundation against the time to come, that they may lay hold on eternal life. | 19. Recondentes sibi ipsis fundamentum bonum in posterum, ut vitam æternam apprehendant. |
| 20. O Timothy, keep that which is committed to thy trust, avoiding profane *and* vain babblings, and oppositions of science falsely so called: | 20. O Timothee, depositum custodi, devitans profanas clamorum inanitates, vaniloquia et oppositiones falsò nominatæ scientiæ. |
| 21. Which some professing, have erred concerning the faith. Grace *be* with thee. Amen. | 21. Quam quidam profitentes aberrarunt a fide. Gratia tecum. Amen. |
| The first to Timothy was written from Laodicea, which is the chiefest city of Phrygia Pacatiana. | Ad Timotheum prima missa fuit ex Laodicea, quæ est metropolis Phrygiæ Pacatianæ. |

17. *Command (or charge) those who are rich.* There being many among Christians who were poor and in a mean condition, it is probable that they were despised (as usually happens) by the rich; and especially this might be common at Ephesus, which was a wealthy city; for in such cities, for the most part, pride is more extensively prevalent. And hence we infer how dangerous is a great abundance of riches. Nor are there wanting good reasons why Paul addresses so severe an admonition to the rich; but it is for the purpose of remedying faults which almost always follow riches in the same manner as the shadow follows the body; and that through the depravity of our natural disposition, for out of the gifts of God we always draw an occasion for sinning.

*That they be not haughty, nor hope in the uncertainty of riches.* He expressly mentions two things against which rich men ought to be on their guard, *pride* and *deceitful hope*, of which the former springs from the latter. Accordingly, Paul appears to have added, in the same place, " nor hope in the uncertainty of riches," in order to point out the source of all pride. For whence comes it, that rich men grow insolent, and take extreme delight in despising others, but because they imagine that they are supremely happy? Vain confidence goes first, and then arrogance follows.

*Rich in this world.* When Paul wishes to correct those faults, he first speaks contemptuously of riches; for the phrase, *in this world,* is intended to lower them in our esteem. All that is in the world has the taste of its nature; so that it is fading, and quickly passes away. The uncertainty and vanity of the hope that is placed in riches are shewn by him from this consideration, that the possession of them is so transitory that it is like a thing unknown; for, while we think that we hold them, they slip out of our hands in a moment. How foolish is it, therefore, to place our hope in them!

*But in the living God.* He who understands this will find no difficulty in withdrawing his hope from riches; for, if it is God alone who supplies us with everything for the necessary purposes of life, we transfer to riches what is his prerogative, when we place hope in them. Now observe that there is an implied contrast, when he affirms that God giveth abundantly to all. The meaning is, that, although we have a full and overflowing abundance of all things, yet we have nothing but from the blessing of God alone; for it is that blessing alone which imparts to us all that is needful.

Hence it follows, that they are egregiously mistaken, who rely on riches, and do not depend entirely on the blessing of God, in which consists a sufficiency of food and of everything else. Hence also we conclude, that we are forbidden to trust in riches, not only because they belong to the use of mortal life, but likewise because they are nothing but smoke; for we are fed, not by bread only, but by the blessing of God. (Deut. viii. 3.)[1]

[1] " It will be useless to say to us, What are the riches of this world? We see that there is no certainty of them. What are honours? They are but smoke. What is even this life? It is but a dream. There is but a turn of the hand, and we become dust and ashes. It will be useless to argue with us on these grounds. All this will serve no purpose, till God has been presented to our minds, till it has been demonstrated to us that we must direct all our affections and confidence to him alone. And that is the reason why all the fine remonstrances urged by the philosophers had no effect. For they spoke of the frailty of this earthly life and the uncertain condition of men. They showed that it was vain to think of finding happiness in our possessions, in our lordships, or in anything else. They showed that it is delusive to think of having anything here below on which we might vaunt ourselves. Those great philosophers knew nothing about God, yet being convinced by experience, discussed and argued ably on these subjects. But still they did no good, because they did not seek the true remedy, to fix the hearts of men on God, and to inform

When he says πλουσίως εἰς ἀπόλαυσιν, *abundantly for enjoyment,* he describes how kind God is to us, and even to all men, and to the brute beasts; for his kindness extends far and wide beyond our necessity. (Ps. xxxvi. 6.)

18. *To do good.* He adds another remedy to the former, for correcting the sinful dispositions of rich men, by stating authoritatively what is the lawful use of riches; for the richer any man is, the more abundant are his means of doing good to others; and because we are always more tardy than we ought to be in giving to the poor, he employs many words in commendation of that virtue.

19. *Laying up for themselves a good foundation.* Besides, he adds an incitement drawn from the promise of a reward; that, by *bestowing* and *communicating,* they will procure for themselves a better treasure than they can have on earth. By the word *foundation* he means a firm and lasting duration; for the spiritual riches which we "lay up for ourselves" in heaven, are not exposed to the ravages of worms or thieves, (Matt. vi. 20,) or fires, but continue always to be placed beyond all danger. On the contrary, nothing on earth is solidly founded; but everything may be said to be in a floating condition.

The inference drawn by Papists from this passage, that we therefore obtain eternal life by the merit of good works, is excessively frivolous. It is true that God accepts as given to himself everything that is bestowed on the poor. (Matt. xxv. 40.) But even the most perfect hardly perform the hundredth part of their duty; and therefore our liberality does not deserve to be brought into account before God. So far are we from rendering full payment, that, if God should call us to a strict account, there is not one of us who would not be a bankrupt. But, after having reconciled us to himself by free grace, he accepts our services, such as they are, and bestows on them a reward which is not due. This recompense, therefore, does not depend on considerations of merit, but on God's gracious acceptance, and is so far from

them, that it is He alone in whom they can find contentment; and till we have come to this, we shall always be involved in many perplexities."— *Fr. Ser.*

being inconsistent with the righteousness of faith, that it may be viewed as an appendage to it.

20. *O Timothy, guard that which is committed to thee.* Though interpreters differ in expounding παραθήκην, *a thing committed*, yet, for my part, I think that it denotes that grace which had been communicated to Timothy for the discharge of his office. It is called " a thing committed," for the same reason that it is called (Matt. xxv. 15,) " a talent ;" for all the gifts which God bestows on us are committed to us on this condition, that we shall one day give an account of them, if the advantage which they ought to have yielded be not lost through our negligence. The Apostle therefore exhorts him to keep diligently what had been given to him, or rather, what had been committed to him in trust ; that he may not suffer it to be corrupted or adulterated, or may not deprive or rob himself of it through his own fault. It frequently happens that our ingratitude or abuse of the gifts of God causes them to be taken from us ; and therefore Paul exhorts Timothy to endeavour to preserve, by a good conscience and by proper use, that which had been " committed" to him.

*Avoiding profane vanities of noises.* The object of the admonition is, that he may be diligent in imparting solid instruction ; and this cannot be, unless he detest ostentation ; for, where an ambitious desire to please prevails, there is no longer any strong desire of edification. For this reason, when he spoke of " guarding the thing committed," he very appropriately added this caution about avoiding profane talkativeness. As to the rendering which the Vulgate gives to κενοφωνίας, *Inanitates vocum*, " vanities of voices," I do not so much object to it, except on the ground of an ambiguity which has led to a wrong exposition ; for " Voces" is commonly supposed to have the same meaning here as " Vocabula," " Words," such as Fate or Fortune.

But, for my part, I think that he describes the high-sounding and verbose and bombastic style of those who, not content with the simplicity of the gospel, turn it into profane philosophy.

The κενοφωνίαι[1] consist, not in single words, but in that swelling language which is so constantly and so disgustingly poured out by ambitious men, who aim at applause rather than the profit of the Church. And most accurately has Paul described it; for, while there is a strange sound of something lofty, there is nothing underneath but "empty" jingle, which he likewise calls "profane;" for the power of the Spirit is extinguished as soon as the Doctors blow their flutes in this manner, to display their eloquence.

In the face of a prohibition so clear and distinct, which the Holy Spirit has given, this plague has nevertheless broken out; and, indeed, it showed itself at the very beginning, but, at length, has grown to such a height in Popery, that the counterfeit mark of theology which prevails there— is a lively mirror of that "profane" and "empty noise" of which Paul speaks. I say nothing about the innumerable errors and follies and blasphemies with which their books and their noisy disputes abound. But even although they taught nothing that was contrary to godliness, yet, because their whole doctrine contains nothing else than big words and bombast, because it is inconsistent with the majesty of Scripture, the efficacy of the Spirit, the gravity of the prophets, and the sincerity of the apostles, it is, on that account, an absolute profanation of real theology.

What, I ask, do they teach about faith, or repentance, or calling on God; about the weakness of men, or the assistance of the Holy Spirit, or the forgiveness of sins by free grace, or about the office of Christ, that can be of any avail for the solid edification of godliness? But on this subject we shall have occasion to speak again in expounding the Second Epistle. Undoubtedly, any person who possesses a moderate share of understanding and of candour, will acknowledge that all the high-sounding terms of Popish Theology, and all the authoritive decisions that make so much noise in their schools, are nothing else than "profane κενοφωνίαι," (empty words,) and that it is impossible to find more accurate terms for describing them than those which

---

[1] Κενοφωνίαι, derived from κενός, "empty," and φωνὴ, "a voice," literally signifies "empty voices" or "words."—*Ed.*

the Apostle has employed. And certainly it is a most righteous punishment of human arrogance, that they who swerve from the purity of Scripture become profane. The doctors of the Church, therefore, cannot be too earnestly attentive to guard against such corruptions, and to defend the youth from them.

The old translation, adopting the reading of καινοφωνίας instead of κενοφωνίας, rendered it *novelties of words ;* and it is evident from the commentaries of the ancients, that this rendering, which is even now found in some Greek copies, was at one time extensively approved ; but the former, which I have followed, is far better.

*And contradictions of science falsely so called.* This also is highly exact and elegant ; for so swollen are the subtleties on which men desirous of glory plume themselves, that they overwhelm the real doctrine of the gospel, which is simple and unpretending. That pomp, therefore, which courts display, and which is received with applause by the world, is called by the Apostle " contradictions." Ambition, indeed, is always contentious, and is the mother of disputes ; and hence it arises that they who are desirous to display themselves are always ready to enter into the arena of debate on any subject. But Paul had this principally in view, that the empty doctrine of the sophists, rising aloft into airy speculations and subtleties, not only obscures by its pretentions the simplicity of true doctrine, but also oppresses and renders it contemptible, as the world is usually carried away by outward show.

Paul does not mean that Timothy should be moved by emulation to attempt something of the same kind, but, because those things which have an appearance of subtlety, or are adapted to ostentation, are more agreeable to human curiosity, Paul, on the contrary, pronounces that " science " which exalts itself above the plain and humble doctrine of godliness—to be *falsely called* and thought a *science.* This ought to be carefully observed, that we may learn boldly to laugh at and despise all that hypocritical wisdom which strikes the world with admiration and amazement, although there is no edification in it ; for, according to Paul, no science is truly and justly so called but that which instructs us in the confidence and fear of God ; that is, in godliness.

21. *Which some professing, have erred concerning the faith.* From the result, also, he demonstrates how dangerous a thing it is, and how much it ought to be avoided. The way in which God punishes the haughtiness of those who, through the desire of obtaining reputation, corrupt and disfigure the doctrine of godliness, is, that he allows them to fall away from soundness of understanding, so that they involve themselves in many absurd errors. We see that this has taken place in Popery ; for, after they began to speculate in a profane manner, about the mysteries of our religion, there followed innumerable monsters of false opinions. *Faith* is here taken, as in some former passages, for the summary of religion and sound doctrine. Warned by such examples, if we abhor revolt from "the faith," let us adhere to the pure word of God, and let us detest sophistry and all useless subtleties, because they are abominable corruptions of religion.

END OF THE FIRST EPISTLE TO TIMOTHY.

# COMMENTARIES

ON

# THE SECOND EPISTLE TO TIMOTHY.

# THE ARGUMENT

ON

# THE SECOND EPISTLE TO TIMOTHY.

IT cannot be absolutely ascertained from Luke's history at what time the former Epistle was written. But I have no doubt that, after that time, Paul had personal communication with Timothy; and it is even possible (if the generally received opinion be believed) that Paul had him for a companion and assistant in many places. Yet it may readily be concluded that he was at Ephesus when this Epistle was written to him; because, towards the close of the Epistle, (2 Tim. iv. 19,) Paul " salutes Priscilla, and Aquila, and Onesiphorus," the last of whom was an Ephesian, and Luke informs us that the other two remained at Ephesus when Paul sailed to Judea, (Acts xviii. 18, 29.)

The chief point on which it turns is to confirm Timothy, both in the faith of the gospel, and in the pure and constant preaching of it. But yet these exhortations derive no small weight from the consideration of the time when he wrote them. Paul had before his eyes the death which he was prepared to endure for the testimony of the gospel. All that we read here, therefore, concerning the kingdom of Christ, the hope of eternal life, the Christian warfare, confidence in confessing Christ, and the certainty of doctrine, ought to be viewed by us as written not with ink but with Paul's own blood; for nothing is asserted by him for which he does not offer the pledge of his death; and therefore this Epistle may be regarded as a solemn subscription and ratification of Paul's doctrine.

It is of importance to remember, however, what we stated in the exposition of the former Epistle, that the Apostle did not write it merely for the sake of one man, but that he exhibited, under the person of one man, a general doctrine, which should afterwards be transmitted from one hand to another. And first, having praised the faith of Timothy, in which he had been educated from his childhood, he exhorts him to persevere faithfully in the doctrine which he had learned, and in the office intrusted to him; and, at the same time, lest Timothy should be discouraged on account of Paul's imprisonment, or the apostasy of others, he boasts of his apostleship and of the reward laid up for him. He likewise praises Onesiphorus, in order to encourage others by his example; and because the condition of those who serve Christ is painful and difficult, he borrows comparisons both from husbandmen and from soldiers, the former of whom do not hesitate to bestow much labour on the cultivation of the soil before any fruit is seen, while the latter lay aside all cares and employments, in order to devote themselves entirely to the life of a soldier and to the command of their general.

Next, he gives a brief summary of his gospel, and commands Timothy to hand it down to others, and to take care that it shall be transmitted to posterity. Having taken occasion from this to mention again his own imprisonment, he rises to holy boldness, for the purpose of animating others by his noble courage; for he invites us all to contemplate, along with him, that crown which awaits him in heaven.

He bids him also abstain from contentious disputes and vain questions, recommending to him, on the contrary, to promote edification; and in order to shew more clearly how enormous an evil it is, he relates that some have been ruined by it, and particularly mentions two, Hymenæus and Philetus, who, having fallen into monstrous absurdity, so as to overturn the faith of the resurrection, suffered the horrible punishment of their vanity. But because falls of that kind, especially of distinguished men and those who enjoyed some reputation, are usually attended by great scandal, he shews that believers ought not to be distressed on account of them, because they who possess the name of Christ do not all belong actually to Christ, and because the Church must be exposed to the misery of dwelling among wicked and ungodly persons in this world. Yet that this may not unduly terrify weak minds, he prudently softens it, by saying that the Lord will preserve till the end his own, whom he has elected.

He afterwards returns to exhort Timothy to persevere faithfully in the discharge of his ministry; and in order to make him more careful, he foretells what dangerous times await the good and the pious, and what destructive men shall afterwards arise; but, in opposition to all this, he confirms him by the hope of a good and successful result. More especially, he recommends to him to be constantly employed in teaching sound doctrine, pointing out the proper use of Scripture, that he may know that he will find in it everything that is necessary for the solid edification of the Church.

Next, he mentions that his own death is at hand, but he does so in the manner of a conqueror hastening to a glorious triumph, which is a clear testimony of wonderful confidence. Lastly, after having besought Timothy to come to him as soon as possible, he points out the necessity arising from his present condition. This is the principal subject in the conclusion of the Epistle.

# COMMENTARIES

ON

# THE SECOND EPISTLE TO TIMOTHY.

## CHAPTER I.

1. Paul, an apostle of Jesus Christ by the will of God, according to the promise of life which is in Christ Jesus,
2. To Timothy, *my* dearly-beloved son: Grace, mercy, *and* peace from God the Father, and Christ Jesus our Lord.

1. Paulus apostolus Iesu Christi per voluntatem Dei, secundum promissionem vitæ, quæ est in Christo Iesu,
2. Timotheo dilecto filio gratia, misericordia, pax a Deo Patre, et Christo Iesu Domino nostro.

1. *Paul an Apostle.* From the very preface we already perceive that Paul had not in view Timothy alone; otherwise he would not have employed such lofty titles in asserting his apostleship; for what purpose would it have served to employ these ornaments of language in writing to one who was fully convinced of the fact? He, therefore, lays claim to that authority over all which belonged to his public character; and he does this the more diligently, because, being near death, he wishes to secure the approbation of the whole course of his ministry,[1] and to seal his doctrine

---

[1] "Although, in all that Paul has left us in writing, we must consider that it is God who speaks to us by the mouth of a mortal man, and that all his doctrine ought to be received with such authority and reverence as if God visibly appeared from heaven, yet still there is in this epistle a special object to be kept in view, that Paul, being in prison, and perceiving his death to be at hand, wished to ratify his faith, as if he had sealed it with his blood. So then, as often as we read this epistle, let the condition in which Paul was at that time come before our eyes; namely, that he was looking for nothing but to die for the testimony of the gospel (which he actually did) as its standard-bearer, in order to give us stronger

which he had laboured so hard to teach, that it may be held sacred by posterity, and to leave a true portrait of it in Timothy.

*Of Jesus Christ by the will of God.* First, according to his custom, he calls himself an "Apostle of Christ." Hence it follows, that he does not speak as a private person, and must not be heard slightly, and for form's sake,[1] like a man, but as one who is a representative of Christ. But because the dignity of the office is too great to belong to any man, except by the special gift and election of God, he at the same time pronounces a eulogy on his calling, by adding that he was ordained *by the will of God.* His apostleship, therefore, having God for its author and defender, is beyond all dispute.

*According to the promise of life.* That his calling may be the more certain, he connects it with the promises of eternal life; as if he had said, "As from the beginning God promised eternal life in Christ, so now he has appointed me to be the minister for proclaiming that promise." Thus also he points out the design of his apostleship, namely, to bring men to Christ, that in him they may find life.

*Which is in Christ Jesus.* He speaks with great accuracy, when he mentions that "the promise of life" was indeed given, in ancient times, to the fathers. (Acts xxvi. 6.) But yet he declares that this life is in Christ, in order to inform us that the faith of those who lived under the Law must nevertheless have looked towards Christ; and that *life,* which was contained in promises, was, in some respects, suspended, till it was exhibited in Christ.

---

assurance of his doctrine, and that will affect us in a more lively manner. Indeed, if we read this epistle carefully, we shall find that the Spirit of God has expressed himself in it in such a manner, with such majesty and power, that we are constrained to be captivated and overwhelmed. For my own part, I know that this epistle has been more profitable to me than any other book of Scripture, and still is profitable to me every day; and if any person shall examine it carefully, there can be no doubt that he will experience the same effect. And if we desire to have a testimony of the truth of God, which pierces our heart, we may well fix on this epistle; for a man must be in a profound sleep, and remarkably stupid, if God do not work in his soul, when he hears the doctrine that shall be drawn from it."—*Fr. Ser.*

[1] "Oui par acquit."

2. *My beloved son.* By this designation he not only testifies his love of Timothy, but procures respect and submission to him; because he wishes to be acknowledged in him, as one who may justly be called his son.[1] The reason of the appellation is, that he had begotten him in Christ; for, although this honour belongs to God alone, yet it is also transferred to ministers, whose agency he employs for regenerating us.

*Grace, mercy.* The word *mercy*, which he employs here, is commonly left out by him in his ordinary salutations. I think that he introduced it, when he poured out his feelings with more than ordinary vehemence. Moreover, he appears to have inverted the order; for, since "mercy" is the cause of "grace," it ought to have come before it in this passage. But still it is not unsuitable that it should be put after *grace*, in order to express more clearly what is the nature of that grace, and whence it proceeds; as if he had added, in the form of a declaration, that the reason why we are loved by God is, that he is merciful. Yet this may also be explained as relating to God's daily benefits, which are so many testimonies of his "mercy;" for, whenever he assists us, whenever he delivers us from evils, pardons our sins, and bears with our weakness, he does so, because he has compassion on us.

| | |
|---|---|
| 3. I thank God, whom I serve from *my* forefathers with pure conscience, that without ceasing I have remembrance of thee in my prayers night and day; | 3. Gratiam habeo Deo, quem colo a progenitoribus in pura conscientia, ut assiduam tui mentionem facio in precibus meis die et noctu, |
| 4. Greatly desiring to see thee, being mindful of thy tears, that I may be filled with joy; | 4. Desiderans te videre, memor tuarum lacrymarum, ut gaudio implear, |
| 5. When I call to remembrance the unfeigned faith that is in thee, which dwelt first in thy grandmother Lois, and thy mother Eunice; and I am persuaded that in thee also. | 5. Memoria repetens eam, quæ in te est, sinceram fidem, quæ habitavit primùm in avia tua Loide, et in matre tua Eunica; persuasum autem habeo quòd etiam in te. |

3. *I give thanks.* The meaning usually assigned to these words is, that Paul "gives thanks to God," and next assigns the cause or ground of thanksgiving; namely, that he is un-

---

[1] "Comme en celuy qui peut a bon droict estre nomme son fils."

ceasingly mindful of Timothy. But let my readers consider whether the following sense do not suit equally well and even better: "Whenever I remember thee in my prayers, (and I do so continually,) I also give thanks concerning thee;" for the particle ὡς most frequently has that meaning;[1] and, indeed, any meaning that can be drawn from a different translation is exceedingly meagre. According to this exposition, prayer will be a sign of carefulness, and thanksgiving a sign of joy; that is, he never thought of Timothy without calling to remembrance the eminent virtues with which he was adorned. Hence arises ground of thanksgiving; for the recollection of the gifts of God is always pleasant and delightful to believers. Both are proofs of real friendship. He calls the *mention* of him (ἀδιάλειπτον) *unceasing*, because he never forgets him when he prays.

*Whom I worship from my ancestors.* This declaration he made in opposition to those well-known calumnies with which the Jews everywhere loaded him, as if he had forsaken the religion of his country, and apostatized from the law of Moses. On the contrary, he declares that he worships God, concerning whom he had been taught by his ancestors, that is, the God of Abraham, who revealed himself to the Jews, who delivered his law by the hand of Moses; and not some pretended God, whom he had lately made for himself.

But here it may be asked, "Since Paul glories in following the religion handed down from his ancestors, is this a sufficiently solid foundation? For hence it follows, that this will be a plausible pretence for excusing all superstitions, and that it will be a crime, if any one depart, in the smallest degree, from the institutions of his ancestors, whatever these are." The answer is easy. He does not here lay down a fixed rule, that every person who follows the religion that he received from his fathers is believed to worship God aright, and, on the other hand, that he who departs from the custom of his ancestors is at all to blame for it. For

[1] "Car le mot Grec se prend plus souvent pour Comme." "For the Greek word generally signifies *as*."

this circumstance must always be taken into account, that Paul was not descended from idolaters, but from the children of Abraham, who worshipped the true God. We know what Christ says, in disapproving of all the false worship of the Gentiles, that the Jews alone maintained the true method of worship. Paul, therefore, does not rest solely on the authority of the fathers, nor does he speak indiscriminately of all his ancestors; but he removes that false opinion, with which he knew that he was unjustly loaded, that he had forsaken the God of Israel, and framed for himself a strange god.

*In a pure conscience.* It is certain that Paul's conscience was not always pure; for he acknowledges that he was deceived by hypocrisy, while he gave loose reins to sinful desire.[1] (Rom. vii. 8.) The excuse which Chrysostom offers for what Paul did while he was a Pharisee, on the ground that he opposed the gospel, not through malice, but through ignorance, is not a satisfactory reply to the objection; for "a pure conscience" is no ordinary commendation, and cannot be separated from the sincere and hearty fear of God. I, therefore, limit it to the present time, in this manner, that he worships the same God as was worshipped by his ancestors, but that now he worships him with pure affection of the heart, since the time when he was enlightened by the gospel.

This statement has the same object with the numerous protestations of the apostles, as recorded in the Acts of the Apostles: "I serve the God of my fathers, believing all things that are written in the law and in the prophets." (Acts xxiv. 14.) Again, "And now I stand to be judged concerning the hope of the promise which was made to our fathers, to which hope our twelve tribes hope to come." (Acts xxvi. 6.) Again, "On account of the hope of Israel I am bound with this chain." (Acts xxviii. 20.)

*In my prayers night and day.* Hence we see how great was his constancy in prayer; and yet he affirms nothing

---

[1] "Quand il se laschoit la bride a convoiter, comme si la chose n'eust point illicite." "When he gave loose reins to lust, as if it had not been an unlawful thing."

about himself but what Christ recommends to all his followers. We ought, therefore, to be moved and inflamed by such examples to imitate them, so far, at least, that an exercise so necessary may be more frequent among us. If any one understand this to mean the daily and nightly prayers which Paul was wont to offer at stated hours, there will be no impropriety in that view; though I give a more simple interpretation, that there was no time when he was not employed in prayer.

5. *Calling to remembrance that unfeigned faith.* Not so much for the purpose of applauding as of exhorting Timothy, the Apostle commends both his own faith and that of his grandmother and mother; for, when one has begun well and valiantly, the progress he has made should encourage him to advance, and domestic examples are powerful excitements to urge him forward. Accordingly, he sets before him *his grandmother Lois and his mother Eunice,* by whom he had been educated from his infancy in such a manner that he might have sucked godliness along with his milk. By this godly education, therefore, Timothy is admonished not to degenerate from himself and from his ancestors.

It is uncertain whether, on the one hand, these women were converted to Christ, and what Paul here applauds was the commencement of faith, or whether, on the other hand, faith is attributed to them apart from Christianity. The latter appears to me more probable; for, although at that time everything abounded with many superstitions and corruptions, yet God had always his own people, whom he did not suffer to be corrupted with the multitude, but whom he sanctified and separated to himself, that there might always exist among the Jews a pledge of this grace, which he had promised to the seed of Abraham. There is, therefore, no absurdity in saying that they lived and died in the faith of the Mediator, although Christ had not yet been revealed to them. But I do not assert anything, and could not assert without rashness.

*And I am persuaded that in thee also.* This clause confirms me in the conjecture which I have just now stated;

for, in my opinion, he does not here speak of the present faith of Timothy. It would lessen that sure confidence of the former eulogium, if he only said that he reckoned the faith of Timothy to resemble the faith of his grandmother and mother. But I understand the meaning to be, that Timothy, from his childhood, while he had not yet obtained a knowledge of the gospel, was imbued with the fear of God, and with such faith as proved to be a living seed, which afterwards manifested itself.

| | |
|---|---|
| 6. Wherefore I put thee in remembrance, that thou stir up the gift of God, which is in thee by the putting on of my hands. | 6. Propterea commonefacio te, ut exsuscites donum Dei, quod in te est, per impositionem manuum mearum. |
| 7. For God hath not given us the spirit of fear; but of power, and of love, and of a sound mind. | 7. Non enim dedit nobis Deus spiritum timiditatis, sed potentiæ et dilectionis et sobrietatis. |
| 8. Be not thou therefore ashamed of the testimony of our Lord, nor of me his prisoner: but be thou partaker of the afflictions of the gospel, according to the power of God ; | 8. Non ergo te pudeat testimonii Domini nostri, neque mei, qui sum vinctus ipsius; sed esto particeps afflictionum Evangelii, secundum potentiam Dei, |
| 9. Who hath saved us, and called *us* with an holy calling, not according to our works, but according to his own purpose and grace, which was given us in Christ Jesus before the world began; | 9. Qui nos servavit ac vocavit vocatione sancta; non secundum opera nostra, sed secundum propositum suum et gratiam, quæ data fuit nobis in Christo Iesu ante tempora sæcularia, |
| 10. But is now made manifest by the appearing of our Saviour Jesus Christ, who hath abolished death, and hath brought life and immortality to light through the gospel: | 10. Revelata autem nunc fuit per apparitionem Servatoris nostri Iesu Christi, qui mortem quidem abolevit, illuminavit autem vitam et immortalitatem per Evangelium, |
| 11. Whereunto I am appointed a preacher, and an apostle, and a teacher of the Gentiles. | 11. In quod positus sum præco et Apostolus, et Doctor Gentium, |
| 12. For the which cause I also suffer these things: nevertheless I am not ashamed; for I know whom I have believed, and am persuaded that he is able to keep that which I have committed unto him against that day. | 12. Quam etiam ob causam hæc patior, sed non pudefio; novi enim, cui crediderim, et persuasus sum quòd potens sit, depositum meum servare in diem illum. |

6. *For which cause I advise thee.* The more abundantly that Timothy had received the grace of God, the more attentive (the Apostle intimates) he ought to be in making progress from day to day. It deserves notice that the words " for which cause" introduce this advice as a conclusion from what has been already said.

*To stir up the gift of God.* This exhortation is highly necessary; for it usually happens, and may be said to be natural, that the excellence of gifts produces carelessness, which is also accompanied by sloth; and Satan continually labours to extinguish all that is of God in us. We ought, therefore, on the other hand, to strive to bring to perfection everything that is good in us, and to kindle what is languid; for the metaphor, which Paul employs, is taken from a fire which was feeble, or that was in course of being gradually extinguished, if strength and flame were not added, by blowing upon it and by supplying new fuel. Let us therefore remember that we ought to apply to use the gifts of God, lest, being unemployed and concealed, they gather rust. Let us also remember that we should diligently profit by them, lest they be extinguished by our slothfulness.

*Which is in thee by the laying on of my hands.* There can be no doubt that Timothy was invited by the general voice of the Church, and was not elected by the private wish of Paul alone; but there is no absurdity in saying, that Paul ascribes the election to himself personally, because he was the chief actor in it. Yet here he speaks of ordination, that is, of the solemn act of conferring the office of the ministry, and not of election. Besides, it is not perfectly clear whether it was the custom, when any minister was to be set apart, that all laid their hands on his head, or that one only did so, in the room and name of all. I am more inclined to the conjecture, that it was only one person who laid on his hands.

So far as relates to the ceremony, the apostles borrowed it from an ancient custom of their nation; or rather, in consequence of its being in use, they retained it; for this is a part of that decent and orderly procedure which Paul elsewhere recommends. (1 Cor. xiv. 40.) Yet it may be doubted if that "laying on of hands" which is now mentioned refers to ordination; because, at that time, the graces of the Spirit, of which he speaks in the 12th chapter of the Epistle to the Romans, and in the 13th of the First Epistle to the Corinthians, were bestowed on many others who were not appointed to be pastors. But, for my own part, I think that it may be easily inferred from the former Epistle, that Paul here speaks of the office of a pastor, for this passage agrees with that, "Do not neglect the grace which was given to thee with the laying on of the hands of the eldership." (1 Tim. iv. 14.)

That point being settled, it is asked, "Was grace given by the outward sign?" To this question I answer, whenever ministers were ordained, they were recommended to God by the prayers of the whole Church, and in this manner grace from God was obtained for them by prayer, and was not given to them by virtue of the sign, although the sign was not uselessly or unprofitably employed, but was a sure pledge of that grace which they received from God's own hand. That ceremony was not a profane act, invented for the sole purpose of procuring credit in the eyes of men, but a lawful consecration before God, which is not performed but by the power of the Holy Spirit. Besides, Paul takes the sign for the whole matter or the whole transaction; for he declares that Timothy was endued with grace, when he was offered to God as a minister. Thus in this mode of expression there is a figure of speech, in which a part is taken for the whole.

But we are again met by another question; for if it was only at his ordination that Timothy obtained the grace necessary for discharging his office, of what nature was the election of a man not yet fit or qualified, but hitherto void and destitute of the gift of God? I answer, it was not then so given to him that he had it not before; for it is certain that he excelled both in doctrine and in other gifts before Paul ordained him to the ministry. But there is no inconsistency in saying, that, when God wished to make use of his services, and accordingly called him, he then fitted and enriched him still more with new gifts, or doubled those which he had previously bestowed. It does not therefore follow that Timothy had not formerly any gift, but it shone forth the more when the duty of teaching was laid upon him.

7. *For God hath not given to us a spirit of cowardice.* It is a confirmation of what he had said immediately before;

and thus he continues to urge Timothy to display the power of the gifts which he had received. He makes use of this argument, that God governs his ministers by *the Spirit of power*, which is the opposite of *cowardice.* Hence it follows, that they ought not to lie down through slothfulness, but, sustained by great confidence and cheerfulness, should exhibit and display, by visible effects, that power of the Spirit.

The following passage occurs in the Epistle to the Romans : " For we have not received a spirit of bondage, to be again in terror ; but we have received the spirit of adoption, by which we cry, Abba, Father." (Rom. viii. 15.) That passage is, at first sight, nearly similar to this ; but yet the context shews that the meaning is different. There he treats of the confidence of adoption which all believers have ; but here he speaks particularly about ministers, and exhorts them, in the person of Timothy, to arouse themselves actively to deeds of valour ; because God does not wish them to perform their office in a cold and lifeless manner, but to press forward powerfully, relying on the efficacy of the Spirit.

*But of power, and of love, and of soberness.* Hence we are taught, first, that not one of us possesses that firmness and unshaken constancy of the Spirit, which is requisite for fulfilling our ministry, until we are endued from heaven with a new power. And indeed the obstructions are so many and so great, that no courage of man will be able to overcome them. It is God, therefore, who endues us with " the spirit of power ;" for they who, in other respects, give tokens of much strength, fall down in a moment, when they are not upheld by the power of the Divine Spirit.

Secondly, we gather from it, that they who have slavish meanness and cowardice, so that they do not venture to do anything in defence of the truth, when it is necessary, are not governed by that Spirit by whom the servants of Christ are guided. Hence it follows, that there are very few of those who bear the title of ministers, in the present day, who have the mark of sincerity impressed upon them ; for, amongst a vast number, where do we find one who, relying on the power of the Spirit, boldly despises all the loftiness which exalts itself against Christ? Do not almost all seek their own interest and their leisure? Do they not sink down dumb as soon as any noise breaks out? The consequence is, that no majesty of God is seen in their ministry. The word *Spirit* is here employed figuratively, as in many other passages.[1]

But why did he afterwards add *love* and *soberness?* In my opinion, it was for the purpose of distinguishing that power of the Spirit from the fury and rage of fanatics, who, while they rush forward with reckless impulse, fiercely boast of having the Spirit of God. For that reason he expressly states that this powerful energy is moderated by " soberness and love," that is, by a calm desire of edifying. Yet Paul does not deny that prophets and teachers were endued with the same Spirit before the publication of the gospel; but he declares that this grace ought now to be especially powerful and conspicuous under the reign of Christ.

8. *Be not ashamed, therefore.* He said this, because the confession of the gospel was accounted infamous; and therefore he forbids that either ambition or the fear of disgrace shall prevent or retard him from the liberty of preaching the gospel. And he infers this from what has been already said; for he who is armed with the power of God will not tremble at the noise raised by the world, but will reckon it honourable that wicked men mark them with disgrace.

And justly does he call the gospel *the testimony of our Lord;* because, although he has no need of our assistance, yet he lays upon us this duty, that we shall give " testimony" to him for maintaining his glory. It is a great and distinguished honour which he confers upon us, and, indeed, upon all, (for there is no Christian that ought not to reckon himself a witness of Christ,) but chiefly pastors and teachers, as Christ said to the apostles,—" Ye shall be witnesses to me."

---

[1] " Le mot d'*Esprit* est yci prins pour les dons qui en procedent, suyvant la figure nommee Metonymie." " The word *Spirit* is here taken for the gifts which proceed from him, agreeably to the figure called Metonymy."

(Acts i. 8.) Accordingly, the more hateful the doctrine of the gospel is in the world, the more earnestly should they labour to confess it openly.

When he adds, *nor of me;* by this word he reminds Timothy not to refuse to be his companion, as in a cause common to both of them ; for, when we begin to withdraw from the society of those who, for the name of Christ, suffer persecution, what else do we seek than that the gospel shall be free from all persecution? Now, though there were not wanting many wicked men who thus ridiculed Timothy,—" Do you not see what has befallen your master ? Do you not know that the same reward awaits you also ? Why do you press upon us a doctrine which you see is hissed at by the whole world ?"—still he must have been cheered by this exhortation,—" You have no reason to be ashamed of me, in that which is not shameful, for I am *Christ's prisoner ;*" that is, " Not for any crime or evil deed, but for his name I am kept in prison."

*But be thou a partaker of the afflictions of the gospel.* He lays down a method by which that which he enjoins may be done ; that is, if Timothy shall prepare himself for enduring the afflictions which are connected with the gospel. Whosoever shall revolt at and shrink from the cross will always be ashamed of the gospel. Not without good reason, therefore, does Paul, while he exhorts to boldness of confession, in order that he may not exhort in vain, speak to him also about bearing the cross.[1]

He adds, *according to the power of God ;* because, but for

---

[1] " He shews, in the first place, that the gospel cannot be without afflictions. Not that God does not call all men to unity in the faith, and the doctrine of the gospel is the message of reconciliation; but yet, on the one hand, there are those who are drawn by the power of his Holy Spirit, while unbelievers remain in their hardness ; and, on the other hand, there is the fire that is kindled, as, when thunders are generated in the air, there must be great troubles, so is it when the gospel is preached. And now, if the gospel brings afflictions, and if our Lord Jesus Christ wishes that what he endured in his person shall be fulfilled in his members, and that every day he shall be, as it were, crucified, is it lawful for us to withdraw from that condition ? Since, therefore, all our hope lies in the gospel, and since we ought to lean upon it, let us ponder what Paul says, that we must lend support to our brethren, when we see that they are assailed, that men trample them under their feet, spit in their face, and insult them, let us

this, and if he did not support us, we should immediately sink under the load. And this clause contains both admonition and consolation. The admonition is, to turn away his eyes from his present weakness, and, relying on the assistance of God, to venture and undertake what is beyond his strength. The consolation is, that, if we endure anything on account of the gospel, God will come forth as our deliverer, that, by his power, we may obtain the victory.

9. *Who hath saved us.* From the greatness of the benefit he shews how much we owe to God; for the salvation which he has bestowed on us easily swallows up all the evils that must be endured in this world. The word *saved*, though it admit of a general signification, is here limited, by the context, to denote eternal salvation. So then he means that they who, having obtained through Christ not a fading or transitory, but an eternal salvation, shall spare their fleeting life or honour rather than acknowledge their Redeemer, are excessively ungrateful.

*And hath called us with a holy calling.* He places the sealing of salvation [1] in the *calling;* for, as the salvation of men was completed in the death of Christ, so God, by the gospel, makes us partakers of it. In order to place in a stronger light the value of this "calling," he pronounces it to be *holy.* This ought to be carefully observed, because, as salvation must not be sought anywhere but in Christ, so, on the other hand, he would have died and risen again without any practical advantage, unless so far as he calls us to a participation of this grace. Thus, after having procured salvation for us, this second blessing remains to be bestowed, that, ingrafting us into his body, he may communicate his benefits to be enjoyed by us.

*Not according to our works, but according to his purpose and grace.* He describes the source both of our calling and of the whole of our salvation. We had not works by which

---

choose to be their companions for enduring the reproaches and base conduct of the world, rather than to be honoured, to be in good reputation and credit, and yet to be estranged from those who suffer for the cause which we have in common with them."—*Fr. Ser.*

[1] "La certitude de salut." "The certainty of salvation."

we could anticipate God; but the whole depends on his gracious purpose and election ; for in the two words *purpose* and *grace* there is the figure of speech called Hypallage,[1] and the latter must have the force of an objection, as if he had said,—" according to his gracious purpose." Although Paul commonly employs the word "purpose" to denote the secret decree of God, the cause of which is in his own power, yet, for the sake of fuller explanation, he chose to add "grace," that he might more clearly exclude all reference to works. And the very contrast proclaims loudly enough that there is no room for works where the grace of God reigns, especially when we are reminded of the election of God, by which he was beforehand with us, when we had not yet been born. On this subject I have spoken more fully in my exposition of the first chapter of the Epistle to the Ephesians ; and at present I do nothing more than glance briefly at that which I have there treated more at large.[2]

*Which was given to us.* From the order of time he argues, that, by free grace, salvation was given to us which we did not at all deserve ; for, if God chose us before the creation of the world, he could not have regard to works, of which we had none, seeing that we did not then exist. As to the cavil of the sophists, that God was moved by the works which he foresaw, it does not need a long refutation. What kind of works would those have been if God had passed us by, seeing that the election itself is the source and beginning of all good works ?

This *giving* of grace, which he mentions, is nothing else than predestination, by which we were adopted to be the sons of God. On this subject I wished to remind my readers, because God is frequently said actually to "give" his grace to us when we receive the effect of it. But here Paul sets before us what God purposed with himself from the beginning. He, therefore, gave that which, not induced by

---

[1] A figure of speech, by which the parts of a proposition seem to be interchanged, ὑπαλλαγή, compounded of ὑπό and ἀλλάσσω, ' I change.'—*Ed.*
[2] See CALVIN's Commentaries on Galatians and Ephesians, pp, 197-201. —*Ed.*

any merit, he appointed to those who were not yet born, and kept laid up in his treasures, until he made known by the fact itself that he purposeth nothing in vain.

*Before eternal ages.* He employs this phrase in the same sense in which he elsewhere speaks of the uninterrupted succession of years from the foundation of the world. (Tit. i. 2.) For that ingenious reasoning which Augustine conducts in many passages is totally different from Paul's design. The meaning therefore is,—" Before times began to take their course from all past ages." Besides, it is worthy of notice, that he places the foundation of salvation in Christ; for, apart from him, there is neither adoption nor salvation; as was indeed said in expounding the first chapter of the Epistle to the Ephesians.

10. *But hath now been revealed by the appearing of our Saviour Jesus Christ.* Observe how appropriately he connects the faith which we have from the gospel with God's secret election, and assigns to each of them its own place. God has now called us by the gospel, not because he has suddenly taken counsel about our salvation, but because he had so determined from all eternity. Christ hath now "appeared"[1] for our salvation, not because the power of saving has been recently bestowed on him, but because this grace was laid up in him for us before the creation of the world. The knowledge of those things is revealed to us by faith; and so the Apostle judiciously connects the gospel with the most ancient promises of God, that novelty may not render it contemptible.

But it is asked; "Were the fathers under the Law ignorant of this grace?" for if it was not revealed but by the coming of Christ, it follows that, before that time, it was concealed. I reply, Paul speaks of the full exhibition of the thing itself on which depended also the faith of the fathers,

---

[1] Τῆς ἐπιφανείας.—" This Theodoret well explains by ἐνανθρωπήσεως, the expression being one especially used by the ancient writers, of the appearance of the gods on earth. So Joseph. Ant. xviii. 3. 4, we have τὴν ἐπιφάνειαν ἐκδιηγεῖται τοῦ 'Ανούβιδος [she relates the appearing of (the god) Anubis.] 'Επιφάνεια here denotes Christ's first appearance in the flesh, though elsewhere the term always means his second appearance to judge the world."—*Bloomfield.*

so that this takes nothing from them. The reason why Abel, Noah, Abraham, Moses, David, and all believers, obtained the same faith with us, was, that they placed their confidence in this "appearance." Thus, when he says that "grace hath been revealed to us by the appearing of Christ," he does not exclude from communion with that grace the fathers who are made partakers with us of this appearing by the same faith. Christ (Heb. xiii. 8) was yesterday as he is to-day; but he did not manifest himself to us, by his death and resurrection, before the time appointed by the Father. To this, as the only pledge and accomplishment of our salvation, both our faith and that of the fathers look with one accord.

*Who hath indeed destroyed death.* When he ascribes to the gospel the manifestation of life, he does not mean that we must begin with the word, leaving out of view the death and resurrection of Christ, (for the word, on the contrary, rests on the subject-matter,) but he only means that the fruit of this grace comes to men in no other way than by the gospel, in accordance with what is said, " God was in Christ, reconciling the world to himself, and hath committed to us the ministry of reconciliation." (2 Cor. v. 19.)

*And hath brought to light life and immortality by the gospel.* It is a high and remarkable commendation of the gospel, that it "bringeth life to light." To *life* he adds *immortality;* as if he had said, "a true and immortal life." But, perhaps, it may be thought better, that by *life* we understand regeneration, that is followed by a blessed *immortality*, which is also the object of hope. And, indeed, this is our "life," not that which we have in common with brute beasts, but that which consists in partaking of the image of God. But because in this world "it doth not appear" (1 John iii. 2) what is the nature, or what is the value of that "life," for the sake of more full expression he has most properly added, "immortality," which is the revelation of that life which is now concealed.

11. *To which I have been appointed.* Not without good reason does he so highly commend the gospel along with his apostleship. Satan labours, beyond all things else,

to banish from our hearts, by every possible method, the faith of sound doctrine; and as it is not always easy for him to do this if he attack us in open war, he steals upon us by secret and indirect methods; for, in order to destroy the credibility of doctrine, he holds up to suspicion the calling of godly teachers.[1] Paul, therefore, having death before his eyes, and knowing well the ancient and ordinary snares of Satan, determined to assert not only the doctrine of the gospel in general, but his own calling. Both were necessary; for, although there be uttered long discourses concerning the dignity of the gospel, they will not be of much avail to us, unless we understand what is the gospel. Many will agree as to the general principle of the undoubted authority of the gospel, who afterwards will have nothing certain that they can follow. This is the reason why Paul expressly wishes to be acknowledged to be a faithful and lawful minister of that life-giving doctrine which he had mentioned.

*A herald, and an apostle, and a teacher of the Gentiles.* For the reasons now stated, he adorns himself with various titles, for expressing one and the same thing. He calls himself a *herald*, whose duty it is, to publish the commands of princes and magistrates. The word *apostle* is here used in its ordinary and restricted meaning. Moreover, because there is a natural relation between a *teacher* and his disciples, he takes to himself also this third name, that they who learn from him may know that they have a master who has been appointed to them by God. And to whom does he declare that he was appointed? To the *Gentiles;* for the main hinge of the controversy was about them, because the Jews denied that the promises of life belonged to any others than to the fleshly children of Abraham. In order, therefore, that the salvation of the Gentiles may not be called in question, he affirms that to them he has been especially sent by God.

12. *For which cause also I suffer these things.* It is well known that the rage of the Jews was kindled against Paul, for this reason more than any other, that he made the gospel

---

[1] "Des Docteurs ou Pasteurs fideles." "Of faithful Teachers or Pastors."

common to the Gentiles. Yet the phrase *for which cause* relates to the whole verse, and therefore must not be limited to the last clause about " the Gentiles."

*But I am not ashamed.* That the prison in which he was bound might not in any degree lessen his authority, he contends, on the contrary, by two arguments. First, he shows that the cause, far from being disgraceful, was even honourable to him ; for he was a prisoner, not on account of any evil deed, but because he obeyed God who called him. It is an inconceivable consolation, when we are able to bring a good conscience in opposition to the unjust judgments of men. Secondly, from the hope of a prosperous issue he argues that there is nothing disgraceful in his imprisonment. He who shall avail himself of this defence will be able to overcome any temptations, however great they may be. And when he says, that he " is not ashamed," he stimulates others, by his example, to have the same courage.

*For I know whom I have believed.* This is the only place of refuge, to which all believers ought to resort, whenever the world reckons them to be condemned and ruined men; namely, to reckon it enough that God approves of them ; for what would be the result, if they depended on men? And hence we ought to infer how widely faith differs from opinion ; because, when Paul says, " I know whom I have believed," he means that it is not enough if you believe, unless you have the testimony of God, and unless you have full certainty of it. Faith, therefore, neither leans on the authority of men, nor rests on God, in such a manner as to hesitate, but must be joined with knowledge; otherwise it would not be sufficiently strong against the innumerable assaults of Satan. He who with Paul enjoys this knowledge, will know, by experience, that, on good grounds, our faith is called " the victory that overcometh the world," (1 John v. 4,) and that on good grounds, it was said by Christ, " The gates of hell shall not prevail against it." (Matt. xvi. 18.) Amidst every storm and tempest, that man will enjoy undisturbed repose, who has a settled conviction that God, " who cannot lie," (Tit. i. 2,) or deceive, hath spoken, and will undoubtedly perform what he hath promised. On the other hand, he who has not this truth sealed on his heart, will be continually shaken hither and thither like a reed.

This passage is highly worthy of attention; because it expresses admirably the power of faith, when it shows that, even in desperate affairs, we ought to give to God such glory as not to doubt that he will be true and faithful; and when it likewise shows that we ought to rely on the word as fully as if God had manifested himself to us from heaven; for he who has not this conviction understands nothing. Let us always remember that Paul does not pursue philosophical speculations in the shade, but, having the reality before his eyes, solemnly declares, how highly valuable is a confident hope of eternal life.

*And am persuaded that he is able.* Because the power and greatness of dangers often fill us with dismay, or at least tempt our hearts to distrust, for this reason we must defend ourselves with this shield, that there is sufficient protection in the power of God. In like manner Christ, when he bids us cherish confident hope, employs this argument, "The Father, who gave you to me, is greater than all," (John x. 29,) by which he means, that we are out of danger, seeing that the Lord, who hath taken us under his protection, is abundantly powerful to put down all opposition. True, Satan does not venture to suggest this thought in a direct form, that God cannot fulfil, or is prevented from fulfilling, what he has promised, (for our senses are shocked by so gross a blasphemy against God,) but, by pre-occupying our eyes and understandings, he takes away from us all sense of the power of God. The heart must therefore be well purified, in order that it may not only taste that power, but may retain the taste of it amidst temptations of every kind.

Now, whenever Paul speaks of the power of God, understand by it what may be called his actual or ($\dot{\epsilon}\nu\epsilon\rho\gamma o\upsilon\mu\dot{\epsilon}\nu\eta\nu$) "effectual" power, as he calls it elsewhere. (Coloss. i. 29.) Faith always connects the power of God with the word, which it does not imagine to be at a distance, but, having inwardly conceived it, possesses and retains it. Thus it is said of Abraham: "He did not hesitate or dispute, but gave glory to God, being fully convinced that what he had promised he was able also to perform." (Rom. iv. 20, 21.)

*What I have intrusted to him.* Observe that he employs this phrase to denote eternal life; for hence we conclude, that our salvation is in the hand of God, in the same manner as there are in the hand of a depositary those things which we deliver to him to keep, relying on his fidelity. If our salvation depended on ourselves,[1] to how many dangers would it be continually exposed? But now it is well that, having been committed to such a guardian, it is out of all danger.

13. Hold fast the form of sound words, which thou hast heard of me, in faith and love which is in Christ Jesus.

14. That good thing which was committed unto thee keep by the Holy Ghost which dwelleth in us.

15. This thou knowest, that all they which are in Asia be turned away from me; of whom are Phygellus and Hermogenes.

16. The Lord give mercy unto the house of Onesiphorus; for he oft refreshed me, and was not ashamed of my chain:

17. But when he was in Rome, he sought me out very diligently, and found me.

18. The Lord grant unto him that he may find mercy of the Lord in that day: and in how many things he ministered unto me at Ephesus, thou knowest very well.

13. Formam habe sanorum sermonum, quos a me audisti in fide et caritate, quæ est in Christo Iesu.

14. Egregium depositum custodi per Spiritum Sanctum, qui inhabitat in nobis.

15. Nosti hoc, quòd aversati me fuerint omnes, qui sunt in Asia, quorum sunt Phygellus et Hermogenes.

16. Det misericordiam Dominus Onesiphori familiæ; quoniam sæpe me refocillavit, et de catena mea non erubuit:

17. Sed quum esset Romæ, studiosius quæsivit me, et invenit.

18. Det ei Dominus, ut inveniat misericordiam apud Dominum in die illo, et quam multa mihi Epheso ministraverit, melius tu nosti.

13. *Hold the form of sound words.* Some explain it thus: "Let thy doctrine be, as it were, a pattern which others may imitate." I do not approve of that view. Equally removed from Paul's meaning is Chrysostom's exposition, that Timothy should have at hand the image of virtues engraven on his heart by Paul's doctrine. I rather think that Paul commands Timothy to hold fast the doctrine which he had learned, not only as to substance, but as to the very form of expression; for ὑποτύ-

[1] " Si nostre salut dependoit de nous, et qu'il fust en nostre garde." " If our salvation depended on us, and were under our protection."

πωσις—the word which Paul employs on this occasion—denotes a lively picture of objects, as if they were actually placed before the eyes. Paul knew how ready men are to depart or fall off from pure doctrine. For this reason he earnestly cautions Timothy not to turn aside from that form of teaching which he had received, and to regulate his manner of teaching by the rule which had been laid down; not that we ought to be very scrupulous about words, but because to misrepresent doctrine, even in the smallest degree, is exceedingly injurious.[1]

Hence we see what kind of theology there is in Popery, which has degenerated so far from the pattern which Paul recommends, that it resembles the riddles of diviners or soothsayers rather than a doctrine taken from the word of God. What taste of Paul's writings, I ask, is there in all the books of the schoolmen? This licentiousness in corrupting doctrine shews that there are great reasons why Paul invites Timothy to hold fast the original and natural form. And he contrasts *sound words* not only with doctrines manifestly wicked, but with useless questions, which, instead of health, bring nothing but disease.

*In faith and love, which is in Christ Jesus.* I am aware that the preposition ἐν, agreeably to the idiom of the Hebrew language, (ב,) is often taken for *with;* but here, I think, the meaning is different. Paul has added this as a mark of sound doctrine, in order that we may know what it contains, and what is the summary of it, the whole of which, according to his custom, he includes under "faith and love." He places both of them *in Christ;* as, indeed, the knowledge of Christ consists chiefly of these two parts; for, although

---

[1] "He was not barely to assert the words of Scripture, but he was to hold fast the summary, or system of the truths he had heard from his spiritual father, and, in a way of dependence on Christ, to show his fidelity and love to his Redeemer. This system of doctrine he was to keep, as a pledge committed to his trust, by the help of the Holy Spirit. Ministers are to hold fast every truth, but, above all, those particular truths which are the peculiar butt of the devil's opposition, and meet with rough treatment in the times in which they live; so doing, they comply with the command which their exalted Master laid upon the pastor of the Church at Philadelphia, and then they may hope for the blessing he promised. (Rev. iii. 8, 10, 11.)"—*Abraham Taylor.*

the words, *which is*, are in the singular number, agreeing with the word *love*, yet it must also be understood as applying to *faith*.

Those who translate it, "*with* faith and love," make the meaning to be, that Timothy should add to sound doctrine the affections of piety and love. I do acknowledge that no man can persevere faithfully in sound doctrine unless he is endued with true faith and unfeigned love. But the former exposition, in my opinion, is more appropriate, namely, that Paul employs these terms for describing more fully what is the nature of "sound words," and what is the subject of them. Now he says that the summary consists in "faith and love," of which the knowledge of Christ is the source and beginning.

14. *Keep the excellent thing committed to thee.* This exhortation is more extensive than the preceding. He exhorts Timothy to consider what God has given to him, and to bestow care and application in proportion to the high value of that which has been committed; for, when the thing is of little value, we are not wont to call any one to so strict an account.

By "that which hath been committed," I understand him to mean both the honour of the ministry and all the gifts with which Timothy was endued. Some limit it to the ministry alone; but I think that it denotes chiefly the qualifications for the ministry, that is, all the gifts of the Spirit, in which he excelled. The word "committed" is employed also for another reason, to remind Timothy that he must, one day, render an account; for we ought to administer faithfully what God has committed to us.

Τὸ καλόν[1] denotes that which is of high or singular value; and, therefore, Erasmus has happily translated it (*egregium*) "excellent," for the sake of denoting its rare worth. I have followed that version. But what is the method of keeping it? It is this. We must beware lest we lose by our indolence what God has bestowed upon us, or lest it be taken away, because we have been ungrateful or have abused it; for there are many who reject the grace of God, and many

---

[1] "Le mot Grec duquel il use, que nous traduisons bon." "The Greek word, which he employs, which we translate good."

who, after having received it, deprive themselves of it altogether. Yet because the difficulty of keeping it is beyond our strength, he therefore adds,—

*By the Holy Spirit.* As if he had said, "I do ask from thee more than thou canst, for what thou hast not from thyself the Spirit of God will supply to thee." Hence it follows, that we must not judge of the strength of men from the commandments of God; because, as he commands by words, so he likewise engraves his words on our hearts, and, by communicating strength, causes that his command shall not be in vain.

*Who dwelleth in us.*[1] By this he means, that the assistance of the Holy Spirit is present to believers, provided that they do not reject it when it is offered to them.

15. *Thou knowest that all that are in Asia have forsaken me.* Those apostasies which he mentions might have shaken the hearts of many, and given rise, at the same time, to many suspicions; as we commonly look at everything in the worst light. Paul meets scandals of this kind with courage and heroism, that all good men may learn to abhor the treachery of those who had thus deserted the servant of Christ, when he alone, at the peril of his life, was upholding the common cause; and that they may not on that account give way,

---

[1] "Seeing that God hath taken up his abode in us, and wishes that we may be his temples, and dwells in those temples by his Holy Spirit, are we afraid that he will not give us power to persevere till the end, that he will not keep us in certain possession of the benefits which we have received from his hand? True, the devil will labour to deprive us of it; but, as our souls will not be a prey to him, because our Lord Jesus Christ has taken them under his protection, having been committed to him by God the Father; so nothing that God has appointed for our salvation will be a prey to Satan. And why? Because we have the Spirit to defend us against all his efforts. And where is that Spirit? We must not go to seek him above the clouds. It is true that he fills the whole earth, and that his majesty dwells above the heavens; but if we feel that he dwells in us, since he has been pleased to exercise his power on such poor creatures as we are, let us know that that power will be sufficient for defending us against the assaults of Satan; that is, provided that we, on our part, are not negligent. For we must not flatter ourselves in our sins, so as to be careless, but must pray to God, committing everything to him, and hoping that he will always strengthen us more and more. And because he has begun to make us ministers of his grace, let us know that he will continue, and in such a way that our salvation and that of our neighbour's shall always be carried forward more and more to his glory."—*Fr. Ser.*

when they learn that Paul is not left destitute of divine assistance.

*Of whom are Phygellus and Hermogenes.* He names two of them, who were probably more celebrated than the rest, that he may shut the door against their slanders; for it is customary with revolters and deserters from the Christian warfare,[1] in order to excuse their own baseness, to forge as many accusations as they can against the good and faithful ministers of the gospel. "Phygellus and Hermogenes," knowing that their cowardice was justly reckoned infamous by believers, and that they were even condemned as guilty of base treachery, would not have hesitated to load Paul with false accusations, and impudently to attack his innocence. Paul, therefore, in order to take away all credit from their lies, brands them with the mark which they deserve.

Thus also, in the present day, there are many who, because they are not here admitted into the ministry, or are stripped of the honour on account of their wickedness,[2] or because we do not choose to support them while they do nothing, or because they have committed theft or fornication, are compelled to fly, and forthwith wander through France and other countries, and, by throwing upon us all the accusations[3] that they can, borrow from them an attestation of their innocence. And some brethren are so silly as to accuse us of cruelty, if any of us paints such persons in their true colours. But it were to be wished that all of them had their forehead marked with a hot iron, that they might be recognised at first sight.

16. *May the Lord grant mercy.* From this prayer we infer, that the good offices done to the saints are not thrown away, even though they cannot recompense them; for, when he prays to God to reward them, this carries in it the force of a promise. At the same time, Paul testifies his gratitude,

[1] "Car c'est la coustume des apostats, et de ceux qui laissent la vocation de Christ." "For it is customary with apostates, and with those who forsake the calling of Christ."

[2] "Pource qu'on les en depose a cause de leur meschancete et vie scandaleuse." "Because they are deposed on account of their wickedness and scandalous life."

[3] "Tous les blasphemes et accusations qu'ils peuvent." "All the blasphemies and accusations that they can."

by desiring that God will grant the remuneration, because he is unable to pay. What if he had possessed abundant means of remuneration ? Undoubtedly he would have manifested that he was not ungrateful.

*To the family of Onesiphorus, for he often refreshed me.* It is worthy of attention, that, although he praises the kindness of *Onesiphorus* alone, yet, on his account, he prays for mercy to the whole *family.* Hence we infer, that "the blessing of God rests, not only on the head of the righteous man," but on all his house. So great is the love of God toward his people, that it diffuses itself over all who are connected with them.

*And was not ashamed of my chain.* This is a proof, not only of his liberality, but likewise of his zeal ; seeing that he cheerfully exposed himself to danger and to the reproach of men, in order to assist Paul.

18. *May the Lord grant to him.* Some explain it thus:— "May God grant to him that he may find mercy with Christ the Judge." And, indeed, this is somewhat more tolerable than to interpret that passage in the writings of Moses: "The Lord rained fire from the Lord," (Gen. xix. 24,) as meaning,—"The Father rained from the Son."[1] Yet it is possible that strong feeling may have prompted Paul, as often happens, to make a superfluous repetition.

*That he may find mercy with the Lord on that day.*[2] This

---

[1] See Calvin's Com. on Genesis, vol. i. p. 512, where that remarkable expression is copiously explained.—*Ed.*

[2] "No Christian can read this passage without being powerfully affected by it; for we see that Paul was, as it were, transported, when he spoke of that coming of our Lord Jesus Christ, and of the final resurrection. He does not say, "May the Lord grant that he may find favour at his coming, on the day of our redemption, when he shall appear again to judge the world!" But he says, "On that day;" as if he presented the Lord Jesus visibly, with his angels. Paul did not speak those things coldly, or like a man, but he rose above all men, that he might be able to exclaim, "That day, that day!" And where is it? True, none of those who wish to be wise in themselves will take any pains to find it; for that saying must be fulfilled,—"Eye hath not seen, ears have not heard, neither hath entered into the heart of man, what God hath prepared for them that love him." (Isa. lxiv. 4.) Let men task their powers to the utmost to know it, it will be to them a dark and mysterious thing, and they will not be able to approach to it. But when we shall embrace the promise which he hath given to us, and after having known that Christ, being risen from the dead,

prayer shews us how much richer a recompense awaits those who, without the expectation of an earthly reward, perform kind offices to the saints, than if they received it immediately from the hand of men. And what does he pray for? "That he may find mercy;" for he who hath been merciful to his neighbours will receive such mercy from God to himself. And if this promise does not powerfully animate and encourage us to the exercise of kindness, we are worse than stupid. Hence it follows, also, that when God rewards us, it is not on account of our merits or of any excellence that is in us; but that the best and most valuable reward which he bestows upon us is, when he pardons us, and shews himself to be, not a stern judge, but a kind and indulgent Father.

## CHAPTER II.

1. Thou therefore, my son, be strong in the grace that is in Christ Jesus.
2. And the things that thou hast heard of me among many witnesses, the same commit thou to faithful men, who shall be able to teach others also.
3. Thou therefore endure hardness, as a good soldier of Jesus Christ.
4. No man that warreth entangleth himself with the affairs of *this* life, that he may please him who hath chosen him to be a soldier.
5. And if a man also strive for masteries, *yet* is he not crowned, except he strive lawfully.
6. The husbandman that laboureth must be first partaker of the fruits.
7. Consider what I say; and the Lord give thee understanding in all things.

1. Tu ergo, fili mi, fortis esto in gratia, quæ est in Christo Iesu.
2. Et quæ a me audisti per multos testes, hæc commenda fidelibus hominibus, qui idonei erunt ad alios etiam docendos.
3. Tu igitur feras afflictiones, ut bonus miles Iesu Christi.
4. Nemo, qui militat, implicatur vitæ negotiis, ut imperatori placeat.
5. Quodsi quis etiam certaverit, non coronatur, nisi legitimè certaverit.
6. Laborare prius agricolam oportet, quam fructus percipiat.
7. Intellige quæ dico; det enim tibi Dominus intellectum in omnibus.

1. *Be strong in the grace.* As he had formerly commanded him to keep, by the Spirit, that which was committed to

displayed his power, not for his own sake, but to gather together all his members, and to unite them to himself, then shall we be able truly to say, That day."—*Fr. Ser.*

him, so now he likewise enjoins him "to be strengthened in grace." By this expression he intends to shake off sloth and indifference; for the flesh is so sluggish, that even those who are endued with eminent gifts are found to slacken in the midst of their course, if they be not frequently aroused.

Some will say: "Of what use is it to exhort a man to 'be strong in grace,' unless free-will have something to do in co-operation?" I reply, what God demands from us by his word he likewise bestows by his Spirit, so that we are strengthened in the grace which he has given to us. And yet the exhortations are not superfluous, because the Spirit of God, teaching us inwardly, causes that they shall not sound in our ears fruitlessly and to no purpose. Whoever, therefore, shall acknowledge that the present exhortation could not have been fruitful without the secret power of the Spirit, will never support free-will by means of it.

*Which is in Christ Jesus.* This is added for two reasons; to shew that the grace comes from Christ alone, and from no other, and that no Christian will be destitute of it; for, since there is one Christ common to all, it follows that all are partakers of his grace, which is said to be in Christ, because all who belong to Christ must have it.

*My son.* This kind appellation, which he employs, tends much to gain the affections, that the doctrine may more effectually obtain admission into the heart.

2. *And which thou hast heard from me.* He again shews how earnestly desirous he is to transmit sound doctrine to posterity; and he exhorts Timothy, not only to preserve its shape and features, (as he formerly did,) but likewise to hand it down to godly teachers, that, being widely spread, it may take root in the hearts of many; for he saw that it would quickly perish if it were not soon scattered by the ministry of many persons. And, indeed, we see what Satan did, not long after the death of the Apostles; for, just as if preaching had been buried for some centuries, he brought in innumerable reveries, which, by their monstrous absurdity, surpassed the superstitions of all the heathens. We need not wonder, therefore, if Paul, in order to guard against an evil of such a nature and of such magnitude, earnestly desires that

his doctrines shall be committed to all godly ministers, who shall be qualified to teach it. As if he had said,—" See that after my death there may remain a sure attestation of my doctrine; and this will be, if thou not only teach faithfully what thou hast learned from me, but take care that it be more widely published by others; therefore, whomsoever thou shalt see fitted for that work, commit to their trust this treasure."

*Commit to believing men.* He calls them *believing men*, not on account of their faith, which is common to all Christians, but on account of their pre-eminence, as possessing a large measure of faith. We might even translate it "*faithful* men;"[1] for there are few who sincerely labour to preserve and perpetuate the remembrance of the doctrine intrusted to them. Some are impelled by ambition, and that of various kinds, some by covetousness, some by malice, and others are kept back by the fear of dangers; and therefore extraordinary faithfulness is here demanded.

*By many witnesses*[2] He does not mean that he produced witnesses in a formal and direct manner[3] in the case of Timothy; but, because some might raise a controversy whether that which Timothy taught had proceeded from Paul, or had been forged by himself, he removes all doubt by this argument, that he did not speak secretly in a corner, but that there were many alive who could testify that Timothy spoke nothing which they had not formerly heard from the mouth of Paul. The doctrine of Timothy would therefore be beyond suspicion, seeing that they had many fellow-disciples, who could bear testimony to it. Hence we learn how greatly a servant of Christ should labour to maintain and defend the purity of doctrine, and not only while he lives, but as long as his care and labour can extend it.

3. *Do thou therefore endure afflictions.* Not without strong necessity has he added this second exhortation; for

[1] "Loyaux et digne auxquels on se fie." "Faithful and trustworthy."
[2] "Entre plusieurs temoins, ou, en presence de plusieurs temoins." "Among many witnesses, or, in presence of many witnesses."
[3] "Il ne veut pas dire qu'il ait appelé des tesmoins, comme c'est la coustume es contrats et autres actes solennels." "He does not mean that he called witnesses, as is customary in contracts and other solemn acts."

they who offer their obedience to Christ must be prepared for "enduring afflictions;" and thus, without patient endurance of evils, there will never be perseverance. And accordingly he adds, "as becomes *a good soldier of Jesus Christ.*" By this term he means that all who serve Christ are warriors, and that their condition as warriors consists, not in inflicting evils, but rather in patience.

These are matters on which it is highly necessary for us to meditate. We see how many there are every day, that throw away their spears, who formerly made a great show of valour. Whence does this arise? Because they cannot become inured to the cross. First, they are so effeminate that they shrink from warfare. Next, they do not know any other way of fighting than to contend haughtily and fiercely with their adversaries; and they cannot bear to learn what it is to "possess their souls in patience." (Luke xxi. 19.)

4. *No man who warreth.* He continues to make use of the metaphor which he had borrowed from warfare. Yet, strictly speaking, he formerly called Timothy "a soldier of Christ" metaphorically; but now he compares profane warfare with spiritual and Christian warfare in this sense. "The condition of military discipline is such, that as soon as a soldier has enrolled himself under a general, he leaves his house and all his affairs, and thinks of nothing but war; and in like manner, in order that we may be wholly devoted to Christ, we must be free from all the entanglements of this world."

*With the affairs of life.* By "the affairs of life"[1] he means the care of governing his family, and ordinary occupations; as farmers leave their agriculture, and merchants their ships and merchandise, till they have completed the time that they agreed to serve in war. We must now apply the comparison to the present subject, that every one who wishes to fight under Christ must relinquish all the hindrances and

---

[1] "By τοῦ βίου πραγματίαις is meant the business of life in general, the plural being used with allusion to the various kinds thereof, as agriculture, trade, manufactures, &c. Now, by the Roman law, soldiers were excluded from *all* such. See Grotius."—*Bloomfield.*

employments of the world, and devote himself unreservedly to the warfare. In short, let us remember the old proverb, *Hoc age*,[1] which means, that in the worship of God, we ought to give such earnestness of attention that nothing else should occupy our thoughts and feelings. The old translation has, " No man that fights for God," &c. But this utterly destroys Paul's meaning.

Here Paul speaks to the pastors of the Church in the person of Timothy. The statement is general, but is specially adapted to the ministers of the word. First, let them see what things are inconsistent with their office, that, freed from those things, they may follow Christ. Next, let them see, each for himself, what it is that draws them away from Christ ; that this heavenly General may not have less authority over us than that which a mortal man claims for himself over heathen soldiers who have enrolled under him.

5. *And if any one strive.* He now speaks of perseverance, that no man may think that he has done enough when he has been engaged in one or two conflicts. He borrows a comparison from wrestlers, not one of whom obtains the prize till he has been victorious in the end. Thus he says : " In a race all run, but one obtaineth the prize ; run so that ye may obtain." (1 Cor. ix. 24.) If any man, therefore, wearied with the conflict, immediately withdraw from the arena to enjoy repose, he will be condemned for indolence instead of being crowned. Thus, because Christ wishes us to strive during our whole life, he who gives way in the middle of the course deprives himself of honour, even though he may have begun valiantly. To *strive lawfully* is to pursue the contest in such a manner and to such an extent as the law requires, that none may leave off before the time appointed.

[1] " Brief, qu'il nous souvienne du proverbe ancien duquel les Latins ont usé en faisant leurs sacrifices, *Hoc age*, c'est a dire, Fay ceci, ou, Pense a ceci, ascavoir que tu as entre mains ; lequel signifie, que quand il est question du service de Dieu, il s'y faut tellement employer, que nous ne soyons ententifs ni affectionnez ailleurs." " In short, let us remember the old proverb which the Latins used in offering their sacrifices, *Hoc age*, that is to say, ' Do this,' or, ' Think of this,' ' Do (or think of) what thou hast in hand;' which means, that when the worship of God is the matter in question, we must be employed in it in such a manner that we shall not give our attention or our heart to anything else."

6. *The husbandman must labour before he receive the fruits.* I am well aware that others render this passage differently; and I acknowledge that they translate, word for word, what Paul has written in Greek; but he who shall carefully examine the context will assent to my view.[1] Besides, the use of (κοπιῶντα) *labouring* instead of (κοπιᾷν) *to labour*, is a well-known Greek idiom; for Greek writers often make use of the participle in place of the infinitive.[2]

The meaning therefore, is, that husbandmen do not gather the fruit, till they have first toiled hard in the cultivation of the soil, by sowing and by other labours. And if husbandmen do not spare their toils, that one day they may obtain fruit, and if they patiently wait for the season of harvest; how much more unreasonable will it be for us to refuse the labours which Christ enjoins upon us, while he holds out so great a reward?

7. *Understand what I say.*[3] He added this, not on account of the obscurity of the comparisons which he has set forth, but that Timothy himself might ponder, how much more excellent is the warfare under the direction of Christ, and how much more abundant the reward; for, when we have studied it incessantly, we scarcely arrive at a full knowledge of it.

[1] "Je scay bien que les autres ont traduit ce passage autrement: Il faut que le laboureur travaillant (ou, qui travaille) prene premier des fruits." "I am well aware that others translate this passage differently: The husbandman labouring (or, who laboureth) must first partake of the fruits."

[2] "The agonistic metaphor now passes into an agricultural one, (such as we find at 1 Cor. ix. 10; James v. 7.) The sense, however, will depend upon what πρῶτον is to be referred to. It is most naturally connected with μεταλαμβάνειν, and such is the construction adopted by the generality of Expositors, ancient and modern. The sense, however, thus arising, either involves what is inconsistent with facts, or (even when helped out by the harsh ellipsis of ἵνα κοπιᾷ, 'in order that he may be enabled to labour,') contains a truth here inapposite; and the *spiritual* application thence deduced is forced and frigid. It is not, however, necessary, with some, to resort to conjecture. We have only to suppose, what is common in his writings, a somewhat harsh transposition, and (with many of the best Expositors) to join πρῶτον with κοπιῶντα, as is required by the course of the argument; the true construction being this:—δεῖ τὸν γεωργὸν πρῶτον κοπιῶντα τῶν καρπῶν μεταλαμβάνειν, where κοπιῶντα is the participle imperfect, and the literal sense is,—It is necessary that the husbandman should first labour, and then enjoy the fruits (of his labour.)"—*Bloomfield.*

[3] "Enten ce que je di, ou, Considere." "Understand what I say, or, Consider what I say."

*The Lord give thee understanding in all things.* The prayer, which now follows, is added by way of correction. Because our minds do not easily rise to that "incorruptible crown" (1 Cor. ix. 25) of the life to come,[1] Paul betakes himself to God, to "give understanding" to Timothy. And hence we infer, that not less are we taught in vain, if the Lord do not open our understandings, than the commandments would be given in vain, if he did not impart strength to perform them. For who could have taught better than Paul? And yet, in order that he may teach with any advantage, he prays that God may train his disciple.

| | |
|---|---|
| 8. Remember that Jesus Christ, of the seed of David, was raised from the dead, according to my gospel: | 8. Memento Iesum Christum excitatum a mortuis, ex semine David, secundum evangelium meum, |
| 9. Wherein I suffer trouble, as an evil-doer, *even* unto bonds; but the word of God is not bound. | 9. In quo laboro usque ad vincula, tanquam maleficus; sed sermo Dei non est vinctus. |
| 10. Therefore I endure all things for the elect's sakes, that they may also obtain the salvation which is in Christ Jesus with eternal glory. | 10. Quamobrem omnia tolero propter electos, ut ipsi quoque salutem consequantur, quæ est in Christo Iesu, cum gloria æterna. |
| 11. *It is* a faithful saying: For if we be dead with *him*, we shall also live with *him:* | 11. Fidelis sermo: si enim commortui sumus, etiam simul cum ipso vivemus: |
| 12. If we suffer, we shall also reign with *him:* if we deny *him*, he also will deny us: | 12. Si sufferimus, etiam simul regnabimus; si negamus, ille quoque negabit nos: |
| 13. If we believe not, *yet* he abideth faithful; he cannot deny himself. | 13. Si increduli sumus, ille fidelis manet; negare se ipsum non potest. |

8. *Remember that Jesus Christ, being raised from the dead.* He expressly mentions some part of his doctrine, which he wished to go down to posterity, entire and uncorrupted. It is probable that he glances chiefly at that part about which he was most afraid; as will also appear clearly from what follows, when he comes to speak about the error of "Hymenæus and Philetus," (ver. 17;) for they denied the resurrection, of which we have a sure pledge in this confession, when they falsely said that it was already past.

How necessary this admonition of Paul was, the ancient histories shew; for Satan put forth all his strength, in order to destroy this article of our faith. There being two parts

---

[1] "De la vie eternelle." "Of eternal life."

of it, that Christ was born "of the seed of David," and that he rose from the dead; immediately after the time of the Apostles, arose Marcion, who laboured to destroy the truth of the human nature in Christ; and afterwards he was followed by the Manichæans; and even, in the present day, this plague is still spreading.

So far as relates to the resurrection, how many have been employed, and with what diversified schemes, in labouring to overthrow the hope of it! This attestation, therefore, means as much as if Paul had said, "Let no one corrupt or falsify my gospel by slanders; I have thus taught, I have thus preached, that Christ, who was born a man of the seed of David, rose from the dead."

*According to my gospel.* He calls it "his gospel," not that he professes to be the author but the minister of it. Now, in the resurrection of Christ we all have a sure pledge of our own resurrection. Accordingly, he who acknowledges that Christ has risen affirms that the same thing will take place with us also; for Christ did not rise for himself, but for us. The head must not be separated from his members. Besides, in the resurrection of Christ is contained the fulfilment of our redemption and salvation; for it is added, *from the dead.* Thus Christ, who was dead, arose. Why? and for what purpose? Here we must come to ourselves, and here too is manifested the power and fruit of both, namely, of his resurrection and of his death; for we must always hold by this principle, that Scripture is not wont to speak of these things coldly, and as matters of history, but makes indirect reference to the fruit.

*Of the seed of David.* This clause not only asserts the reality of human nature in Christ, but also claims for him the honour and name of the Messiah. Heretics deny that Christ was a real man, others imagine that his human nature descended from heaven, and others think that there was in him nothing more than the appearance of a man.[1] Paul exclaims, on the contrary, that he was "of the seed of David;"

---

[1] "Que seulement il y avoit en luy une apparence d'homme, et non pas une vraye nature humaine." "That there was in him only an appearance of man, and not a real human nature."

by which he undoubtedly declares that he was a real man, the son of a human being, that is, of Mary. This testimony is so express, that the more heretics labour to get rid of it, the more do they discover their own impudence. The Jews and other enemies of Christ deny that he is the person who was formerly promised; but Paul affirms that he is the son of David, and that he is descended from that family from which the Messiah ought to descend.[1]

9. *In which I am a sufferer.* This is an anticipation, for his imprisonment lessened the credit due to his gospel in the eyes of ignorant people. He, therefore, acknowledges that, as to outward appearance, he was imprisoned like a criminal; but adds, that his imprisonment did not hinder the gospel from having free course; and not only so, but that what he suffers is advantageous to the elect, because it tends to confirm them. Such is the unshaken courage of the martyrs of Christ, when the consciousness of being engaged in a good cause lifts them up above the world; so that, from a lofty position, they look down with contempt, not only on bodily pains and agonies, but on every kind of disgrace.

Moreover, all godly persons ought to strengthen themselves with this consideration, when they see the ministers

[1] "If we wish to be victorious over all the temptations of Satan, we must have great steadfastness, and must know that it is not at random that we believe in Jesus Christ, that this is not a doubtful matter, but that he came to us from God to be our Redeemer. And for this reason Paul here points out that he is of the lineage of David, and of his seed; for we know the promises that are contained in the Holy Scriptures, namely, that the whole world should be blessed in the seed of Abraham. Now, God confirmed this to David, by shewing that from him the Redeemer should proceed, that is, from the tribe of Judah, and from the house of David. Thus, the reason why Paul claims for him this title is, that, having the promises which God had formerly made to the fathers, concerning that Redeemer who hath been given to us, we may not doubt that we ought to receive him with full conviction, and have no reason to doubt whether he is, or is not, the Messiah. Why? He is descended from the house of David; and, although at that time, it had no royal dignity, yet that defect could not lessen the glory of our Lord Jesus Christ, but, on the contrary, was fitted to confirm more fully our belief that it was he who should be sent. And why? The Prophet Isaiah did not say that he would be born in a palace, or that he would be brought up in great splendour; but he said, that he would grow as a small twig (Isa. xi. 1) from the root of Jesse; as if he had said, that, although Jesus Christ was of royal lineage, nevertheless his parents were poor, and were held of no account in worldly matters, having no rank or grandeur."—*Fr. Ser.*

of the gospel attacked and outraged by adversaries, that they may not, on that account, cherish less reverence for doctrine, but may give glory to God, by whose power they see it burst through all the hindrances of the world. And, indeed, if we were not excessively devoted to the flesh, this consolation alone must have been sufficient for us in the midst of persecutions, that, if we are oppressed by the cruelty of the wicked, the gospel is nevertheless extended and more widely diffused; for, whatever they may attempt, so far are they from obscuring or extinguishing the light of the gospel, that it burns the more brightly. Let us therefore bear cheerfully, or at least patiently, to have both our body and our reputation shut up in prison, provided that the truth of God breaks through those fetters, and is spread far and wide.

10. *Wherefore I endure all things for the sake of the elect.* From the effect he shews, that his imprisonment is so far from being a ground of reproach, that it is highly profitable to the elect. When he says that he endures *for the sake of the elect*,[1] this demonstrates how much more he cares for the edification of the Church than for himself; for he is prepared, not only to die, but even to be reckoned in the number of wicked men, that he may promote the salvation of the Church.

In this passage Paul teaches the same doctrine as in Col. i. 24, where he says, that he " fills up what is wanting in the sufferings of Christ, for his body, which is the Church." Hence the impudence of the Papists is abundantly refuted,

---

[1] "It might be replied, that it is superfluous that Paul should ' endure for the elect.' ' Cannot God save those whom he elected and adopted before the creation of the world, without the assistance of men? Has the immutable decree of God any need of human help, or of creatures? Why then does Paul say that he endures on account of the elect?' Now, it is true that God will conduct his people to the inheritance which is prepared for them; but yet he is pleased to make use of the labour of men. Not that he is under a necessity of borrowing anything from us, but he confers on us this honour by his undeserved goodness, and wishes that we should be instruments of his power. Thus Paul does not boast that the salvation of the children of God depends on his steadfastness or on the afflictions which he had to endure; but he only means that God wishes to conduct his people by means of the word, and that he employs men whom he has chosen for that purpose, as for his own work, and makes them instruments of the power of his Holy Spirit."—*Fr. Ser.*

who infer from these words that the death of Paul was a satisfaction for our sins; as if he claimed anything else for his death, than that it would confirm the faith of the godly, for he immediately adds an exposition, by affirming that the salvation of believers is found in Christ alone. But if any of my readers wishes to see a more extended illustration of this subject, let him consult my Commentary on the chapter which I have just now quoted—the first of the Epistle to the Colossians.

*With eternal glory.* This is the end of the salvation which we obtain in Christ; for our salvation is to live to God, which salvation begins with our regeneration, and is completed by our perfect deliverance, when God takes us away from the miseries of this mortal life, and gathers us into his kingdom. To this salvation is added the participation of heavenly, that is, divine glory; and, therefore, in order to magnify the grace of Christ, he gave to salvation the name of "eternal glory."

11. *A faithful saying.* He makes a preface to the sentiment which he is about to utter; because nothing is more opposite to the feeling of the flesh, than that we must die in order to live, and that death is the entrance into life; for we may gather from other passages, that Paul was wont to make use of a preface of this sort, in matters of great importance, or hard to be believed.

*If we die with him, we shall also live with him.* The general meaning is, that we shall not be partakers of the life and glory of Christ, unless we have previously died and been humbled with him; as he says, that all the elect were "predestinated that they might be conformed to his image." (Rom. viii. 29.) This is said both for exhorting and comforting believers. Who is not excited by this exhortation, that we ought not to be distressed on account of our afflictions, which shall have so happy a result? The same consideration abates and sweetens all that is bitter in the cross; because neither pains, nor tortures, nor reproaches, nor death ought to be received by us with horror, since in these we share with Christ; more especially seeing that all these things are the forerunners of a triumph.

By his example, therefore, Paul encourages all believers to receive joyfully, for the name of Christ, those afflictions in which they already have a taste of future glory. If this shocks our belief, and if the cross itself so overpowers and dazzles our eyes, that we do not perceive Christ in them, let us remember to present this shield, "It is a faithful saying." And, indeed, where Christ is present, we must acknowledge that life and happiness are there. We ought, therefore, to believe firmly, and to impress deeply on our hearts, this fellowship, that we do not die apart, but along with Christ, in order that we may afterwards have life in common with him; that we suffer with him, in order that we may be partakers of his glory. By *death* he means all that outward mortification of which he speaks in 2 Cor. iv. 10.[1]

12. *If we deny him, he will also deny us.* A threatening is likewise added, for the purpose of shaking off sloth; for he threatens that they who, through the dread of persecution, leave off the confession of his name, have no part or lot with Christ. How unreasonable is it, that we should esteem more highly the transitory life of this world than the holy and sacred name of the Son of God! And why should he reckon among his people those who treacherously reject him? Here the excuse of weakness is of no value;[2] for, if men did not willingly deceive themselves with vain flatteries, they would constantly resist, being endued with the spirit of strength and courage. Their base denial of Christ proceeds not only from weakness, but from unbelief; because it is in consequence of being blinded by the allurements of the world, that they do not at all perceive the life which is in the kingdom of God. But this doctrine has more need of being meditated on than of being explained; for the words of Christ are perfectly clear, "Whoever shall deny me, him will I also deny." It remains that every one consider with himself, that this is no childish terror, but the judge seriously pronounces what will be found, at the appointed time, to be true.

---

[1] The reader will do well to consider the author's Commentary on that remarkable passage.—*Ed.*

[2] "On ne gaigne rien yci de se defendre et excuser, en alleguant son infirmité." "Here nothing is gained by defending and excusing ourselves on the ground of our weakness."

13. *If we are unbelieving, he remaineth faithful.* The meaning is, that our base desertion takes nothing from the Son of God or from his glory; because, having everything in himself, he stands in no need of our confession. As if he had said, "Let them desert Christ who will, yet they take nothing from him; for when they perish, he remaineth unchanged."

*He cannot deny himself.* This is a still stronger expression. "Christ is not like us, to swerve from his truth." Hence it is evident, that all who deny Christ are disowned by him. And thus he drives away from wicked apostates the flatteries with which they soothe themselves; because, being in the habit of changing their hue, according to circumstances, they would willingly imagine that Christ, in like manner, assumes various forms, and is liable to change; which Paul affirms to be impossible. Yet, at the same time, we must firmly believe what I stated briefly on a former passage, that our faith is founded on the eternal and unchangeable truth of Christ, in order that it may not waver through the unsteadfastness or apostasy of men.

| 14. Of these things put *them* in remembrance, charging *them* before the Lord that they strive not about words to no profit, *but* to the subverting of the hearers.<br>15. Study to shew thyself approved unto God, a workman that needeth not to be ashamed, rightly dividing the word of truth.<br>16. But shun profane *and* vain babblings; for they will increase unto more ungodliness.<br>17. And their word will eat as doth a canker; of whom is Hymeneus and Philetus;<br>18. Who concerning the truth have erred, saying that the resurrection is past already; and overthrow the faith of some. | 14. Hæc admone, contestans coram Domino, ne verbis disceptent, ad nullam utilitatem, ad subversionem audientium.<br>15. Stude te ipsum probatum exhibere Deo, operarium non erubescentem, rectè secantem sermonem veritatis.<br>16 Cæterum profanas clamorum inanitates omitte; ad majorem enim proficiunt impietatem.<br>17. Et sermo eorum, ut gangræna, pastionem habebit, quorum de numero est Hymenæus et Philetus,<br>18. Qui circa veritatem aberrarunt, dicentes resurrectionem jam esse factam, et subvertunt quorundam fidem. |

14. *Remind them of these things.* The expression ($\tau a \hat{\upsilon} \tau a$) *these things,* is highly emphatic. It means that the summary of the gospel which he gave, and the exhortations which he added to it, are of so great importance, that a good

minister ought never to be weary of exhibiting them; for they are things that deserve to be continually handled, and that cannot be too frequently repeated. "They are things (he says) which I wish you not only to teach once, but to take great pains to impress on the hearts of men by frequent repetition." A good teacher ought to look at nothing else than edification, and to give his whole attention to that alone.[1] On the contrary, he enjoins him not only to abstain from useless questions, but likewise to forbid others to follow them.[2]

*Solemnly charging them before the Lord, not to dispute about words.* Λογομαχεῖν means to engage earnestly in contentious disputes, which are commonly produced by a foolish desire of being ingenious. *Solemn charging before the Lord* is intended to strike terror;[3] and from this severity we learn how dangerous to the Church is that knowledge which leads to debates, that is, which disregards piety, and tends to ostentation. Of this nature is the whole of that speculative theology, as it is called, that is found among the Papists.

*For no use.* On two grounds, λογομαχία, or "disputing about words," is condemned by him. It is of no advantage, and it is exceedingly hurtful, by disturbing weak minds. Although in the version I have followed Erasmus, because it did not disagree with Paul's meaning, yet I wish to in-

---

[1] "When any person comes to the sermon, let it not be to hear something that tickles the ears, or that gives pleasure; but let it be to make progress in the fear of God, and in humility, and to excite to prayer, and to confirm him in patience. If we have heard an exhortation to-day, and if to-morrow it is repeated to us, let us not think that this is superfluous, let us not be annoyed at it; for every person who carefully examines this subject will find it to be highly necessary for him to be reminded of the lesson which he had learned, that he may practise it well. If, therefore, God refreshes our memory with it, he has conferred on us a great favour. That is what we have to remark on this passage, when Paul says, 'Remind them of these things.' For undoubtedly he intended to prevent what we frequently meet with, when it is said, 'We have heard this before. Is not that a very common remark? Where is the little child that does not know it?' Such things are said by those who would wish to be fed with useless questions. But here the Holy Spirit desires that what is useful should be brought forward every day, because we have not sufficiently understood it, and because it must be put in practice."—*Fr. Ser.*

[2] "Mais de defendre aussi aux autres qu'ils ne s'y amusent point." "But likewise to forbid others to entertain themselves with them."

[3] "Est pour donner crainte a ceux qui voudroyent faire autrement." "Is intended to strike terror into those who would wish to act differently."

form my readers that Paul's words may be explained in this manner, "That which is useful for nothing." The Greek words are, εἰς οὐδὲν χρήσιμον, and I read χρήσιμον in the accusative case, and not in the nominative. The style will thus flow more agreeably; as if he had said, "Of what use is it, when no good comes from it, but much evil? for the faith of many is subverted."

Let us remark, first, that, when a manner of teaching does no good, for that single reason it is justly disapproved; for God does not wish to indulge our curiosity, but to instruct us in a useful manner. Away with all speculations, therefore, which produce no edification!

But the second is much worse, when questions are raised, which are not only unprofitable, but tend *to the subversion of the hearers.* I wish that this were attended to by those who are always armed for fighting with the tongue, and who, in every question are looking for grounds of quarrelling, and who go so far as to lay snares around every word or syllable. But they are carried in a wrong direction by ambition, and sometimes by an almost fatal disease; which I have experienced in some. What the Apostle says about *subverting* is shown, every day, by actual observation, to be perfectly true; for it is natural, amidst disputes, to lose sight of the truth; and Satan avails himself of quarrels as a pretence for disturbing weak persons, and overthrowing their faith.

15. *Study to shew thyself to be approved by God.* Since all disputes about doctrine arise from this source, that men are desirous to make a boast of ingenuity before the world, Paul here applies the best and most excellent remedy, when he commands Timothy to keep his eyes fixed on God; as if he had said; "Some aim at the applause of a crowded assembly, but do thou study to approve thyself and thy ministry to God." And indeed there is nothing that tends more to check a foolish eagerness for display, than to reflect that we have to deal with God.

*A workman that doth not blush.* Erasmus translates ἀνεπαίσχυντον, "that ought not to blush." I do not find fault with that rendering, but prefer to explain it actively, "that doth not blush;" both because that is the more ordinary meaning of the word as used by Greek writers, and because I consider it to agree better with the present passage. There is an implied contrast. Those who disturb the Church by contentions break out into that fierceness, because they are ashamed of being overcome, and because they reckon it disgraceful that there should be anything that they do not know. Paul, on the contrary, bids them appeal to the judgment of God.

And first, he bids them be not lazy disputants, but *workmen.* By this term he indirectly reproves the foolishness of those who so greatly torment themselves by doing nothing. Let us therefore be "workmen" in building the Church, and let us be employed in the work of God in such a manner that some fruit shall be seen; then we shall have no cause to "blush;" for, although in debating we be not equal to talkative boasters, yet it will be enough that we excel them in the desire of edification, in industry, in courage, and in the efficacy of doctrine. In short, he bids Timothy labour diligently, that he may not be ashamed before God; whereas ambitious men dread only this kind of shame, to lose nothing of their reputation for acuteness or profound knowledge.

*Dividing aright the word of truth.* This is a beautiful metaphor, and one that skilfully expresses the chief design of teaching. "Since we ought to be satisfied with the word of God alone, what purpose is served by having sermons every day, or even the office of pastors? Has not every person an opportunity of reading the Bible?"[1] But Paul assigns to

---

[1] "We shall find fanatics who think that it is a loss of time to come to the Church to be taught. 'What? Is not all the doctrine of God contained in the Bible? What more can be said on the subject?' It is making them little children (they will say) to come here to be taught; but grown people may dispense with it. What? Must there be all this preaching? There are but two points in Scripture, that we ought to love God and to love our neighbour. We have not heard these things merely from those who come to relate them; but the most distinguished scholars of those who vomited out these blasphemies have themselves declared them to us. I could name the day when it was said, and the houses, and the hour, and the people who were present, and how wicked men poured out their venom and their passion against God, to overthrow and destroy all religion, if it were possible; that is but too well known. On the contrary, Paul shews us here, that if we have only the Holy Scripture, it is not enough that each of us read it in private, but the doctrine drawn from it must be preached to us in order that we may be well informed."—*Fr. Ser*

teachers the duty of dividing or cutting,[1] as if a father, in giving food to his children, were dividing the bread, by cutting it into small pieces.

He advises Timothy to "cut aright," lest, when he is employed in cutting the surface, as unskilful people are wont to do, he leave the pith and marrow untouched. Yet by this term I understand, generally, an allotment of the word which is judicious, and which is well suited to the profit of the hearers. Some mutilate it, others tear it, others torture it, others break it in pieces, others, keeping by the outside, (as we have said,) never come to the soul of doctrine.[2] To all these faults he contrasts the "dividing aright," that is, the manner of explaining which is adapted to edification; for that is the rule by which we must try all interpretation of Scripture.

16. *But avoid profane and unmeaning noises.* My opinion as to the import of these words has been stated in my commentary on the last chapter of the First Epistle to Timothy; and my readers will find it there.[3]

*For they will grow to greater ungodliness.* That he may more effectually deter Timothy from that profane and noisy talkativeness, he states that it is a sort of labyrinth, or rather a deep whirlpool, from which they cannot go out, but into which men plunge themselves more and more.

17. *And their word will eat as a gangrene.* I have been told by Benedict Textor, a physician, that this passage is badly translated by Erasmus, who, out of two diseases quite different from each other, has made but one disease; for, instead of "gangrene," he has used the word "cancer." Now Galen, in many passages throughout his writings, and especially where he lays down definitions in his small work "On unnatural swellings," distinguishes the one from the other. Paul Aegineta, too, on the authority of Galen, thus in his sixth book defines a "cancer;" that it is "an unequal swelling, with inflated extremities, loathsome to the sight, of a leaden colour, and unaccompanied by pain." Next, he enumerates two kinds, as other physicians do; for he says that

---

[1] "De couper et tailler." "Of cutting and carving."
[2] "A l'ame de la doctrine."         [3] See p. 173.

some "cancers" are concealed and have no ulcer; while others, in which there is a preponderance of the black bile from which they originate, are ulcerous.

Of the "gangrene," on the other hand, Galen, both in the small work already quoted, and in his second book to Glauco, Aëtius in his fourteenth book, and the same Ægineta in his fourth book, speak to the following effect; that it proceeds from great phlegmons or inflammations, if they fall violently on any member, so that the part which is destitute of heat and vital energy tends to destruction. If that part be quite dead, the Greek writers call the disease σφάκελος, the Latins *sideratio,* and the common people call it St. Anthony's fire.

I find, indeed, that Cornelius Celsus draws the distinction in this manner, that "cancer" is the genus, and "gangrene" the species; but his mistake is plainly refuted from numerous passages in the works of physicians of high authority. It is possible, also, that he was led astray by the similarity between the Latin words "cancer" and "gangræna." But in the Greek words there can be no mistake of that kind; for κάρκινος is the name which corresponds to the Latin word "cancer," and denotes both the animal which we call a crab, and the disease; while grammarians think that γάγγραινα is derived ἀπο τοῦ γραίνειν, which means "to eat." We must therefore abide by the word "gangrene," which Paul uses, and which best agrees with what he says as to "eating" or "consuming."

We have now explained the etymology; but all physicians pronounce the nature of the disease to be such, that, if it be not very speedily counteracted, it spreads to the adjoining parts, and penetrates even to the bones, and does not cease to consume, till it has killed the man. Since, therefore, "gangrene" is immediately followed by (νέκρωσις) mortification, which rapidly infects the rest of the members till it end in the universal destruction of the body; to this mortal contagion Paul elegantly compares false doctrines; for, if you once give entrance to them, they spread till they have completed the destruction of the Church. The contagion being so destructive, we must meet it early, and not wait till it has gathered strength by progress ; for there will then be no time for rendering assistance. The dreadful extinction of the gospel among the Papists arose from this cause, that, through the ignorance or slothfulness of the pastors, corruptions prevailed long and without control, in consequence of which the purity of doctrine was gradually destroyed.

*Of the number of whom are Hymenæus and Philetus.* He points out with the finger the plagues themselves, that all may be on their guard against them ; for, if those persons who aim at the ruin of the whole Church are permitted by us to remain concealed, then to some extent we give them power to do injury. It is true that we ought to conceal the faults of brethren, but only those faults the contagion of which is not widely spread. But where there is danger to many, our dissimulation is cruel, if we do not expose in proper time the hidden evil. And why ? Is it proper, for the sake of sparing one individual, that a hundred or a thousand persons shall perish through my silence ? Besides, Paul did not intend to convey this information to Timothy alone, but he intended to proclaim to all ages and to all nations the wickedness of the two men, in order to shut the door against their base and ruinous doctrine.

18. *Who, concerning the truth have erred, saying that the resurrection is already past.* After having said that they had departed from " the truth," he specifies their error, which consisted in this, that they gave out that " the resurrection was already past." In doing this, they undoubtedly contrived a sort of allegorical resurrection, which has also been attempted in this age by some filthy dogs. By this trick Satan overthrows that fundamental article of our faith concerning the resurrection of the flesh. Being an old and worthless dream, and being so severely condemned by Paul, it ought to give us the less uneasiness. But when we learn that, from the very beginning of the gospel, *the faith of some was subverted,* such an example ought to excite us to diligence, that we may seize an early opportunity of driving away from ourselves and others so dangerous a plague ; for, in consequence of the strong inclination of men to vanity,

there is no absurdity so monstrous that there shall not be some men who shall lend their ear to it.

19. Nevertheless the foundation of God standeth sure, having this seal, The Lord knoweth them that are his. And, Let every one that nameth the name of Christ depart from iniquity.
20. But in a great house there are not only vessels of gold and of silver, but also of wood and of earth; and some to honour, and some to dishonour.
21. If a man therefore purge himself from these, he shall be a vessel unto honour, sanctified, and meet for the master's use, *and* prepared unto every good work.

19. Firmum tamen fundamentum Dei stat, habens sigillum hoc, Novit Dominus, qui sint sui; et, Discedat ab injustitia, quicunque invocat nomen Christi.
20. In magna quidem domo non solum sunt vasa aurea et argentea, sed etiam lignea et fictilia, et alia quidem in honorem, alia in contumeliam.
21. Si quis ergo expurgaverit se ipsum ab his, erit vas in honorem sanctificatum, et utile Domino ad omne opus bonum comparatum.

19. *Nevertheless the foundation of God standeth firm.* We know too well, by experience, how much scandal is produced by the apostasy of those who at one time professed the same faith with ourselves. This is especially the case with those who were extensively known, and who had a more brilliant reputation than others; for, if any of the common people apostatize, we are not so deeply affected by it. But they who in the ordinary opinion of men held a distinguished rank, having been formerly regarded as pillars, cannot fall in this manner, without involving others in the same ruin with themselves; at least, if their faith has no other support. This is the subject which Paul has now in hand; for he declares that there is no reason why believers should lose heart, although they see those persons fall, whom they were wont to reckon the strongest.

He makes use of this consolation, that the levity or treachery of men cannot hinder God from preserving his Church to the last. And first he reminds us of the election of God, which he metaphorically calls a *foundation*, expressing by this word the firm and enduring constancy of it. Yet all this tends to prove the certainty of our salvation, if we are of the elect of God. As if he had said, "The elect do not depend on changing events, but rest on a solid and immovable foundation; because their salvation is in the hand of God." For as "every plant which the heavenly

Father hath not planted must be rooted up," (Matt. xv. 13,) so a root, which has been fixed by his hand, is not liable to be injured by any winds or storms.

First of all, therefore, let us hold this principle, that, amidst so great weakness of our flesh, the elect are nevertheless beyond the reach of danger, because they do not stand by their own strength, but are founded on God. And if foundations laid by the hand of men have so much firmness, how much more solid will be that which has been laid by God himself? I am aware that some refer this to doctrine, "Let no man judge of the truth of it from the unsteadfastness of men;" but it may easily be inferred from the context, that Paul speaks of the Church of God, or of the elect.

*Having this seal.* The word *signaculum* (which denotes either "a seal" or "the print of a seal") having led into a mistake some people who thought that it was intended to denote a mark or impress, I have translated it *sigillum*, (a seal,) which is less ambiguous. And, indeed, Paul means, that under the secret guardianship of God, as a signet, is contained the salvation of the elect, as Scripture testifies that they are "written in the book of life." (Ps. lxix. 28; Philip. iv. 3.)

*The Lord knoweth who are his.* This clause, together with the word *seal*, reminds us, that we must not judge, by our own opinion, whether the number of the elect is great or small; for what God hath sealed he wishes to be, in some respect, shut up from us. Besides, if it is the prerogative of God to *know who are his*, we need not wonder if a great number of them are often unknown to us, or even if we fall into mistakes in making the selection.

Yet we ought always to observe why and for what purpose he makes mention of a *seal;* that is, when we see such occurrences, let us instantly call to remembrance what we are taught by the Apostle John, that "they who went out from us were not of us." (1 John ii. 19.) Hence arises a twofold advantage. First, our faith will not be shaken, as if it depended on men; nor shall we be even dismayed, as often happens, when unexpected events take place. Secondly, being convinced that the Church shall nevertheless be safe, we shall more patiently endure that the reprobate go away into their own lot, to which they were appointed; because there will remain the full number, with which God is satisfied. Therefore, whenever any sudden change happens among men, contrary to our opinion and expectation, let us immediately call to remembrance, " The Lord knoweth who are his."

*Let every one that calleth on the name of Christ depart from iniquity.* As he formerly met the scandal by saying, " Let not the revolt of any man produce excessive alarm in believers;" so now, by holding out this example of hypocrites, he shews that we must not sport with God by a feigned profession of Christianity. As if he had said, " Since God thus punishes hypocrites by exposing their wickedness, let us learn to fear him with a sincere conscience, lest anything of that kind should happen to us. Whoever, therefore, calleth upon God, that is, professeth to be, and wisheth to be reckoned, one of the people of God, let him keep at a distance from all iniquity."[1] For to "call on the name of Christ" means here to glory in Christ's honourable title, and to boast of belonging to his flock; in the same manner as to have " the name of a man called on a woman" (Isa. iv. 1) means that the woman is accounted to be his lawful wife; and to have " the name of Jacob called on" all his posterity (Gen. xlviii. 16)

[1] " Let us not therefore be distressed by all the scandals that may arise. And yet let us study to walk in fear, not abusing the goodness of our God, but knowing that, since he hath separated us from the rest of the world, we must live as being in his house and as being his, in the same manner as he hath given to us the outward mark of baptism, that we may also have the signature of his Holy Spirit; for he is ' the earnest,' as Paul calls him, of our election, he is the pledge which we possess that we are called to the heavenly inheritance. Let us therefore pray to God that he may sign and seal in our hearts his gracious election, by his Holy Spirit, and, at the same time, that he may keep us sealed and as shut up under the shadow of his wings; and if poor reprobates go astray and are lost, and if the devil drives them along, and if they do not rise again when they fall, but are cast down and ruined, let us, on our part, pray to God to keep us under his protection, that we may know what it is to obey his will, and to be supported by him. Though the world strive to shake us, let us lean on this foundation, that the Lord knoweth who are his; and let us never be drawn aside from this, but let us persevere and profit more and more, till God withdraw us from the present state into his kingdom, which is not liable to change."—*Fr. Ser.*

means that the name of the family shall be kept up in uninterrupted succession, because the race is descended from Jacob.

20. *In a great house.* He now goes farther, and demonstrates by a comparison, that, when we see some who, for a time, made a show of distinguished piety and zeal, fall back shamefully, so far from being troubled on account of it, we ought rather to acknowledge that this arrangement is seemly and adapted to the providence of God. Who will find fault with a large house, in which there is abundance of every kind of furniture, and which accordingly contains not only those articles which are fitted for purposes of display, but likewise those which are of a meaner sort? This diversity is even ornamental, if, while the side-board and the table glitter with gold and silver, the kitchen is furnished with vessels of wood and of earthenware. Why then should we wonder if God, the head of the family, so rich and so abundantly supplied with everything, has in this world, as in a large house, various kinds of men, as so many parts of furniture?

Commentators are not agreed, however, whether the "great house" means the Church alone, or the whole world. And, indeed, the context rather leads us to understand it as denoting the Church; for Paul is not now reasoning about strangers, but about God's own family. Yet what he says is true generally, and in another passage the same Apostle extends it to the whole world; that is, at Rom. ix. 21, where he includes all the reprobate under the same word that is here used. We need not greatly dispute, therefore, if any person shall apply it simply to the world. Yet there can be no doubt that Paul's object is to shew that we ought not to think it strange, that bad men are mixed with the good, which happens chiefly in the Church.

21. *If any man shall cleanse himself from these.* If the reprobate are "vessels for dishonour," they have that dishonour confined to themselves, but they do not disfigure the house, or bring any disgrace on the head of the family, who, while he has a variety of articles of furniture, appropriates each vessel to its proper use. But let us learn, by their

example, to apply them to better and worthier uses; for in the reprobate, as in mirrors, we perceive how detestable is the condition of man, if he do not sincerely promote the glory of God. Such examples, therefore, afford to us good ground for exhortation to devote ourselves to a holy and blameless life.

There are many who misapply this passage, for the sake of proving that what Paul elsewhere (Rom. ix. 16) declares to belong "to God that sheweth mercy," is actually within the power of "him that willeth and him that runneth." This is exceedingly frivolous; for Paul does not here argue about the election of men, in order to shew what is the cause of it, as he does in the ninth chapter of the Epistle to the Romans; but only means that we are unlike wicked men, whom we perceive to have been born to their perdition. It is consequently foolish to draw an inference from these words, about the question whether it is in a man's power to place himself in the number of the children of God, and to be the author of his own adoption. That is not the present question. Let this short warning suffice against those who bid a man cause himself to be predestinated; as if Paul enjoined men to do what they must have done before they were born, and even before the foundations of the world were laid.

Others, who infer from these words that free-will is sufficient for preparing a man, that he may be fit and qualified for obeying God, do not at first sight appear to be so absurd as the former; yet there is no solidity in what they advance. The Apostle enjoins that men who desire to consecrate themselves to the Lord cleanse themselves from the pollution of wicked men; and throughout the Scriptures God gives the same injunction; for we find nothing here but what we have seen in many passages of Paul's writings, and especially in the Second Epistle to the Corinthians, "Be ye clean, that bear the vessels of the Lord."[1] Beyond all controversy, we are called to holiness. But the question about the calling

---

[1] This quotation is taken from Isa. lii. 11, but the passage to which our author, quoting from memory, makes reference, is 2 Cor. vi. 17, where the words of Isaiah have undergone considerable variation. See CALVIN's Com. on Corinthians, vol. ii. p. 261.—*Ed.*

and duty of Christians is totally different from the question about their power or ability. We do not deny that it is demanded from believers that they purify themselves; but elsewhere the Lord declares that this is their duty, while he promises by Ezekiel that he will send " clean waters, that we may be cleansed." (Ezek. xxxvi. 25.) Wherefore we ought to supplicate the Lord to cleanse us, instead of vainly trying our strength in this matter without his assistance.

*A vessel sanctified for honour* means, set apart for honourable and magnificent purposes. In like manner, what is *useful* to the head of the family is put for that which is applied to agreeable purposes. He afterwards explains the metaphor, when he adds, that we must be *prepared for every good work.* Away with the wild language of fanatics, " I will contribute to the glory of God, as Pharaoh did; for is it not all one, provided that God be glorified ?" For here God explicitly states in what manner he wishes us to serve him, that is, by a religious and holy life.

| | |
|---|---|
| 22. Flee also youthful lusts: but follow righteousness, faith, charity, peace, with them that call on the Lord out of a pure heart. | 22. Juveniles cupiditates fuge; sequere autem justitiam, fidem, dilectionem, pacem cum omnibus invocantibus Dominum ex puro corde. |
| 23. But foolish and unlearned questions avoid, knowing that they do gender strifes. | 23. Stultas verò et ineruditas quæstiones vita, sciens quòd generant pugnas. |
| 24. And the servant of the Lord must not strive; but be gentle unto all *men*, apt to teach, patient; | 24. Atqui servum Domini non oportet pugnare; sed placidum esse erga omnes, propensum ad docendum, tolerantem malorum, |
| 25. In meekness instructing those that oppose themselves; if God peradventure will give them repentance to the acknowledging of the truth; | 25. Cum mansuetudine erudientem (*vel, castigantem*) eos qui obsistunt, si quando det illis Deus pœnitentiam in agnitionem veritatis, |
| 26. And *that* they may recover themselves out of the snare of the devil, who are taken captive by him at his will. | 26. Et excitationem (*vel, reditum ad sanam mentem*) a laqueo diaboli, a quo capti tenentur ad ipsius voluntatem. |

22. *Flee youthful desires.* This is an inference from what goes before; for, after mentioning useless questions, and having been led by this circumstance to censure Hymenæus and Philetus, whose ambition and vain curiosity had led them away from the right faith, he again exhorts Timothy to keep at a distance from so dangerous a plague. And for this purpose he advises him to avoid " youthful desires."

By this term he does not mean either a propensity to uncleanness, or any of those licentious courses or sinful lusts in which young men frequently indulge, but any impetuous passions to which the excessive warmth of that age is prone. If some debate has arisen, young men more quickly grow warm, are more easily irritated, more frequently blunder through want of experience, and rush forward with greater confidence and rashness, than men of riper age. With good reason, therefore, does Paul advise Timothy, being a young man, to be strictly on his guard against the vices of youth, which otherwise might easily drive him to useless disputes.

*But follow righteousness.* He recommends the opposite feelings, that they may restrain his mind from breaking out into any youthful excesses; as if he had said, "These are the things to which thou oughtest to give thy whole attention, and thy whole exertions." And first he mentions *righteousness*, that is, the right way of living; and afterwards he adds *faith* and *love,* in which it principally consists. *Peace* is closely connected with the present subject; for they who delight in the questions which he forbids must be contentious and fond of debating.

*With all that call on the Lord.* Here, by a figure of speech, in which a part is taken for the whole, "calling on God" is taken generally for worship, if it be not thought preferable to refer it to profession. But this is the chief part of the worship of God, and for that reason "calling on God" often signifies the whole of religion or the worship of God. But when he bids him seek "peace with all that call upon the Lord," it is doubtful whether, on the one hand, he holds out all believers as an example, as if he had said, that he ought to pursue this in common with all the true worshippers of God, or, on the other hand, he enjoins Timothy to cultivate peace with them. The latter meaning appears to be more suitable.

23. *But avoid foolish and uninstructive questions.* He calls them *foolish,* because they are *uninstructive;* that is, they contribute nothing to godliness, whatever show of acuteness they may hold out. When we are wise in a useful manner, then alone are we truly wise. This ought to be

carefully observed; for we see what foolish admiration the world entertains for silly trifles, and how eagerly it runs after them. That an ambition to please may not urge us to seek the favour of men by such display, let us always remember this remarkable testimony of Paul, that questions, which are held in high estimation, are nevertheless foolish, because they are unprofitable.

*Knowing that they beget quarrels.* Next, he expresses the evil which they commonly produce. And here he says nothing else than what we experience every day, that they give occasion for jangling and debates. And yet the greater part of men, after having received so many instructions, do not at all profit by them.

24. *But the servant of the Lord must not fight.* Paul's argument is to this effect: "The servant of God must stand aloof from contentions; but foolish questions are contentions; therefore whoever desires to be a 'servant of God,' and to be accounted such, ought to shun them." And if superfluous questions ought to be avoided on this single ground, that it is unseemly for a servant of God to fight, how impudently do they act, who have the open effrontery of claiming applause for raising incessant controversies? Let the theology of the Papists now come forth; what else will be found in it than the art of disputing and fighting? The more progress any man has made in it, the more unfit will he be for serving Christ.

*But gentle towards all,*[1] *qualified for teaching.* When he bids the servant of Christ be "gentle," he demands a virtue which is opposite to the disease of contentions. To the same purpose is what immediately follows, that he be διδακ-τικός, "qualified for teaching." There will be no room for

---

[1] "When he says, that we must be 'gentle towards all,' he means that we ought to be easy and affable in receiving all who come to be taught in the gospel; for if we do not give them access, it is like shutting the door against them, so that they shall never have it in their power to approach to God. We must, therefore, have that mildness and humanity dwelling in us, so as to be ready to receive all who wish to be instructed. And, therefore, he adds, that we must be 'qualified for teaching;' as if he had said, that those things are connected with each other, gentleness and skill in teaching. The reason is, if a man be fierce and inaccessible, it will never be possible for us to receive instruction from him. He who wishes

instruction, if he have not moderation and some equability of temper. What limit will be observed by a teacher, when he is warmed for fighting? The better a man is qualified for teaching, the more earnestly does he keep aloof from quarrels and disputes.

*Patient to the bad.*[1] The importunity of some men may sometimes produce either irritation or weariness; and for that reason he adds, " bearing with them," at the same time pointing out the reason why it is necessary; namely, because a godly teacher ought even to try whether it be possible for him to bring back to the right path obstinate and rebellious persons, which cannot be done without the exercise of gentleness.

25. *If sometime God grant to them repentance.* This expression, " If sometime," or " If perhaps," points out the difficulty of the case, as being nearly desperate or beyond hope. Paul therefore means that even towards the most unworthy we must exercise *meekness;* and although at first there be no appearance of having gained advantage, still we must make the attempt. For the same reason he mentions that " God will grant it." Since the conversion of a man is in the hand of God, who knows whether they who to-day appear to be unteachable shall be suddenly changed by the power of God, into other men? Thus, whoever shall consider that repentance is the gift and work of God, will cherish more earnest hope, and, encouraged by this confidence, will bestow more toil and exertion for the instruction of rebels. We should view it thus, that our duty is, to be employed in sowing and watering, and, while we do this, we must look for the increase from God. (1 Cor. iii. 6.) Our

to be a good teacher must conduct himself with civility, and must have some way of drawing those who come to him, so as to gain their affections; and that cannot be, unless he have that 'gentleness' of which Paul speaks. Thus we see how he intended to confirm what he had briefly stated, that a man who is quarrelsome, and addicted to disputes and contentions, is in no degree a servant of God. And why? As servants of God, must we not labour to gain poor ignorant persons? And that cannot be, unless we are mild, unless we hear patiently what they say, unless we bear with their weakness, until by little and little they are edified. If we have not that, it is like casting them off."—*Fr. Ser.*

[1] " Portant patiemment les mauvais." " Patiently bearing with the bad."

labours and exertions are thus of no advantage in themselves; and yet, through the grace of God, they are not fruitless.

*To the knowledge of the truth.* We may learn from this what is the actual repentance of those who for a time were disobedient to God; for Paul declares that it begins with " the knowledge of the truth." By this he means that the understanding of man is blinded, so long as it stands out fiercely against God and his doctrine.

26. *And deliverance from the snare of the devil.* Illumination is followed by deliverance from the bondage of the devil; for unbelievers are so intoxicated by Satan, that, being asleep, they do not perceive their distresses. On the other hand, when the Lord shines upon us by the light of his truth, he wakens us out of that deadly sleep, breaks asunder the snares by which we were bound, and, having removed all obstacles, trains us to obedience to him.

*By whom they are held captive.* A truly shocking condition, when the devil has so great power over us, that he drags us, as captive slaves, here and there at his pleasure. Yet such is the condition of all those whom the pride of their heart draws away from subjection to God. And this tyrannical dominion of Satan we see plainly, every day, in the reprobate; for they would not rush with such fury and with brutal violence into every kind of base and disgraceful crimes, if they were not drawn by the unseen power of Satan. That is what we saw at Eph. ii. 2,[1] that, Satan exerts his energy in unbelievers.

Such examples admonish us to keep ourselves carefully under the yoke of Christ, and to yield ourselves to be governed by his Holy Spirit. And yet a captivity of this nature does not excuse wicked men, so that they do not sin, because it is by the instigation of Satan that they sin; for, although their being carried along so resistlessly to that which is evil proceeds from the dominion of Satan, yet they do nothing by constraint, but are inclined with their whole heart to that to which Satan drives them. The result is, that their captivity is voluntary.

See CALVIN's Com. on Galatians and Ephesians, p. 220.—*Ed.*

## CHAPTER III.

1. This know also, that in the last days perilous times shall come:

2. For men shall be lovers of their own selves, covetous, boasters, proud, blasphemers, disobedient to parents, unthankful, unholy,

3. Without natural affection, truce-breakers, false accusers, incontinent, fierce, despisers of those that are good,

4. Traitors, heady, high-minded, lovers of pleasures more than lovers of God;

5. Having a form of godliness, but denying the power thereof: from such turn away.

6. For of this sort are they which creep into houses, and lead captive silly women laden with sins, led away with divers lusts;

7. Ever learning, and never able to come to the knowledge of the truth.

1. Illud autem scito, quòd extremis diebus instabunt tempora periculosa (*vel. gravia.*)

2. Erunt enim homines sui amantes, avari, fastuosi. superbi, maledici, parentibus immorigeri, ingrati, impii,

3. Carentes affectu, nescii fœderis, calumniatores, intemperantes, immites, negligentes bonorum,

4. Proditores, præcipites, inflati, voluptatum amantes potius quam Dei;

5. Habentes formam pietatis, quum vim ejus abnegarint; et istos aversare.

6. Ex iis enim sunt qui subintrant in familias, et captivas ducunt mulierculas oneratas peccatis, quæ ducuntur concupiscentiis variis,

7. Semper discentes, quum tamen nunquam ad cognitionem veritatis pervenire valeant.

1. *But know this.* By this prediction he intended still more to sharpen his diligence; for, when matters go on to our wish, we become more careless; but necessity urges us keenly. Paul, therefore informs him, that the Church will be subject to terrible diseases, which will require in the pastors uncommon fidelity, diligence, watchfulness, prudence, and unwearied constancy; as if he enjoined Timothy to prepare for arduous and deeply anxious contests which awaited him. And hence we learn, that, so far from giving way, or being terrified, on account of any difficulties whatsoever, we ought, on the contrary, to arouse our hearts for resistance.

*In the last days.* Under "the last days," he includes the universal condition of the Christian Church. Nor does he compare his own age with ours, but, on the contrary, informs Timothy what will be the future condition of the kingdom of Christ; for many imagined some sort of condition that would be absolutely peaceful, and free from any annoyance.[1]

[1] " Why does the holy Apostle, both here and elsewhere, speak of the

In short, he means that there will not be, even under the gospel, such a state of perfection, that all vices shall be banished, and virtues of every kind shall flourish; and that therefore the pastors of the Christian Church will have quite as much to do with wicked and ungodly men as the prophets and godly priests had in ancient times. Hence it follows, that there is no time for idleness or for repose.

2. *For men will be.* It is proper to remark, first, in what he makes the hardship of those "dangerous" or "troublesome" times to consist; not in war, nor in famine, nor in diseases, nor in any calamities or inconveniences to which the body is incident, but in the wicked and depraved actions of men. And, indeed, nothing is so distressingly painful to godly men, and to those who truly fear God, as to behold such corruptions of morals; for, as there is nothing which they value more highly than the glory of God, so they cannot but suffer grievous anguish when it is attacked or despised.

Secondly, it ought to be remarked, who are the persons of whom he speaks. They whom he briefly describes are not external enemies, who openly assail the name of Christ, but domestics, who wish to be reckoned among the members of the Church; for God wishes to try his Church to such an extent as to carry within her bosom such plagues, though she abhors to entertain them. So then, if in the present day many whom we justly abhor are mingled with us, let us learn to groan patiently under that burden, when we are informed that this is the lot of the Christian Church.

Next, it is wonderful that those persons, whom Paul pro-

---

'last days,' when he forewarns believers that they must prepare themselves, and make provision for many troubles and annoyances? It is because this fancy was so common, that matters would go much better than before; because, formerly, the prophets, when speaking of the kingdom of our Lord Jesus Christ, said that everything would be astonishingly reformed, that the world would obey God, that his majesty would be adored by the high and the low, that every mouth would sing his praise, and every knee would bow before him. In short, when we hear such promises, we think that we must be in a state of angelical holiness, now that Christ has appeared. Many concluded, in their mistaken fancy, that, since the coming of the Redeemer, nothing but the most correct virtue and modesty would ever be seen, and that everything would be so thoroughly regulated, that there would be no more vices in the world."—*Fr. Ser.*

nounces to be guilty of so many and so aggravated acts of wickedness, can keep up the appearance of piety, as he also declares. But daily experience shows that we ought not to regard this as so wonderful; for such is the amazing audacity and wickedness of hypocrites, that, even in excusing the grossest crimes, they are excessively impudent, after having once learned falsely to shelter themselves under the name of God. In ancient times, how many crimes abounded in the life of the Pharisees? And yet, as if they had been pure from every stain, they enjoyed a reputation of eminent holiness.

Even in the present day, although the lewdness of the Popish clergy is such that it stinks in the nostrils of the whole world, still, in spite of their wickedness, they do not cease to arrogate proudly to themselves all the rights and titles of saints. Accordingly, when Paul says that hypocrites, though they are chargeable with the grossest vices, nevertheless deceive under a mask of piety, this ought not to appear strange, when we have examples before our eyes. And, indeed, the world deserves to be deceived by those wicked scoundrels, when it either despises or cannot endure true holiness. Besides, Paul enumerates those vices which are not visible at first sight, and which are even the ordinary attendants of pretended holiness. Is there a hypocrite who is not proud, who is not a lover of himself, who is not a despiser of others, who is not fierce and cruel, who is not treacherous? But all these are concealed from the eyes of men.[1]

To spend time in explaining every word would be superfluous; for the words do not need exposition. Only let my readers observe that $\varphi\iota\lambda\alpha\upsilon\tau\iota\alpha$, *self-love*, which is put first, may be regarded as the source from which flow all the vices that follow afterwards. He who loveth himself claims a superiority in everything, despises all others, is cruel, indulges in covetousness, treachery, anger, rebellion against parents, neglect of what is good, and such like. As it was

---

[1] " Mais ce sont tous vices cachez, et qui n'apparoissent pas devant les yeux des hommes." " But all these are concealed vices, and do not show themselves before the eyes of men."

the design of Paul to brand false prophets with such marks, that they might be seen and known by all; it is our duty to open our eyes, that we may see those who are pointed out with the finger.

5. *From those turn away.* This exhortation sufficiently shows that Paul does not speak of a distant posterity, nor foretell what would happen many ages afterwards ; but that, by pointing out present evils, he applies to his own age what he had said about "the last times ;" for how could Timothy " turn away" from those who were not to arise till many centuries afterwards ? So then, from the very beginning of the gospel, the Church must have begun to be affected by such corruptions.

6. *Of those are they who creep into families.* You would say, that here Paul intentionally draws a lively picture of the order of monks. But without saying a single word about monks, those marks by which Paul distinguishes false and pretended teachers are sufficiently clear; creeping into houses, snares for catching silly women, mean flattery, imposing upon people by various superstitions. These marks it is proper to observe carefully, if we wish to distinguish between useless drones and faithful ministers of Christ. These former are here marked by so black a coal, that it is of no use for them to shuffle. To "creep into families" means to enter stealthily, or to seek an entrance by cunning methods.

*And lead captive silly women laden with sins.* Now, he speaks of "women" rather than men, because the former are more liable to be led astray in this manner. He says that they "are led captive," because false prophets of this sort, through various tricks, gain their ear, partly by prying curiously into all their affairs, and partly by flattery. And this is what he immediately adds, "laden with sins ;" for, if they had not been bound by the chain of a bad conscience, they would not have allowed themselves to be led away, in every possible manner, at the will of others.

*By various sinful desires.* I consider "sinful desires" to denote generally those foolish and light desires by which women, who do not seek God sincerely, and yet wish to be reckoned religious and holy, are carried away. There is no end of the methods adopted by them, when, departing from a good conscience, they are constantly assuming new masks. Chrysostom is more disposed to refer it to disgraceful and immodest desires; but, when I examine the context, I prefer the former exposition; for it immediately follows—

7. *Always learning, while yet they never can come to the knowledge of the truth.* That fluctuation between various desires, of which he now speaks, is when, having nothing solid in themselves, they are tossed about in all directions. They "learn," he says, as people do who are under the influence of curiosity, and with a restless mind, but in such a manner as never to arrive at any certainty or truth. It is ill-conducted study, and widely different from knowledge. And yet such persons think themselves prodigiously wise; but what they know is nothing, so long as they do not hold the truth, which is the foundation of all knowledge.

| | |
|---|---|
| 8. Now as Jannes and Jambres withstood Moses, so do these also resist the truth: men of corrupt minds, reprobate concerning the faith. | 8. Quemadmodum autem Iannes et Iambres restiterunt Mosi, ita et hi resistunt veritati, homines corrupti mente, reprobi circa fidem. |
| 9. But they shall proceed no further: for their folly shall be manifest unto all *men*, as theirs also was. | 9. Sed non proficient amplius; amentia enim eorum manifesta erit omnibus, sicut et illorum fuit. |
| 10. But thou hast fully known my doctrine, manner of life, purpose, faith, long-suffering, charity, patience, | 10. Tu autem assectatus es meam doctrinam, institutionem, propositum, fidem, tolerantiam, dilectionem, patientiam, |
| 11. Persecutions, afflictions, which came unto me at Antioch, at Iconium, at Lystra; what persecutions I endured: but out of *them* all the Lord delivered me. | 11. Persequutiones, afflictiones, quæ mihi acciderunt Antiochæ, Iconii, Lystris, quas, inquam, persequutiones sustinuerim; sed ex omnibus eripuit me Dominus. |
| 12. Yea, and all that will live godly in Christ Jesus shall suffer persecution. | 12. Et omnes, qui piè volunt in Christo Iesu vivere, persequutionem patientur. |

8. *And as Jannes and Jambres resisted Moses.* This comparison confirms what I have already said about the "last times;" for he means that the same thing happens to us under the gospel, which the Church experienced almost from her very commencement, or at least since the law was published. In like manner the Psalmist also speaks largely about the unceasing battles of the Church. "Often did they

fight against me from my youth, now let Israel say. The wicked ploughed upon my back, they made long their furrows." (Ps. cxxix. 1, 3.) Paul reminds us, that we need not wonder if adversaries rise up against Christ to oppose his gospel, since Moses likewise had those who contended with him; for these examples drawn from a remote antiquity yield us strong consolation.

It is generally believed, that the two who are mentioned, "Jannes and Jambres," were magicians put forward by Pharaoh. But from what source Paul learned their names is doubtful, except that it is probable, that many things relating to those histories were handed down, the memory of which God never permitted to perish. It is also possible that in Paul's time there were commentaries on the prophets that gave more fully those narratives which Moses touches very briefly. However that may be, it is not at random that he calls them by their names. The reason why there were two of them may be conjectured to have been this, that, because the Lord had raised up for his people two leaders, Moses and Aaron, Pharaoh determined to place against them the like number of magicians.

9. *But they shall not proceed further.* He encourages Timothy for the contest, by the confident hope of victory; for, although false teachers give him annoyance, he promises that they shall be, within a short time, disgracefully ruined.[1]

[1] " Thus we see, that the Holy Spirit, by the mouth of Paul, holds out two reasons to fortify us. When we see that Satan opposes, and that the truth of God is not received by all, but that there are bad men who labour to pervert everything, and who slander and falsify the truth, here are consolations provided for us. In the first place, that our Lord treats us in the same manner as he has treated the Church in all ages, that those who lived before us were not better situated in this respect; for God tried them by sending false pastors, or rather by giving free scope to Satan for sending them. Let us know what has happened since the law was published. Here is Moses, who was before the other prophets. Yet already the war was begun, and that evil has never ceased. If we must now endure the like, let us bear it with patience; for it is not reasonable to expect that our condition shall be better or easier than that of Moses, and of others who followed him. That is one argument. The second is, that the result shall be prosperous and successful. Although we dislike fighting, and though it appears as if the truth of God were about to perish utterly, let us wait till God come forth in defence of it; for he will cause wicked men to be completely disgraced. After they have triumphed, God

Yet the event does not agree with this promise; and the Apostle appears to make a totally different declaration, a little afterwards, when he says that they will grow worse and worse. Nor is there any force in the explanation given by Chrysostom, that they will grow worse every day, but will do no injury to any person; for he expressly adds, "deceived and deceiving;" and, indeed, the truth of this is proved by experience. It is more correct to say, that he looked at them in various aspects; for the affirmation, that they will not make progress, is not universal; but he only means, that the Lord will discover their madness to many whom they had, at first, deceived by their enchantments.

*For their folly shall be manifest to all.* When he says, *to all*, it is by a figure of speech, in which the whole is taken for a part. And, indeed, they who are most successful in deceiving do, at first, make great boasting, and obtain loud applause; and, in short, it appears as if nothing were beyond their power. But speedily their tricks vanish into air; for the Lord opens the eyes of many, so that they begin to see what was concealed from them for a time. Yet never is the "folly" of false prophets discovered to such an extent as to be known to all. Besides, no sooner is one error driven away than new errors continually spring up.

Both admonitions are therefore necessary. That godly teachers may not despair, as if it were in vain for them to make war against error, they must be instructed about the prosperous success which the Lord will give to his doctrine. But that they may not think, on the other hand, that they are discharged from future service, after one or two battles, they must be reminded that there will always be new occasion for fighting. But on this second point we shall speak afterwards; at present, let it suffice us, that he holds out to Timothy the sure hope of a successful issue, that he may be the more encouraged to fight. And he confirms this by the example which he had quoted; for, as the truth of God prevailed against the tricks of the magicians, so he promises that

will, undoubtedly, discover their baseness, and we shall see how God takes care to support his cause, though that may not be evident for a time."—*Fr. Ser.*

the doctrine of the gospel shall be victorious against every kind of errors that may be invented.

10. *But thou hast followed.*[1] In order to urge Timothy, he employs this argument also, that he is not an ignorant and untaught soldier, because Paul carried him through a long course of training. Nor does he speak of doctrine only; for those things which he likewise enumerates add much weight, and he gives to us, in this sentence, a very lively picture of a good teacher, as one who does not, by words only, train and instruct his disciples, but, so to speak, opens his very breast to them, that they may know, that whatever he teaches, he teaches sincerely. This is what is implied in the word *purpose.* He likewise adds other proofs of sincere and unfeigned affection, such as *faith, mildness, love, patience.* Such were the early instructions which had been imparted to Timothy in the school of Paul. Yet he does not merely bring to remembrance what he had learned from him, but bears testimony to his former life, that in this manner he may urge him to perseverance; for he praises him as an imitator of his own virtues; as if he had said, "Thou hast been long accustomed to follow my instructions; I ask nothing more than that thou shouldst go on as thou hast begun." It is his wish, however, that the example of his "faith, love, and patience" should be constantly before the eyes of Timothy; and for that reason he dwells chiefly on his persecutions, which were best known to him.

11. *But out of them all the Lord delivered me.* It is a consolation which mitigates the bitterness of afflictions, that they always have a happy and joyful end. If it be objected, that the success of which he boasts is not always visible, I acknowledge that this is true, so far as relates to the feeling of the flesh; for Paul had not yet been delivered. But when God sometimes delivers us, he testifies, in this manner, that

---

[1] " Having spoken of the troubles which were to befall the Church, and having exhorted Timothy to be firm, so as not to shrink from them, the Apostle adds, that now, for a long time, he must have been prepared for all this, because he had been taught in a good school. 'Thou hast known intimately,' like one who had followed him step by step; for such is the import of the word which Paul uses: 'Thou hast known well the course which I have pursued.' "—*Fr. Ser.*

he is present with us, and will always be present; for from the feeling, or actual knowledge, of present aid, our confidence ought to be extended to the future. The meaning, therefore, is as if he had said, " Thou hast known by experience that God hath never forsaken me, so that thou hast no right to hesitate to follow my example."

12. *And all who wish to live a godly life.*[1] Having mentioned his own persecutions, he likewise adds now, that nothing has happened to him which does not await all the godly.[2] And he says this, partly that believers may prepare themselves for submitting to this condition, and partly that good men may not view him with suspicion on account of the persecutions which he endures from wicked persons; as it frequently happens that the distresses to which men are subjected lead to unfavourable opinions concerning them; for he whom men regard with aversion is immediately declared by the common people to be hated by God.

By this general statement, therefore, Paul classes himself with the children of God, and, at the same time, exhorts all the children of God to prepare for enduring persecutions; for, if this condition is laid down for "all who wish to live a godly life in Christ," they who wish to be exempt from persecutions must necessarily renounce Christ. In vain shall we endeavour to detach Christ from his cross; for it may be said to be natural that the world should hate Christ even in his members. Now hatred is attended by cruelty, and hence arise persecutions. In short, let us know that we are Christians on this condition, that we shall be liable to many tribulations and various contests.

But it is asked, Must all men be martyrs? for it is evident that there have been many godly persons who have never suffered banishment, or imprisonment, or flight, or any kind of persecution. I reply, it is not always in one way that Satan persecutes the servants of Christ. But yet it is absolutely unavoidable that all of them shall have the world for

---

[1] " Et tous ceux aussi qui veulent vivre en la crainte de Dieu." "And all those also who wish to live in the fear of God."

[2] " Que rien ne luy est advenu que tous fideles ne doyvent aussi attendre." "That nothing has happened to him which all believers must not also look for."

their enemy in some form or other, that their faith may be tried and their steadfastness proved; for Satan, who is the continual enemy of Christ, will never suffer any one to be at peace during his whole life; and there will always be wicked men that are thorns in our sides. Moreover, as soon as zeal for God is manifested by a believer, it kindles the rage of all ungodly men; and, although they have not a drawn sword, yet they vomit out their venom, either by murmuring, or by slander, or by raising a disturbance, or by other methods. Accordingly, although they are not exposed to the same assaults, and do not engage in the same battles, yet they have a warfare in common, and shall never be wholly at peace and exempt from persecutions.

13. But evil men and seducers shall wax worse and worse, deceiving, and being deceived.

14. But continue thou in the things which thou hast learned, and hast been assured of, knowing of whom thou hast learned *them;*

15. And that from a child thou hast known the holy scriptures, which are able to make thee wise unto salvation through faith which is in Christ Jesus.

16. All scripture *is* given by inspiration of God, and *is* profitable for doctrine, for reproof, for correction, for instruction in righteousness;

17. That the man of God may be perfect, throughly furnished unto all good works.

13. Mali autem homines et impostores proficient in pejus, errantes, et mittentes in errorem.

14. Tu autem mane in iis, quæ didicisti, et quæ credita sunt tibi, sciens a quo didiceris;

15. Et quòd a pueritia Sacras litteras novisti, quæ possunt te eruditum reddere ad salutem per fidem, quæ est in Christo Iesu.

16. Omnis Scriptura divinitus inspirata est ac utilis ad doctrinam, ad redargutionem, ad correctionem, ad institutionem, quæ est in justitia.

17. Ut integer sit Dei homo, ad omne opus bonum formatus.

13. *But wicked men and impostors.* This is the most bitter of all persecutions, when we see wicked men, with their sacrilegious hardihood, with their blasphemies and errors, gathering strength. Thus Paul says elsewhere, that Ishmael persecuted Isaac, not by the sword, but by mockery. (Gal. iv. 29.) Hence also we may conclude, that, in the preceding verse, it was not merely one kind of persecution that was described, but that the Apostle spoke, in general terms, of those distresses which the children of God are compelled to endure, when they contend for the glory of their Father.

I stated, a little before, in what respect they *shall grow worse and worse;* for he foretells not only that they will make obstinate resistance, but that they will succeed in injuring and corrupting others. One worthless person will always be more effectual in destroying, than ten faithful teachers in building, though they labour with all their might. Nor are there ever wanting the tares which Satan sows for injuring the pure corn; and even when we think that false prophets are driven away, others continually spring up in other directions.

Again, as to the power of doing injury,[1] it is not because falsehood, in its own nature, is stronger than truth, or that the tricks of Satan exceed the energy of the Spirit of God; but because men, being naturally inclined to vanity and errors, embrace far more readily what agrees with their natural disposition, and also because, being blinded by a righteous vengeance of God, they are led, as captive slaves, at the will of Satan.[2] And the chief reason, why the plague of wicked doctrines is so efficacious, is, that the ingratitude of men deserves that it should be so. It is highly necessary for godly teachers to be reminded of this, that they may be prepared for uninterrupted warfare, and may not be discouraged by delay, or yield to the haughtiness and insolence of adversaries.

14. *But as for thee, continue in those things which thou hast learned.* Although wickedness prevail, and push its way forward, he advises Timothy nevertheless to stand firm. And undoubtedly this is the actual trial of faith, when we offer unwearied resistance to all the contrivances of Satan, and do not alter our course for every wind that blows, but remain steadfast on the truth of God, as on a sure anchor.

*Knowing from whom thou hast learned them.* This is said for the purpose of commending the certainty of the doctrine; for, if any one has been wrong instructed, he ought not to persevere in it. On the contrary, we ought to unlearn all that we have learned apart from Christ, if we wish to be his

---

[1] "Si on demande d'où vient ceste puissance et facilité de nuire?" "If it be asked, Whence comes this power and facility of doing injury?"

[2] "Satan les tire, d'un costé et d'autre, a son plaisir." "Satan leads them, on one side or another, at his pleasure."

disciples; as, for example, it is the commencement of our pure instruction in the faith, to reject and forget all the instruction of Popery. The Apostle therefore does not enjoin Timothy to defend indiscriminately the doctrine which has been delivered to him, but only that which he knows to be truth; by which he means, that he must make a selection.[1] Besides, he does not claim this as a private individual, that what he has taught shall be reckoned to be a divine revelation; but he boldly asserts his own authority to Timothy, who, he was aware, knew that his fidelity and his calling had been proved. And if he was fully convinced that he had been taught by an Apostle of Christ, he concluded that therefore it was not a doctrine of man, but of Christ.

This passage teaches us, that we ought to be as careful to guard against obstinacy in matters that are uncertain, (such as all the doctrines of men are,) as to hold with unshaken firmness the truth of God. Besides, we learn from it, that faith ought to be accompanied by prudence, that it may distinguish between the word of God and the word of men, so that we may not adopt at random everything that is brought forward. Nothing is more inconsistent with the nature of faith than light credulity, which allows us to embrace everything indiscriminately, whatever it may be, and from whomsoever it proceeds; because it is the chief foundation of faith, to know that it has God for its author.

*And which have been intrusted to thee.*[2] When he adds, that the doctrine had been intrusted to Timothy, this gives (αὔξησιν) additional force to the exhortation; for to "commit a thing in trust" is something more than merely to deliver it. Now Timothy had not been taught as one of the common people, but in order that he might faithfully deliver into the hands of others what he had received.

15. *And that from (thy) childhood.* This was also no ordinary addition, that he had been accustomed, from his

---

[1] " Par lequel mot il signifie qu'il est requis d'user de jugement et discretion en cest endroit." " By this word, he means that it is necessary to use judgment and discretion in that matter."

[2] " Et qui te sont commises, ou desquelles plene assurance t'a este donnee." " And which have been intrusted to thee, or of which full assurance hath been given to thee."

infancy, to the reading of the Scripture; for this long habit may make a man much more strongly fortified against every kind of deception. It was therefore a judicious caution observed in ancient times, that those who were intended for the ministry of the word should be instructed, from their infancy, in the solid doctrine of godliness, that, when they came to the performance of their office, they might not be untried apprentices. And it ought to be reckoned a remarkable instance of the kindness of God, if any person, from his earliest years, has thus acquired a knowledge of the Scriptures.

*Which are able to make thee wise unto salvation.* It is a very high commendation of the Holy Scriptures, that we must not seek anywhere else the wisdom which is sufficient for salvation; as the next verse also expresses more fully. But he states, at the same time, what we ought to seek in the Scripture; for the false prophets also make use of it as a pretext; and therefore, in order that it may be useful to us for salvation, it is necessary to understand the right use of it.

*Through faith, which is in Christ Jesus.* What if any one give his whole attention to curious questions? What if he adhere to the mere letter of the law, and do not seek Christ? What if he pervert the natural meaning by inventions that are foreign to it? For this reason he directs us to the faith of Christ as the design, and therefore as the sum, of the Scriptures; for on faith depends also what immediately follows.

16. *All Scripture;* or, *the whole of Scripture;* though it makes little difference as to the meaning. He follows out that commendation which he had glanced at briefly. First, he commends the Scripture on account of its authority; and secondly, on account of the utility which springs from it. In order to uphold the authority of the Scripture, he declares that it *is divinely inspired;* for, if it be so, it is beyond all controversy that men ought to receive it with reverence. This is a principle which distinguishes our religion from all others, that we know that God hath spoken to us, and are fully convinced that the prophets did not speak at their own

suggestion, but that, being organs of the Holy Spirit, they only uttered what they had been commissioned from heaven to declare. Whoever then wishes to profit in the Scriptures, let him, first of all, lay down this as a settled point, that the Law and the Prophets are not a doctrine delivered according to the will and pleasure of men, but dictated by the Holy Spirit.

If it be objected, " How can this be known?" I answer, both to disciples and to teachers, God is made known to be the author of it by the revelation of the same Spirit. Moses and the prophets did not utter at random what we have received from their hand, but, speaking at the suggestion of God, they boldly and fearlessly testified, what was actually true, that it was the mouth of the Lord that spake. The same Spirit, therefore, who made Moses and the prophets certain of their calling, now also testifies to our hearts, that he has employed them as his servants to instruct us. Accordingly, we need not wonder if there are many who doubt as to the Author of the Scripture ; for, although the majesty of God is displayed in it, yet none but those who have been enlightened by the Holy Spirit have eyes to perceive what ought, indeed, to have been visible to all, and yet is visible to the elect alone. This is the first clause, that we owe to the Scripture the same reverence which we owe to God ; because it has proceeded from him alone, and has nothing belonging to man mixed with it.

*And is profitable.* Now follows the second part of the commendation, that the Scripture contains a perfect rule of a good and happy life. When he says this, he means that it is corrupted by sinful abuse, when this usefulness is not sought. And thus he indirectly censures those unprincipled men who fed the people with vain speculations, as with wind. For this reason we may, in the present day, condemn all who, disregarding edification, agitate questions which, though they are ingenious, are also useless. Whenever ingenious trifles of that kind are brought forward, they must be warded off by this shield, that " Scripture is profitable." Hence it follows, that it is unlawful to treat it in an unprofitable manner ; for the Lord, when he gave us the Scriptures, did not intend either to gratify our curiosity, or to encourage ostentation, or to give occasion for chatting and talking, but to do us good; and, therefore, the right use of Scripture must always tend to what is profitable.[1]

*For instruction.* Here he enters into a detailed statement of the various and manifold advantages derived from the Scriptures. And, first of all, he mentions *instruction*, which ranks above all the rest; for it will be to no purpose that you exhort or reprove, if you have not previously instructed. But because "instruction," taken by itself, is often of little avail, he adds *reproof* and *correction*.

It would be too long to explain what we are to learn from the Scriptures; and, in the preceding verse, he has given a brief summary of them under the word *faith*. The most valuable knowledge, therefore, is " faith in Christ." Next follows instruction for regulating the life, to which are added the excitements of exhortations and reproofs. Thus he who knows how to use the Scriptures properly, is in want of nothing for salvation, or for a holy life. *Reproof* and *correction* differ little from each other, except that the latter proceeds from the former; for the beginning of repentance is the knowledge of our sinfulness, and a conviction of the judgment of God. *Instruction in righteousness* means the rule of a good and holy life.

17. *That the man of God may be perfect.* *Perfect* means here a blameless person, one in whom there is nothing defective; for he asserts absolutely, that the Scripture is sufficient for perfection. Accordingly, he who is not satisfied

[1] " Who is it that by nature will not desire his happiness and his salvation? And where could we find it but in the Holy Scripture, by which it is communicated to us? Woe to us if we will not listen to God when he speaks to us, seeing that he asks nothing but our advantage. He does not seek his own profit, for what need has he of it? We are likewise reminded not to read the Holy Scripture so as to gratify our fancies, or to draw from it useless questions. Why? Because it is profitable for salvation, says Paul. Thus, when I expound the Holy Scripture, I must be guided by this consideration, that those who hear me may receive profit from the doctrine which I teach, that they may be edified for salvation. If I have not that desire, and do not aim at the edification of those who hear me, I am a sacrilegious person, profaning the word of God. On the other hand, they who read the Scripture, or who come to the sermon to listen, if they are in search of some foolish speculation, if they come here to take their amusement, are guilty of having profaned a thing so holy."—*Fr. Ser.*

with Scripture desires to be wiser than is either proper or desirable.

But here an objection arises. Seeing that Paul speaks of the Scriptures, which is the name given to the Old Testament, how does he say that it makes a man thoroughly perfect? for, if it be so, what was afterwards added by the apostles may be thought superfluous. I reply, so far as relates to the substance, nothing has been added; for the writings of the apostles contain nothing else than a simple and natural explanation of the Law and the Prophets, together with a manifestation of the things expressed in them. This eulogium, therefore, is not inappropriately bestowed on the Scriptures by Paul; and, seeing that its instruction is now rendered more full and clear by the addition of the Gospel, what can be said but that we ought assuredly to hope that the usefulness, of which Paul speaks, will be much more displayed, if we are willing to make trial and receive it?

## CHAPTER IV.

1. I charge *thee* therefore before God, and the Lord Jesus Christ, who shall judge the quick and the dead at his appearing and his kingdom;
2. Preach the word; be instant in season, out of season; reprove, rebuke, exhort, with all long-suffering and doctrine.
3. For the time will come when they will not endure sound doctrine; but after their own lusts shall they heap to themselves teachers, having itching ears;
4. And they shall turn away *their* ears from the truth, and shall be turned unto fables.

1. Obtestor igitur ego coram Deo et Domino Iesu Christo, qui judicaturus est vivos et mortuos in apparitione sua et in regno suo:
2. Prædica sermonem, insta tempestivè, intempestivè; argue, increpa, hortare cum omni lenitate et doctrina.
3. Nam erit tempus, quum sanam doctrinam non sustinebunt; sed juxta concupiscentias suas coacervabunt sibi doctores, ut qui prurient auribus,
4. Et a veritate quidem aures avertent, ad fabulas autem convertentur.

1. *I charge thee, therefore, before God and the Lord Jesus Christ.* It is proper to observe carefully the word *therefore*, by means of which he appropriately connects Scripture with preaching. This also refutes certain fanatics, who haughtily boast that they no longer need the aid of teachers, because

the reading of Scripture is abundantly sufficient. But Paul, after having spoken of the usefulness of Scripture, infers not only that all ought to read it, but that teachers ought to administer it, which is the duty enjoined on them. Accordingly, as all our wisdom is contained in the Scriptures, and neither ought we to learn, nor teachers to draw their instructions, from any other source; so he who, neglecting the assistance of the living voice, shall satisfy himself with the silent Scripture, will find how grievous an evil it is to disregard that way of learning which has been enjoined by *God* and *Christ.* Let us remember, I say, that the reading of Scripture is recommended to us in such a manner as not to hinder, in the smallest degree, the ministry of pastors; and, therefore, let believers endeavour to profit both in reading and in hearing; for not in vain hath God ordained both of them.

Here, as in a very weighty matter, Paul adds a solemn charge, exhibiting to Timothy God as the avenger, and Christ as the judge, if he shall cease to discharge his office of teaching. And, indeed, in like manner as God showed by an inestimable pledge, when he spared not his only-begotten Son, how great is the care which he has for the Church, so he will not suffer to remain unpunished the negligence of pastors, through whom souls, which he hath redeemed at so costly a price, perish or are exposed as a prey.

*Who shall judge the living and the dead.* More especially the Apostle fixes attention on the judgment of Christ; because, as we are his representatives, so he will demand a more strict account of evil administration. By "the living and the dead" are meant those whom he shall find still alive at his coming, and likewise those who shall have died. There will therefore be none that escape his judgment.

*The appearance of Christ and his kingdom* mean the same thing; for although he now reigns in heaven and earth, yet hitherto his reign is not clearly manifested, but, on the contrary, is obscurely hidden under the cross, and is violently assailed by enemies. His kingdom will therefore be established at that time when, having vanquished his enemies, and either removed or reduced to nothing every opposing power, he shall display his majesty.

2. *Be instant in season, out of season.* By these words he recommends not only constancy, but likewise earnestness, so as to overcome all hindrances and difficulties; for, being, by nature, exceedingly effeminate or slothful, we easily yield to the slightest opposition, and sometimes we gladly seek apologies for our slothfulness. Let us now consider how many arts Satan employs to stop our course, and how slow to follow, and how soon wearied are those who are called. Consequently the gospel will not long maintain its place, if pastors do not urge it earnestly.

Moreover, this earnestness must relate both to the pastor and to the people; to the pastor, that he may not devote himself to the office of teaching merely at his own times and according to his own convenience, but that, shrinking neither from toils nor from annoyances, he may exercise his faculties to the utmost. So far as regards the people, there is constancy and earnestness, when they arouse those who are asleep, when they lay their hands on those who are hurrying in a wrong direction, and when they correct the trivial occupations of the world. To explain more fully in what respects the pastor must " be instant," the Apostle adds—

*Reprove, rebuke, exhort.* By these words he means, that we have need of many excitements to urge us to advance in the right course; for if we were as teachable as we ought to be, a minister of Christ would draw us along by the slightest expression of his will. But now, not even moderate exhortations, to say nothing of sound advices, are sufficient for shaking off our sluggishness, if there be not increased vehemence of reproofs and threatenings.

*With all gentleness and doctrine.* A very necessary exception; for reproofs either fall through their own violence, or vanish into smoke, if they do not rest on *doctrine*. Both exhortations and reproofs are merely aids to doctrine, and, therefore, have little weight without it. We see instances of this in those who have merely a large measure of zeal and bitterness, and are not furnished with solid doctrine. Such men toil very hard, utter loud cries, make a great noise, and all to no purpose, because they build without a foundation. I speak of men who, in other respects, are good, but with little learning, and excessive warmth; for they who employ all the energy that they possess in battling against sound doctrine, are far more dangerous, and do not deserve to be mentioned here at all.

In short, Paul means that reproofs are founded on doctrine, in order that they may not be justly despised as frivolous. Secondly, he means that keenness is moderated by gentleness; for nothing is more difficult than to set a limit to our zeal, when we have once become warm. Now when we are carried away by impatience, our exertions are altogether fruitless. Our harshness not only exposes us to ridicule, but also irritates the minds of the people. Besides, keen and violent men are generally unable to endure the obstinacy of those with whom they are brought into intercourse, and cannot submit to many annoyances and insults, which nevertheless must be digested, if we are desirous to be useful. Let severity be therefore mingled with this seasoning of gentleness, that it may be known to proceed from a peaceful heart.

3. *For there will be a time.*[1] From the very depravity of men he shews how careful pastors ought to be; for soon shall the gospel be extinguished, and perish from the remembrance of men, if godly teachers do not labour with all their might to defend it. But he means that we must avail ourselves of the opportunity, while there is any reverence for Christ; as if one should say that, when a storm is at hand, we must not labour remissly, but must hasten with all diligence, because there will not afterwards be an equally fit season.

*When they will not endure sound doctrine.* This means that they will not only dislike and despise, but will even hate, sound doctrine; and he calls it "sound (or healthful) doctrine," with reference to the effect produced, because it actually instructs to godliness. In the next verse he pronounces the same doctrine to be *truth,* and contrasts it with

---

[1] "Car un temps viendra." "For a time will come."

*fables*, that is, useless imaginations, by which the simplicity of the gospel is corrupted.

First, let us learn from it, that the more extraordinary the eagerness of wicked men to despise the doctrine of Christ, the more zealous should godly ministers be to defend it, and the more strenuous should be their efforts to preserve it entire; and not only so, but also by their diligence to ward off the attacks of Satan. And if ever this ought to have been done, the great ingratitude of men has now rendered it more than necessary; for they who at first receive the gospel warmly, and make a show of some kind of uncommon zeal, afterwards contract dislike, which is by and by followed by loathing; others, from the very outset, either reject it furiously, or, contemptuously lending an ear, treat it with mockery; while others, not suffering the yoke to be laid on their neck, kick at it, and, through hatred of holy discipline, are altogether estranged from Christ, and, what is worse, from being friends become open enemies. So far from this being a good reason why we should be discouraged and give way, we ought to fight against such monstrous ingratitude, and even to strive with greater earnestness than if all were gladly embracing Christ offered to them.

Secondly, having been told that men will thus despise and even reject the word of God, we ought not to stand amazed as if it were a new spectacle, when we see actually accomplished that which the Holy Spirit tells us will happen. And indeed, being by nature prone to vanity, it is no new or uncommon thing, if we lend an ear more willingly to fables than to truth.

Lastly, the doctrine of the gospel, being plain and mean in its aspect, is unsatisfactory partly to our pride, and partly to our curiosity. And how few are there who are endued with spiritual taste, so as to relish newness of life and all that relates to it! Yet Paul foretells some greater impiety of one particular age, against which he bids Timothy be early on his guard.

*Shall heap up to themselves teachers.* It is proper to observe the expression, *heap up*, by which he means that the madness of men will be so great, that they will not be satisfied with a few deceivers, but will desire to have a vast multitude ; for, as there is an unsatiable longing for those things which are unprofitable and destructive, so the world seeks, on all sides and without end, all the methods that it can contrive and imagine for destroying itself ; and the devil has always at hand a sufficiently large number of such teachers as the world desires to have. There has always been a plentiful harvest of wicked men, as there is in the present day ; and therefore Satan never has any lack of ministers to deceive men, as he never has any lack of the means of deceiving.

Indeed, this monstrous depravity, which almost constantly prevails among men, deserves that God, and his healthful doctrine, should be either rejected or despised by them, and that they should more gladly embrace falsehood. Accordingly, that false teachers frequently abound, and that they sometimes multiply like a nest of hornets, should be ascribed by us to the righteous vengeance of God. We deserve to be covered and choked by that kind of filth, seeing that the truth of God finds no place in us, or, if it has found entrance, is immediately driven from its possession ; and since we are so much addicted to fabulous notions, that we never think that we have too great a multitude of deceivers. Thus what an abomination of Monks is there in Popery ! If one godly pastor were to be supported, instead of ten Monks and as many priests, we should presently hear nothing else than complaints about the great expense.[1]

The disposition of the world is therefore such that, by "heaping up" with insatiable desire innumerable deceivers, it desires to banish all that belongs to God. Nor is there any other cause of so many errors than that men, of their own accord, choose to be deceived rather than to be properly instructed. And that is the reason why Paul adds the expression, *itching ears.*[2] When he wishes to assign a cause

[1] " Incontinent on n'orroit autre chose que plaintes de la trop grande despense."

[2] " The greater part cannot endure corrections, or threatenings, or even simple doctrine. When we denounce vices, though we do not employ violent language, they think that all is lost. Never was the world so obstinately wicked as it now is, and those who have made a profession of the

for so great an evil, he makes use of an elegant metaphor, by which he means, that the world will have ears so refined, and so excessively desirous of novelty, that it will collect for itself various instructors, and will be incessantly carried away by new inventions. The only remedy for this vice is, that believers be instructed to adhere closely to the pure doctrine of the gospel.

5. But watch thou in all things, endure afflictions, do the work of an evangelist, make full proof of thy ministry.

6. For I am now ready to be offered, and the time of my departure is at hand.

7. I have fought a good fight, I have finished *my* course, I have kept the faith:

8. Henceforth there is laid up for me a crown of righteousness, which the Lord, the righteous Judge, shall give me at that day; and not to me only, but unto all them also that love his appearing.

5. Tu verò vigila in omnibus, perfer afflictiones, opus fac Evangelistæ, ministerium tuum probatum redde.

6. Ego enim jam immolor, et tempus meæ resolutionis instat.

7. Bonum certamen certavi, cursum consummavi, fidem servavi.

8. Quod superest, reposita est mihi justitiæ corona, quam reddet mihi Dominus in illa die justus judex, nec solum mihi, sed etiam omnibus, qui diligunt adventum ejus.

5. *But watch thou in all things.* He proceeds with the former exhortation, to the effect that the more grievous the diseases are, the more earnestly Timothy may labour to cure them; and that the nearer dangers are at hand, the more diligently he may keep watch. And because the ministers of Christ, when they faithfully discharge their office, are immediately called to engage in combats, he at the same time reminds Timothy to be firm and immoveable in enduring adversity.[1]

gospel appear to endeavour, as far as they can, to destroy the grace of God. For we are not speaking about Papists only, who fight furiously against us, but of those who adhere to the Protestant Reformation of the Gospel. We see that they would wish to be like unbridled calves. (They care not about a yoke, or government, or anything of that sort.) Let them be allowed to do what they please, let blasphemies and all licentious conduct be permitted; it is all one, provided that they have no form of ceremony, and that they despise the Pope and idolaters. This is the way in which many who make a profession of the gospel would wish to be governed; but the reason is, that they have 'itching ears.'"—*Fr. Ser.*

[1] "When the devil has raised his standard, and when scandals and disturbances abound everywhere, we cannot be sufficiently attentive to guard against them, unless we are fortified by patience, and are not discouraged by the adversity which we must endure. If this warning ever was advan-

*Do the work of an Evangelist.* That is, "Do that which belongs to an evangelist." Whether he denotes generally by this term any ministers of the gospel, or whether this was a special office, is doubtful; but I am more inclined to the second opinion, because from Eph. iv. 11 it is clearly evident that this was an intermediate class between apostles and pastors, so that the evangelists ranked as assistants next to the apostles. It is also more probable that Timothy, whom Paul had associated with himself as his closest companion in all things, surpassed ordinary pastors in rank and dignity of office, than that he was only one of their number. Besides, to mention an honourable title of office tends not only to encourage him, but to recommend his authority to others; and Paul had in view both of these objects.

*Render thy ministry approved.* If we read this clause as in the old translation, "Fulfil thy ministry," the meaning will be: "Thou canst not fully discharge the office intrusted to thee but by doing those things which I have enjoined. Wherefore see that you fail not in the middle of the course." But because πληροφορεῖν commonly means "to render certain" or "to prove," I prefer the following meaning, which is also most agreeable to the context,—that Timothy, by watching, and by patiently enduring afflictions, and by constant teaching, will succeed in having the truth of his

---

tageous, how exceedingly necessary is it at the present day! Has not the world arrived at the highest pitch of iniquity? We see that the majority furiously reject the gospel. As to others who pretend to welcome the gospel, what sort of obedience do they render to it? There is so much contempt and so much pride, that, as soon as vices are reproved, or more sharpness is used than suits the taste of those who would wish to have full permission to act wickedly, and whose sole aim is to destroy everything, they are filled with spite. Although Papists will permit their preaching Friars to cry out and storm against them, and at the same time do nothing but steep themselves in lies to their destruction, they who openly declare that they wish the reformation of the gospel cannot endure to be reproved when it is necessary, but gnash their teeth against God, and fulfil what Paul says to the Corinthians, that if deceivers came to impose upon them, they would bear with all tyranny, and would be quiet when they were buffeted; but if we teach them faithfully in the name of God, and for their salvation, they are so fastidious that a single word will provoke them to rebellion; and if we persevere in doing our duty, war will be immediately declared. Would to God that these things were not so visible amongst us as they are!"—*Fr. Ser.*

ministry established, because from such marks all will acknowledge him to be a good and faithful minister of Christ.

6. *For I am now offered as a sacrifice.* He assigns the reason for the solemn protestation which he employed. As if he had said, " So long as I lived, I stretched out my hand to thee ; my constant exhortations were not withheld from thee; thou hast been much aided by my advices, and much confirmed by my example ; the time is now come, that thou shouldst be thine own teacher and exhorter, and shouldst begin to swim without support : beware lest any change in thee be observed at my death."

*And the time of my dissolution is at hand.*[1] We must attend to the modes of expression by which he denotes his death. By the word *dissolution* he means that we do not altogether perish when we die ; because it is only a separation of the soul from the body. Hence we infer, that death is nothing else than a departure of the soul from the body— a definition which contains a testimony of the immortality of the soul.

" Sacrifice" was a term peculiarly applicable to the death of Paul, which was inflicted on him for maintaining the truth of Christ ; for, although all believers, both by their obedient life and by their death, are victims or offerings acceptable to God, yet martyrs are sacrificed in a more excellent manner, by shedding their blood for the name of Christ. Besides, the word σπένδεσθαι, which Paul here employs, does not denote every kind of sacrifice, but that which serves for ratifying covenants. Accordingly, in this passage, he means the same thing which he states more clearly when he says, " But if I am offered on the sacrifice of your faith, I rejoice." (Philip. ii. 17.) For there he means that the faith of the Philippians was ratified by his death, in precisely the same manner that covenants were ratified in ancient times by sacrifices of slain beasts ; not that the certainty of our faith is founded, strictly speaking, on the steadfastness of the martyrs, but because it tends greatly to confirm us. Paul has

[1] " Car de moy je m'en vay maintenant estre sacrifié." " For, for my part, I am going to be now sacrificed."

here adorned his death by a magnificent commendation, when he called it the ratification of his doctrine, that believers, instead of sinking into despondency—as frequently happens—might be more encouraged by it to persevere.

*The time of dissolution.* This mode of expression is also worthy of notice, because he beautifully lessens the excessive dread of death by pointing out its effect and its nature. How comes it that men are so greatly dismayed at any mention of death, but because they think that they perish utterly when they die? On the contrary, Paul, by calling it "Dissolution," affirms that man does not perish, but teaches that the soul is merely separated from the body. It is with the same object that he fearlessly declares that "the time is at hand," which he could not have done unless he had despised death; for although this is a natural feeling, which can never be entirely taken away, that man dreads and shrinks from death, yet that terror must be vanquished by faith, that it may not prevent us from departing from this world in an obedient manner, whenever God shall call us.

7. *I have fought the good fight.* Because it is customary to form a judgment from the event, Paul's fight might have been condemned on the ground that it did not end happily. He therefore boasts that it is excellent, whatever may be the light in which it is regarded by the world. This declaration is a testimony of eminent faith; for not only was Paul accounted wretched in the opinion of all, but his death also was to be ignominious. Who then would not have said that he fought without success? But he does not rely on the corrupt judgments of men. On the contrary, by magnanimous courage he rises above every calamity, so that nothing opposes his happiness and glory; and therefore he declares "the fight which he fought" to be good and honourable.

*I have finished my course.* He even congratulates himself on his death, because it may be regarded as the goal or termination of his course. We know that they who run a race have gained their wish when they have reached the goal. In this manner also he affirms that to Christ's combatants death is desirable, because it puts an end to their labours; and, on the other hand, he likewise declares that we ought never to rest in this life, because it is of no advantage to have run well and constantly from the beginning to the middle of the course, if we do not reach the goal.

*I have kept the faith.*[1] This may have a twofold meaning, either that to the last he was a faithful soldier to his captain, or that he continued in the right doctrine. Both meanings will be highly appropriate; and indeed he could not make his fidelity acceptable to the Lord in any other way than by constantly professing the pure doctrine of the gospel. Yet I have no doubt that he alludes to the solemn oath taken by soldiers; as if he had said that he was a good and faithful soldier to his captain.

8. *Henceforth there is laid up for me the crown of righteousness.* Having boasted of having fought his fight, and finished his course, and kept the faith, he now affirms that he has not laboured in vain. Now it is possible to put forth strenuous exertion, and yet to be defrauded of the reward which is due. But Paul says that his reward is sure. This certainty arises from turning his eyes to the day of the resurrection, and this is what we also ought to do; for all around we see nothing but death, and therefore we ought not to keep our eye fixed on the outward appearance of the world, but, on the contrary, to hold out to our minds the coming of Christ. The consequence will be, that nothing can detract from our happiness.

*Which the Lord the righteous Judge will render to me.* Because he mentions "the crown of righteousness" and "the righteous Judge," and employs the word "render," the Papists endeavour, by means of this passage, to build up the

[1] "This word 'Faith' may indeed be taken for Fidelity; as if he had said that he was loyal to our Lord Jesus Christ, and that he never flinched, that he always performed what belonged to his office. But we may also take this word Faith in its ordinary meaning, that Paul did not turn aside from the pure simplicity of the gospel, and even that he relied on the promises of salvation which had been given to him, and, having preached to others, shewed that he was in earnest in what he spoke. For, indeed, all the loyalty which God demands from us proceeds from our adhering firmly to his word, and being founded on it in such a manner that we shall not be moved by any storm or tempest that may arise."—*Fr. Ser.*

merits of works in opposition to the grace of God. But their reasoning is absurd. Justification by free grace, which is bestowed on us through faith, is not at variance with the rewarding of works, but, on the contrary, those two statements perfectly agree, that a man is justified freely through the grace of Christ, and yet that God will render to him the reward of works; for as soon as God has received us into favour, he likewise accepts our works, so as even to deign to give them a reward, though it is not due to them.

Here two blunders are committed by the Papists; first, in arguing that we deserve something from God, because we do well by virtue of our free-will; and secondly, in holding that God is bound to us, as if our salvation proceeded from anything else than from his grace. But it does not follow that God owes anything to us, because he renders righteously what he renders; for he is righteous even in those acts of kindness which are of free grace. And he "renders the reward" which he has promised, not because we take the lead by any act of obedience, but because, in the same course of liberality in which he has begun to act toward us, he follows up his former gifts by those which are afterwards bestowed. In vain, therefore, and to no purpose, do the Papists labour to prove from this, that good works proceed from the power of free-will; because there is no absurdity in saying that God crowns in us his own gifts. Not less absurdly and foolishly do they endeavour, by means of this passage, to destroy the righteousness of faith; since the goodness of God—by which he graciously embraces a man, not imputing to him his sins —is not inconsistent with that rewarding of works which he will render by the same kindness with which he made the promise.[1]

[1] "The Papists themselves ought to observe carefully what was said by one of those whom they call their Doctors. 'How would God render the crown as a righteous Judge, if he had not first given grace as a merciful Father? And how would there have been righteousness in us, had it not been preceded by the grace which justifies us? And how would that crown have been rendered as due, had not all that we have—been given when it was not due?' These are the words of Augustin; and although the Papists do not choose to keep by the Holy Scripture, they ought at least not to be so base as to renounce that which they pretend to hold. But even this is

*And not to me only.* That all the rest of the believers might fight courageously along with him, he invites them to a participation of the crown; for his unshaken steadfastness could not have served for an example to *us,* if the same hope of obtaining the crown had not been held out to us.

*To all who love his coming.*[1] This is a singular mark which he employs in describing believers. And, indeed, wherever faith is strong, it will not permit their minds to fall asleep in this world, but will elevate them to the hope of the last resurrection. His meaning therefore is, that all who are so much devoted to the world, and who love so much this fleeting life, as not to care about the coming of Christ, and not to be moved by any desire of it, deprive themselves of immortal glory. Woe to our stupidity, therefore, which exercises such power over us, that we never think seriously about the coming of Christ, to which we ought to give our whole attention. Besides, he excludes from the number of believers those in whom the coming of Christ produces terror and alarm; for it cannot be loved unless it be regarded as pleasant and delightful.

| | |
|---|---|
| 9. Do thy diligence to come shortly unto me: | 9. Da operam, ut ad me venias cito. |
| 10. For Demas hath forsaken me, having loved this present world, and is departed unto Thessalonica; Crescens to Galatia, Titus unto Dalmatia. | 10. Demas enim me reliquit, amplexus hoc sæculum, et profectus est Thessalonicam, Crescens in Galatiam, Titus in Dalmatiam. |
| 11. Only Luke is with me. Take Mark, and bring him with thee: for he is profitable to me for the ministry. | 11. Lucas est solus mecum. Marcum assume, ut tecum adducas; est enim mihi utilis in ministerium. |
| 12. And Tychicus have I sent to Ephesus. | 12. Tychicum autem misi Ephesum. |
| 13. The cloak that I left at Troas | 13. Pænulam, quam Troade re- |

not all. It is true that it is a doctrine which well deserves to be embraced, that God cannot be a righteous Judge to save us, unless he have been previously declared to be in the highest degree a merciful Father; that there will be no righteousness in us but that which he has placed there; and that he cannot reward us but by crowning his gifts. But it is also true, that, though God has given us grace to serve him, though we have laboriously done, according to our ability, all that was possible for us, though we have done so well that God accepts of it all; still there will be much to censure in all the best works that we have done, and the greatest virtue that can be perceived in us will be vicious."—*Fr. Ser.*

[1] "Son apparition." "His appearing."

with Carpus, when thou comest, bring *with thee*, and the books, *but* especially the parchments.

liqui apud Carpum, quum venies, affer, et libros et membranas.

9. *Make haste, to come to me quickly.* As he knew that the time of his death was at hand, there were many subjects—I doubt not—on which he wished to have a personal interview with Timothy for the good of the Church; and therefore he does not hesitate to desire him to come from a country beyond the sea. Undoubtedly there must have been no trivial reason why he called him away from a church over which he presided, and at so great a distance. Hence we may infer how highly important are conferences between such persons; for what Timothy had learned in a short space of time would be profitable, for a long period, to all the churches; so that the loss of half a year, or even of a whole year, was trivial compared with the compensation gained. And yet it appears from what follows, that Paul called Timothy with a view to his own individual benefit likewise; although his own personal matters were not preferred by him to the advantage of the Church, but it was because it involved the cause of the gospel, which was common to all believers; for as he defended it from a prison, so he needed the labours of others to aid in that defence.

10. *Having embraced this world.* It was truly base in such a man to prefer the love of this world to Christ. And yet we must not suppose that he altogether denied Christ, or gave himself up either to ungodliness or to the allurements of the world; but he merely preferred his private convenience, or his safety, to the life of Paul. He could not have assisted Paul without many troubles and vexations, attended by imminent risk of his life; he was exposed to many reproaches, and must have submitted to many insults, and been constrained to leave off the care of his own affairs; and, therefore, being overcome by his dislike of the cross, he resolved to consult his own interests. Nor can it be doubted, that he enjoyed a propitious gale from the world. That he was one of the leading men may be conjectured on this ground, that Paul mentions him amidst a very few (at Coloss.

CHAP. IV. 13. THE SECOND EPISTLE TO TIMOTHY. 265

iv. 14,) and likewise in the Epistle to Philemon, (ver. 24,) where also he is ranked among Paul's assistants ; and, therefore, we need not wonder if he censures him so sharply on this occasion, for having cared more about himself than about Christ.

Others, whom he afterwards mentions, had not gone away from him but for good reasons, and with his own consent. Hence it is evident that he did not study his own advantage, so as to deprive churches of their pastors, but only to obtain from them some relief. Undoubtedly he was always careful to invite to come to him, or to keep along with him, those whose absence would not be injurious to other churches. For this reason he had sent *Titus to Dalmatia*, and some to one place and some to another, when he invited Timothy to come to him. Not only so, but in order that the church at Ephesus may not be left destitute or forlorn during Timothy's absence, he sends *Tychicus* thither, and mentions this circumstance to Timothy, that he may know that that church will not be in want of one to fill his place during his absence.

13. *Bring the cloak which I left at Troas*. As to the meaning of the word φελόνη,[1] commentators are not agreed ; for some think that it is a chest or box for containing books, and others that it is a garment used by travellers, and fitted for defending against cold and rain. Whether the one interpretation or the other be adopted, how comes it that Paul should give orders to have either a garment or a chest brought to him from a place so distant, as if there were not workmen, or as if there were not abundance both of cloth and timber? If it be said, that it was a chest filled with books, or manuscripts, or epistles, the difficulty will be solved ; for such materials could not have been procured at any price. But, because many will not admit the conjecture, I willingly translate it by the word *cloak*. Nor is there any absurdity in saying that Paul desired to have it brought from so great a distance, because that garment, through long use, would

---

[1] " Quant au mot Grec, lequel on traduit manteline." " As to the Greek word which is translated mantle or cloak."

be more comfortable for him, and he wished to avoid expense.¹

Yet (to own the truth) I give the preference to the former interpretation; more especially because Paul immediately afterwards mentions *books and parchments.* It is evident from this, that the Apostle had not given over reading, though he was already preparing for death. Where are those who think that they have made so great progress that they do not need any more exercise? Which of them will dare to compare himself with Paul? Still more does this expression refute the madness of those men who—despising books, and condemning all reading—boast of nothing but their own (ἐνθουσιασμοὺς) divine inspirations.² But let us know that this passage gives to all believers³ a recommendation of constant reading, that they may profit by it.⁴

Here some one will ask, " What does Paul mean by asking for a robe or cloak, if he perceived that his death was at hand?" This difficulty also induces me to interpret the word as denoting a chest, though there might have been some use of the "cloak" which is unknown in the present day; and therefore I give myself little trouble about these matters.

14. Alexander the coppersmith did me much evil; the Lord reward him according to his works:

14. Alexander faber ærarius multis me malis affecit: reddat illi Dominus juxta facta ipsius.

¹ " Et aussi qu'il vouloit eviter la despense d'en achever une autre."
" And also because he wished to avoid the expense of buying another."
² " De leurs inspirations Divines."
³ " Above all, let those whose office it is to instruct others look well to themselves; for however able they may be, they are very far from approaching Paul. This being the case, let them resolve to commit themselves to God, that he may give them grace to have still more ample knowledge of his will, to communicate to others what they have received. And when they have faithfully taught during their whole life, and when they are at the point of death, let them still desire to profit, in order to impart to their neighbours what they know; and let great and small, doctors and the common people, philosophers and idiots, rich and poor, old and young,—let all be exhorted by what is here taught them, to profit during their whole life, in such a manner that they shall never slacken their exertions, till they no longer see in part or in a mirror, but behold the glory of God face to face.—*Fr. Ser.*
⁴ " Comme un moyen ordonné de Dieu pour profiter." " As a method appointed by God for profiting."

15. Of whom be thou ware also; for he hath greatly withstood our words.

16. At my first answer no man stood with me, but all *men* forsook me: *I pray God* that it may not be laid to their charge.

17. Notwithstanding the Lord stood with me, and strengthened me; that by me the preaching might be fully known, and *that* all the Gentiles might hear: and I was delivered out of the mouth of the lion.

18. And the Lord shall deliver me from every evil work, and will preserve *me* unto his heavenly kingdom: to whom *be* glory for ever and ever. Amen.

19. Salute Prisca and Aquila, and the household of Onesiphorus.

20. Erastus abode at Corinth: but Trophimus have I left at Miletum sick.

21. Do thy diligence to come before winter. Eubulus greeteth thee, and Pudens, and Linus, and Claudia, and all the brethren.

22. The Lord Jesus Christ *be* with thy spirit. Grace *be* with you. Amen.

The second *epistle* unto Timotheus, ordained the first bishop of the church of the Ephesians, was written from Rome, when Paul was brought before Nero the second time.

15. Quem et tu cave; vehementer enim restitit sermonibus nostris.

16. In prima defensione nemo mihi affuit, sed omnes me deseruerunt: ne illis imputetur.

17. Sed Dominus mihi affuit, et corroboravit me, ut per me præconium confirmaretur, et audirent omnes Gentes.

18. Et ereptus fui ex ore leonis, et eripiet me Dominus ex omni facto (*vel, opere*) malo, servabitque in regnum suum cœleste, cui gloria in sæcula sæculorum.' Amen.

19. Saluta Priscam et Aquilam et familiam Onesiphori.

20. Erastus mansit Corinthi: Trophimum autem reliqui in Mileto languentem.

21. Da operam, ut ante hyemem venias. Salutat te Eubulus et Pudens et Linus et Claudia et fratres omnes.

22. Dominus Iesus Christus cum spiritu tuo. Gratia vobiscum. Amen.

Scripta e Roma secunda ad Timotheum, qui primus Ephesi ordinatus fuit Episcopus, quum Paulus iterum sisteretur Cæsari Neroni.

14. *Alexander the coppersmith.* In this man was exhibited a shocking instance of apostasy. He had made profession of some zeal in advancing the reign of Christ, against which he afterwards carried on open war. No class of enemies is more dangerous or more envenomed than this. But from the beginning, the Lord determined that his Church should not be exempted from this evil, lest our courage should fail when we are tried by any of the same kind.

*Hath done me many evil things.* It is proper to observe, what are the "many evils" which Paul complains that Alexander brought upon him. They consisted in this, that he opposed his doctrine. Alexander was an artificer, not prepared by the learning of the schools for being a great disputer; but domestic enemies have always been abundantly able to do injury. And the wickedness of such men always obtains credit in the world, so that malicious and impudent ignorance sometimes creates trouble and difficulty greater than the highest abilities accompanied by learning. Besides, when the Lord brings his servants into contest with persons of this low and base class, he purposely withdraws them from the view of the world, that they may not indulge in ostentatious display.

From Paul's words, (ver. 15,) *for he vehemently opposed our discourses*, we may infer that he had committed no greater offence than an attack on sound doctrine; for if Alexander had wounded his person, or committed an assault on him, he would have endured it patiently; but when the truth of God is assailed, his holy breast burns with indignation, because, in all the members of Christ that saying must hold good, " The zeal of thy house hath eaten me up." (Ps. lxix. 9.) And this is also the reason of the stern imprecation into which he breaks out, that *the Lord may reward him according to his works*. A little afterwards, when he complains that *all had forsaken him*, (ver. 16,) still he does not call down the vengeance of God on them, but, on the contrary, appears as their intercessor, pleading that they may obtain pardon. So mild and so merciful to all others, how comes it that he shows himself so harsh and inexorable towards this individual ? The reason is this. Because some had fallen through fear and weakness, he desires that the Lord would forgive them; for in this manner we ought to have compassion on the weakness of brethren. But because this man rose against God with malice and sacrilegious hardihood, and openly attacked known truth, such impiety had no claim to compassion.

We must not imagine, therefore, that Paul was moved by excessive warmth of temper, when he broke out into this imprecation; for it was from the Spirit of God, and through a well regulated zeal, that he wished eternal perdition to Alexander, and mercy to the others. Seeing that it is by the guidance of the Spirit that Paul pronounces a heavenly judgment from on high, we may infer from this passage, how dear to God is his truth, for attacking which he punishes so severely. Especially, it ought to be observed how detestable a crime it is, to fight with deliberate malice against the true religion.

But lest any person, by falsely imitating the Apostle, should rashly utter similar imprecations, there are three things here that deserve notice. First, let us not avenge the injuries done to ourselves, lest self-love and a regard to our private advantage should move us violently, as frequently happens. Secondly, while we maintain the glory of God, let us not mingle with it our own passions, which always disturb good order. Thirdly, let us not pronounce sentence against every person without discrimination, but only against reprobates, who, by their impiety, give evidence that such is their true character; and thus our wishes will agree with God's own judgment; otherwise there is ground to fear that the same reply may be made to us that Christ made to the disciples who thundered indiscriminately against all who did not comply with their views, " Ye know not of what spirit ye are." (Luke ix. 55.) They thought that they had Elijah as their supporter, (2 Kings i. 10,) who prayed to the Lord in the same manner; but because they differed widely from the spirit of Elijah, the imitation was absurd. It is therefore necessary, that the Lord should reveal his judgment before we burst forth into such imprecations; and wish that by his Spirit he should restrain and guide our zeal. And whenever we call to our remembrance the vehemence of Paul against a single individual, let us also recollect his amazing meekness towards those who had so basely forsaken him, that we may learn, by his example, to have compassion on the weakness of our brethren.

Here I wish to put a question to those who pretend that Peter presided over the church at Rome. Where was he at that time? According to their opinion, he was not dead; for they tell us, that exactly a year intervened between his death and that of Paul. Besides, they extend his pontificate to seven years. Here Paul mentions his first defence: his second appearance before the court would not be quite so soon. In order that Peter may not lose the title of Pope, must he endure to be charged with the guilt of so shameful a revolt? Certainly, when the whole matter has been duly examined, we shall find that everything that has been believed about his Popedom is fabulous.

17. *But the Lord assisted me.* He adds this, in order to remove the scandal which he saw might arise from that base desertion of his cause.[1] Though the church at Rome had failed to perform its duty, he affirms that the gospel had suffered no loss by it, because, leaning on heavenly power, he was himself fully able to bear the whole burden, and was so far from being discouraged by the influence of that fear which seized on all, that it became only the more evident that the grace of God has no need of receiving aid from any other quarter. He does not boast of his courage, but gives thanks to the Lord; that, when reduced to extremities, he did not give way nor lose heart under so dangerous a temptation. He therefore acknowledges that he was supported by the arm of the Lord, and is satisfied with this, that the inward grace of God served for a shield to defend him against every assault. He assigns the reason—

*That the proclamation might be confirmed.* The word "proclamation" is employed by him to denote the office of publishing the gospel among the Gentiles, which was especially assigned to him;[2] for the preaching of others did not so much resemble a proclamation, in consequence of being confined to the Jews. And with good reason does he make use of this word in many passages. It was no small confirmation of his ministry, that, when the whole world foamed with madness against him, and on the other hand, all human assistance failed him, still he remained unshaken. Thus he gave practical demonstration that his apostleship was from Christ.

---

[1] "De ce que plusieurs l'avoyent ainsi lachement abandonné en la defense de sa cause." "From many having so basely deserted them in the defence of his cause."

[2] "Le mot Grec signifie proprement une publication et proclamation qui se fait solennellement et comme a son de trompe." "The Greek word properly denotes a publication or proclamation which is made solemnly, and, as it were, with the sound of a trumpet."

He now describes the manner of the confirmation, *that all the Gentiles might hear* that the Lord had so powerfully assisted him; for from this event they might infer that both their own calling and that of Paul were from the Lord.

*And I was delivered out of the mouth of the lion.* By the word "lion," many suppose that he means Nero. For my part, I rather think that he makes use of this expression to denote danger in general; as if he had said, "out of a blazing fire," or "out of the jaws of death." He means that it was not without wonderful assistance from God, that he escaped, the danger being so great that but for this he must have been immediately swallowed up.

18. *And the Lord will deliver me from every evil work.* He declares, that he hopes the same for the future; not that he will escape death, but that he will not be vanquished by Satan, or turn aside from the right course. This is what we ought chiefly to desire, not that the interests of the body may be promoted, but that we may rise superior to every temptation, and may be ready to suffer a hundred deaths rather than that it should come into our mind to pollute ourselves by any "evil work." Yet I am well aware, that there are some who take the expression *evil work* in a passive sense, as denoting the violence of wicked men, as if Paul had said, "The Lord will not suffer wicked men to do me any injury." But the other meaning is far more appropriate, that he will preserve him pure and unblemished from every wicked action; for he immediately adds, *to his heavenly kingdom,* by which he means that that alone is true salvation, when the Lord—either by life or by death—conducts us into his kingdom.

This is a remarkable passage for maintaining the uninterrupted communication of the grace of God, in opposition to the Papists. After having confessed that the beginning of salvation is from God, they ascribe the continuation of it to free-will; so that in this way perseverance is not a heavenly gift, but a virtue of man. And Paul, by ascribing to God this work of "preserving us to his kingdom," openly affirms that we are guided by his hand during the whole course of our life, till, having discharged the whole of our warfare, we obtain the victory. And we have a memorable instance of this in Demas, whom he mentioned a little before, because, from being a noble champion of Christ, he had become a base deserter. All that follows has been seen by us formerly, and therefore does not need additional exposition.

END OF THE SECOND EPISTLE TO TIMOTHY.

# COMMENTARIES

ON

# THE EPISTLE TO TITUS.

TO TWO EMINENT SERVANTS OF CHRIST,

# WILLIAM FARELL AND PETER VIRET,

HIS DEARLY BELOVED BRETHREN AND COLLEAGUES,

# JOHN CALVIN

OFFERS HIS SALUTATIONS.

My Commentary—which now goes forth, bearing the inscription of your name—is, indeed, a small gift ; yet I fully believe that it will be acceptable to you, for this reason, that the subject of the Epistle induced me to make this Dedication. The task of putting the finishing hand to that building which Paul had begun in Crete, but left incomplete—was undertaken by Titus. I occupy nearly the same position with regard to you.

When you had made some progress in rearing this church with vast exertions, and at great risk, after some time had elapsed I came, first as your assistant, and afterwards was left as your successor, that I might endeavour to carry forward, to the best of my ability, that work which you had so well and so successfully begun. This work, I and my colleagues are endeavouring to perform, if not with so great progress as might have been desired, yet heartily and faithfully, according to our small ability.

To return to you, in consequence of holding the same relation to you which Paul assigned to Titus, I have been led to consider this similarity as a good reason for selecting you above all others, for dedicating to you this labour of mine. Meanwhile, to the present age, and perhaps to posterity, it will, at least, be some evidence of that holy union and friend-

[1] " Et compagnons en l'œuvre de nostre Seigneur." " And colleagues in the work of our Lord."

ship which exists between us. I think that there has never been, in ordinary life, a circle of friends so sincerely bound to each other as we have been in our ministry. With both of you I discharged here the office of pastor; and so far was there from being any appearance of envy, that you and I seemed to be one. We were afterwards separated by places; for you, Farell, were invited by the church of Neufchastel, which you had rescued from the tyranny of Popery, and brought into obedience to Christ; and you, Viret, are held in the same relation by the church of Lausanne.

While each of us occupies his own position, our union brings together the children of God into the fold of Christ, and even unites them in his body; while it scatters not only those outward enemies who openly carry on war with us, but those nearer and domestic enemies, by whom we are inwardly assailed. For I reckon this also to be one of the benefits resulting from being closely related, that filthy dogs, whose bites cannot succeed so far as to tear and rend the Church of Christ, do nothing more than bark against it with all their might. And, indeed, we cannot too thoroughly despise their insolence, since we can, with truth, glory before God, and have proved to men by the clearest evidence, that we cultivate no other society or friendship than that which has been consecrated to the name of Christ, which has hitherto been advantageous to his Church, and which has no other aim than that all may be at one with us in Him.

Farewell, my most excellent and most upright brethren. May the Lord Jesus continue to bless your pious labours!

GENEVA, 29*th November* 1549.

# THE ARGUMENT

ON

# THE EPISTLE TO TITUS.

PAUL, having only laid the foundations of the church in Crete, and hastening to go to another place, (for he was not the pastor of a single island only, but the Apostle of the Gentiles,) had given charge to Titus to prosecute this work as an Evangelist. It is evident from this Epistle that, immediately after Paul's departure, Satan laboured not only to overthrow the government of the Church, but likewise to corrupt its doctrine.

There were some who, through ambitious motives, wished to be elevated to the rank of pastors, and who, because Titus did not comply with their wicked desires, spoke unfavourably of him to many persons. On the other hand, there were Jews who, under the pretence of supporting the Mosaic law, introduced a great number of trifles; and such persons were listened to with eagerness and with much acceptance. Paul therefore writes with this design, to arm Titus with his authority, that he may be able to bear so great a burden; for undoubtedly there were some who fearlessly despised him as being but one of the ordinary rank of pastors. It is also possible that complaints about him were in circulation, to the effect that he assumed more authority than belonged to him, when he did not admit pastors till he had made trial and ascertained their fitness.

Hence we may infer, that this was not so much a private epistle of Paul to Titus, as it was a public epistle to the Cretans. It is not probable that Titus is blamed for having with too great indulgence raised unworthy persons to the office of bishop, or that, as an ignorant man and a novice, he is told what is that kind of doctrine in which he ought to instruct the people; but because due honour was not rendered to him, Paul clothes him with his own authority, both in ordaining ministers and in the whole government of the Church. Because there were many who foolishly desired to have another form of doctrine than that which he delivered, Paul approves of this alone—rejecting all others—and exhorts him to proceed as he had begun.

First, then, he shows what sort of persons ought to be chosen for being ministers.[1] Among other qualifications, he requires that a minister shall be well instructed in sound doctrine, that by means of it he may resist adversaries. Here he takes occasion to censure some vices of the Cretans, but especially rebukes the Jews, who made some kind of holiness to consist in a distinction of food, and in other outward ceremonies. In order to refute their fooleries, he contrasts with them the true exercises of piety and Christian life; and, with the view of pressing them more closely, he describes what are the duties which belong to every one in his calling. These duties he enjoins Titus diligently and constantly to inculcate. On the other hand, he admonishes others not to be weary of hearing them, and shows that this is the design of the redemption and salvation obtained through Christ. If any obstinate person oppose, or refuse to obey, he bids him set that person aside. We now see that Paul has no other object in view than to support the cause of Titus, and to stretch out the hand to assist him in performing the work of the Lord.

---

[1] "Pour estre ministres et pasteurs de l'Eglise." "To be ministers and pastors of the Church."

# COMMENTARIES

ON

# THE EPISTLE TO TITUS.

## CHAPTER I.

1. Paul, a servant of God, and an apostle of Jesus Christ, according to the faith of God's elect, and the acknowledging of the truth which is after godliness;
2. In hope of eternal life, which God, that cannot lie, promised before the world began;
3. But hath in due times manifested his word through preaching, which is committed unto me, according to the commandment of God our Saviour;
4. To Titus, *mine* own son after the common faith: Grace, mercy, *and* peace from God the Father, and the Lord Jesus Christ our Saviour.

1. Paulus servus Dei, Apostolus autem Iesu Christi, secundum fidem electorum Dei et agnitionem veritatis ejus, quæ secundum pietatem est,
2. In spe (*vel, propter spem*) vitæ æternæ, quam promisit is, qui mentiri non potest, Deus, ante tempora secularia;
3. Manifestavit autem propriis temporibus sermonem suum (*vel, per sermonem*) in prædicatione, quæ mihi commissa est secundum ordinationem Servatoris nostri Dei:
4. Tito germano filio, secundum communem fidem, gratia, misericordia, pax a Deo Patre et Domino Iesu Christo Servatore nostro.

1. *A servant of God.* This extended and laborious commendation of his apostleship shows that Paul had in view the whole Church, and not Titus alone; for his apostleship was not disputed by Titus, and Paul is in the habit of proclaiming the titles of his calling, in order to maintain his authority. Accordingly, just as he perceives those to whom he writes to be disposed, he deals largely or sparingly in those ornaments. Here his design was, to bring into subjection those who had haughtily rebelled; and for this reason he extols his apostleship in lofty terms. He therefore writes this

Epistle, not that it may be read in solitude by Titus in his closet, but that it may be openly published.

*An Apostle of Jesus Christ.* First, he calls himself "a servant of God," and next adds the particular kind of his ministry, namely, that he is "an Apostle of Christ;" for there are various ranks among the servants of God. Thus he descends from the general description to the particular class. We ought also to keep in remembrance what I have said elsewhere, that the word *servant* means something else than ordinary subjection, (on account of which all believers are called "servants of God,") and denotes a minister who has received a particular office. In this sense the prophets were formerly distinguished by this title, and Christ himself is the chief of the prophets: "Behold my servant, I have chosen him." (Isa. xlii. 1.) Thus David, with a view to his royal dignity, calls himself "a servant of God." Perhaps, also, it is on account of the Jews that he designates himself "a servant of God;" for they were wont to lower his authority by alleging the law against him. He therefore wishes to be accounted an Apostle of Christ in such a manner that he may likewise glory in being a servant of the eternal God. Thus he shows not only that those two titles are quite consistent with each other, but that they are joined by a bond which cannot be dissolved.

*According to the faith of the elect of God.*[1] If any one

---

[1] "If faith be the fruit of election, the prescience of faith does not influence the electing act of God. It is called 'the faith of God's elect;' Paul an apostle of Jesus Christ, according to the faith of God's elect, (Tit. i. 1,) that is, settled in this office to bring the elect of God to faith. If men be chosen by God upon the foresight of faith, or not chosen till they have faith, they are not so much God's elect as God is their elect: they choose God by faith, before God chooseth them by love. It had not been the faith of God's elect, that is, of those already chosen, but the faith of those that were to be chosen by God afterwards. Election is the cause of faith, and not faith the cause of election. Fire is the cause of heat, and not heat of fire; the sun is the cause of day, and not the day the cause of the rising of the sun. Men are not chosen because they believe, but they believe because they are chosen. The Apostle did ill else to appropriate that to the elect, which they had no more interest in by virtue of their election than the veriest reprobate in the world. If the foresight of what works might be done by his creatures was the motive of his choosing them, why did he not choose the devils to redemption, who could have done him better service, by the strength of their nature, than the whole mass of

doubt about his apostleship, he procures credit for it by a very strong reason, connecting it with the salvation " of the elect of God." As if he had said, " There is a mutual agreement between my apostleship and the faith of the elect of God; and, therefore, it will not be rejected by any man who is not a reprobate and opposed to the true faith."

By " the elect" he means not only those who were at that time alive, but all that had been from the beginning of the world; for he declares that he teaches no doctrine which does not agree with the faith of Abraham and of all the fathers. So, then, if any person in the present day wishes to be accounted a successor of Paul, he must prove that he is the minister of the same doctrine. But these words contain also an implied contrast, that the gospel may suffer no damage from the unbelief and obstinacy of many; for at that time, as well as in the present day, weak minds were greatly disturbed by this scandal, that the greater part of those who boasted of the title of the Church rejected the pure doctrine of Christ. For this reason Paul shows that, though all indiscriminately boast of the name of God, there are many of that multitude who are reprobates; as he elsewhere (Rom. ix. 7) affirms, that not all who are descended from Abraham according to the flesh, are the lawful children of Abraham.

*And the knowledge of that truth.* I consider the copulative *and* to be here equivalent to *that is;* so that the passage might run thus: " according to the faith of the elect of God, that is, the knowledge of that truth which is according to godliness." This clause explains what is the nature of that "faith" which he has mentioned, though it is not a full definition of it, but a description framed so as to apply to the present context. For the purpose of maintaining that his apostleship is free from all imposture and error, he solemnly declares that it contains nothing but known and ascertained truth, by which men are instructed in the pure worship of God. But as every word has its own weight, it is highly proper to enter into a detailed explanation.

Adam's posterity? Well, then, there is no possible way to lay the original foundation of this act of election and preterition in anytning but the absolute sovereignty of God."—*Charnock.*

First, when "faith" is called "knowledge," it is distinguished not only from opinion, but from that shapeless faith which the Papists have contrived; for they have forged an implicit faith destitute of all light of the understanding. But when Paul describes it to be a quality which essentially belongs to faith—to know the truth, he plainly shews that there is no faith without knowledge.

The word *truth* expresses still more clearly the certainty which is demanded by the nature of faith; for faith is not satisfied with probable arguments, but holds what is true. Besides, he does not speak of every kind of truth, but of the heavenly doctrine, which is contrasted with the vanity of the human understanding. As God has revealed himself to us by means of that truth, so it is alone worthy of the honour of being called "the truth"—a name which is bestowed on it in many parts of Scripture. "And the Spirit will lead you into all truth." (John xvi. 13.) "Thy word is the truth." (John xvii. 17.) "Who hath bewitched you that ye should not obey the truth?" (Gal. iii. 1.) "Having heard the word of the truth, the gospel of the Son of God." (Col. i. 5.) "He wisheth all to come to the knowledge of the truth." (1 Tim. ii. 4.) "The Church is the pillar and foundation of the truth." (1 Tim. iii. 15.) In a word, that truth is the right and sincere knowledge of God, which frees us from all error and falsehood. So much the more ought it to be valued by us, since nothing is more wretched than to wander like cattle during our whole life.

*Which is according to godliness.* This clause especially limits "the truth" of which he had spoken, but at the same time commends the doctrine of Paul from the fruit and end of it, because it has no other object than that God should be worshipped in a right manner, and that pure religion should flourish among men. In this manner he defends his doctrine from every suspicion of vain curiosity, as he did before Felix, (Acts xxiv. 10,) and afterwards before Agrippa, (Acts xxvi. 1;) for, since all questions which do not tend to edification ought justly to be suspected and even hated by good men, the only lawful commendation of doctrine is this, that it instructs us to fear God and to bow before him with reverence. And hence we are also informed, that the greater progress any one has made in godliness, he is so much the better disciple of Christ; and that he ought to be reckoned a true theologian who edifies consciences in the fear of God.

2. *In the hope* (or, on account of the hope) *of eternal life.* This undoubtedly denotes the cause; for that is the force of the Greek preposition ἐπί, *upon;* and therefore it may be translated, "On account of the hope," or "On the hope." True religion and the practice of godliness—begin with meditation or the heavenly life; and in like manner, when Paul (Col. i. 5) praises the faith and love of the Colossians, he makes the cause and foundation of them to be "the hope laid up in heaven." The Sadducees and all who confine our hope to this world, whatever they may pretend, can do nothing else than produce contempt of God, while they reduce men to the condition of cattle. Accordingly, it ought always to be the aim of a good teacher, to turn away the eyes of men from the world, that they may look up to heaven. I readily acknowledge that we ought to value the glory of God more highly than our salvation; but we are not now discussing the question which of these two ought to be first in order. All that I say is—that men never seek God in a right manner till they have confidence to approach to him; and, therefore, that we never apply our mind to godliness till we have been instructed about the hope of the heavenly life.[1]

[1] "Thus he shews that it will never be possible for men to dedicate themselves entirely to the service of God, if they do not think more about God than about all things else. In short, there is no living root, no faith, no religion, till we have been led to heaven; that is, till we know that God has not created us to keep us here in an earthly life with brute beasts, but that he has adopted us to be his heritage, and reckons us to be his children. If, therefore, we do not look up to heaven, it is impossible that we shall have true devotion to surrender ourselves to God, or that there shall be any faith or Christianity in us. And that is the reason why—among all who, in the present day, are accounted Christians, and give themselves out to be such—there are very few who have this true mark, which Paul has here given to all the children of God. It is because all are occupied with the present life, and are so firmly bound to it, that they cannot rise higher. Now perceiving this vice to be so common, so much the more ought we to guard against it, and break the force of that which we cannot altogether destroy, till we come into close fellowship with God, which will only be, when the hope of eternal life shall be actually and sincerely formed in our hearts."—*Fr. Ser.*

*Which God promised before the times of ages.* As Augustine translated the words, πρὸ χρόνων αἰωνίων to mean—not "the times of ages" but "eternal times," he gives himself great uneasiness about "the eternity of times," till at length he explains "eternal times" as denoting those which go beyond all antiquity. As to the meaning, he and Jerome and other commentators agree, that God determined, before the creation of the world, to give that salvation which he hath now manifested by the gospel. Thus Paul would have used the word *promise* incorrectly instead of *decree;* for before men existed there was no one to whom he could promise.

For this reason, while I do not reject this exposition, yet when I take a close survey of the whole matter, I am constrained to adopt a different interpretation—that eternal life was promised to men many ages ago, and not only to those who lived at that time, but also for our own age. It was not for the benefit of Abraham alone, but with a view to all who should live after him, that God said, "In thy seed shall all nations be blessed." (Gen. xxii. 18.) Nor is this inconsistent with what he says, in another sense, (2 Tim. i. 9) that salvation was given to men "before the times of ages." The meaning of the word is still the same in both passages; for, since the Greek word αἰών denotes an uninterrupted succession of time from the beginning to the end of the world, Paul declares, in that passage, that salvation was given or decreed for the elect of God before times began to flow. But because in this passage he treats of the promise, he does not include all ages, so as to lead us back beyond the creation of the world, but shews that many ages[1] have elapsed since salvation was promised.

If any person prefer to view "the times of ages" as a concise expression for the ages themselves, he is at liberty to do so. But because salvation was given by the eternal election of God before it was promised, the act of giving salvation is put in that passage (2 Tim. i. 9) before all ages, and therefore we must supply the word *all.* But here it means nothing more than that the promise is more ancient than a long course of ages, because it began immediately

---

[1] "Beaucoup de centeines d'ans." "Many centuries of years."

after the creation of the world. In the same sense he shews that the gospel, which was to have been proclaimed when Christ rose from the dead, had been promised in the Scriptures by the prophets; for there is a wide difference between the promise which was formerly given to the fathers and the present exhibition of grace.

*Who cannot lie.* This expression (ἀψευδής) is added for glorifying God, and still more for confirming our faith. And, indeed, whenever the subject treated of is our salvation, we ought to recollect that it is founded on the word of Him who can neither deceive nor lie. Moreover, the only proof of the whole of religion is—the unchangeable truth of God.[1]

3. *But hath manifested.* There was indeed some manifestation of this kind, when God in ancient times spake by his prophets; but because Christ publicly displayed by his coming those things which they had obscurely predicted, and the Gentiles were afterwards admitted into the fellowship of the covenant, in this sense Paul says that what had formerly been exhibited in part "hath now been manifested."

*In his own times.* This has the same meaning as "the fulness of times." (Gal. iv. 4.) He reminds us that the time

---

[1] "What a strange sort of men are these, that will endure to be so exposed, so scorned, so trampled upon, as they that bear the Christian name commonly are? What is the reason of it? What account will a reasonable man give, why he will so expose himself? I will tell you the reason. 'Therefore we labour and suffer reproach, because we hope in God, in the living God, and we are pretty well persuaded we shall not finally be losers; we shall not have an ill bargain of it at last.' As the same Apostle, when he writes himself 'an Apostle and servant of Jesus Christ,' seems to allow, that he was to doom himself to all the sufferings and calamities that the enemies of the Christian cause could load him with and lay upon him, for his assuming to himself such names of 'an Apostle and servant of Jesus Christ.' But why should Paul,—that wise and prudent man, that learned man, that man of so considerable reputation among his own countrymen—why should he come to be written among the Apostles and servants of Jesus Christ? Why, saith he, it is in hope of eternal life, which God, that cannot lie, hath promised. (Tit. i. 1, 2.) I avow myself an Apostle and servant of Jesus Christ upon this inducement, and for this reason; and so I mean to continue unto the end. It is the hope of eternal life, which God, that cannot lie, hath promised to me. He whose nature doth not allow him to deceive, to whom it is impossible to lie, I firmly and securely hope in him; and, therefore, I will readily dispose myself to encounter all the difficulties and hardships which the service of Jesus Christ can lay me open to."—*Howe.*

when it pleased the Lord to do this—must have been the most seasonable time for doing it; and he mentions this for the purpose of meeting the rashness of men, who have always the hardihood to inquire why it was not sooner, or why it is to-day rather than to-morrow. In order therefore that our curiosity may not exceed proper bounds, he shews that the "times" are placed in the hand, and at the disposal, of God, in such a manner that we ought to think that he does everything in the proper order and at the most seasonable time.

*His word.* Or, *by his word;* for it is not uncommon with Greek writers to supply the preposition *by.* Or, he calls Christ the Word; if it be not thought preferable to supply something for the sake of completing the sentence. Were it not that the second exposition is a little forced, in other respects I should give it the preference. Thus John says, " What we have heard, what we have seen with our eyes, what our hands have handled of the Word of life; and the life was manifested." (1 John i. 1, 2.) I therefore prefer what is a simple meaning, that God hath manifested the word concerning the life by the preaching of the gospel.

*The preaching,* of which he speaks, is the gospel proclaimed, as the chief thing which we hear in it is—that Christ is given to us, and that in him there is life.

*Which hath been committed to me.* Because all are not indiscriminately fit for so important an office, and no man ought to thrust himself into it, he asserts his calling, according to his custom. Here we ought to learn—what we have often remarked on other occasions—that the honour is not due to any man, till he has proved that God has ordained him; for even the ministers of Satan proudly boast that God has called them, but there is no truth in their words. Now Paul states nothing but what is known and proved, when he mentions his calling.

Besides, from this passage we learn for what purpose they were made apostles. It was for the sake of publishing the gospel, as he says elsewhere, " Woe to me if I preach not the gospel, for a dispensation is committed unto me." (1 Cor. ix. 16, 17.) Accordingly, they who enact dumb show, in the midst of idleness and luxury, are excessively impudent in boasting that they are the successors of the apostles.

*Of God our Saviour.* He applies the same epithet to the Father and to Christ, so that each of them is our Saviour, but for a different reason; for the Father is called our Saviour, because he redeemed us by the death of his Son, that he might make us heirs of eternal life; and the Son, because he shed his blood as the pledge and the price of our salvation. Thus the Son hath brought salvation to us from the Father, and the Father hath bestowed it through the Son.

4. *To Titus, my own son, according to the common faith.* Hence it is evident in what sense a minister of the word is said to beget spiritually those whom he brings to the obedience of Christ, that is, so that he himself is also begotten. Paul declares himself to be the father of Titus, with respect to his faith; but immediately adds, that this faith is common to both, so that both of them alike have the same Father in heaven. Accordingly, God does not diminish his own prerogative, when he pronounces those to be spiritual fathers along with himself, by whose ministry he regenerates whom he chooses; for of themselves they do nothing, but only by the efficacy of the Spirit. As to the remainder of the verse, the exposition of it will be found in the Commentaries on the former Epistles, and especially on the First Epistle to Timothy.[1]

| 5. For this cause left I thee in Crete, that thou shouldest set in order the things that are wanting, and ordain elders in every city, as I had appointed thee: | 5. Hujus rei gratia reliqui te in Creta, ut, quæ desunt, pergas corrigere, et constituas oppidatim presbyteros, quemadmodum tibi ordinavi: |
|---|---|
| 6. If any be blameless, the husband of one wife, having faithful children, not accused of riot, or unruly. | 6. Si quis est a crimine immunis, unius uxoris vir, liberos habens fideles, non infames ob lasciviam, non immorigeros. |

5. *For this reason I left thee in Crete.* This preface clearly proves, that Titus is not so much admonished on his own account as recommended to others, that no one may hinder him. Paul testifies that he has appointed him in his own room; and on that account all should acknowledge and receive him with reverence as the Apostle's deputy. The

[1] See p. 21.

apostles had no fixed place assigned to them, but were charged to spread the gospel through the whole world; and for this reason, when they left one city or district to go to another, they were wont to place fit men as their substitutes, to complete the work which they had begun. Thus Paul affirms that he founded the church of the Corinthians, but that there were other workmen,[1] who must build on his foundation, that is, carry forward the building.

This, indeed, belongs to all pastors; for the churches will always stand in need of increase and progress, as long as the world shall endure. But in addition to the ordinary office of pastors, the care of organizing the church was committed to Titus. Till the churches have been already organized, and reduced to some order, pastors were not usually appointed over them. But Titus held some additional charge, which consisted in giving a form to churches that had not yet been properly arranged, and in appointing a fixed kind of government accompanied by discipline. Having laid the foundation, Paul departed; and then it became the duty of Titus to carry the work higher, that the building might have fair proportions.

This is what he calls *correcting those things which are still wanting*. The building of the Church is not a work so easy that it can be brought all at once to perfection. How long Paul was in Crete—is uncertain; but he had spent some time there, and had faithfully devoted his labours to erect the kingdom of Christ. He did not lack the most consummate skill that can be found in man; he was unwearied in toil; and yet he acknowledged that he left the work rough and incomplete. Hence we see the difficulty; and, indeed, we find, by experience, in the present day, that it is not the labour of one or two years to restore fallen churches to a tolerable condition. Accordingly, those who have made diligent progress for many years—must still be attentive to correct many things.[2]

---

[1] "Mais que les autres estoyent maçons ou charpentiers." "But that the others were masons and carpenters."

[2] "Those who are guided by ambition would wish to be thought clever people on the first day; they would wish to enjoy such reputation as to have it thought that they discharged their duty so faithfully that nothing

Here it is highly proper to observe the modesty of Paul who willingly permits another person to complete the work which he had begun. And, indeed, although Titus is greatly inferior to him, he does not refuse to have him for (ἐπανορ-θωτήν) a "corrector," to give the finishing hand to his work. Such ought to be the dispositions of godly teachers; not that every one should labour to make everything bend to his own ambitious views, but that they should strive to assist each other, and that, when any one has laboured more successfully, he should be congratulated and not envied by all the rest.

And yet we must not imagine that Paul intended that Titus should correct those things which he had left undone, either through ignorance, or forgetfulness, or carelessness, but those things which he could not finish on account of the shortness of the time. In short, he enjoined Titus to make that correction which he would himself have made, if he had remained longer in Crete; not by varying—not by changing anything, but by adding what was wanting; because the difficulty of such a work does not allow every part of it to be done in a single day.

*And appoint presbyters in each city.*[1] In the spiritual

more could be desired. On the contrary, when we have laboured during our whole life to edify the Church of God, still we shall not succeed to the full extent. Let us therefore know that we must not presume so far on our industry or our virtues, that he who is endued with more abundant graces can suddenly have edified the Church of God to perfection; but we must assist each other. He who is farthest advanced must know that he cannot do everything, and must bend his shoulders and ask assistance from those whom God has appointed, and must be well pleased that others make progress, provided that all aim at serving God and advancing the kingdom of our Lord Jesus Christ. If we look well to ourselves, there will always be reason to grieve, because we are very far from having performed our duty. And those who make themselves believe this or that, and say, 'Here is a church so well reformed that nothing more is needed'—are mistaken; for if they knew what reformation is, they would beware of thinking that there was no room for finding fault. Whatever pains we take in arranging matters, and bringing them into order, there are indeed many things which, when once begun, will follow in a regular train; but as to reaching perfection, we are very far from it."—*Fr. Ser.*

"Κατὰ πόλιν. Not 'in every city,' but 'in each city or town,' (literally, 'city by city,') of all those which had Christian congregations. Of such there might be several in this 'hundred-citied isle;' though the name πόλις was often given to towns; and there is reason to think that not a few of the Cretan cities were no better."—*Bloomfield.*

building this nearly comes next to doctrine, that pastors be ordained, to take charge of governing the Church; and therefore Paul mentions it here in preference to everything else. It is a point which ought to be carefully observed, that churches cannot safely remain without the ministry of pastors, and that consequently, wherever there is a considerable body of people, a pastor should be appointed over it. And yet he does not say that each town shall have a pastor, so that no place shall have more than one; but he means that no towns shall be destitute of pastors

*Presbyters* or elders. It is well known, that it was not on account of age, that they received this appellation; for sometimes those who were still young—such as Timothy—were admitted to this rank. But in all languages it has been customary to apply this honourable designation to all rulers. Although we may conclude, from 1 Tim. v. 17, that there were two classes of presbyters, the context will immediately show, that here none other than teachers are meant, that is, those who were ordained to teach; for immediately afterwards, he will call the same persons "bishops."

But it may be thought that he gives too much power to Titus, when he bids him appoint ministers for all the churches. That would be almost royal power. Besides, this method takes away from each church the right of choosing, and from the College of Pastors the power of judging; and thus the sacred administration of the Church would be almost wholly profaned. The answer is easy. He does not give permission to Titus, that he alone may do everything in this matter, and may place over the churches those whom he thinks fit to appoint to be bishops; but only bids him preside, as moderator, at the elections, which is quite necessary. This mode of expression is very common. In the same manner, a consul, or regent, or dictator is said to have created consuls, on account of having presided over the public assembly in electing them. Thus also Luke relates that Paul and Barnabas ordained elders in every church. (Acts xiv. 23.) Not that they alone, in an authoritative manner, appointed pastors which the churches had neither approved nor known; but that they ordained fit men, who had been chosen or desired by the people. From this passage we do indeed learn, that there was not at that time such equality among the ministers of Christ but that some one had authority and deliberative voice above others; but this has nothing to do with the tyrannical and profane custom which prevails in Popery as to Collations. The apostles had a widely different mode of procedure.

6. *If any one is blameless.* In order that no one may be angry with Titus, as if he were too rigorous or severe in rejecting any, Paul takes the whole blame to himself;[1] for he declares that he has expressly commanded, that no one may be admitted, unless he be such a person as is here described. Accordingly, as he testified, a little before, that he had invested Titus with authority to preside in the appointment of pastors, that others might allow to him that right; so he now relates the injunction which he had given, lest the severity of Titus should be exposed to the ill-will of the ignorant, or the slanders of wicked men.

As this passage presents to us a lively portrait of a lawful bishop, we ought to observe it carefully; but, on the other hand, as almost everything that is here contained has been explained by me in the Commentary on the First Epistle to Timothy, it will be enough at present to touch on it slightly. When he says, that a bishop must be ἀνέγκλητος, *blameless*, he does not mean one who is exempt from every vice, (for no such person could at any time be found,) but one who is marked by no disgrace that would lessen his authority. He means, therefore, that he shall be a man of unblemished reputation.[2]

[1] "Prend sur soy toute l'envie, voulant qu'on luy impute tout ce que Tite fera en cest endroit." "Takes all the blame on himself, wishing that to him may be imputed all that Titus shall do in this matter."

[2] "It is true, that the servants of God will never be without blame; as he even says, that they cannot avoid walking amidst disgrace and reproach. It is true, that Paul lived so virtuously that no fault could be found with him, and that too, before he came to the faith of Jesus Christ; so that he lived without reproach, and was a mirror and a jewel of holiness. Indeed, he knew not what he did, for hitherto he had not been directed by the Spirit of God; but he led a life so good that it was not liable to any reproach. And yet he tells us that he was pointed at with the finger, was mocked at, was reproached, was even accursed among believers, whose ingratitude was such that in his absence he was reviled and

*The husband of one wife.* The reason why this rule is laid down—has been explained by us in the Commentary on the First Epistle to Timothy.[1] Polygamy was so common among the Jews, that the wicked custom had nearly passed into a law. If any man had married two wives before he made a profession of Christianity, it would have been cruel to compel him to divorce one of them; and therefore the apostles endured what was in itself faulty, because they could not correct it. Besides, they who had involved themselves by marrying more than one wife at a time, even though they had been prepared to testify their repentance by retaining but one wife, had, nevertheless, given a sign of their incontinence, which might have been a brand on their good name. The meaning is the same as if Paul had enjoined them to elect those who had lived chastely in marriage—had been satisfied with having a single wife, and had forbidden those who had manifested the power of lust by marrying many wives. At the same time, he who, having become an unmarried man by the death of his wife, marries another, ought, nevertheless, to be accounted " the husband of one wife;" for the apostle does not say, that they shall choose him who has been, but him who is, " the husband of one wife."

*Having believing children.* Seeing that it is required that a pastor shall have prudence and gravity, it is proper that those qualities should be exhibited in his family; for how shall that man who cannot rule his own house—be able to govern the church! Besides, not only must the bishop himself be free from reproach, but his whole family ought to be a sort of mirror of chaste and honourable discipline; and, therefore, in the First Epistle to Timothy, he not less strictly enjoins their wives what they ought to be.[2]

loaded with many slanders. So it is with the servants of God. But when Paul demands that they shall be without crime, he means that we should inquire and ascertain if the life of a man be pure and without blame, and if he continues to conduct himself in that manner. Although we cannot shut the mouths of all slanderers, that they shall not revile us, yet we must be without crime; for it is said, that we shall be reviled as evil-doers, but we shall be pure and innocent. And in what way? Before God we shall have this testimony, that he approves of us, and that all the talk against us is a lie."—*Fr. Ser.*

[1] See p. 76.   [2] See p. 87.

First, he demands that the children shall be "believers;" whence it is obvious that they have been educated in the sound doctrine of godliness, and in the fear of the Lord. Secondly, that they shall not be devoted to luxury, that they may be known to have been educated to temperance and frugality. Thirdly, that they shall *not be disobedient;* for he who cannot obtain from his children any reverence or subjection—will hardly be able to restrain the people by the bridle of discipline.

| | |
|---|---|
| 7. For a bishop must be blameless, as the steward of God; not self-willed, not soon angry, not given to wine, no striker, not given to filthy lucre; | 7. Oportet enim episcopum esse a crimine immunem, tanquam Dei œconomum, non præfractum, non iracundum, non vinosum, non percussorem, non turpiter lucro deditum; |
| 8. But a lover of hospitality, a lover of good men, sober, just, holy, temperate; | 8. Sed hospitalem, studiosum benignitatis, temperantem, justum, sanctum, moderatum, |
| 9. Holding fast the faithful word as he hath been taught, that he may be able by sound doctrine both to exhort and to convince the gainsayers. | 9. Tenacem fidelis sermonis, qui secundum doctrinam est, ut potens sit et exhortari per doctrinam sanam, et contradicentes convincere. |

7. *For a bishop ought to be blameless, as a governor of the house of God.* He again repeats, that they who aspire to the office of a bishop ought to retain an unspotted reputation; and he confirms it by this argument, that, because the Church is the house of God, every person who is appointed to govern it—is constituted, as it were, governor of the house of God. Now, he would be ill spoken of among men, who should take a scandalous and infamous person, and make him his steward; and therefore it would be far more base and intolerable to appoint such persons to be rulers of the household of God. The Latin word *dispensator* (steward or manager)—employed in the old translation, and retained by Erasmus—does not at all express Paul's meaning; for, in order that greater care may be exercised in the election, he adorns the office of a bishop with this honourable eulogy, that it is a government of the house of God, as he says to Timothy, "That thou mayest know how thou oughtest to conduct thyself in the house of God, which is the church of the living God, the pillar and foundation of truth." (1 Tim. iii. 15.)

This passage plainly shows that there is no distinction

between a presbyter and a bishop; for he now calls indiscriminately, by the latter name, those whom he formerly called presbyters; and farther, in conducting this very argument, he employs both names in the same sense, without any distinction; as Jerome has remarked, both in his Commentary on this passage, and in his Epistle to Evagrius. And hence we may perceive how much greater deference has been paid to the opinions of men than ought to have been paid to them; for the language of the Holy Spirit has been set aside, and the custom introduced by the arbitrary will of man has prevailed. For my own part, I do not find fault with the custom which has existed from the very beginning of the Church, that each assembly of bishops shall have one moderator;[1] but that the name of office which God has given to all, shall be conveyed to one alone, and that all the rest shall be deprived of it, is both unreasonable and absurd. Besides, to pervert the language of the Holy Spirit—in such a manner that the same words shall have a different meaning from what he intended—is excessive and profane hardihood.[2]

*Not self-willed.* With good reason does he condemn this vice in a bishop, whose duty it is not only to receive kindly those who come to him of their own accord, but also to allure those who withdraw themselves, that he may conduct all in like manner to Christ. Now, αὐθάδεια (as Plato says in one of his Epistles to Dion) τῆς ἐρημίας ἐστὶ ξύνοικος, that is, "self-will is closely allied to solitude;" for society and friendship cannot be cherished, when every man pleases himself to such an extent as to refuse to yield and accommodate himself to others. And, indeed, every (αὐθάδης) "self-willed" person, as soon as an occasion presents itself, will instantly become a fanatic.

[1] "Un gouverneur ou superintendant." "A governor or superintendent."
[2] "Those whom he formerly called presbyters he now calls bishops, (which means overseers or superintendents,) and he gives this name to all whose duty it is to preach the word of God. And so it was a corruption and abuse in Popery—that is, in the ancient Church—that one individual was called bishop; for that was to change the language of the Holy Spirit, and we ought to speak in accordance with the Scripture. Now we see that Satan labours incessantly to draw us aside from the simplicity of the word of God."—*Fr. Ser.*

8. *But hospitable, devoted to kindness.* Hence it is evident how destructive is that plague which tears the Church by quarrels. With this vice he contrasts, first, docility, and next, gentleness and modesty towards all; for a bishop will never teach well, who is not also ready to learn. Augustine praises highly a saying of Cyprian: " Let him be as patient to learn as skilful to teach." Besides, bishops often need advice and warnings. If they refuse to be admonished, if they reject good advices, they will immediately fall headlong to the grievous injury of the Church. The remedy against these evils, therefore, is, that they be not wise to themselves.

I have chosen to translate φιλάγαθον *devoted to kindness*, rather than with Erasmus, " a lover of good things;" for this virtue, accompanied by hospitality, appears to be contrasted by Paul with covetousness and niggardliness. He calls that man *just*, who lives among men without doing harm to any one. *Holiness* has reference to God; for even Plato draws this distinction between the two words.

9. *Holding fast the faithful word.* This is the chief gift in a bishop, who is elected principally for the sake of teaching; for the Church cannot be governed in any other way than by the word. "The faithful word" is the appellation which he gives to that doctrine which is pure, and which has proceeded from the mouth of God. He wishes that a bishop should hold it fast, so as not only to be well instructed in it, but to be constant in maintaining it. There are some fickle persons who easily suffer themselves to be carried away to various kinds of doctrine; while others are cast down by fear, or moved by any occurrence to forsake the defence of the truth. Paul therefore enjoins that those persons shall be chosen who, having cordially embraced the truth of God, and holding it firmly, never allow it to be wrested from them, or can be torn from it. And, indeed, nothing is more dangerous than that fickleness of which I have spoken, when a pastor does not stedfastly adhere to that doctrine of which he ought to be the unshaken defender. In short, in a pastor there is demanded not only learning, but such zeal for pure doctrine as never to depart from it.

But what is meant by *according to instruction* or *doctrine?*[1] The meaning is, that it is useful for the edification of the Church; for Paul is not wont to give the name of "doctrine" to anything that is learned and known without promoting any advancement of godliness; but, on the contrary, he condemns as vain and unprofitable all the speculations which yield no advantage, however ingenious they may be in other respects. Thus, "He that teacheth, let him do it in doctrine;" that is, let him labour to do good to the hearers. (Rom. xii. 7.) In short, the first thing required in a pastor is, that he be well instructed in the knowledge of sound doctrine; the second is, that, with unwavering firmness of courage, he hold by the confession of it to the last; and the third is, that he make his manner of teaching tend to edification, and do not, through motives of ambition, fly about through the subtleties of frivolous curiosity, but seek only the solid advantage of the Church.

*That he may be able.* The pastor ought to have two voices: one, for gathering the sheep; and another, for warding off and driving away wolves and thieves. The Scripture supplies him with the means of doing both; for he who is deeply skilled in it will be able both to govern those who are teachable, and to refute the enemies of the truth. This twofold use of Scripture Paul describes when he says, *That he may be able to exhort and to convince adversaries.* And hence let us learn, first, what is the true knowledge of a bishop, and, next, to what purpose it ought to be applied. That bishop is truly wise, who holds the right faith; and he makes a proper use of his knowledge, when he applies it to the edification of the people.

This is remarkable applause bestowed on the word of God, when it is pronounced to be sufficient, not only for governing the teachable, but for subduing the obstinacy of enemies. And, indeed, the power of truth revealed by the Lord is such that it easily vanquishes all falsehoods. Let the Popish bishops now go and boast of being the successors of the apostles, seeing that the greater part of them are so ignorant

---

[1] "Selon instruction ou doctrine."

of all doctrine, as to reckon ignorance to be no small part of their dignity.

10. For there are many unruly and vain talkers and deceivers, specially they of the circumcision :

11. Whose mouths must be stopped ; who subvert whole houses, teaching things which they ought not, for filthy lucre's sake.

12. One of themselves, *even* a prophet of their own, said, The Cretians *are* alway liars, evil beasts, slow bellies.

10. Sunt enim multi immorigeri et vaniloqui et mentium seductores, maximè qui sunt ex Circumcisione,

11. Quibus oportet obturare os, qui totas domos subvertunt, docentes quæ non oportet, turpis lucri gratia.

12. Dixit quidam ex ipsis, proprius eorum propheta, Cretenses semper mendaces, malæ bestiæ, ventres pigri.

10. *For there are many unruly.*[1] After having laid down a general rule, which ought to be everywhere observed, in order that Titus may be more attentive to adhere to it, he holds out to him the urgent necessity which ought to excite him more than all things else. He warns him that he has to deal with many obstinate and incorrigible persons, that many are puffed up with vanity and idle talk, that many are deceivers ; and that therefore they ought to choose, on the other hand, such leaders as are qualified and well prepared to oppose them. For, if the children of this world, when dangers arise, increase their solicitude and watchfulness, it would be disgraceful for us, when Satan is using his utmost efforts, to remain careless and inactive, as if we were in a state of peace.

*Unruly.* Instead of (inobedientes) *disobedient*, which is the rendering in the old translation for ἀνυπότακτοι, Erasmus translates it (intractabiles) *incorrigible.* He means those who cannot endure to be brought to obey, and who throw off the yoke of subjection. He gives the appellation of *vain talkers*,[2] not only to the authors of false doctrines, but to those who, addicted to ambitious display, occupy themselves with nothing but useless subtleties. Ματαιολογία[3] (vain talking) is contrasted with useful and solid doctrine, and therefore includes all trivial and frivolous speculations, which contain nothing but empty bombast, because

---

[1] " Car il y en a plusieurs qui ne se peuvent ranger." " For there are many of them who cannot submit."

[2] " Parlans vanitez." " Speaking vanities."

[3] " Vanite de paroles." " Vanity of words."

they contribute nothing to piety and the fear of God. And such is all the scholastic theology that is found, in the present day, in Popery. Yet he calls the same persons *deceivers of minds.* It may be thought preferable to view this as relating to a different class of persons; but, for my own part, I think that it means the same class; for the teachers of such trifles entice and fascinate the minds of men, so as no longer to receive sound doctrine.

*Chiefly they who are of the circumcision.* He says that they are chiefly of the Jews; for it is highly requisite that such plagues shall be known by all. We ought not to listen to those who plead that we should spare the reputation of this or that individual, when the matter in question is the great danger of the whole Church. And so much the greater danger was to be apprehended from that nation, because it claimed superiority above others on account of the sacredness of its lineage. This is therefore the reason why Paul reproves the Jews more sharply, in order to take from them the power of doing injury.

11. *Whose mouth must be stopped.* A good pastor ought therefore to be on the watch, so as not to give silent permission to wicked and dangerous doctrines to make gradual progress, or to allow wicked men an opportunity of spreading them. But it may be asked, "How is it possible for a bishop to constrain obstinate and self-willed men to be silent? For such persons, even though they are vanquished in argument, still do not hold their peace; and it frequently happens that, the more manifestly they are refuted and vanquished, they become the more insolent; for not only is their malice strengthened and inflamed, but they give themselves up to indolence." I reply, when they have been smitten down by the sword of God's word, and overwhelmed by the force of the truth, the Church may command them to be silent; and if they persevere, they may at least be banished from the society of believers, so that they shall have no opportunity of doing harm.[1] Yet by " shutting the

---

[1] " If we mark such persons, and point them out with the finger, everybody will avoid them, and thus they will be prevented from doing harm. This is what Paul had in his eye. Following his example, when we see

mouth" Paul simply means—"to refute their vain talking, even though they should not cease to make a noise; for he who is convicted by the word of God, however he may chatter, has nothing to say.

*Who overturn whole houses.* If the faith of one individual were in danger of being overturned, (for we are speaking of the perdition of a single soul redeemed by the blood of Christ) the pastor should immediately gird himself for the combat; how much less tolerable is it to see whole houses overturned?

*Teaching things which they ought not.* The manner in which they were overturned is described in these words. Hence we may infer how dangerous it is to make even the smallest departure from sound doctrine; for he does not say that the doctrines, by which they overturned the faith of many, were openly wicked; but we may understand by this designation every kind of corruptions, when there is a turning aside from the desire of edification. Thus it is in reality, that, amidst so great weakness of the flesh, we are exceedingly prone to fall; and hence it arises, that Satan easily and speedily destroys, by his ministers, what godly teachers had reared with great and long-continued toil.

He next points out the source of the evil, a desire *of dishonest gain;* by which he reminds us how destructive a plague avarice is in teachers; for, as soon as they give themselves up to the pursuit of gain, they must labour to

people who can do nothing but contrive measures for disturbing and ruining the Church, and who are altogether addicted to evil, it is true that, if we can bring them back in a gentle manner to the right path, we should endeavour to do so. But if they persist, and if we perceive that they are obstinate in their malice, we must not be wiser than the Holy Spirit. They must be known, they must be exposed, and their baseness must be held up to public view, that they may be abhorred, and that others may withdraw from them, as we have formerly seen in other passages. As for those who murmur when we make use of such liberty, they shew plainly that they aim at nothing but confusion in the Church. They do indeed make a show of having some regard to humanity. 'And must we degrade people, and hold them up to scorn, as if we wished to put them to shame?' We answer, Must we leave the poor Church of God in the power of wolves and robbers? Must all the flock be scattered, the blood of our Lord Jesus Christ trampled under foot, and souls which he has redeemed at so costly a price go to perdition, and all order be set aside; and must we nevertheless be silent and shut our eyes?"—*Fr. Ser.*

obtain the favour and countenance of men. This is quickly followed by the corruption of pure doctrine.

12. *One of themselves, a prophet of their own.* I have no doubt that he who is here spoken of is Epimenides, who was a native of Crete; for, when the Apostle says that this author was "one of themselves," and was "a prophet of their own," he undoubtedly means that he belonged to the nation of the Cretans. Why he calls him a Prophet—is doubtful. Some think that the reason is, that the book from which Paul borrowed this passage bears the title Περὶ Χρησμῶν, " concerning oracles." Others are of opinion that Paul speaks ironically, by saying that they have such a Prophet—a Prophet worthy of a nation which refuses to listen to the servants of God. But as poets are sometimes called by the Greeks (προφῆται) " prophets," and as the Latin authors call them Vates, I consider it to denote simply a teacher. The reason why they were so called appears to have been, that they were always reckoned to be (γένος θεῖον καὶ ἐνθουσιαστικόν) " a divine race and moved by divine inspiration." Thus also Adimantus, in the Second Book of Plato's treatise Περὶ Πολιτείας, after having called the poets (υἱοὺς θεῶν) " sons of the gods," adds, that they also became their prophets. For this reason I think that Paul accommodates his style to the ordinary practice. Nor is it of any importance to inquire on what occasion Epimenides calls his countrymen liars, namely, because they boast of having the sepulchre of Jupiter; but seeing that the poet takes it from an ancient and well-known report, the Apostle quotes it as a proverbial saying.[1]

From this passage we may infer that those persons are superstitious, who do not venture to borrow anything from heathen authors. All truth is from God; and consequently, if wicked men have said anything that is true and just, we

[1] The Greek hexameter verse which Paul quotes has been rendered into Latin hexameter by CALVIN himself, and into a French couplet by his translator; and it may be worth while to set down the quotation in the three languages:—
  Greek.—Κρῆτες ἀεὶ ψεῦσται, κακὰ θηρία, γαστέρες ἀργαί.
  Latin.—Mendax, venter iners, semper mala bestia Cres est.
  French.—Tousjours menteuse, et tousjours male-beste,
    Ventre sans coeur, et fay-neant est Crete.—*Ed.*

ought not to reject it; for it has come from God. Besides, all things are of God; and, therefore, why should it not be lawful to dedicate to his glory everything that can properly be employed for such a purpose? But on this subject the reader may consult Basil's discourse[1] πρὸς τοὺς νέους, ὅπως ἂν ἐξ ἑλλ. κ.τ.λ.

| | |
|---|---|
| 13. This witness is true: wherefore rebuke them sharply, that they may be sound in the faith; | 13. Testimonium hoc est verum. Quamobrem argue eos severè, ut sani sint in fide, |
| 14. Not giving heed to Jewish fables, and commandments of men, that turn from the truth. | 14. Neque attendant Judaicis fabulis, et præceptis hominum aversantium veritatem. |
| 15. Unto the pure all things *are* pure: but unto them that are defiled and unbelieving *is* nothing pure; but even their mind and conscience is defiled. | 15. Omnia quidem pura puris; inquinatis autem et infidelibus nihil purum, sed inquinatæ sunt eorum mens et conscientia. |
| 16. They profess that they know God; but in works they deny *him*, being abominable, and disobedient, and unto every good work reprobate. | 16. Deum profitentur se nosse, operibus verò negant, quum sint abominabiles, inobsequentes, et ad omne opus bonum reprobi. |

13. *This testimony is true.*[2] How worthless soever the

[1] " Qu'il lise l'oraison que Basile en a faite, remonstrant aux jeunes gens comment ils se doyvent aider des livres des autheurs profanes." "Let him read Basil's discourse on this subject, instructing young persons how they ought to avail themselves of the assistance to be derived from heathen authors."

[2] " The general character of the Cretans, noticed in Paul's Epistle to Titus, is confirmed by the testimony of antiquity. The Apostle, writing to Titus, who had been left in Crete to regulate the affairs of the Christian Church in that island, complains of many disorderly men there,— 'many unruly and vain talkers and deceivers, who subvert whole houses, (or families,) teaching things which they ought not, for filthy lucre's sake, (Tit. i. 10, 11); and he quotes the following verse from 'one of themselves, a prophet of their own,' namely, Epimenides, who was a Cretan poet, and whose writings were by the ancients termed χρησμοὶ or 'oracles,'

Κρῆτες ἀεὶ ψεῦσται, κακὰ θηρία, γαστέρες ἀργαί.

The general import of which passage is, that 'the Cretans were a false people, and united in their character the ferocity of the wild beast with the luxury of the domesticated one.' The circumstance of Paul's styling Epimenides 'a prophet' is sufficiently explained by the fact of the words Poet and Prophet being often used promiscuously by the Greeks and Romans,—probably because their poets pretended to be inspired, and were by some believed to be so. The Apostle adds, that the testimony of Epimenides is but too true, 'this witness is true.' How true the first part of it is, with respect to their deceit and lying, the following facts will attest. From the time of Homer, the island of Crete was regarded as the scene of fiction. Many authors affirm that, as a people, its inhabitants were

witness may have been,¹ yet the truth which has been spoken
by him is acknowledged by Paul. The inhabitants of Crete,
of whom he speaks with such sharpness, were undoubtedly
very wicked. The Apostle, who is wont to reprove mildly
those who deserved to be treated with extreme severity,
would never have spoken so harshly of the Cretans, if he
had not been moved by very strong reasons. What term
more reproachful than these opprobrious epithets can be
imagined ; that they were " lazy, devoted to the belly, destitute of truth, evil beasts ?" Nor are these vices charged
against one or a few persons, but he condemns the whole
nation.

It was truly a wonderful purpose of God, that he called a
nation so depraved, and so infamous on account of its vices,
to be among the first who should partake of the gospel ; but
his goodness is not less worthy of admiration, in having bestowed heavenly grace on those who did not even deserve to
live in this world.² In that country so corrupt, as if in the
midst of hell, the Church of Christ held a position, and did
not cease to be extended, though it was infected by the corruption of the evils which prevailed there ; for here Paul not
only reproves those who were strangers to the faith, but expressly reproves those who had made a profession of Christianity. Perceiving that these vices so hateful have already
taken root, and are spreading far and wide, he does not spare
the reputation of the whole nation, that he may attempt the
care of those whom there was some hope of healing.

*Wherefore rebuke them sharply.* Of that circumspection
and prudence with which a bishop ought to be endowed, it
is not the least part, that he regulate his manner of teaching by the dispositions and conduct of men. We must not
deal with obstinate and unruly persons in the same manner
as with those who are meek and teachable ; for, in instruct-

infamous for their violation of truth; and at length their falsehood became so notorious, that Κρητίζειν, to Cretise, or imitate the Cretans, was a
proverbial expression among the ancients for *lying.*"—*Horne's Intro-
duction.*

¹ " Combien que l'autheur soit profane et de nulle authorite." " Although the author is a heathen and of no authority."
² " De vivre en ce monde."

ing the latter, we ought to use such mildness as is suitable to their teachable disposition, while the stubbornness of the former must be severely corrected, and (as the saying is) for a bad knot there must be a bad wedge.[1] The reason why Titus ought to be more sharp and severe in rebuking them has been already stated, namely, that they are "evil beasts."

*That they may be sound in the faith.* Whether the "soundness" or "healthfulness" is here contrasted with the diseases which he has mentioned, or whether he simply commands them to remain in the sound faith, is uncertain. I prefer the latter view. As they already are exceedingly vicious, and may easily be corrupted more and more, he wishes them to be more closely and strictly kept within the pure faith.[2]

14. *And may not listen to Jewish fables.* He now shews in what "sound faith" consists—when it is not corrupted by any "fables." But in guarding against the danger he prescribes this remedy—not to give ear to them; for God wishes us to be so attentive to his word, that there shall be no entrance for trifles. And, indeed, when the truth of God has once gained admission, all that can be brought against it will be so tasteless, that it will not attract our minds. If, therefore, we wish to preserve the faith uncontaminated, let us learn carefully to restrain our senses, so that they may not give themselves up to strange contrivances; for, as soon as any person shall begin to listen to fables, he will lose the purity of faith.

[1] "A un mauvais noeud il faut un mauvais coin."

[2] "We have to observe that here, in a single word, Paul declares to us by what means men may defend themselves. It is, by keeping the purity of faith. If, then, we do not turn aside from the simple doctrine of the gospel, but wish to be governed according to the will of God; if we are not carried away by our volatile passions, and do not walk according to our grovelling appetites; in short, if we are good scholars of our God, and reckon it enough to have received the doctrine which he teaches us; if that be the case, we shall be fortified against all evil. It is true, the devil will seek to poison the whole world with his venom, and will spread his filth everywhere, so that the world will be full of so many corruptions that every place shall be infected by them. But however that may be, we must not turn aside from the simplicity of our faith, and must always seek to be instructed simply by our God. When we follow this course, though the devil may contrive all that he can, still we shall be fortified against all evil."—*Fr. Ser.*

All trivial inventions he calls "fables," or, as we would say, "trifles;" for what he immediately adds, about "the commandments of men," has the same meaning. And he calls those men *enemies of the truth* who, not satisfied with the pure doctrine of Christ, mix up with them their own fooleries; for all that men of themselves contrive ought to be accounted "fabulous."

He attributes this vice chiefly to the Jews, because, under the pretence of the divine law, they introduced superstitious ceremonies. The Gentiles, being aware that they had been wretchedly deceived during their whole life, more easily renounced their former course of life; while the Jews, having been educated in the true religion, obstinately defended the ceremonies to which they had been accustomed, and could not be convinced that the Law had been abrogated. In this manner they disturbed all churches, because, as soon as the gospel began to make its appearance anywhere, they did not cease to corrupt its purity by mixing it with their leaven. Accordingly, Paul not only forbids them, in general terms, to degenerate from sound doctrine, but points out, as with the finger, the present evil which needed to be remedied, that they may be on their guard against it.

15. *To the pure all things indeed are pure.* He glances at one class of fabulous opinions; for the choice of the kinds of food, (such as was temporarily enjoined by Moses,) together with purifications and washings, were insisted on as being still necessary, and they even made holiness to consist almost wholly in these minute observances. How dangerous to the Church this was, we have already explained. First, a snare of bondage was laid on the consciences; and next, ignorant persons, bound by this superstition, had a veil drawn over their eyes, which hindered them from advancing in the pure knowledge of Christ. If any of the Gentiles refused to submit to this yoke, because he had not been accustomed to it, the Jews vehemently contended for it, as if it had been the chief article of religion. Not without good reason, therefore, does Paul firmly oppose such corrupters of the gospel. In this passage, indeed, he not only refutes their error, but wittily laughs at their folly, in labouring anxiously, without

any advantage, about abstaining from certain kinds of food and things of that nature.

In the first clause of this verse he upholds Christian liberty, by asserting, that to believers nothing is unclean; but at the same time he indirectly censures the false apostles who set no value on inward purity, which alone is esteemed by God. He therefore rebukes their ignorance, in not understanding that Christians are pure without the ceremonies enjoined by the Law; and next he chastises their hypocrisy, in disregarding uprightness of heart, and occupying themselves with useless exercises. But as the subject now in hand is not the health of the body, but peace of conscience, he means nothing else than that the distinction of the kinds of food, which was in force under the Law, has now been abolished. For the same reason it is evident, that they do wrong, who impose religious scruples on consciences in this matter; for this is not a doctrine intended for a single age, but an eternal oracle of the Holy Spirit, which cannot lawfully be set aside by any new law.

Accordingly, this must be true till the end of the world, that there is no kind of food which is unlawful in the sight of God; and, therefore, this passage is fitly and appropriately quoted in opposition to the tyrannical law of the Pope, which forbids the eating of flesh on certain days. And yet I am not unacquainted with the sophistical arguments which they employ. They affirm, that they do not forbid the eating of flesh, because they allege that it is unclean, (for they acknowledge that all kinds of food are in themselves clean and pure,) but that abstinence from flesh is enjoined on another ground, that it has a tendency to tame the lust of the flesh; as if the Lord had forbidden to eat swine's flesh, because he judged swine to be unclean. Even under the Law the fathers reckoned that everything which God created is in itself pure and clean; but they held that they were unclean for this reason, that the use of them was unlawful, because God had forbidden it. All things are, therefore, pronounced by the Apostle to be pure, with no other meaning than that the use of all things is free, as regards the conscience. Thus, if any law binds the consciences to any necessity of abstaining from certain kinds of food, it wickedly takes away from believers that liberty which God had given them.

*But to the polluted and unbelieving nothing is pure.* This is the second clause, in which he ridicules the vain and useless precautions of such instructors. He says that they gain nothing by guarding against uncleanness in certain kinds of food, because they cannot touch anything that is clean to them. Why so? Because they are "polluted," and, therefore, by their only touching those things which were otherwise pure, they become "polluted."

To the "polluted" he adds the "unbelieving,"[1] not as being a different class of persons; but the addition is made for the sake of explanation. Because there is no purity in the sight of God but that of faith, it follows that all unbelievers are unclean. By no laws or rules, therefore, will they obtain that cleanness which they desire to have; because, being themselves "polluted," they will find nothing in the world that is clean to them.[2]

*But their mind and conscience are polluted.* He shows the fountain from which flows all the filth which is spread over the whole life of man; for, unless the heart be well

---

[1] "The Apostle joins "defiled" and "unbelieving," to intimate that, without a true belief, nothing is clean. The understanding and the conscience are polluted. Both the man and his doings are impure."—*Hervey.*

[2] "It is a dreadful condemnation pronounced on men, when it is said that nothing is clean to them—that all is polluted and defiled, till God has renewed them. So far are we from being able to bring anything that is acceptable to him, that we can neither eat nor drink, nor put on our clothes, nor walk a single step, without corruption; and, what is more, by dwelling in the world we infect all the creatures. And this is the reason why they must call for vengeance at the last day against all unbelievers and reprobates. We have, therefore, good reason to be dissatisfied with ourselves, and to be ashamed, when we see that they become hateful on our account, and that we are so polluted as to have infected everything that God had appropriated to our use, and even that there is nothing in us but all corruption—nothing but a God cursed and disowned. When we are thus humbled, let us know, on the other hand, the inestimable blessing which God bestows on us, when he brings us back to himself, and, after having cleansed us, causes us to use all his blessings and bounties with purity of heart, and when we are assured that it is lawful for us to eat and drink, provided that we do so with all sobriety, and in a reasonable manner."—*Fr. Ser.*

purified, although men consider works to have great splendour, and a sweet smell, yet with God they will excite disgust by their abominable smell and by their filthiness. "The Lord looketh on the heart," (1 Sam. xvi. 7,) and "his eyes are on the truth." (Jer. v. 3.) Whence it arises, that those things which are lofty before men are abomination before God.

The *mind* denotes the understanding, and the *conscience* relates rather to the affections of the heart. But here two things ought to be observed ; first, that man is esteemed by God, not on account of outward works, but on account of the sincere desire of the heart ; and, secondly, that the filth of infidelity is so great, that it pollutes not only the man, but everything that he touches. On this subject let the reader consult Hag. ii. 11-14. In like manner Paul teaches that " all things are sanctified by the word," (1 Tim. iv. 5,) because men use nothing in a pure manner till they receive it by faith from the hand of God.

16. *They profess that they know God.* He treats those persons as they deserve ; for hypocrites, who give their whole attention to minute observances, despise fearlessly what constitutes the chief part of the Christian life. The consequence is, that they display their vanity, while contempt of God is manifested in open crimes. And this is what Paul means ; that they who wish to be seen abstaining from one kind of food—indulge in wantonness and rebellion, as if they had shaken off the yoke ; that their conduct is disgraceful and full of wickedness, and that not a spark of virtue is visible in their whole life.

*For they are abominable, disobedient, and to every good work reprobate.* When he calls them (βδελυκτούς)[1] abomi-

---

[1] " 1. They are said to be βδιλυκτοί, abominable, or shamefully addicted to all manner of evil. The word in the original, denotes the heinousness of those practices in which they allow themselves ; and is derived from a word that signifies to send forth an offensive smell. For all sentiments of right and good are not so totally lost and obliterated among mankind, but that there are some things which even pagans would detest. 2. They are said to be also ἀπιθεῖς, disobedient, which expression imports perseverance and obstinacy in an evil course. They will by no means—by no importunity—by no arguments whatever, be dissuaded from practices so unjustifiable and detestable in their own nature. They

*nable,* he seems to allude to their pretended holiness, to which they gave their earnest attention. But Paul declares that they gain no advantage, for they do not cease to be profane and detestable. With good reason does he accuse them of *disobedience;* for nothing can be more haughty than hypocrites, who exert themselves so laboriously about ceremonies, in order that they may have it in their power to despise with impunity the chief requirements of the law. We may appropriately interpret the word (ἀδόκιμοι) *reprobate,* in an active signification; as if he had said, that they who wish to be thought so sagacious instructors in trifles—are destitute of judgment and understanding as to good works.

## CHAPTER II.

1. But speak thou the things which become sound doctrine:

2. That the aged men be sober, grave, temperate, sound in faith, in charity, in patience.

3. The aged women likewise, that *they be* in behaviour as becometh holiness, not false accusers, not given to much wine, teachers of good things;

4. That they may teach the young women to be sober, to love their husbands, to love their children,

1. Tu verò loquere quæ decent sanam doctrinam.

2. Senes ut sobrii sint, graves, temperantes, sani fide, dilectione, patientia.

3. Anus similiter ut sint in habitu religiosè decoro, non calumniatrices, non multo vino servientes, honesti magistræ,

4. Quo adolescentulas temperantiam doceant, ut ament maritos et liberos,

are resolved to run on, whatever it costs them—to continue in sin, and in the profession of religion at the same time, which is the greatest absurdity imaginable. 3. They are said, lastly, to be πρὸς πᾶν ἔργον ἀγαθὸν ἀδόκιμοι, reprobate to every good work; which signifies a disinclination to everything that is good, to everything that is worthy of praise. The word may be taken, as it is observed, either actively or passively, and so may signify not only to be disappointed by others, but to disapprove themselves; in which latter sense we must, at present, principally understand the phrase. They disapprove all that which claims their approbation and esteem; and are disaffected to all that good which the religion they profess would oblige them to the practice of. The expression, therefore, does not so much signify their omission of what is good, as their disinclination to it; but it further denotes that, if they do anything at all in religion, it is what they neither delight in, nor can endure. 'Every good work' is an expression of such latitude, that it may comprehend all the works of piety, mercy, and common justice. And so it is fit we should understand it in this place. Whatever they do of this kind, their hearts are averse to it, and they bear a disaffected mind to it all. And such as here described, persons may be found to be, notwithstanding their profession."—*Howe.*

5. *To be* discreet, chaste, keepers at home, good, obedient to their own husbands, that the word of God be not blasphemed.

5. Sint temperantes, puræ, domus custodes, benignæ, subjectæ suis maritis, ne sermo Dei malè audiat.

1. *But speak thou the things which become sound doctrine.* He points out the remedy for driving away fables, namely, that Titus should devote himself to edification. He gives the appellation of *sound doctrine* to that which may instruct men to godliness; for all trifles vanish away, when that which is solid is taught. When he enjoins him to speak those things which agree with " sound doctrine," it is as if he had said, that Titus must be continually employed in this preaching; for to mention these things once or twice would not be enough. And Paul does not speak of the discourse of a single day; but so long as Titus shall hold the office of pastor, he wishes him to be employed in teaching this doctrine.

" Sound doctrine" is so called from the effect produced by it; as, on the contrary, he says, that unskilful men dote about questions which do no good. *Sound,* therefore, means wholesome, that which actually feeds souls. Thus, by a single word, as by a solemn proclamation, he banishes from the Church all speculations which serve rather to promote ostentation than to aid godliness,[1] as he did in both of the Epistles to Timothy.

---

[1] " Let the doctrine which proceeds from thy mouth be sound. For he expressly uses this word, because it is the means of upholding us in true integrity, that the word of God, which is preached to us, be our spiritual pasture. This will not be perceived at first sight, but such is the fact. And why do we not perceive it? Because we are too sensual and earthly. For when we are in want of food for our body, we are immediately terrified, we become alarmed, we have not a moment of repose, for it touches us nearly. We are sensitive as to this fading life, but we are insensible to all that affects our souls; there is such brutal stupidity that we do not know our wants, though they press heavily upon us. Yet let it be observed that there is nothing but weakness in us, if we are not fed with the doctrine of God. And that is the reason why it is called ' s o u n d,' for in this consists the health of our souls. As our bodies are kept in their proper condition by well-regulated nourishment, so our souls are supported by that doctrine which serves not only for nourishment but for medicine. For we are full of vices which are worse than diseases; and therefore our soul must be purged, and we must be healed of them. The method of doing this is, that we profit by the word of God. And so it is not without good reason that Paul gives to it this designation, that it is ' sound,' or that it is ' wholesome.' "—*Fr. Ser.*

He makes "sound doctrine" to consist of two parts. The first is that which magnifies the grace of God in Christ, from which we may learn where we ought to seek our salvation; and the second is that by which the life is trained to the fear of God, and inoffensive conduct. Although the former, which includes faith, is far more excellent, and therefore ought to be more zealously inculcated; yet Paul, in writing to Timothy, was not careful about attending to order; for he had to deal with an intelligent man, to whom he would offer an insult, if he dictated to him word by word, as is usually done to apprentices or beginners. Under the person of Titus, indeed, he instructs the whole church of Crete; yet he attends to the rules of propriety, that he may not appear to distrust his prudence. Besides, the reason why he is longer in his exhortations is, that they who gave their whole attention to idle questions—needed especially to be exhorted to the practice of a good and holy life; for nothing is better fitted to restrain the wandering curiosity of men than to know in what duties[1] they ought to be employed.

2. *That aged men be sober.* He begins with particular duties, that the discourse may be better adapted to the instruction of the people. And he does so, not only that he may accommodate himself to their capacity, but that he may press every one more closely; for a general doctrine produces a less powerful impression; but when, by holding out a few cases, he has instructed every person about his duty, there is no one who may not easily conclude, that the Lord has sufficiently instructed him as to the work in which he ought to be employed. We must not therefore, look for a regular method here; for Paul's design was only to state briefly what were the subjects concerning which godly teachers ought to speak, and not to undertake to treat largely of those subjects.

"Aged men" are mentioned by him in the first place. He wishes them to be "sober," because excessive drinking is a vice too common among the old. *Gravity*, which he next mentions, is procured by well-regulated morals. No-

---

[1] "En quels devoirs et bonnes œuvres." "In what duties and good works."

thing is more shameful than for an old man to indulge in youthful wantonness, and, by his countenance, to strengthen the impudence of the young. In the life of old men, therefore, let there be displayed (σεμνότης) "a becoming gravity," which shall constrain the young to modesty. This will be followed chiefly by *temperance,* which he immediately adds.

*Sound in faith.* I do not know whether the word "sound" or "healthy" contains an indirect allusion to the various diseases of old men, with which he contrasts this health of the soul; at least, I think so, though I do not affirm it. With good reason does he include in these three parts—*faith, love, patience*—the sum of Christian perfection. By *faith* we worship God; for neither calling upon him, nor any exercises of godliness, can be separated from it. *Love* extends to all the commandments of the second table. Next follows *patience* as the seasoning of "faith" and "love;" for without "patience" faith would not long endure, and many occurrences are taking place every day—instances of unhandsome conduct or evil temper, which irritate us so much that we should not only be languid, but almost dead, to the duties of love towards our neighbour, if the same "patience" did not support us.

3. *That aged women in like manner.* We very frequently see, that females advanced in age either continue to dress with the lightness of youthful years, or have something superstitious in their apparel, and seldom hit the golden mean. Paul wished to guard against both extremes, by enjoining them to follow a course that is agreeable both to outward propriety and to religion; or, if you choose to express it in simpler language, to give evidence, by their very dress, that they are holy and godly women.

He next corrects other two vices, to which they are often addicted, when he forbids them to be *slanderers* and *slaves to much wine.* Talkativeness is a disease of women, and it is increased by old age. To this is added, that women never think that they are eloquent enough, if they are not given to prattling and to slander—if they do not attack the characters of all. The consequence is, that old women, by their slanderous talkativeness, as by a lighted torch, frequently set on fire many houses. Many are also given to drinking, so that, forgetting modesty and gravity, they indulge in an unbecoming wantonness.

4. *That they may teach young women temperance.* That they may be more attentive to duty, he shows that it is not enough if their own life be decent, if they do not also train *young women*, by their instructions, to a decent and chaste life. He therefore adds, that by their example they should train to temperance and gravity those younger women whom the warmth of youth might otherwise lead into imprudence.

*To love their husbands and their children.* I do not agree with those who think that this is a recapitulation of the advices which elderly women should give to those who are younger; for a careful perusal of the context will enable any one easily to perceive that Paul goes on in explaining the duties of women, which apply equally to those who are older. Besides, the construction would be inappropriate, σωφρονίζωσι, σώφρονας εἶναι.[1] Yet while he instructs elderly females what they ought to be, he at the same time holds out to the younger the example which they ought to follow. Thus he indiscriminately teaches both. In short, he wishes women to be restrained, by conjugal love and affection for their children, from giving themselves up to licentious attachments, he wishes them to rule their own house in a sober and orderly manner, forbids them to wander about in public places, bids them be chaste, and at the same time modest, so as to be subject to the dominion of their husbands; for those who excel in other virtues sometimes take occasion from them to act haughtily, so as to be disobedient to their husbands.

When he adds, *that the word of God may not be evil spoken of*, it is supposed that this relates strictly to women who were married to unbelieving husbands, who might judge of

---

[1] "Ἵνα σωφρονίζωσι τὰς νίας. "These words point at the chief purpose of the instructions—namely, that they should teach them to be σώφρονις, acting as monitresses and regulators of their morals. Those instructions (as appears from what follows) were to turn on the domestic duties suitable to young married women, and each in the order of importance. The first is, as it were, their cardinal virtue; for it was well said by Socrates, (Ap. Stob. p. 488,) εὐσέβεια γυναικεία, ὁ πρὸς τὸν ἄνδρα ἔρως, ('female piety is love to her husband.') In like manner, modesty is, by Pericles, in his Funeral Oration (Thucyd. ii. 45) called 'the virtue of the female sex.'"—*Bloomfield.*

the gospel from the wicked conduct of their wives; and this appears to be confirmed by 1 Pet. iii. 1. But what if he does not speak of husbands alone? And, indeed, it is probable that he demands such strictness of life as not to bring the gospel into the contempt of the public by their vices. As to the other parts of the verse, the reader will find them explained in the Commentary on the First Epistle to Timothy.[1]

| | |
|---|---|
| 6. Young men likewise exhort to be sober-minded. | 6. Juniores similiter hortare, ut temperantes sint, |
| 7. In all things shewing thyself a pattern of good works: in doctrine *shewing* uncorruptness, gravity, sincerity, | 7. In omnibus teipsum exhibens exemplar bonorum operum in doctrina, integritatem, gravitatem, |
| 8. Sound speech, that cannot be condemned; that he that is of the contrary part may be ashamed, having no evil thing to say of you. | 8. Sermonem sanum, irreprehensibilem, ut adversarius pudefiat, nihil habens, quod de vobis obloquatur: |
| 9. *Exhort* servants to be obedient unto their own masters, *and* to please *them* well in all *things;* not answering again; | 9. Servos, ut dominis suis subjecti sint, in omnibus placere studentes, non responsatores, |
| 10. Not purloining, but shewing all good fidelity; that they may adorn the doctrine of God our Saviour in all things. | 10. Non furaces, sed fidem omnem ostendentes bonam, ut doctrinam Servatoris nostri Dei ornent in omnibus. |

6. *Exhort likewise younger men.* He merely enjoins that young men be instructed to be *temperate;* for temperance, as Plato shows, cures the whole understanding of man. It is as if he had said, "Let them be well regulated and obedient to reason."

7. *In all things shewing thyself.* For doctrine will otherwise carry little authority, if its power and majesty do not shine in the life of the bishop,[2] as in a mirror. He wishes, therefore, that the teacher may be a pattern, which his scholars may copy.[3]

[1] See p. 135.
[2] "En la vie du pasteur." "In the life of the pastor."
[3] "As if he had said, that the man who has the office and duty of proclaiming the word of God ought to preach throughout his whole life, since God has chosen him to that condition; when it shall be seen how he governs, when it is found that it is an approbation of the doctrine which he teaches, and that he profits and edifies not only by the mouth, showing what ought to be done, but likewise by his example, when it shall be known that he speaks in sincerity, and not in hypocrisy, that he may be edified by it.

*A pattern of good works in doctrine, uprightness, gravity.* In the original Greek the style is here involved and obscure, and this creates ambiguity. First, he makes use of the words *in doctrine,* and then adds, in the accusative case, *integrity, gravity,* &c.¹ Without mentioning the interpretations given by others, I shall state that which appears to me to be the most probable. First, I connect these words, *of good works in doctrine;* for, after having enjoined Titus that, in teaching, he shall inculcate the practice of good works, he wishes that good works, which correspond to this doctrine, may be visible in his life; and consequently the preposition *in* means that they shall be suitable, or shall correspond, to the doctrine. What follows is in no degree obscure; for, in order that he may exhibit a representation of his doctrine in morals, he bids him be "upright and grave."

8. *Sound speech, unblamable.*² "Sound speech" relates (in my opinion) to ordinary life and familiar conversation; for it would be absurd to interpret it as relating to public instruction, since he only wishes that Titus, both in his actions and in his words, shall lead a life that agrees with his preaching. He therefore enjoins that his words shall be pure and free from all corruption.

*Unblamable* may apply either to the words or the person of Titus. I prefer the latter view, that the other nouns in the accusative case (which the Greek syntax easily allows) may depend upon it in this sense—"that thou mayest shew thyself unblamable in gravity, in integrity, and in sound words."

*That the adversary may be ashamed.* Although a Christian

And would to God that this were duly observed; for the truth of God would be received with greater reverence than it is. But however that may be, we shall not be held excused, since God wishes to make use of us so as to regulate others, and to direct our life in such a manner that, when they shall follow as with one accord, we may strive to honour God, and give no occasion to despise the sacred word, since God has made us instruments, and wishes that his doctrine should be received from us, as if he spoke in his own person."—*Fr. Ser.*

¹ "At ἐν τῇ διδασκαλίᾳ ἀδιαφθορίαν repeat παρεχόμενος in the sense ἐνδεικνύ-μενος."—*Bloomfield.*
² "Irreprehensible, ou qu'on ne puisse condamner." "Unblamable, or that cannot be condemned."

man ought to look at other objects, yet this must not be neglected, to shut the mouth of wicked men, as we are everywhere taught that we should give no occasion for slander. Everything that they can seize on as improper in our conduct is maliciously turned against Christ and his doctrine. The consequence is, that, through our fault, the sacred name of God is exposed to insult. Accordingly, the more we perceive that we are keenly observed by enemies, let us be the more attentive to guard against their calumnies, and thus let their malignity strengthen in us the desire of doing well.

9. *Servants, that they be subject to their masters.* It has been already said that Paul merely glances at some things by way of example, and does not explain the whole of these subjects, as if he undertook, expressly, to handle them. Accordingly, when he enjoins servants *to please their masters in all things,* this desire of pleasing must be limited to those things which are proper, as is evident from other passages of a similar nature, in which an exception is expressly added, to the effect that nothing should be done but according to the will of God.

It may be observed that the Apostle dwells chiefly on this point, that they who are under the authority of others shall be obedient and submissive. With good reason he does this, for nothing is more contrary to the natural disposition of man than subjection, and there was danger lest they should take the gospel as a pretext for becoming more refractory, as reckoning it unreasonable that they should be subject to the authority of unbelievers. So much the greater care and diligence ought pastors to use for either subduing or checking this rebellious spirit.

10. *Not thievish, but shewing all good faith.* He censures two vices that are common among servants, petulant replies, and a propensity to steal.[1] The comedies are full of instances

---

[1] "Here we see how strictly Paul observed those of whom he was speaking. For the slaves who were in that age were addicted to pillage; and besides, they were contradictory, as if they had not dreaded the strokes with which they were chastised. We find that they sometimes grew hardened, because their masters did not use them gently, but treated them as brute beasts, struck them, teased them, put them to the torture, and frequently beat them, when they were absolutely naked, so that the blood

of excessively ready talk, by which servants cheat their masters. Nor was it without reason that an exchange of names took place in ancient times, by which "servant" and "thief" became convertible terms. Thus prudence requires that we make our instructions apply to the morals of each individual.

By *faith* he means fidelity to their masters; and therefore, to *shew all faith* is to act faithfully, without using fraud or doing injury, in transacting the affairs of their masters.

*That they may adorn the doctrine of God our Saviour in all things.* This ought to be a very sharp spur of exhortation to us, when we learn that our becoming conduct adorns the doctrine of God, which, at the same time, is a mirror of his glory. And, indeed, we see that this usually happens; as, on the other hand, our wicked life brings disgrace upon it; for men commonly judge of us from our works. But this circumstance ought also to be observed, that God deigns to receive an "ornament" from slaves, whose condition was so low and mean that they were wont to be scarcely accounted men; for he does not mean "servants," such as we have in the present day, but slaves,[1] who were bought with money, and held as property, like oxen or horses. And if the life of those men is an ornament to the Christian name, much more let those who are in honour take care that they do not stain it by their baseness.

| | |
|---|---|
| 11. For the grace of God that bringeth salvation hath appeared to all men, | 11. Apparuit enim gratia Dei salutaris omnibus hominibus, |
| 12. Teaching us, that, denying ungodliness and worldly lusts, we should live soberly, righteously, and godly, in this present world; | 12. Instituens nos, ut, abnegata impietate et mundanis cupiditatibus, temperanter et justè et piè vivamus in hoc sæculo, |
| 13. Looking for that blessed hope, and the glorious appearing of the great God and our Saviour Jesus Christ; | 13. Expectantes beatam spem et apparitionem gloriæ magni Dei et Servatoris nostri Iesu Christi, |

flowed on all sides. Being thus hardened to evil, we must not be astonished if they had such corruption as to take revenge on their masters when they had any opportunity. But now Paul does not fail to exhort them to please their masters, that is, in everything that was good and right—an exception which he makes in other passages."—*Fr. Ser.*

[1] "Des esclaves ou serfs." "Slaves or serfs."

| 14. Who gave himself for us, that he might redeem us from all iniquity, and purify unto himself a peculiar people, zealous of good works. | 14. Qui dedit seipsum pro nobis, ut redimeret nos ab omni iniquitate, et purificaret sibi populum peculiarem studiosum bonorum operum. |
|---|---|
| 15. These things speak, and exhort, and rebuke with all authority. Let no man despise thee. | 15. Hæc loquere et exhortare, et argue cum omni auctoritate. Nemo te contemnat. |

11. *For the grace of God*[1] *hath appeared.* He argues from the design of redemption, which he shews to be a desire to live a godly and upright life. Hence it follows, that the duty of a good teacher is rather to exhort to a holy life than to occupy the minds of men with useless questions. "He hath redeemed us," says Zacharias in his song,—"that we may serve him in holiness and righteousness all the days of our life." (Luke i. 74, 75.) For the same reason Paul says, *the grace of God hath appeared, teaching us;* for he means that it ought to hold the place of instruction to us to regulate our life well. What is proclaimed concerning the mercy of God is seized by some as an occasion of licentiousness; while others are hindered by slothfulness from meditating on "newness of life." But the manifestation of the grace of God unavoidably carries along with it exhortations to a holy life.

*Bringing salvation to all men.*[2] That it is common to all

[1] "We have seen that we ought to preach daily that grace which was declared at the coming of our Lord Jesus Christ. This is a wonderful mystery, that God was manifested in the flesh, and that, at the same time, he hath shewn to us his heavenly glory, that we may be united to it. In this manner all pastors ought to be employed; for when they shall unceasingly illustrate that wisdom which God hath declared to us in the person of his Son, it is certain that the time will not be lost. And this is what Paul says in another passage, (Eph. iii. 18,) that it is the height, and depth, and length, and breadth, and thickness of all knowledge. When we shall have extended our views to explore as far as possible—when we shall descend into the depth to search out all that is concealed from us—when we shall go beyond the length and breadth of the sea, we shall have a wisdom (he says) as high and as deep, as long and as broad as this, when we shall know the infinite love of God which God hath showed to us in the person of his only-begotten Son."—*Fr. Ser.*

[2] "We now see why Paul speaks of *all men,* and thus we may judge of the folly of some who pretend to expound the Holy Scriptures, and do not understand their style, when they say, 'And God wishes that every person should be saved; the grace of God hath appeared for the salvation of every person; it follows, then, that there is free-will, that there is no election, that none have been predestinated to salvation.' If those men spoke, it ought to be with a little more caution. Paul did not mean in this passage,

is expressly testified by him on account of the slaves of whom he had spoken. Yet he does not mean individual men, but rather describes individual classes, or various ranks of life. And this is not a little emphatic, that the grace of God hath let itself down even to the race of slaves; for, since God does not despise men of the lowest and most degraded condition, it would be highly unreasonable that we should be negligent and slothful to embrace his goodness.

12. *Teaching us that, denying ungodliness.* He now lays down the rule for regulating our life well, and how we ought to begin, namely, with renouncing our former life, of which he enumerates two parts, "ungodliness and worldly desires." Under *ungodliness*, I include not only superstitions, in which they had gone astray, but irreligious contempt of God, such as reigns in men, till they have been enlightened in the knowledge of the truth. Although they have some profession of religion, yet they never fear and reverence God sincerely and honestly, but, on the contrary, have consciences that are useless, so that nothing is further from their thoughts than that they ought to serve God.[1]

or in 1 Tim. ii. 6, anything else than that the great are called by God, though they are unworthy of it; that men of low condition, though they are despised, are nevertheless adopted by God, who stretches out his hand to receive them. At that time, because kings and magistrates were mortal enemies of the gospel, it might be thought that God had rejected them, and that they cannot obtain salvation. But Paul says that the door must not be shut against them, and that, eventually, God may choose some of this company, though their case appear to be desperate. Thus, in this passage, after speaking of the poor slaves who were not reckoned to belong to the rank of men, he says that God did not fail, on that account, to show himself compassionate towards them, and that he wishes that the gospel should be preached to those to whom men do not deign to utter a word. Here is a poor man, who shall be rejected by us; we shall hardly say, God bless him! and God addresses him in an especial manner, and declares that he is his Father, and does not merely say a passing word, but stops him to say, 'Thou art of my flock, let my word be thy pasture, let it be the spiritual food of thy soul.' Thus we see that this word is highly significant, when it is said that the grace of God hath appeared fully to all men."—*Fr. Ser.*

[1] "It presents us with the strongest motives to obedience. 'The grace of God teacheth us to deny ungodliness.' What chains bind faster and closer than love? Here is love to our nature in his incarnation; love to us, though enemies, in his death and passion; encouragements to obedience by the proffers of pardon for former rebellions. By the disobedience of man God introduces his redeeming grace, and engages his creature to more ingenuous and excellent returns than his innocent state could oblige

By *worldly desires*[1] he means all the affections of the flesh; because we look at nothing but the world, till the Lord has drawn us to himself. Meditation on the heavenly life begins with regeneration. Before we have been regenerated, our desires lean towards the world, and rest on the world.

*That we may live temperately, and righteously, and piously.* As he formerly mentioned those three, when he wished to give a comprehensive summary of Christian life, so he now makes it to consist of those three, " piety, righteousness, and temperance." " Piety" is religion towards God. " Righteousness" has place among men. He who is endowed with both of these lacks nothing for perfect virtue; and, indeed, in the law of God there is absolute perfection, to which nothing whatever can be added. But as the exercises of godliness may be regarded as appendages to the first table, so " temperance," which Paul mentions in this passage, aims at nothing else than keeping the law, and, as I said before about patience,[2] is added to the former as a seasoning. Nor does the Apostle contradict himself, when at one time he describes patience, and at another time temperance, as the perfection of a holy life; for they are not distinct virtues, since σωφροσύνη (here translated temperance) includes patience under it.

He adds, *in this world*,[3] because the Lord has appointed the present life for the trial of our faith. Although the fruit of good actions is not yet visible, yet the hope should

him to. In his created state he had goodness to move him, he hath the same goodness now to oblige him as a creature, and a greater love and mercy to oblige him as a repaired creature; and the terror of justice is taken off, which might envenom his heart as a criminal. In his revolted state he had misery to discourage him; in his redeemed state he hath love to attract him. Without such a way, black despair had seized upon the creature exposed to a remediless misery; and God would have had no returns of love from the best of his earthly works; but if any sparks of ingenuity be left, they will be excited by the efficacy of this argument."— *Charnock.*

[1] " On the expression τὰς κοσμικὰς ἐπιθυμίας the best comment is 1 John ii. 16. Σωφρόνως denotes virtue as regards ourselves; δικαίως, as regards our fellow-creatures; and εὐσεβῶς, as respects God. Similar divisions are found in passages of the classical writers cited by the commentators."— *Bloomfield.*   [2] See p. 311.

[3] " En ce present monde." " In this present world."

be sufficient for stimulating us to doing well; and this is what he immediately adds,—

13. *Looking for that blessed hope.* From the hope of future immortality he draws an exhortation, and indeed, if that hope be deeply seated in our mind, it is impossible that it should not lead us to devote ourselves wholly to God. On the contrary, they who do not cease to live to the world and to the flesh never have actually tasted what is the worth of the promise of eternal life; for the Lord, by calling us to heaven, withdraws us from the earth.

*Hope* is here put for the thing hoped for, otherwise it would be an incorrect mode of expression. He gives this appellation to the blessed life which is laid up for us in heaven. At the same time he declares when we shall enjoy it, and what we ought to contemplate, when we desire or think of our salvation.

*And the appearing of the glory of the great God and Saviour.* I interpret the *glory of God* to mean not only that by which he shall be glorious in himself, but also that by which he shall then diffuse himself on all *sides*, so as to make all his elect partakers of it. He calls God *great*, because his greatness—which men, blinded by the empty splendour of the world, now extenuate, and sometimes even annihilate, as far as lies in their power—shall be fully manifested on the last day. The lustre of the world, while it appears great to our eyes, dazzles them so much that " the glory of God " is, as it were, hidden in darkness. But Christ, by his coming, shall chase away all the empty show of the world—shall no longer obscure the brightness, shall no longer lessen the magnificence, of his glory. True, the Lord demonstrates his majesty every day by his works; but because men are prevented by their blindness from seeing it, it is said to be hidden in obscurity. Paul wishes that believers may now contemplate by faith that which shall be manifested on the last day, and therefore that God may be magnified, whom the world either despises, or, at least, does not esteem according to his excellence.

It is uncertain whether these words should be read together thus, " the glory of our Lord Jesus Christ, the great

God and our Saviour," or separately, as of the Father and the Son, "the glory of the great God, and of our Saviour, the Lord Jesus Christ."[1] The Arians, seizing on this latter sense, have endeavoured to prove from it, that the Son is less than the Father, because here Paul calls the Father *the great God* by way of distinction from the Son. The orthodox teachers of the Church, for the purpose of shutting out this slander, eagerly contended that both are affirmed of Christ. But the Arians may be refuted in a few words and by solid argument; for Paul, having spoken of the revelation of the glory of "the great God," immediately added "Christ," in order to inform us, that that revelation of glory will be in his person; as if he had said that, when Christ shall appear, the greatness of the divine glory shall then be revealed to us.

Hence we learn, first, that there is nothing that ought to render us more active or cheerful in doing good than the hope of the future resurrection; and, secondly, that believers ought always to have their eyes fixed on it, that they may not grow weary in the right course; for, if we do not wholly

---

[1] "Of these words the most natural sense, and that required by the 'proprietas linguæ,' is, beyond all doubt, the one assigned by almost all the ancients from Clem. Alex. downwards, and by the early modern expositors, as Erasmus, Grotius, and Beza, and also by some eminent expositors and theologians of later times, as Bishops Pearson and Bull, Wolff, Matthæi, and Bishop Middleton, namely, 'Looking for (or rather, looking forward to; comp. Job ii. 9, and see Grotius) the blessed hope, even the glorious appearing of our great God and Saviour Jesus Christ.' The cause of the ambiguity in our common version is ably pointed out, and the above version established on the surest grounds, by Bishop Middleton and Professor Scholefield. But, besides the argument founded on the 'propriety of language,' that of Beza, who urges that ἐπιφάνεια is nowhere used of God, but Christ, is unanswerable. So in an able critique on Dr. Channing's works, in the British Critic, the Reviewer justly maintains that 'Christ must be the God here spoken of, because it is his "glorious appearing" which all Christians here are said to expect; but of God the Father we are expressly told that him "no man hath seen, nor can see."' Other convincing arguments for the construction here laid down may be seen in Dr. Routh's Reliquiæ Sacræ, vol. ii. p. 26. The reader is also particularly referred to Clem. Alex. Cohort. ad Gentes, sub init., where verses 11-14 are cited by that Father, and the view of Σωτῆρος here maintained is adopted. The whole of the context there is deserving of great attention, as containing such plain and repeated attestations to the divinity of Jesus Christ as can rarely be found. The passage itself may be seen in Bishop Bull's Def. Fid. Nic., p. 87."—*Bloomfield.*

depend upon it, we shall continually be carried away to the vanities of the world. But, since the coming of the Lord to judgment might excite terror in us, Christ is held out to us as our "Saviour," who will also be our judge.

14. *Who gave himself for us.* This is another argument of exhortation, drawn from the design or effect of the death of Christ, who offered himself for us, that he might redeem us from the bondage of sin, and purchase us to himself as his heritage. His grace, therefore, necessarily brings along with it "newness of life," (Rom. vi. 4,) because they who still are the slaves of sin make void the blessing of redemption; but now we are released from the bondage of sin, in order that we may serve the righteousness of God; and, therefore, he immediately added,—

*A peculiar people, zealous of good works;* by which he means that, so far as concerns us, the fruit of redemption is lost, if we are still entangled by the sinful desires of the world. And in order to express more fully, that we have been consecrated to good works by the death of Christ, he makes use of the word *purify;* for it would be truly base in us to be again polluted by the same filth from which the Son of God hath washed us by his blood.[1]

15. *Speak these things, and exhort, and reprove.* This conclusion is of the same meaning as if he enjoined Titus to dwell continually on that doctrine of edification, and never to grow weary, because it cannot be too much inculcated. He likewise bids him add the spurs of "exhortations and reproofs;" for men are not sufficiently admonished as to their duty, if they be not also vehemently urged to the per-

[1] "Christ expiated sin, not encouraged it; he died to make your peace, but he died to make you holy; 'to purify a people to himself,' (Tit. ii. 14.) The ends of Christ's death cannot be separated. He is no atoner, where he is not a refiner. It is as certain as any word the mouth of God hath spoken, that 'there is no peace to the wicked,' (Isa. xlviii. 22.) A guilty conscience, and an impure, will keep up the amity with Satan, and enmity with God. He that allows himself in any sin deprives himself of the benefit of reconciliation. This reconciliation must be mutual; as God lays down his wrath against us, so we must throw down our arms against him. As there was a double enmity, one rooted in nature, another declared by wicked works; or rather, one enmity in its root, and another in its exercise, (Col. i. 21,) so there must be an alteration of state, and an alteration of acts."—*Charnock.*

formance of it. He who understands those things which the Apostle has formerly stated, and who has them always in his mouth, will have ground not only for teaching, but likewise for correcting.

*With all authority.* I do not agree with Erasmus, who translates ἐπιταγή "diligence in commanding." There is greater probability in the opinion of Chrysostom, who interprets it to mean severity against more atrocious sins; though I do not think that even he has hit the Apostle's meaning; which is, that Titus should claim authority and respect for himself in teaching these things. For men given to curious inquiries, and eager about trifles, dislike the commandments to lead a pious and holy life as being too common and vulgar. In order that Titus may meet this disdain, he is enjoined to add the weight of his authority to his doctrine. It is with the same view (in my opinion) that he immediately adds,—

*Let no man despise thee.* Others think that Titus is instructed to gain the ear of men, and their respect for him, by the integrity of his life; and it is indeed true that holy and blameless conduct imparts authority to instruction. But Paul had another object in view; for here he addresses the people rather than Titus. Because many had ears so delicate, that they despised the simplicity of the gospel; because they had such an itch for novelty, that hardly any space was left for edification; he beats down the haughtiness of such men, and strictly charges them to desist from despising, in any way, sound and useful doctrine. This confirms the remark which I made at the outset, that this Epistle was written to the inhabitants of Crete rather than to any single individual.

## CHAPTER III.

| 1. Put them in mind to be subject to principalities and powers, to obey magistrates, to be ready to every good work, | 1. Admone illos, ut principatibus et potestatibus subditi sint, ut magistratibus pareant, ut ad omne opus bonum sint parati, |
|---|---|
| 2. To speak evil of no man, to be | 2. Ne de quoquam malè dicant, |

no brawlers, *but* gentle, shewing all meekness unto all men.

3. For we ourselves also were sometimes foolish, disobedient, deceived, serving divers lusts and pleasures, living in malice and envy, hateful, *and* hating one another.

ut sint non pugnaces, humani, omnem exhibentes mansuetudinem erga omnes homines.

3. Nam eramus et nos stulti quondam, inobedientes, errantes, servientes cupiditatibus et voluntatibus variis, in malitia et invidia degentes, odiosi, invicem odio prosequentes.

1. *Remind them to be subject to principalities and powers.* From many passages it is evident that the Apostles had great difficulty in keeping the common people subject to the authority of magistrates and princes. We are all by nature desirous of power; and the consequence is, that no one willingly is subject to another. Besides, perceiving that nearly all the principalities and powers of the world[1] were at that time opposed to Christ, they thought them unworthy of receiving any honour. The Jews especially, being an untamable race, did not cease to mutiny and rage. Thus, after having spoken of particular duties, Paul now wishes to give a general admonition to all, to observe peaceably the order of civil government, to submit to the laws, to obey magistrates. That subjection to princes, and that obedience to magistrates, which he demands, is extended to edicts, and laws, and other parts of civil government.

What he immediately adds, *To be ready for every good work,* may be applied to the same subject; as if he had said, "All who do not refuse to lead a good and virtuous life, will cheerfully yield obedience to magistrates." For, since they have been appointed for the preservation of mankind, he who desires to have them removed, or shakes off their yoke, is an enemy of equity and justice, and is therefore devoid of all humanity. Yet if any prefer to interpret it without any immediate relation to the context, I have no objection; and indeed there can be no doubt that, in this sentence, he recommends to them kind offices towards their neighbours throughout their whole life.

2. *To speak evil of no one.* He now lays down the method of maintaining peace and friendship with all men. We know that there is nothing to which the disposition of every man

[1] "Toutes les principautes et puissances du monde."

is more prone than to despise others in comparison of himself. The consequence is, that many are proud of the gifts of God; and this is accompanied by contempt for their brethren, which is immediately followed by insult. He therefore forbids Christians to glory over others, or to reproach them, whatever may be their own superior excellence. Yet he does not wish them to flatter the vices of wicked men; he only condemns the propensity to slander.

*Not given to fighting.* As if he had said, "Quarrels and contentions must be avoided." The old translation has therefore rendered it better, *Not quarrelsome;* for there are other ways of fighting than the sword or the fist. And from what follows it is evident that this is the meaning; for he points out the remedies for the evil, when he enjoins them *to be kind, and to shew all meekness towards all men;* for "kindness" is contrasted with the utmost rigour of law, and "meekness" with bitterness. If, therefore, we are disposed to avoid every kind of contentions and fighting, let us learn, first, to moderate many things by gentleness, and next to bear with many things; for they who are excessively severe and ill-tempered carry with them a fire to kindle strife.

He says, *towards all men,* in order to intimate that he should bear with even the lowest and meanest persons. Believers, holding wicked men in contempt, did not think them worthy of any forbearance. Such severity, which arises from nothing else than pride, Paul wished to correct.

3. *For we ourselves*[1] *also were formerly foolish.* Nothing

---

[1] "We ourselves, who had the oracles of God, that had greater privileges than others, were carried out with as strong an impetus naturally, till grace stopped the tide, and, after stopping, turned it against nature. When the mind was thus prepossessed, and the will made the lusts of the flesh its work and trade, there was no likelihood of any co-operation with God, in fulfilling his desires, till the bent of the heart was changed from the flesh and its principles. The heart is stone before grace. No stone can co-operate with any that would turn it into flesh, since it hath no seed, causes, or principles of any fleshly nature in it. Since we are overwhelmed by the rubbish of our corrupted estate, we can no more co-operate to the removal of it than a man buried under the ruins of a fallen house can contribute to the removal of that great weight that lies upon him. Neither would a man in that state help such a work, because his lusts are plea-

is better adapted to subdue our pride, and at the same time to moderate our severity, than when it is shewn that everything that we turn against others may fall back on our own head; for he forgives easily who is compelled to sue for pardon in return. And indeed, ignorance of our own faults is the only cause that renders us unwilling to forgive our brethren. They who have a true zeal for God, are, indeed, severe against those who sin; but, because they begin with themselves, their severity is always attended by compassion. In order that believers, therefore, may not haughtily and cruelly mock at others, who are still held in ignorance and blindness, Paul brings back to their remembrance what sort of persons they formerly were; as if he had said, "If such fierce treatment is done to those on whom God has not yet bestowed the light of the gospel, with equally good reason might you have been at one time harshly treated. Undoubtedly you would not have wished that any person should be so cruel to you; exercise now, therefore, the same moderation towards others."

In the words of Paul, there are two things that need to be understood. The first is, that they who have now been enlightened by the Lord, being humbled by the remembrance of their former ignorance, should not exalt themselves proudly over others, or treat them with greater harshness and severity than that which, they think, ought to have been exercised towards themselves, when they were what those now are. The second is, that they should consider, from what has taken place in their own persons, that they who to-day are strangers may to-morrow be received into the Church, and, having been led to amendment of their sinful practices, may become partakers of the gifts of God, of which they are now destitute. There is a bright mirror of both in believers, who "at one time were darkness, and afterwards began to be light in the Lord." (Eph. v. 8.) The knowledge of their former condition should therefore dispose them to ($\sigma\upsilon\mu\pi\acute{a}\theta\epsilon\iota\alpha\nu$) fellow-feeling. On the other

---

sures; he serves his lusts, which are pleasures as well as lusts, and therefore served with delight."—*Charnock.*

hand, the grace of God, which they now enjoy, is a proof that others may be brought to salvation.

Thus we see that we must be humbled before God, in order that we may be gentle towards brethren; for pride is always cruel and disdainful of others. In another passage, (Gal. vi. 1,) where he exhorts us to mildness, he advises every one to remember his own weakness. Here he goes farther, for he bids us remember those vices from which we have been delivered, that we may not pursue too keenly those which still dwell in others.

Besides, seeing that here Paul describes briefly the natural disposition of men, such as it is before it is renewed by the Spirit of God, we may behold, in this description, how wretched we are while we are out of Christ. First, he calls unbelievers *foolish,* because the whole wisdom of men is mere vanity, so long as they do not know God. Next, he calls them *disobedient,* because, as it is faith alone that truly obeys God, so unbelief is always wayward and rebellious; although we might translate ἀπειθεῖς *unbelieving,* so as to describe the kind of "foolishness." Thirdly, he says that unbelievers *go astray;* for Christ alone is "the way" and the "light of the world." (John viii. 12; xiv. 6.) All who are estranged from God must therefore wander and go astray during their whole life.

Hitherto he has described the nature of unbelief; but now he likewise adds the fruits which proceed from it, namely, *various desires and pleasures, envy, malice,* and such like. It is true that each person is not equally chargeable with every vice; but, seeing that all are the slaves of wicked desires, although some are carried away by one and others by another desire, Paul embraces in a general statement[1] all

[1] "The Apostle speaks of what naturally we all were. This, then, is a most merciful influence that is given forth in the regenerating work. It is as if God should have said, I see those poor creatures are perishing, not only tending to hell, but carrying with them their own hell into hell, 'hell being at last cast into hell' (as the expression in the Revelation is.) It is a throwing hell into hell, when a wicked man comes to hell; for he was his own hell before. God, beholding this forlorn case of wretched creatures, saith, I must either renew them or lose them; I must either transform them, or they must perish: they are in the fire of hell already. Such and such we were, but of his mercy he saved us by the washing of regeneration,

the fruits that are anywhere produced by unbelief. This subject is explained towards the close of the first chapter of the Epistle to the Romans.

Moreover, since Paul, by these marks, distinguishes the children of God from unbelievers, if we wish to be accounted believers, we must have our heart cleansed from all envy, and from all malice; and we must both love and be beloved. It is unreasonable that those desires should reign in us, which are here called "various," for this reason, in my opinion, that the lusts by which a carnal man is driven about are like opposing billows, which, by fighting against each other, turn the man hither and thither, so that he changes and vacillates almost every moment. Such, at least, is the restlessness of all who abandon themselves to carnal desires; because there is no stability but in the fear of God.

4. But after that the kindness and love of God our Saviour toward man appeared,

5. Not by works of righteousness which we have done, but according to his mercy he saved us, by the washing of regeneration, and renewing of the Holy Ghost;

6. Which he shed on us abundantly through Jesus Christ our Saviour;

7. That, being justified by his grace, we should be made heirs according to the hope of eternal life.

4. Sed postquam bonitas et amor erga homines apparuit Servatoris nostri Dei,

5. Non ex operibus, quæ essent in justitia, quæ nos fecissemus, sed secundum suam misericordiam salvos nos fecit per lavacrum regenerationis ac renovationis Spiritus sancti,

6. Quod (*vel*, *quem*) effudit in nos opulenter per Iesum Christum Servatorem nostrum,

7. Ut justificati illius gratia, heredes efficeremur secundum spem vitæ æternæ.

Either the principal clause in this sentence is, that "God hath saved us by his mercy," or the language is elliptical. Thus it will be proper to supply, that they were changed for the better, and became new men, in consequence of God having mercy upon them; as if he had said, When God regenerated you by his Spirit, then did you begin to differ from others. But since there is a complete sense in the

---

and renewing by the Holy Ghost. O! the compassionate influence that is shed upon a soul in this case! The balmy dews that descend from heaven upon a distempered soul, which quench the flames of lust, and which implant and invigorate (after their implantation) a divine principle, in-create a new life, that leads to God and Christ, and the way of holiness and heaven at last."—*Howe*.

words of Paul, there is no necessity for making any addition. He classes himself along with others, in order that the exhortation may be more efficacious.

4. *But after that the goodness and love towards man appeared.* First, it might be asked,—" Did the goodness of God begin to be made known to the world at the time when Christ was manifested in the flesh? For certainly, from the beginning, the fathers both knew and experienced that God was good, and kind, and gracious to them; and therefore this was not the first manifestation of his goodness, and fatherly love towards us."

The answer is easy. In no other way did the fathers taste the goodness of God under the Law, than by looking at Christ, on whose coming all their faith rested. Thus the goodness of God is said to have *appeared,* when he exhibited a pledge of it, and gave actual demonstration, that not in vain did he so often promise salvation to men. " God so loved the world," says John, " that he gave his only-begotten Son." (John iii. 16.) Paul also says in another passage, " Hereby God confirmeth his love towards us, that, while we were enemies, Christ died for us." (Rom. v. 8.) It is a customary way of speaking in Scripture, that the world was reconciled to God through the death of Christ, although we know that he was a kind Father in all ages. But because we find no cause of the love of God toward us, and no ground of our salvation, but in Christ, not without good reason is God the Father said to have shewn his goodness to us in him.

Yet there is a different reason for it in this passage, in which Paul speaks, not of that ordinary manifestation of Christ which took place when he came as a man into the world, but of the manifestation which is made by the gospel, when he exhibits and reveals himself, in a peculiar manner, to the elect. At the first coming of Christ, Paul was not renewed; but, on the contrary, Christ was raised in glory, and salvation through his name shone upon many, not only in Judea, but throughout the neighbouring countries, while Paul, blinded by unbelief, laboured to extinguish this grace by every means in his power. He therefore means that the grace of God "appeared" both to himself and to others, when they were enlightened in the knowledge of the gospel. And indeed, in no other way could these words apply; for he does not speak indiscriminately about the men of his age, but specially addresses those who had been separated from the ordinary ranks; as if he had said, that formerly they resembled those unbelievers who were still plunged in darkness, but that now they differ from them, not through their own merit, but by the grace of God; in the same manner as he beats down all the haughtiness of the flesh by the same argument. "Who maketh thee to differ," or to be more highly esteemed than others? (1 Cor. iv. 7.)

*Goodness and love.* He has with propriety assigned the first rank to "goodness," which prompts God to love us; for God will never find in us anything which he ought to love, but he loves us because he is good and merciful. Besides, although he testifies his goodness and love to all, yet we know it by faith only, when he declares himself to be our Father in Christ. Before Paul was called to the faith of Christ, he enjoyed innumerable gifts of God, which might have given him a taste of God's fatherly kindness; he had been educated, from his infancy, in the doctrine of the law; yet he wanders in darkness, so as not to perceive the goodness of God, till the Spirit enlightened his mind, and till Christ came forth as the witness and pledge of the grace of God the Father, from which, but for him, we are all excluded. Thus he means that the kindness of God is not revealed and known but by the light of faith.

5. *Not by works.*[1] Let us remember that here Paul ad-

[1] "Perhaps the reader will give me leave to add a short expository lecture upon the most distinguished parts of this very important paragraph. I.—We have the cause of our redemption; not works of righteousness which we have done, but the kindness, the love, the mercy, of God our Saviour. To these, to these alone, every child of man must ascribe both his fruition of present, and his expectation of future blessedness. II.—The effects, which are—1. Justification, being justified, having our sins forgiven and our persons accepted through the righteousness of Christ imputed; all this without any the least deserving quality in us, solely by his grace and most unmerited goodness. 2. Sanctification, expressed by 'the washing of regeneration'—that washing in the Redeemer's blood which cleanses the soul from guilt, as the washing of water cleanseth the body from filth, which reconciles to God, gives peace of conscience, and thereby

dresses his discourse to believers, and describes the manner in which they entered into the kingdom of God. He affirms that by their works they did not at all deserve that they should become partakers of salvation, or that they should be reconciled to God through faith; but he says that they obtained this blessing solely through the mercy of God. We therefore conclude from his words, that we bring nothing to God, but that he goes before us by his pure grace, without any regard to works. For when he says,—"Not by works which we have done," he means, that we can do nothing but sin till we have been renewed by God. This negative statement depends on the former affirmation, by which he said that they were foolish and disobedient, and led away by various desires, till they were created anew in Christ; and indeed, what good work could proceed from so corrupt a mass?

It is madness, therefore, to allege that a man approaches to God by his own "preparations," as they call them. During the whole period of life they depart further and further from him, until he puts forth his hand, and brings them back into that path from which they had gone astray. In short, that we, rather than others, have been admitted to enjoy the salvation of Christ, is altogether ascribed by Paul to the mercy of God, because there were no works of righteousness in us. This argument would have no weight, if he did not take for granted, that everything that we attempt to do before we believe, is unrighteous and hateful to God.

*Which we had done.* To argue from the preterite tense of this verb, that God looks at the future merits of men when he calls them, is sophistical and foolish. "When Paul," say they, "denies that God is induced by our merits to bestow his grace upon us, he limits the statement to the past time; and therefore, if it is only for the righteousness going before

lays the foundation of an universal spiritual change—the renewing of the Holy Ghost, whose influences, testifying of Christ, and applying his merits, introduce an improvement into all the faculties of the mind, something like that annual renovation and general smile which the return of spring diffuses over the face of nature. III.—The end and consummation of all—that we should be made heirs of the heavenly kingdom, and live more in the assured hope, hereafter in the full enjoyment, of eternal life."—*Hervey.*

that no room is left, future righteousness is admitted to consideration. But they assume a principle, which Paul everywhere rejects, when he declares that election by free grace is the foundation of good works. If we owe it entirely to the grace of God, that we are fit for living a holy life, what future works of ours will God look upon? If, previously to our being called by God, iniquity holds such dominion over us, that it will not cease to make progress till it come to its height, how can God be induced, by a regard to our future righteousness, to call us? Away then with such trifling! When Paul spoke of past works, his sole object was to exclude all merits. The meaning of his words is as if he had said,—"If we boast of any merit, what sort of works had we?" This maxim holds good, that men would not be better than they were before, if the Lord did not make them better by his calling.

*He hath saved us.* He speaks of faith, and shews that we have already obtained salvation. Although, so long as we are held by the entanglements of sin, we carry about a body of death, yet we are certain of our salvation, provided that we are ingrafted into Christ by faith, according to that saying,—" He that believeth in the Son of God hath passed from death into life." (John v. 24.) Yet, shortly afterwards, by introducing the word *faith,* the Apostle will shew that we have not yet actually attained what Christ procured for us by his death. Hence it follows, that, on the part of God, our salvation is completed, while the full enjoyment of it is delayed till the end of our warfare. And that is what the same Apostle teaches in another passage, that "we are saved by hope." (Rom. viii. 24.)

*By the washing of regeneration.* I have no doubt that he alludes, at least, to baptism, and even I will not object to have this passage expounded as relating to baptism; not that salvation is contained in the outward symbol of water, but because baptism seals to us the salvation obtained by Christ. Paul treats of the exhibition of the grace of God, which, we have said, has been made by faith. Since therefore a part of revelation consists in baptism, that is, so far as it is intended to confirm our faith, he properly makes mention of it. Besides, baptism—being the entrance into the Church, and the symbol of our ingrafting into Christ—is here appropriately introduced by Paul, when he intends to shew in what manner the grace of God appeared to us; so that the strain of the passage runs thus :—" God hath saved us by his mercy, the symbol and pledge of which he gave in baptism, by admitting us into his Church, and ingrafting us into the body of his Son."

Now the Apostles are wont to draw an argument from the Sacraments, to prove that which is there exhibited under a figure, because it ought to be held by believers as a settled principle, that God does not sport with us by unmeaning figures, but inwardly accomplishes by his power what he exhibits by the outward sign; and therefore, baptism is fitly and truly said to be "the washing of regeneration." The efficacy and use of the sacraments will be properly understood by him who shall connect the sign and the thing signified, in such a manner as not to make the sign unmeaning and inefficacious, and who nevertheless shall not, for the sake of adorning the sign, take away from the Holy Spirit what belongs to him. Although by baptism wicked men are neither washed nor renewed, yet it retains that power, so far as relates to God, because, although they reject the grace of God, still it is offered to them. But here Paul addresses believers, in whom baptism is always efficacious, and in whom, therefore, it is properly connected with its truth and efficacy. But by this mode of expression we are reminded that, if we do not wish to annihilate holy baptism, we must prove its efficacy by "newness of life." (Rom. vi. 4.)

*And of the renewing of the Holy Spirit.*[1] Though he

---

[1] "It remaineth that we declare what is the office of the same, what he is unto us, as the Holy Spirit; for although the Spirit of God be of infinite, essential, and original holiness, as God, and so may be called Holy in himself; though other spirits which were created be either actually now unholy, or of defectible sanctity at first, and so having the name of spirit common unto them, he may be termed holy, that he may be distinguished from them; yet I conceive he is rather called the Holy Spirit, 'or the Spirit of Holiness,' (Rom. i. 4,) because of the three persons in the blessed Trinity, it is his particular office to sanctify or make us holy. As, therefore, what our Saviour did and suffered for us belonged to that office of a Redeemer which he took upon him; so whatsoever the Holy Ghost worketh

mentioned the sign, that he might exhibit to our view the grace of God, yet, that we may not fix our whole attention on the sign, he immediately sends us to the Spirit, that we may know that we are washed by his power, and not by water, agreeably to what is said,—"I will sprinkle on you clean waters, even my Spirit." (Ezek. xxxvi. 25, 27.) And indeed, the words of Paul agree so completely with the words of the Prophet, that it appears clearly that both of them say the same thing. For this reason I said at the commencement, that Paul, while he speaks directly about the Holy Spirit, at the same time alludes to baptism. It is therefore the Spirit of God who regenerates us, and makes us new creatures; but because his grace is invisible and hidden, a visible symbol of it is beheld in baptism.

Some read the word "renewing" in the accusative case, thus:—"through the washing of regeneration and (through) the renewing of the Holy Spirit." But the other reading —"through the washing of regeneration and of the renewing of the Holy Spirit"—is, in my opinion, preferable.

6. *Which he shed*, (or, *whom he shed.*) In the Greek, the relative may apply either to the "washing" or to the "Spirit;" for both of the nouns—λουτρόν and Πνεῦμα—are neuter. It makes little difference as to the meaning; but the metaphor will be more elegant, if the relative be applied to (λουτρόν) the "washing." Nor is it inconsistent with this opinion, that all are baptized without any distinction; for, while he shews that the "washing" is "shed," he speaks not of the sign, but rather of the thing signified, in which the truth of the sign exists.

When he says, *abundantly*, he means that, the more any of us excels in the abundance of the gifts which he has re-

---

in order to the same salvation, we look upon as belonging to his office. And because without holiness it is impossible to please God, because we all are impure and unholy, and the purity and holiness which is required in us to appear in the presence of God, whose eyes are pure, must be wrought in us by the Spirit of God, who is called Holy, because he is the cause of this holiness in us, therefore we acknowledge the office of the Spirit of God to consist in the sanctifying of the servants of God, and the declaration of this office, added to the description of his nature, to be a sufficient explication of the object of faith contained in this article—'I believe in the Holy Ghost.'"—*Bp. Pearson on the Creed.*

ceived, so much the more is he under obligations to the mercy of God, which alone enriches us; for in ourselves we are altogether poor, and destitute of everything good. If it be objected that not all the children of God enjoy so great abundance, but, on the contrary, the grace of God drops sparingly on many; the answer is, that no one has received so small a measure that he may not be justly accounted rich; for the smallest drop of the Spirit (so to speak) resembles an ever-flowing fountain, which never dries up. It is therefore a sufficient reason for calling it "abundance," that, how small soever the portion that has been given to us, it is never exhausted.

*Through Jesus Christ.*[1] It is he alone in whom we are adopted; and therefore, it is he alone, through whom we are made partakers of the Spirit, who is the earnest and witness of our adoption. Paul therefore teaches us by this word, that the Spirit of regeneration is bestowed on none but those who are the members of Christ.

7. *That being justified by his grace.* If we understand "regeneration" in its strict and ordinary meaning, it might be thought that the Apostle employs the word "justified" instead of "regenerated;" and this is sometimes the meaning of it, but very seldom; yet there is no necessity which constrains us to depart from its strict and more natural signification. The design of Paul is, to ascribe to the grace of God all that we are, and all that we have, so that we may not exalt ourselves proudly against others. Thus he now extols the mercy of God, by ascribing to it entirely the cause of our salvation. But because he had spoken of the vices of unbelievers, it would have been improper to leave out the grace of regeneration, which is the medicine for curing them.

[1] "When we wish to ascertain the method of our salvation, we must begin with the Son of God. For it is he who hath washed us by his blood—it is he who hath obtained righteousness for us by his obedience—it is he who is our Advocate, and through whom we now find grace—it is he who procured for us the adoption by which we are made children and heirs of God. Let us carefully observe that we must seek all the parts of our salvation in Jesus Christ; for we shall not find a single drop of it anywhere else."—*Fr. Ser.*

Still this does not prevent him from returning immediately to praise divine mercy; and he even mingles both blessings together—that our sins have been freely pardoned, and that we have been renewed so as to obey God. This, at least, is evident, that Paul maintains that "justification" is the free gift of God; and the only question is, what he means by the word *justified.* The context seems to demand that its meaning shall be extended further than to the imputation of righteousness; and in this larger sense it is seldom (as I have said) employed by Paul; yet there is nothing that hinders the meaning of it from being limited to the forgiveness of sins.

When he says, *by his grace,* this applies both to Christ and to the Father; and we ought not to contend for either of these expositions, because it will always hold good, that, by the grace of God, we have obtained righteousness through Christ.

*Heirs according to the hope of eternal life.* This clause is added by way of exposition. He had said that we have been saved through the mercy of God.[1] But our salvation is as yet hidden; and therefore he now says that we are heirs of life, not because we have arrived at the present possession of it, but because hope brings to us full and complete certainty of it. The meaning may be thus summed up. "Having been dead, we were restored to life through the grace of Christ, when God the Father bestowed on us his Spirit, by whose power we have been purified and renewed. Our salvation consists in this; but, because we are still in the world, we do not yet enjoy 'eternal life,' but only obtain it by 'hoping.'"

8. *This is* a faithful saying, and these things I will that thou affirm constantly, that they which have believed in God might be careful to maintain good works. These things are good and profitable unto men.

9. But avoid foolish questions, and genealogies, and contentions, and strivings about the law; for they are unprofitable and vain.

8. Fidelis sermo: de his volo, ut confirmes, quo bonis operibus præesse (*vel, bona opera extollere, vel, illis dare primatum*) curent, qui crediderunt Deo. Hæc enim honesta sunt et utilia hominibus.

9. Stultas autem quæstiones et genealogias et contentiones ac pugnas legales omitte; sunt enim inutiles ac supervacuæ.

[1] "Par la grace et misericorde de Dieu." "By the grace and mercy of God."

8. *A faithful saying.* He employs this mode of expression, when he wishes to make a solemn assertion, as we have seen in both of the Epistles to Timothy. (1 Tim. i. 15; iii. 1; 2 Tim. ii. 11.) And therefore he immediately adds:—

*I wish thee to affirm these things.*[1] Διαβεβαιοῦσθαι, under a passive termination, has an active signification, and means "to affirm anything strongly." Titus is therefore enjoined to disregard other matters, and to teach those which are certain and undoubted—to press them on the attention of their hearers—to dwell upon them—while others talk idly about things of little importance. Hence also, we conclude that a bishop must not make any assertions at random, but must assert those things only which he has ascertained to be true. "Affirm these things," says he, "because they are true and worthy of credit." But we are reminded, on the other hand, that it is the duty and office of a bishop to affirm strongly, and maintain boldly, those things which are believed on good grounds, and which edify godliness.

*That they who have believed God may be careful to excel in good works,* (or, *to extol good works,* or, *to assign to them the highest rank.*) He includes all the instructions which he formerly gave concerning the duty of every person, and the desire of leading a religious and holy life; as if he contrasted the fear of God, and well-regulated conduct, with idle speculations. He wishes the people to be instructed in such a manner that "they who have believed God" may be solicitous, above all things, about good works.

But, as the verb προΐστασθαι is used in various senses by

[1] "Meaning, 'and I would have you constantly insist on these truths; so that those who have believed in God may maintain good works.' The cause of the obscurity, and consequent diversity of interpretation, arose from the Apostle not having here shewn *how* it should be, that the doctrine of salvation by grace should produce holiness of life. But he has done it in another kindred passage, namely, Eph. ii. 9, 10, where, after having at large treated on the subject of salvation by grace, (as here,) adding that it is not of works, lest any man should boast, he subjoins, αὐτοῦ γάρ ἐσμεν, κ. τ. λ., where the γὰρ refers to a clause omitted, q. d. (Yet works must be done,) for, &c. Hence it would seem that καλῶν ἔργων here must have the same sense as ἔργοις ἀγαθοῖς there; and consequently it must not be limited, with many eminent commentators, to works of benevolence, still less to the business of our avocation, but be extended to good works of every kind."—*Bloomfield.*

Greek authors, this passage also gives scope for various interpretations. Chrysostom explains it to mean, that they should endeavour to relieve their neighbours by giving alms. Προΐστασθαι does sometimes mean "to give assistance;" but in that case the syntax would require us to understand that the "good works" should be aided, which would be a harsh construction. The meaning conveyed by the French word *avancer,* "to go forward," would be more appropriate. What if we should say,—"Let them strive as those who have the pre-eminence?" That is also one meaning of the word. Or, perhaps, some one will prefer what I have enclosed in brackets: "Let them be careful to assign the highest rank to good works." And certainly it would not be unsuitable that Paul should enjoin that those things should prevail in the life of believers, because they are usually disregarded by others.

Whatever may be the ambiguity of the expression, the meaning of Paul is sufficiently clear, that the design of Christian doctrine is, that believers should exercise themselves in good works.[1] Thus he wishes them to give to it their study and application; and, when the Apostle says, φροντίζωσι, ("let them be careful,") he appears to allude elegantly to the useless contemplations of those who speculate without advantage, and without regard to active life.

Yet he is not so careful about good works as to despise the root—that is, faith—while he is gathering the fruits. He takes account of both parts, and, as is highly proper, assigns the first rank to faith; for he enjoins those "who believed in God" to be zealous of "good works;" by which he means that faith must go before in such a manner that good works may follow.

*For these things are honourable.* I refer this to the doctrine rather than to the works, in this sense: "It is excellent and useful that men be thus instructed; and, therefore,

---

[1] "The original word προΐστασθαι has a beauty and an energy, which, I believe, it is impossible for our language to preserve by any literal translation. It implies, that a believer should not only be exercised in, but eminent for, all good works; should shew others the way, and outstrip them in the honourable race; be both a pattern and a patron of universal godliness."—*Hervey.*

those things which he formerly exhorted Titus to be zealous in affirming are the same things that are good and useful to men." We might translate τὰ καλά either " good," or " beautiful," or " honourable ;" but, in my opinion, it would be best to translate it " excellent." He states indirectly that all other things that are taught are of no value, because they yield no profit or advantage ; as, on the contrary, that which contributes to salvation is worthy of praise.

9. *But avoid foolish questions.* There is no necessity for debating long about the exposition of this passage. He contrasts " questions" with sound and certain doctrine. Although it is necessary to seek, in order to find, yet there is a limit to seeking, that you may understand what is useful to be known, and, next, that you may adhere firmly to the truth, when it has been known. Those who inquire curiously into everything, and are never at rest, may be truly called Questionarians. In short, what the schools of the Sorbonne account worthy of the highest praise—is here condemned by Paul ; for the whole theology of the Papists is nothing else than a labyrinth of questions. He calls them *foolish ;* not that, at first sight, they appear to be such, (for, on the contrary, they often deceive by a vain parade of wisdom,) but because they contribute nothing to godliness.

When he adds *genealogies,* he mentions one class of " foolish questions ;" for instance, when curious men, forgetting to gather fruit from the sacred histories, seize on the lineage of races, and trifles of that nature, with which they weary themselves without advantage. Of that folly we spoke towards the beginning of the First Epistle to Timothy.[1]

He properly adds *contentions ;* because in " questions" the prevailing spirit is ambition ; and, therefore, it is impossible but that they shall immediately break forth into " contention" and quarrels ; for there every one wishes to be the conqueror. This is accompanied by hardihood in affirming about things that are uncertain, which unavoidably leads to debates.

*And fightings about the law.* He gives this disdainful appellation to those debates which were raised by the Jews

[1] See p. 23.

under the pretence of the law; not that the law of itself produces them, but because the Jews, pretending to defend the law, disturbed the peace of the Church by their absurd controversies about the observation of ceremonies, about the distinction of the kinds of food and things of that nature.

*For they are unprofitable and unnecessary.* In doctrine, therefore, we should always have regard to usefulness, so that everything that does not contribute to godliness shall be held in no estimation. And yet those sophists, in babbling about things of no value, undoubtedly boasted of them as highly worthy and useful to be known; but Paul does not acknowledge them to possess any usefulness, unless they tend to the increase of faith and to a holy life.

10. A man that is an heretick, after the first and second admonition, reject;
11. Knowing that he that is such is subverted, and sinneth, being condemned of himself.
12. When I shall send Artemas unto thee, or Tychicus, be diligent to come unto me to Nicopolis; for I have determined there to winter.
13. Bring Zenas the lawyer and Apollos on their journey diligently, that nothing be wanting unto them.
14. And let ours also learn to maintain good works for necessary uses, that they be not unfruitful.

15. All that are with me salute thee. Greet them that love us in the faith. Grace *be* with you all. Amen.
 It was written to Titus, ordained the first bishop of the church of the Cretians, from Nicopolis of Macedonia.

10. Hæreticum hominem post unam et alteram admonitionem fuge.
11. Sciens, quòd eversus sit, qui est ejusmodi, et peccet, a se ipso damnatus.
12. Quum misero ad te Artemam vel Tychicum, da operam, ut ad me venias Nicopolim; illic enim decrevi hyemare.
13. Zenam Legis peritum et Apollo studiosè deducito, ne quid illis desit.
14. Discant autem et nostri, bonis præesse (*vel*, (*ut prius*) *dare illis principatum, ut emineant*), in necessarios usus, ne sint infructuosi.

15. Salutant te, qui mecum sunt, omnes. Saluta eos qui nos diligunt in fide. Gratia cum omnibus vobis. Amen.
 Ad Titum, qui primus Cretensium Ecclesiæ ordinatus fuit Episcopus, scripsit ex Nicopoli Macedoniæ.

10. *Avoid an heretical man.* This is properly added; because there will be no end of quarrels and disputes, if we wish to conquer obstinate men by argument; for they will never want words, and they will derive fresh courage from impudence, so that they will never grow weary of fighting. Thus, after having given orders to Titus as to the form of doctrine which he should lay down, he now forbids him to

waste much time in debating with heretics, because battle would lead to battle and dispute to dispute. Such is the cunning of Satan, that, by the impudent talkativeness of such men, he entangles good and faithful pastors, so as to draw them away from diligence in teaching. We must therefore beware lest we become engaged in quarrelsome disputes; for we shall never have leisure to devote our labours to the Lord's flock, and contentious men will never cease to annoy us.

When he commands him to *avoid* such persons, it is as if he said that he must not toil hard to satisfy them, and even that there is nothing better than to cut off the handle for fighting which they are eager to find. This is a highly necessary admonition; for even they who would willingly take no part in strifes of words are sometimes drawn by shame into controversy, because they think that it would be shameful cowardice to quit the field. Besides, there is no temper, however mild, that is not liable to be provoked by the fierce taunts of enemies, because they look upon it as intolerable that those men should attack the truth, (as they are accustomed to do,) and that none should reply. Nor are there wanting men who are either of a combative disposition, or excessively hot-tempered, who are eager for battle. On the contrary, Paul does not wish that the servant of Christ should be much and long employed in debating with heretics.

We must now see what he means by the word *heretic*. There is a common and well-known distinction between a heretic and a schismatic. But here, in my opinion, Paul disregards that distinction: for, by the term "heretic" he describes not only those who cherish and defend an erroneous or perverse doctrine, but in general all who do not yield assent to the sound doctrine which he laid down a little before. Thus under this name he includes all ambitious, unruly, contentious persons, who, led away by sinful passions, disturb the peace of the Church, and raise disputings. In short, every person who, by his overweening pride, breaks up the unity of the Church, is pronounced by Paul to be a "heretic."

But we must exercise moderation, so as not instantly to declare every man to be a "heretic" who does not agree with our opinion. There are some matters on which Christians may differ from each other, without being divided into sects. Paul himself commands that they shall not be so divided, when he bids them keep their harmony unbroken, and wait for the revelation of God. (Philip. iii. 16.) But whenever the obstinacy of any person grows to such an extent, that, led by selfish motives, he either separates from the body, or draws away some of the flock, or interrupts the course of sound doctrine, in such a case we must boldly resist.

In a word, a heresy or sect and the unity of the Church—are things totally opposite to each other. Since the unity of the Church is dear to God, and ought to be held by us in the highest estimation, we ought to entertain the strongest abhorrence of heresy. Accordingly, the name of sect or heresy, though philosophers and statesmen reckon it to be honourable, is justly accounted infamous among Christians. We now understand who are meant by Paul, when he bids us dismiss and avoid heretics. But at the same time we ought to observe what immediately follows,—

*After the first and second admonition;* for neither shall we have a right to pronounce a man to be a heretic, nor shall we be at liberty to reject him, till we have first endeavoured to bring him back to sound views.[1] He does not mean any "admonition" whatever, or that of a private individual, but an "admonition" given by a minister, with the public authority of the Church; for the meaning of the Apostle's words is as if he had said, that heretics must be rebuked with solemn and severe censure.

They who infer from this passage, that the supporters of wicked doctrines must be restrained by excommunication alone, and that no rigorous measures beyond this must be used against them, do not argue conclusively. There is a difference between the duties of a bishop and those of a magistrate. Writing to Titus, Paul does not treat of the office of a magistrate, but points out what belongs to a

[1] "Au droit chemin." "To the right road."

bishop.[1] Yet moderation is always best, that, instead of being restrained by force and violence, they may be corrected by the discipline of the Church, if there be any ground to believe that they can be cured.

11. *Knowing that he who is such is ruined.* He declares that man to be "ruined," as to whom there is no hope of repentance, because, if our labour could bring back any man to the right path, it should by no means be withheld. The metaphor is taken from a building, which is not merely decayed in some part, but completely demolished, so that it is incapable of being repaired.

He next points out the sign of this ruin—an evil conscience, when he says, that they who do not yield to admonitions *are condemned by themselves;* for, since they obstinately reject the truth, it is certain that they sin wilfully and of their own accord, and therefore it would be of no advantage to admonish them.

At the same time, we learn from Paul's words that we must not rashly or at random pronounce any man to be a heretic; for he says, "Knowing that he who is such is ruined." Let the bishop therefore beware lest, by indulging his passionate temper, he treat with excessive harshness, as a heretic, one whom he does not yet know to be such.

13. *Zenas a lawyer.* It is uncertain whether "Zenas" was a Doctor of the Civil Law or of the Law of Moses; but as we may learn from Paul's words that he was a poor man and needed the help of others, it is probable that he belonged to the same rank with *Apollo,* that is, an expounder of the Law of God among the Jews. It more frequently happens that such persons are in want of the necessaries of life than those who conduct causes in civil courts. I have said that Zenas's poverty may be inferred from the words of Paul, because the expression, *conduct him,* means here to supply him with the means of accomplishing his journey, as is evident from what follows.

14. *And let ours also learn to excel in good works.*[2] That

---

[1] "Ce qu'il convient au Pasteur de faire." "What it belongs to the pastor to do."

[2] "As he said before, let them apply their mind to it. He contrasts

the Cretans, on whom he lays this burden, may not complain of being loaded with the expense, he reminds them that they must not *be unfruitful,* and that therefore they must be warmly exhorted to be zealous in good works. But of this mode of expression[1] we have already spoken. Whether, therefore, he enjoins them to excel in good works, or to assign the highest rank to good works, he means that it is useful for them to have an opportunity afforded for exercising liberality, that they may not "be unfruitful" on this ground, that there is no opportunity, or that it is not demanded by necessity. What follows has been already explained in the other Epistles.

this with the foolish presumption but too common among those who thought that they were clever men, when they had speculated on this and the other subject. You have fine speculations, says he, but yet consider what is the true excellence of the children of God; it is to shew that they have profited well in doing good, and that this is the subject to which they have given their study. And then he says, *Let them learn;* as if he had said, Hitherto you have employed your time very ill, for there was nothing but foolish ambition, you yielded too far to your vain fancy. You must now follow a different course. Henceforth you must excel in doing good, and not in rambling talk. Instead of being led by curiosity and ambition, let every man be employed in doing good to his neighbours. Let every man consider what is his ability; and according to the power which God has given us, let us serve one another. Thus shall we shew that it is not in vain that we have received the gospel."—*Fr. Ser.*

[1] See p. 337.

END OF THE EPISTLE TO TITUS.

# COMMENTARIES

ON

# THE EPISTLE TO PHILEMON.

# COMMENTARIES

ON

# THE EPISTLE TO PHILEMON.

1. Paul, a prisoner of Jesus Christ, and Timothy *our* brother, unto Philemon our dearly beloved, and fellow-labourer,

2. And to our beloved Apphia, and Archippus our fellow-soldier, and to the church in thy house:

3. Grace to you, and peace, from God our Father, and the Lord Jesus Christ.

4. I thank my God, making mention of thee always in my prayers,

5. Hearing of thy love and faith, which thou hast toward the Lord Jesus, and toward all saints;

6. That the communication of thy faith may become effectual, by the acknowledging of every good thing which is in you in Christ Jesus.

7. For we have great joy and consolation in thy love, because the bowels of the saints are refreshed by thee, brother.

1. Paulus vinctus Christi Iesu et Timotheus frater Philemoni amico et cooperario nostro,

2. Et Apphiæ dilectæ, et Archippo commilitoni nostro, et Ecclesiæ, quæ domi tuæ est.

3. Gratia vobis et pax a Deo Patre nostro et Domino Iesu Christo.

4. Gratias ago Deo meo, semper memoriam tui faciens in precibus meis,

5. Audiens tuam dilectionem et fidem, quam habes erga Dominum Iesum et erga omnes sanctos,

6, Ut communicatio fidei tuæ efficax sit cognitione omnis boni, quod in vobis est erga Christum Iesum.

7. Gratiam enim habemus multam et consolationem super dilectione tua, quia viscera sanctorum per te refocillata sunt, frater.

THE singular loftiness of the mind of Paul, though it may be seen to greater advantage in his other writings which treat of weightier matters, is also attested by this Epistle, in which, while he handles a subject otherwise low and mean, he rises to God with his wonted elevation. Sending back a runaway slave and thief, he supplicates pardon for him. But in pleading this cause, he discourses about Christian forbearance[1] with such ability, that he appears to speak about the interests of the whole Church rather than the private affairs of a single individual. In behalf of a man of the lowest condition, he demeans himself so modestly and humbly, that nowhere else is the meekness of his temper painted in a more lively manner.

1. *A prisoner of Jesus Christ.* In the same sense in which he elsewhere calls himself an Apostle of Christ, or a minister of Christ, he now calls himself "a prisoner of Christ;" because the chains by which he was bound on account of the gospel, were the ornaments or badges of that embassy which he exercised for Christ. Accordingly, he mentions them for the sake of strengthening his authority; not that he was afraid of being despised, (for Philemon undoubtedly had so great reverence and esteem for him, that there was no need of assuming any title,) but because he was about to plead the cause of a runaway slave, the principal part of which was entreaty for forgiveness.

*To Philemon our friend and fellow-labourer.* It is probable that this "Philemon" belonged to the order of pastors; for the title with which he adorns him, when he calls him *fellow-labourer*, is a title which he is not accustomed to bestow on a private individual.

2. *And to Archippus our fellow-soldier.* He next adds "Archippus," who appears also to have been a minister of the Church; at least, if he be the same person who is mentioned towards the conclusion of the Epistle to the Colossians, (iv. 17,) which is not at all improbable; for the designation—"fellow-soldier"—which he bestows on this latter individual, belongs peculiarly to ministers. Although the condition of a soldier belongs to all Christians universally, yet because teachers may be regarded as standard-bearers in the warfare, they ought to be ready more than all others to fight, and Satan usually gives them greater annoyance. It is also possible, that Archippus attended

---

[1] "De la douceur, moderation, et humanite." "Of gentleness, moderation, and kindness."

and shared in some contests which Paul maintained; and, indeed, this is the very word that Paul makes use of, whenever he mentions persecutions.

*And to the Church which is in thy house.* By employing these terms, he bestows the highest praise on the family of Philemon. And certainly it is no small praise of a householder, that he regulates his family in such a manner as to be an image of the Church, and to discharge also the duty of a pastor within the walls of his dwelling. Nor must we forget to mention that this good man had a wife of the same character; for she, too, not without reason, is commended by Paul.

4. *I give thanks to my God.* It deserves attention, that he at the same time prays for that very thing for which he "gives thanks." Even the most perfect, so long as they live in the world, never have so good ground for congratulation as not to need prayers, that God may grant to them, not only to persevere till the end, but likewise to make progress from day to day.

5. *Hearing of thy love and faith.* This praise, which he bestows on Philemon, includes briefly the whole perfection of a Christian man. It consists of two parts, faith in Christ, and love towards our neighbours; for to these all the actions and all the duties of our life relate. Faith is said to be in Christ, because to him it especially looks; in like manner as in no other way than through him alone can God the Father be known, and in no other than in Him can we find any of the blessings which faith seeks.

*And towards all saints.* He does not thus limit this *love* to the *saints*, as if there ought to be none towards others; for, since the doctrine of "love" is, that "we should not despise our flesh," (Isa. lviii. 7,) and that we should honour the image of God which is engraven on our nature, undoubtedly it includes all mankind. But since they that are of the household of faith are united with us by a closer bond of relationship, and since God peculiarly recommends them to us, for this reason they justly hold the highest rank.

The arrangement of the passage is somewhat confused;

but there is no obscurity in the meaning, except that it is doubtful whether the adverb *always* (in the 4th verse) is connected with the first clause, "I give thanks always to my God," or with the second clause, "making mention of thee always in my prayers." The meaning may be brought out in this manner, that, whenever the Apostle offered prayer for Philemon, he interwove thanksgiving with it; that is, because Philemon's piety afforded ground of rejoicing; for we often pray for those in whom nothing is to be found but what gives occasion for grief and tears. Yet the second mode of pointing is generally preferred, that Paul "gives thanks for Philemon, and always makes mention of him in his prayers." Let my readers be at full liberty to judge for themselves; but, for my own part, I think that the former meaning is more appropriate.

In the rest of the passage there is an inversion of the natural order; for, after having spoken of "love" and "faith," he adds, "towards Christ and towards saints," while, on the contrary, the contrast would demand that "Christ" should be put in the second part of the clause as the object to which our faith looks.[1]

6. *That the communication of thy faith may be effectual.* This clause is somewhat obscure; but I shall endeavour to elucidate it in such a manner that my readers may somewhat understand Paul's meaning. First, it ought to be known that the Apostle is not continuing to give the praise of Philemon, but that, on the contrary, he expresses those blessings for which he prays to God. These words are connected with what he had formerly said, that he "makes mention of him in his prayers." (Verse 4.) What blessing then did he ask for Philemon? That his faith, exercising itself by good works, might be proved to be true, and not

---

[1] It has sometimes occurred to me, that the intricacy of this passage might be removed, first, by the transposition suggested by CALVIN, and, next, by transposing the 5th verse so as to place it before the 4th. "Hearing of thy love towards all saints, and of thy faith which thou hast towards the Lord Jesus, I give thanks unto my God, making mention of thee always in my prayers, That the communication of thy faith may be effectual, through the knowledge of every good thing which is in thee towards Christ Jesus."—*Ed.*

unprofitable. He calls it "the communication of faith," because it does not remain inactive and concealed within, but is manifested to men by actual effects. Although faith has a hidden residence in the heart, yet it communicates itself to men by good works. It is, therefore, as if he had said, "That thy faith, by communicating itself, may demonstrate its efficacy in every good thing.

*The knowledge of every good thing* denotes experience. He wishes that, by its effects, faith may be proved to be effectual. This takes place, when the men with whom we converse know our godly and holy life; and therefore he says, *of every good thing which is in you;* for everything in us that is good makes known our faith.

*Towards Christ Jesus.* The phrase εἰς Χριστόν may be explained to mean "through Christ." But, for my own part, if I were at liberty, I would rather translate it as equivalent to ἐν Χριστῷ, "in Christ;" for the gifts of God dwell in us in such a manner, that nevertheless, we are partakers of them only so far as we are members of Christ. Yet because the words *in you* go before, I am afraid that the harshness of the expression would give offence. Accordingly, I have not ventured to make any alteration in the words, but only wished to mention it to my readers, that, after full consideration, they may choose either of those meanings which they prefer.

7. *We have much grace and consolation.* Although this reading is found in the majority of Greek copies, yet I think that it ought to be translated *joy;* for, since there is little difference between χάριν and χαράν, it would be easy to mistake a single letter. Besides, Paul elsewhere employs the word χάριν to mean "joy;" at least, if we believe Chrysostom on this matter. What has "grace" to do with con-"solation?"

*For thy love.* It is plain enough what he means, that he has great joy and consolation, because Philemon administered relief to the necessities of the godly. This was singular love, to feel so much joy on account of the benefit received by others. Besides, the Apostle does not only speak of his personal joy, but says that many rejoiced on account of the kindness and benevolence with which Philemon had aided religious men.

*Because the bowels of the saints have been refreshed by thee, brother.* "To refresh the bowels" is an expression used by Paul to mean, to give relief from distresses, or to aid the wretched in such a manner that, having their minds composed, and being free from all uneasiness and grief, they may find repose. "The bowels" mean the affections, and ἀνάπαυσις denotes tranquillity; and therefore they are greatly mistaken who torture this passage so as to make it refer to the belly and the nourishment of the body.

| | |
|---|---|
| 8. Wherefore, though I might be much bold in Christ to enjoin thee that which is convenient, | 8. Quapropter multam in Christo fiduciam habens imperandi tibi quod decet. |
| 9. Yet, for love's sake, I rather beseech *thee*, being such an one as Paul the aged, and now also a prisoner of Jesus Christ. | 9. Propter caritatem magis rogo, quum talis sim, nempe Paulus senex; nunc vero etiam vinctus Iesu Christi. |
| 10. I beseech thee for my son Onesimus, whom I have begotten in my bonds: | 10. Rogo autem te pro filio meo, quem genui in vinculis meis, Onesimo, |
| 11. Which in time past was to thee unprofitable, but now profitable to thee and to me: | 11. Qui aliquando tibi inutilis fuit, nunc autem et mihi et tibi utilis. |
| 12. Whom I have sent again: thou therefore receive him that is mine own bowels; | 12. Quem remisi; tu vero illum, hoc est, mea viscera, suscipe. |
| 13. Whom I would have retained with me, that in thy stead he might have ministered unto me in the bonds of the gospel. | 13. Quem ego volebam apud me ipsum retinere, ut pro te mihi ministraret in vinculis evangelii. |
| 14. But without thy mind would I do nothing; that thy benefit should not be as it were of necessity, but willingly. | 14. Sed absque tua sententia nihil volui facere, ut non quasi secundum necessitatem esset bonum tuum, sed voluntarium. |

8. *Wherefore, while I have great confidence in Christ to command thee.* That is, "though I have authority so that I might justly command thee, yet thy love makes me prefer to entreat thee."

9. *Being such a one.* He claims the right to command on two grounds, that he is *an elder*, and that he is *a prisoner for Christ*. He says that, on account of Philemon's love, he chooses rather to entreat, because we interpose authority in commanding those things which we wish to extort by

necessity even from the unwilling, but there is no need of commanding those who willingly obey. And because they who are ready of their own accord to do their duty listen more willingly to a calm statement of what is necessary to be done than to the exercise of authority, with good reason does Paul, when he has to deal with an obedient man, use entreaty. By his example he shows that pastors should endeavour to draw disciples gently rather than to drag them by force; and indeed, when, by condescending to entreaty, he foregoes his right, this has far greater power to obtain his wish than if he issued a command. Besides, he claims nothing for himself, but in Christ, that is, on account of the office which he has received from him; for he does not mean that they whom Christ has appointed to be apostles are destitute of authority.

*What is proper.* By adding this, he means that teachers have not power to enact whatever they please, but that their authority is confined within these limits, that they must not command anything but " what is proper," and, in other respects, consistent with every man's duty. Hence (as I said a little before) pastors are reminded that the hearts of their people must be soothed with all possible gentleness, wherever this method is likely to be more advantageous, but yet so as to know that they who are treated so gently have nothing less exacted from them than what they ought to do.

The designation, " elder," here, denotes not age, but office. He calls himself an apostle for this reason, that the person with whom he has to deal, and with whom he talks familiarly, is a fellow-labourer in the ministry of the word.

10. *I beseech thee for my son.* Since less weight is commonly attached to those prayers which are not founded in some cause of just commendation, Paul shows that Onesimus is so closely related to him as to afford a good reason for supplicating in his behalf. Here it is of importance to consider how deep is his condescension, when he gives the name of " son" to a slave, and a runaway, and a thief.

When he says that Onesimus has been *begotten by him,*

this must be understood to mean, that it was done by his ministry, and not by his power. To renew a soul of man and form it anew to the image of God—is not a human work, and it is of this spiritual regeneration that he now speaks. Yet because the soul is regenerated by faith, and "faith is by hearing," (Rom. x. 17,) on that account he who administers the doctrine holds the place of a parent. Moreover, because the word of God preached by man is the seed of eternal life, we need not wonder that he from whose mouth we receive that seed is called a father. Yet, at the same time, we must believe that, while the ministry of a man is efficacious in regenerating the soul, yet, strictly speaking, God himself regenerates by the power of his Spirit. These modes of expression, therefore, do not imply any opposition between God and man, but only show what God does by means of men. When he says that he had *begotten him in his bonds*, this circumstance adds weight to the commendation.

12. *Receive him, that is, my bowels.* Nothing could have been more powerful for assuaging the wrath of Philemon; for if he had refused to forgive his slave, he would thus have used cruelty against "the bowels" of Paul. This is remarkable kindness displayed by Paul, that he did not hesitate to receive, as it were into his bowels, a contemptible slave, and thief, and runaway, so as to defend him from the indignation of his master. And, indeed, if the conversion of a man to God were estimated by us, at its proper value, we too would embrace, in the same manner, those who should give evidence that they had truly and sincerely repented.

13. *Whom I was desirous to keep beside me.* This is another argument for the purpose of appeasing Philemon, that Paul sends him back a slave, of whose services, in other respects, he stood greatly in need. It would have been extreme cruelty, to disdain so strong affection manifested by Paul. He likewise states indirectly, that it will be a gratification to himself to have Onesimus sent back to him rather than that he should be harshly treated at home.

*That he might minister to me instead of thee in the bonds*

*of the gospel.* He now mentions other circumstances : first, Onesimus will supply the place of his master, by performing this service; secondly, Paul himself, through modesty, was unwilling to deprive Philemon of his right ; and, thirdly, Philemon will receive more applause, if, after having had his slave restored to him, he shall willingly and generously send him back. From this last consideration we infer, that we ought to aid the martyrs of Christ by every kind office in our power, while they are labouring for the testimony of the gospel ; for if exile, imprisonment, stripes, blows, and violent seizing of our property, are believed by us to belong to the gospel, as Paul here calls them, whoever refuses to share and partake of them separates himself even from Christ. Undoubtedly the defence of the gospel belongs alike to all. Accordingly, he who endures persecution, for the sake of the gospel, ought not to be regarded as a private individual, but as one who publicly represents the whole Church. Hence it follows, that all believers ought to be united in taking care of it, so that they may not, as is frequently done, leave the gospel to be defended in the person of one man.

14. *That thy benefit might not be by constraint.* This is drawn from the general rule, that no sacrifices are acceptable to God but those which are freely offered. Paul speaks of almsgiving in the same manner. (2 Cor. ix. 7.) Τὸ ἀγαθόν is here put for " acts of kindness," and willingness is contrasted with constraint, when there is no other opportunity of putting to the test a generous and cheerful act of the will ; for that duty which is generously performed, and not through influence exercised by others, is alone entitled to full praise. It is also worthy of observation, that Paul, while he acknowledges that Onesimus was to blame in past time, affirms that he is changed ; and lest Philemon should have any doubt that his slave returns to him with a new disposition and different conduct, Paul says that he has made full trial of his repentance by personal knowledge.

| 15. For perhaps he therefore departed for a season, that thou shouldest receive him for ever ; | 15. Fortè enim ideo separatus fuit ad tempus, ut perpetuò eum retineres ; |
|---|---|

| | |
|---|---|
| 16. Not now as a servant, but above a servant, a brother beloved, specially to me, but how much more unto thee, both in the flesh and in the Lord? | 16. Non jam ut servum, sed super servum fratrem dilectum maximè mihi, quantò magis tibi et in carne et in Domino? |
| 17. If thou count me therefore a partner, receive him as myself. | 17. Si igitur me habes consortem, suscipe eum tanquam me. |
| 18. If he hath wronged thee, or oweth *thee* aught, put that on mine account; | 18. Si verò qua in re te læsit, vel aliquid debet, id mihi imputa. |
| 19. I Paul have written *it* with mine own hand, I will repay *it*: albeit I do not say to thee how thou owest unto me even thine own self besides. | 19. Ego Paulus scripsi mea manu, ego solvam, ut ne dicam tibi, quòd et te ipsum mihi debes. |

15. *For perhaps he was separated.* If we are angry on account of offences committed by men, our minds ought to be soothed, when we perceive that those things which were done through malice have been turned to a different end by the purpose of God. A joyful result may be regarded as a remedy for evils, which is held out to us by the hand of God for blotting out offences. Thus Joseph—when he takes into consideration, that the wonderful providence of God brought it about, that, though he was sold as a slave, yet he was elevated to that high rank, from which he could provide food for his brethren and his father—forgets the treachery and cruelty of his brethren, and says, that he was sent before on their account. (Gen. xlv. 5.)

Paul therefore reminds Philemon that he ought not to be so greatly offended at the flight of his slave, for it was the cause of a benefit not to be regretted. So long as Onesimus was at heart a runaway, Philemon, though he had him in his house, did not actually enjoy him as his property; for he was wicked and unfaithful, and could not be of real advantage. He says, therefore, that he was a wanderer for a little time, that, by changing his place, he might be converted and become a new man. And he prudently softens everything, by calling the flight a departure, and adding, that it was only *for a time.*

*That thou mightest receive him for ever.* Lastly, he contrasts the perpetuity of the advantage with the short duration of the loss.

16. *But above a servant, a beloved brother.* He next brings

forward another advantage of the flight, that Onesimus has not only been corrected by means of it, so as to become a useful slave, but that he has become the " brother" of his master.

*Especially to me.* Lest the heart of Onesimus, wounded by the offence which was still fresh, should be reluctant to admit the brotherly appellation, Paul claims Onesimus first of all, as his own " brother." Hence he infers that Philemon is much more closely related to him, because both of them had the same relationship in the Lord according to the Spirit, but, according to the flesh, Onesimus is a member of his family. Here we behold the uncommon modesty of Paul, who bestows on a worthless slave the title of a brother, and even calls him a dearly beloved brother to himself. And, indeed, it would be excessive pride, if we should be ashamed of acknowledging as our brother those whom God accounts to be his sons.

*How much more to thee.* By these words he does not mean that Philemon is higher in rank according to the Spirit; but the meaning is, " Seeing that he is especially a brother to me, he must be much more so to thee; for there is a twofold relationship between you."

We must hold it to be an undoubted truth, that Paul does not rashly or lightly (as many people do) answer for a man of whom he knows little, or extol his faith before he has ascertained it by strong proofs; and therefore in the person of Onesimus there is exhibited a memorable example of repentance. We know how wicked the dispositions of slaves were, so that scarcely one in a hundred ever came to be of real use. As to Onesimus, we may conjecture from his flight, that he had been hardened in depravity by long habit and practice. It is therefore uncommon and wonderful virtue to lay aside the vices by which his nature was polluted, so that the Apostle can truly declare that he has now become another man.

From the same source proceeds a profitable doctrine, that the elect of God are sometimes brought to salvation by a method that could not have been believed, contrary to general expectation, by circuitous windings, and even by labyrinths. Onesimus lived in a religious and holy family, and, being banished from it by his own evil actions, he deliberately, as it were, withdraws far from God and from eternal life. Yet God, by hidden providence, wonderfully directs his pernicious flight, so that he meets with Paul.

17. *If, therefore, thou holdest me to be thy associate.* Here he lowers himself still further, by giving up his right and his honour to a runaway, and putting him in his own room, as he will shortly afterwards offer himself to be his cautioner. He reckoned it to be of vast importance that Onesimus should have a mild and gentle master, that immoderate severity might not drive him to despair. That is the object which Paul toils so earnestly to accomplish. And his example warns us how affectionately we ought to aid a sinner who has given us proof of his repentance. And if it is our duty to intercede for others, in order to obtain forgiveness for those who repent, much more should we ourselves treat them with kindness and gentleness.

18. *If in any thing he hath done thee injury.* Hence we may infer that Onesimus had likewise stolen something from his master, as was customary with fugitives; and yet he softens the criminality of the act, by adding, *or if he oweth thee anything.* Not only was there a bond between them recognised by civil law, but the slave had become indebted to his master by the wrong which he had inflicted on him. So much the greater, therefore, was the kindness of Paul, who was even ready to give satisfaction for a crime.

19. *Not to tell thee that thou owest to me thyself.* By this expression he intended to describe how confidently he believes that he will obtain it; as if he had said, "There is nothing that thou couldest refuse to give me, even though I should demand thyself." To the same purpose is what follows about lodging and other matters, as we shall immediately see.

There remains one question. How does Paul—who, if he had not been aided by the churches, had not the means of living sparingly and frugally — promise to pay money? Amidst such poverty and want this does certainly appear to be a ridiculous promise; but it is easy to see that, by this form of expression, Paul beseeches Philemon not to ask anything back from his slave. Though he does not speak ironically, yet, by an indirect figure, he requests him to blot out and cancel this account. The meaning, therefore, is—"I wish that thou shouldest not contend with thy slave, unless thou choosest to have me for thy debtor in his stead." For he immediately adds that Philemon is altogether his own; and he who claims the whole man as his property, need not give himself uneasiness about paying money.

| | |
|---|---|
| 20. Yea, brother, let me have joy of thee in the Lord: refresh my bowels in the Lord. | 20. Certè frater, ego te fruar in Domino: refocilla mea viscera in Domino. |
| 21. Having confidence in thy obedience, I wrote unto thee, knowing that thou wilt also do more than I say. | 21. Persuasus de tua obedientia scripsi tibi, sciens etiam, quòd supra id, quod scribo, facturus sis. |
| 22. But withal prepare me also a lodging: for I trust that through your prayers I shall be given unto you. | 22. Simul verò præpara mihi hospitium; spero enim quòd etiam per vestras precationes donabor vobis. |
| 23. There salute thee Epaphras, my fellow-prisoner in Christ Jesus; | 23. Salutant te Epaphras concaptivus meus in Christo Iesu: |
| 24. Marcus, Aristarchus, Demas, Lucas, my fellow-labourers. | 24. Marcus, Aristarchus, Demas, Lucas, cooperarii mei. |
| 25. The grace of our Lord Jesus Christ be with your spirit. Amen. | 25. Gratia Domini nostri Iesu Christi cum spiritu vestro. Amen. |
| Written from Rome to Philemon by Onesimus a servant. | Ad Philemonem missa fuit e Roma per Onesimum servum. |

20. *Yea, brother.* This affirmation is used in order to increase the ardour of the exhortation; as if he had said—"Now shall it be clearly proved that there hath been no variance between thee and me, but that, on the contrary, thou art sincerely attached to me, and that all that thou hadst is at my disposal, if thou pardon offences and receive into favour him who is so closely related to me."

*Refresh my bowels in the Lord.* He again repeats the same form of expressions which he had previously employed. Hence we infer that the faith of the gospel does not overturn civil government, or set aside the power and authority which masters have over slaves. For Philemon was not a man of the ordinary rank, but a fellow-labourer of Paul in cultivating Christ's vineyard; and yet that power over a slave which was permitted by the law is not taken away, but he is only commanded to receive him kindly by granting forgiveness, and is even humbly besought by Paul to restore him to his former condition.

When Paul pleads so humbly in behalf of another, we are reminded how far distant they are from true repentance who obstinately excuse their vices, or who, without shame and without tokens of humility, acknowledge indeed that they have sinned, but in such a manner as if they had never sinned. When Onesimus saw so distinguished an apostle of Christ plead so eagerly in his behalf, he must undoubtedly have been much more humbled, that he might bend the heart of his master to be merciful to him. To the same purpose is the excuse which he offers (ver. 21) for writing so boldly, because he knew that Philemon would do more than he had been requested.

21. *But at the same time prepare for me a lodging.* This confidence must have powerfully excited and moved Philemon; and next, he holds out to him the hope of being gratified by his own arrival. Although we do not know whether or not Paul was afterwards released from prison, yet there is no absurdity in this statement, even though he was disappointed of the hope which he cherished about God's temporal kindness. He had no confident hope of his release, further than if it pleased God. Accordingly, he always kept his mind in suspense, till the will of God was made known by the result.

*That through your prayers I shall be given to you.* Here it deserves notice, that he says that everything that believers obtain " through their prayers," is " given" to them; for hence we infer that our prayers, though they are not unsuccessful, yet have no power through their own merit; for what is yielded to them is of free grace.

24. *Demas.* This is the same person who afterwards for-

sook him, as he complains in the Second Epistle to Timothy (iv. 10.) And if one of Paul's assistants, having become weary and discouraged, was afterwards drawn aside by the vanity of the world, let no man reckon too confidently on the zeal of a single year; but, considering how large a portion of the journey still remains to be accomplished, let him pray to God for steadfastness.

END OF THE COMMENTARIES ON THE
EPISTLE TO PHILEMON.

# TRANSLATION

OF

## CALVIN'S VERSION

OF

# THE EPISTLES TO TIMOTHY, TITUS, AND PHILEMON.

A TRANSLATION OF CALVIN'S VERSION

OF THE

# FIRST EPISTLE OF PAUL TO TIMOTHY.

## CHAPTER I.

1 PAUL, an apostle of Jesus Christ, according to the appointment of God our Saviour, and of the Lord Jesus Christ our
2 hope; to Timothy my own son in the faith, grace, mercy, peace, from God our Father, and our Lord Jesus Christ.
3 As I besought thee to remain at Ephesus, when I set out for Macedonia, I wish that thou shouldst charge some not to teach
4 differently;[1] and not to give heed to fables and to genealogies that have no end, which produce questions rather than the edification of God, which consisteth in faith.
5 Now, the end of the commandment is love, out of a pure
6 heart, and of a good conscience, and of faith unfeigned; from which some, having gone astray, have turned aside to idle talk-
7 ing, wishing to be teachers of the law, not understanding what
8 they say, nor concerning what things they affirm. But we know
9 that the law is good, if one use it lawfully; knowing this, that the law is not made for the righteous man, but for the unrighteous and disobedient, for the ungodly and for sinners, for the unholy and profane, for murderers of fathers and murderers
10 of mothers, for manslayers, for fornicators, for sodomites, for robbers, for liars, for perjurers, and if there be anything else
11 that is contrary to sound doctrine; according to the gospel of the glory of the blessed God, which hath been intrusted to me.
12 And I give thanks to our Lord Jesus Christ, who hath made me powerful, because he reckoned me faithful, by putting me
13 into the ministry; who was formerly a blasphemer and a persecutor, and an oppressor, but I obtained mercy, because I did
14 it ignorantly in unbelief. And the grace of our Lord aboundeth beyond measure, with faith and love, which is in Christ Jesus.
15 It is a faithful saying, and worthy of being fully accepted, that Christ Jesus came into the world, to save sinners, of whom I am

[1] "Autrement, ou, diverse doctrine." "Differently, or, different doctrine."

16 the first; but for this cause I obtained mercy, that in me the first, Jesus Christ might show all compassion, for a pattern to
17 those who should believe in him to eternal life. Now to the King eternal, immortal, invisible, the only wise God, (be) honour and glory for ever and ever. Amen.
18 This commandment I recommend to thee, son Timothy, according to the prophecies which went before concerning thee,
19 that by them thou mayest war a good warfare; holding faith and a good conscience, from which some, having turned aside
20 concerning faith, have made shipwreck; of whom are Hymenæus and Alexander, whom I have delivered to Satan, that they may learn not to blaspheme.

## CHAPTER II.

1 I exhort therefore, that, above all, supplications, entreaties,
2 intercessions, and thanksgivings, be made for all men; for kings, and for all who are placed in authority, that we lead a peace-
3 ful and quiet life, with all godliness and decency; for this is
4 good and acceptable before God our Saviour; who wishes that all men may be saved and come to the knowledge of the truth.
5 For there is one God, and one Mediator between God and men,
6 the man Christ Jesus, who gave himself the price of redemption
7 for all, (that there might be) a testimony in due time; for which I have been appointed a herald and an apostle, (I speak the truth in Christ, I lie not,) a teacher of the Gentiles in faith and truth.
8 I wish therefore that men may pray in every place, lifting
9 up pure hands, without wrath and disputing. In like manner also that women adorn themselves in decent apparel, with modesty and sobriety, not with plaited hair, or gold, or pearls,
10 or costly raiment; but (which becometh women professing
11 godliness) by good works. Let the woman learn in silence with
12 all subjection. But I suffer not the woman to teach, nor to
13 assume authority over the man, but to be silent. For Adam
14 was first created, then Eve. And Adam was not deceived; but
15 the woman, being deceived, was guilty of the trangression. Yet she shall be saved through child-bearing, if they continue in faith, and love, and sanctification, with sobriety.

## CHAPTER III.

1 It is a true saying, If a man desireth the office of a bishop, he
2 desireth an excellent work. A bishop, therefore, must be blameless, the husband of one wife, sober, temperate, modest,
3 hospitable, able to teach; not addicted to wine, not a striker,

not wickedly desirous of gain, but mild, not quarrelsome, not
4 covetous ; who ruleth well his own house, who hath his children
5 in subjection with all reverence. (And if a man know not
how to rule his own house, how shall he take charge of the
6 church of God?) Not a novice, lest, being swelled with pride,
7 he fall into condemnation of the devil. He must also have a
good report from those who are without, lest he fall into reproach and the snare of the devil.
8 In like manner, the deacons must be grave, not doubletongued, not given to much wine, not wickedly desirous of
9 gain; holding the mystery of faith in a pure conscience.
10 And let these be first tried, next let them minister when they
11 have been found blameless. In like manner, their wives must
12 be grave, not slanderers, sober, faithful in all things. Let the
deacons be husbands of one wife, who rule their children and
13 their houses in a becoming manner; for they who have served
well procure for themselves a good (or, honourable) degree, and
much liberty in the faith which is in Christ Jesus.
14 These things I write to thee, hoping to come to thee soon ;
15 and, if I shall delay, that thou mayest see how thou oughtst
to conduct thyself in the house of God ; which is the Church
16 of the living God, the pillar and foundation of truth. And,
without controversy, great is the mystery of godliness; God
was manifested in the flesh, seen by angels, preached to the
Gentiles, obtained belief in the world, was received into glory.

## CHAPTER IV.

1 Now, the Spirit plainly saith, that, in the latter times, some
will revolt from the faith, giving heed to deceiving spirits and
2 to doctrines of devils ; speaking lies in hypocrisy, having their
3 conscience seared with a hot iron ; forbidding to enter into
marriages, commanding to abstain from some kinds of food,
which God hath created to be received with thanksgiving by
4 believers, and by those that know the truth ; because every
creature of God is good, and nothing is to be rejected which is
5 received with thanksgiving ; for it is sanctified by the word of
God and prayer.
6 Exhibiting these things to the brethren, thou shalt be a good
minister of Jesus Christ, nourished by the words of faith, which
7 thou hast followed.[1] But avoid profane and old women's fables,
8 and, on the contrary, exercise thyself to godliness. For bodily
exercise is of little profit; but godliness is profitable for all
things, having the promises of the present life, and of that

---

[1] " Que tu as soigneusement suivie." " Which thou hast carefully followed."

9, 10 which is to come. It is a faithful saying, and worthy of being cordially embraced. For in this we both labour and suffer reproaches, because we have hope fixed on the living God, who is the Saviour of all men, especially of believers.

11, 12 Instruct and teach these things. Let no man despise thy youth; but be thou an example of the believers, in word,
13 in conversation, in love, in spirit, in faith, in chastity. Till I come, apply thyself to reading, to exhortation, to doctrine.
14 Neglect not the gift which is in thee, which was given to thee by prophecy with the laying on of the hands of the presbytery.
15, 16 Take heed to these things; give attention to them, that thy profiting may be manifest to all men, (or, *in all things*.) Give heed to thyself, and to the doctrine; continue in them; for, if thou shalt do this, thou shalt both save thyself and them that hear thee.

## CHAPTER V.

1 Do not harshly rebuke an elder, but exhort him as a father,
2 the younger as brethren; the older women as mothers; the younger as sisters, with all chastity.
3, 4 Honour widows that are really widows. Now, if any widow hath children or grandchildren, let them learn first to exercise piety toward their own house, and to requite their
5 parents; for this is good and acceptable before God. Now, she who is really a widow and desolate hopeth in God, and
6 continueth in prayers and supplications night and day. But she who spendeth her time in luxury is dead while she liveth.
7, 8 And enjoin these things, that they may be blameless. And if any person do not provide for his own, and especially for those of his own household, he hath denied the faith, and is worse than an infidel.
9, 10 Let a widow be chosen, not under sixty years of age, who hath been the wife of one man; having attestation for good works, if she hath brought up children, if she hath been hospitable, if she hath washed the feet of the saints, if she hath relieved the
11 afflicted, if she hath been diligent in every good work. But refuse younger widows; for, when they have begun to be wan-
12, 13 ton against Christ, they wish to be married; having condemnation, because they have renounced their first faith. And at the same time, being idle, they learn to go about from house to house; and not only are idle, but also tattlers and busybodies, speaking things which they ought not.
14 I wish the younger (widows), therefore, to be married, to bear children, to take charge of the house, to give no occasion
15, 16 to the adversary, that he may have ground for slandering; for some have already turned aside after Satan. And if any be-

lieving man or believing woman hath widows, let him or her relieve them; and let not the church be burdened, that it may relieve those who are really widows.

17 Let the elders[1] that rule well be reckoned worthy of double honour, especially those who labour in word and doctrine.
18 For the scripture saith, Thou shalt not muzzle the ox that treadeth out the corn, (Deut. xxv. 4,) and, The labourer is
19 worthy of his hire. (Matt. x. 10.) Against an elder receive
20 not an accusation, unless by two or three witnesses. Those that sin rebuke in presence of all,[2] that others also may fear.
21 I adjure thee before God, and the Lord Jesus Christ, and the elect angels, that thou observe these things without hastiness of judgment, doing nothing by turning to this side or that.
22 Lay not hands suddenly on any man, neither partake of other
23 men's sins; keep thyself pure. No longer drink water, but use a little wine on account of thy stomach, and of thy frequent ill health.
24 The sins of some men are visible beforehand, hastening to
25 judgment; and in some they follow after. In like manner, also, the good works are visible beforehand; and those that are otherwise cannot be concealed.

## CHAPTER VI.

1 Let all who are slaves under the yoke reckon their own masters worthy of all honour, that the name of God and his
2 doctrine may not be blasphemed. And they who have believing masters, let them not despise them because they are brethren; but let them serve so much the more, because they are believers and beloved, and partakers of the benefit. These things teach and exhort.
3 If any man teacheth otherwise (*or, other things*), and consenteth not to the healthful words of our Lord Jesus Christ,
4 and to that doctrine which is according to godliness, he is puffed up, knowing nothing, but sickening after questions and debates of words, out of which spring envy, strife, slanders,
5 unfounded suspicions, useless disputes of men corrupt in understanding, and that are destitute of the truth, thinking that gain is godliness. Withdraw thyself from such.
6, 7 But godliness with sufficiency[3] is great gain. For we brought nothing into the world; it is certain that neither can
8 we carry anything out. And having food and raiment, we

---

[1] "Les prestres ou anciens." "The presbyters or elders."
[2] "Repren publiquement." "Rebuke publicly."
[3] "Avec suffisance, ou, contentement." "With sufficiency, or, with contentment."

9 shall be content with these. For they who wish to be rich fall
into temptation and a snare, and into numerous and hurtful
10 follies, which plunge men into ruin and destruction. For the
root of all evils is avarice, which some eagerly desiring, have
gone astray from the faith, and have entangled themselves
with many sorrows.
11 But thou, O man of God, flee these things, and follow after
12 righteousness, piety, faith, love, patience, meekness. Fight
the good fight of faith; lay hold on eternal life, to which also
thou art called, and hast confessed a good confession before
many witnesses.
13 I charge (*or, command*) thee before God, who quickeneth all
things, and before Christ Jesus, who testified a good confession
14 before Pontius Pilate, that thou keep the commandment without spot and unblameably, till the revelation of our Lord Jesus
15 Christ; which shall be manifested in due season by the blessed
16 and only Prince, the King of kings, and Lord of lords, who
alone hath immortality, who inhabiteth unapproachable light,
whom no man hath seen or can see, to whom be honour and
everlasting power (*or, everlasting dominion*). Amen.
17 Command (*or, charge*) those who are rich, that they be not
haughty, nor hope in the uncertainty of riches, but in the living
18 God, who supplieth all things abundantly for enjoyment; to
do good, to be rich in good works, ready to distribute (*or, to*
19 *bestow*), willingly imparting, laying up for themselves a good
foundation for the future, that they may lay hold on eternal
life.
20 O Timothy, guard that which is committed to thee, avoiding
profane vanities of noises, idle talking, and contradictions of
science falsely so called, which some professing, have erred concerning the faith. Grace (be) with thee. Amen.

The first (Epistle) to Timothy was sent from Laodicea,
which is the chief city of Phrygia Pacatiana.

A TRANSLATION OF CALVIN'S VERSION

OF THE

# SECOND EPISTLE OF PAUL TO TIMOTHY.

### CHAPTER I.

1 PAUL, an apostle of Jesus Christ by the will of God, accord-
2 ing to the promise of life, which is in Christ Jesus, to Timothy, my beloved son,[1] grace, mercy, peace, from God the Father, and from Christ Jesus our Lord.
3 I give thanks to God, whom I worship from my ancestors, in a pure conscience, as I make continual mention of thee in
4 my prayers night and day, desiring to see thee, being mind-
5 ful of thy tears, that I may be filled with joy; calling to remembrance that unfeigned faith which is in thee, which dwelt first in thy grandmother Lois, and in thy mother Eunice, and I am persuaded that (it dwelleth) in thee also.[2]
6 For which cause I advise thee to stir up the gift of God,
7 which is in thee, by the laying on of my hands; for God hath not given to us a spirit of cowardice, but of power, and of love, and
8 of soberness. Be not ashamed, therefore, of the testimony of our Lord, nor of me, who am his prisoner; but be thou a partaker of the afflictions of the gospel, according to the power
9 of God; who hath saved us and hath called us with a holy calling; not according to our works, but according to his pur-
10 pose and grace, which was given to us in Christ Jesus before eternal ages, but hath now been revealed by the appearing of our Saviour Jesus Christ, who hath indeed destroyed death, and hath brought to light life and immortality by the gos-
11 pel, to which I have been appointed a herald, and an apostle,
12 and a teacher of the Gentiles; for which cause also I suffer these things, but I am not ashamed; for I know whom I have believed, and am persuaded that he is able to keep what I have intrusted to him till that day.
13 Hold the form of sound words, which thou hast heard from

[1] " Mon tres-cher fils."  " My dearly-beloved son."
[2] " Et suis certain qu'en toy aussi."  " And am certain that in thee also."

14 me, in faith and love which is in Christ Jesus. Guard the excellent thing committed to thee by the Holy Spirit, who dwelleth in us.
15 Thou knowest this, that all that are in Asia have forsaken
16 me; of whom are Phygellus and Hermogenes. May the Lord grant mercy to the family of Onesiphorus; for he often re-
17 freshed me, and was not ashamed of my chain; but when he was in Rome, he sought me out diligently, and found me.
18 May the Lord grant to him that he may find mercy with the Lord on that day; and how many things he ministered to me at Ephesus, thou knowest well.[1]

## CHAPTER II.

1 Thou therefore, my son, be strong in the grace which is in
2 Christ Jesus. And what things thou hast heard from me by many witnesses, these commit thou to believing men, who shall
3 be able to teach others also. Do thou therefore endure afflic-
4 tions, as a good soldier of Jesus Christ. No man who warreth entangleth himself with the affairs of life, that he may please
5 his general. And if any one also strive, he is not crowned, un-
6 less he strive lawfully. The husbandman must labour before
7 he receive the fruits. Understand what I say; and may the Lord give thee understanding in all things!
8 Remember that Jesus Christ, of the seed of David, hath been
9 raised from the dead, according to my gospel; in which I am a sufferer, as an evil-doer, even to bonds, but the word of God is
10 not bound. Wherefore I endure all things for the sake of the elect, that they also may obtain the salvation which is in Christ Jesus
11 with eternal glory. It is a faithful saying; for if we die with
12 him, we shall also live with him; if we suffer, we shall also
13 reign with him;[2] if we deny him,[3] he will also deny us; if we are unbelieving, he remaineth faithful; he cannot deny himself.
14 Remind them of these things, solemnly charging them before the Lord not to dispute about words, for no use, (but) for
15 the subversion of the hearers. Study to shew thyself to be approved by God, a workman that doth not blush, dividing aright
16 the word of truth. But avoid profane and unmeaning noises;
17 for they will grow to greater ungodliness. And their word will eat as a gangrene; of the number of whom are Hymenæus and

---

[1] "Et tout ce en quoy il m'a servi en Ephese tu le cognois tres-bien." "And all that in which he served me at Ephesus thou knowest very well."
[2] "Avec luy."
[3] "Si nous le renions."

18 Philetus, who concerning the truth have erred, saying that the resurrection is already past, and subvert the faith of some.
17 Nevertheless, the foundation of God standeth firm, having this seal, The Lord knoweth who are his, and, Let every one that
20 calleth on the name of Christ depart from iniquity. Now, in a great house there are not only vessels of gold and silver, but also of wood and of earth; and some to honour and some to dis-
21 honour. If any one, therefore, shall cleanse himself from these, he shall be a vessel sanctified for honour, and useful for the Lord, being prepared for every good work.
22 Flee youthful desires; but follow righteousness, faith, love,
23 peace, with all that call on the Lord out of a pure heart. But avoid foolish and uninstructive questions, knowing that they
24 beget quarrels. But the servant of the Lord must not fight, but must be gentle towards all, qualified for teaching, patient
25 to the bad, instructing (*or, chastising*) those who resist, if some time God give to them repentance for the acknowledgment of
26 the truth, and deliverance (*or, return to a sound mind*) from the snare of the devil, by whom they are held captive at his will.

## CHAPTER III.

1 But know this, that in the last days there will arise danger-
2 ous (*or, troublesome*) times. For men will be lovers of themselves, covetous, proud, slanderers, disobedient to parents,
3 unthankful, unholy; without natural affection,[1] covenant-breakers, false accusers, intemperate, fierce, despisers of those
4 that are good; traitors, rash, haughty, lovers of pleasures
5 rather than of God; having a form of godliness, while they
6 deny the power of it. Turn away from those persons; for of those are they who creep into families, and lead captive silly women laden with sins, who are led away by various sinful
7 desires; always learning, while yet they never can come to the knowledge of the truth.
8 And as Jannes and Jambres resisted Moses, so do these also resist the truth, men corrupted in understanding, reprobate
9 concerning the faith. But they shall not proceed further; for the madness of the latter shall be manifest to all, as was also
10 that of the former. But thou hast closely followed my doctrine, instruction,[2] purpose, faith, meekness, love, patience;
11 persecutions, afflictions, which befell me at Antioch, at Iconium, at Lystra; what persecutions I endured; but out of

---

[1] "Sans affection naturelle."
[2] "Mon institution, ou, ma conduite, ou, ma maniere de faire." "My instruction, or, my conduct, or, my manner of acting."

12, 13 them all the Lord delivered me. And all who wish to live a godly life in Christ Jesus shall suffer persecution. But wicked men and impostors will grow worse and worse, going astray, and leading others astray.

14 But as for thee, continue in those things which thou hast learned, and which have been intrusted to thee, knowing from
15 whom thou hast learned them; and that from (thy) childhood thou hast known the holy scriptures, which are able to make thee wise to salvation, through faith which is in Christ Jesus.
16 All scripture (*or, the whole of scripture*) is divinely inspired, and is profitable for doctrine, for reproof, for correction, for instruc-
17 tion, which is in righteousness; that the man of God may be perfect, being made ready for every good work.

## CHAPTER IV.

1 I adjure thee, therefore, before God and the Lord Jesus Christ, who shall judge the living and the dead, at his appear-
2 ing and his kingdom. Preach the word; apply thyself in season, out of season; reprove, rebuke, exhort, with all gentle-
3 ness and doctrine. For there will be a time, when they will not endure sound doctrine, but, having itching ears, shall heap
4 up to themselves according to their sinful desires; and they shall turn away their ears from the truth, and shall be turned to fables.
5 But watch thou in all things, endure afflictions, do the work
6 of an evangelist, render thy ministry approved. For I am now offered as a sacrifice, and the time of my dissolution is at
7 hand. I have fought the good fight, I have finished the course,
8 I have kept the faith. Henceforth there is laid up for me the crown of righteousness, which the Lord, the righteous Judge, will render to me on that day, and not to me only, but likewise to all who love his coming.
9, 10 Make haste to come to me quickly. For Demas hath forsaken me, having embraced this world, and is gone away to
11 Thessalonica, Crescens to Galatia, Titus to Dalmatia. Luke alone is with me. Take Mark, and bring him with thee; for
12 he is profitable to me for the ministry. And I have sent
13 Tychicus to Ephesus. When thou shalt come, bring the cloak which I left at Carpus, and the books, and the parchments.
14 Alexander the coppersmith hath done me many evil things;
15 may the Lord reward him according to his works! Of whom beware thou also; for he vehemently opposed our discourses.
16 At my first defence no man assisted me, but all forsook me;
17 may it not be laid to their charge! But the Lord assisted and

strengthened me, that through me the proclamation might be confirmed, and that all the Gentiles might hear; and I was
18 delivered out of the mouth of the lion. And the Lord will deliver me from every evil work, and will preserve me to his heavenly kingdom, to whom be glory for ever and ever! Amen.
19 Salute Prisca and Aquila, and the family of Onesiphorus.
20 Erastus remained at Corinth; but I left Trophimus at Mile-
21 tum sick. Make haste to come before winter. Eubulus salut-
22 eth thee, and Pudens, and Linus, and Claudia, and all the brethren. The Lord Jesus Christ (be) with thy spirit. Grace be with thee. Amen.

This Second (Epistle) was written from Rome to Timothy, who was the first bishop ordained at Ephesus, when Paul was brought the second time before Cæsar Nero.

# TRANSLATION OF CALVIN'S VERSION

OF THE

# EPISTLE OF PAUL TO TITUS.

## CHAPTER I.

1 PAUL, a servant of God, and an apostle of Jesus Christ, according to the faith of the elect of God, and (*or, that is,*) the
2 knowledge of that truth which is according to godliness; in the hope (*or, on account of the hope*) of eternal life, which God,
3 who cannot lie, promised before eternal ages; but hath manifested in his own times his word (*or, by his word,*) in the preaching which hath been committed to me, according to the
4 appointment of God our Saviour; to Titus, my own son, according to the common faith, grace, mercy, peace, from God the Father, and from the Lord Jesus Christ our Saviour.
5 For this reason I left thee in Crete, that thou mightest continue to correct those things which are still wanting,[1] and mightst ordain presbyters[2] in each city, as I appointed thee:
6 if any one is blameless, the husband of one wife, having believing children, not accused of licentiousness, not disobedient.
7 For a bishop ought to be blameless, as a governor of the house of God; not self-willed, not passionate, not given to wine, not
8 a striker, not wickedly desirous of gain; but hospitable, de-
9 voted to kindness, prudent, just, holy, temperate; holding fast the faithful word, which is according to instruction, that he may be able both to exhort by sound doctrine, and to convince adversaries.
10 For there are many unruly,[3] and vain talkers, and deceivers
11 of minds, chiefly they who are of the circumcision; whose mouth must be stopped, who overturn whole houses, teaching things which they ought not, for the sake of dishonest
12 gain. One of themselves, a prophet of their own, said, The
13 Cretans are always liars, evil beasts, lazy bellies. This testimony is true; wherefore rebuke them sharply, that they may

---

[1] "La cause pourquoy je t'ay laissé en Crete, C'est afin que tu poursuyves de corriger les choses qui restent." "The reason why I left thee in Crete, is in order that thou mayest continue to correct the things that are wanting."
[2] "Des prestres, ou anciens." "Presbyters, or elders."
[3] "Car il y en a plusieurs qui ne se peuvent ranger." "For there are many of them who cannot submit to authority."

14 be sound in the faith, and may not give heed to Jewish fables, and to commandments of men who turn aside from the truth.
15 To the pure all things indeed are pure; but to the polluted and unbelieving nothing is pure, but their mind and conscience
16 are polluted. They profess that they know God, but in works they deny him; for they are abominable, disobedient, and to every good work reprobate.

## CHAPTER II.

1 But speak thou the things which become sound doctrine;
2 that aged men be sober, grave, temperate, sound in faith, in
3 love, in patience; that aged women, in like manner, wear raiment which becomes religious persons, that they be not slanderers, not slaves to much wine, (that they be) teachers of
4 what is good; that they may teach the young women temper-
5 ance, to love their husbands and their children, to be temperate, chaste, keepers of the house, kind, subject to their husbands, that the word of God may not be evil spoken of.
6, 7 Exhort likewise younger men to be temperate; in all things shewing thyself a pattern of good works; in doctrine,
8 (shewing) integrity, gravity; sound speech, unblameable, that the adversary may be ashamed, having nothing evil to say of you.
9 Exhort servants to be subject to their own masters, endea-
10 vouring to please them in all things, not answering again; not thievish, but shewing all good faith, that they may adorn the doctrine of God our Saviour in all things.
11 For the grace of God hath appeared, bringing salvation to
12 all men, teaching us that, denying ungodliness and worldly desires, we should live temperately and righteously and piously, in
13 this world; looking for the blessed hope and the appearing of
14 Jesus Christ, the great God and our Saviour; who gave himself for us, that he might redeem us from all iniquity, and purify to himself a peculiar[1] people, zealous of good works.[2]
15 Speak these things, and exhort, and rebuke with all authority. Let no man despise thee.

## CHAPTER III.

1 Remind them to be subject to principalities and powers, to
2 obey magistrates, to be ready for every good work; to speak evil of no one, not to be given to fighting, (to be) kind, shew-

---

[1] "Ou, propre a luy." "Or, belonging to him."
[2] "Adonné a bonnes oeuvres." "Devoted to good works."

3 ing all meekness towards all men. For we ourselves were also formerly foolish, disobedient, going astray, serving various desires and pleasures, living in malice and envy, hateful,[1] and hating one another.
4 But after that the goodness and love of God our Saviour to-
5 wards men appeared, not by works, which were in righteousness, which we had done, but according to his mercy, he saved us, by the washing of regeneration and of the renewing of the
6 Holy Spirit, which (*or, whom*) he shed abundantly on us,
7 through Jesus Christ our Saviour, that, being justified by his grace, we might be made heirs according to the hope of eternal life.
8 A faithful saying: I wish thee to affirm these things, that they who have believed in God may be careful to excel in good works, (*or, to extol good works, or, to assign to them the*
9 *highest rank.*) For these things are honourable and profitable to men. But avoid foolish questions, and genealogies, and contentions, and fightings about the law; for they are unprofitable and unnecessary.
10 Avoid an heretical man after the first and second admonition;
11 knowing that he who is such is ruined, being condemned by himself.
12 When I shall send to thee Artemas, or Tychicus, hasten to come to me to Nicopolis; for I have determined to winter
13 there. Be careful to help forward Zenas the lawyer, and
14 Apollo, that they may not be in want of anything. And let ours also learn to excel in good works, (or, as formerly, *to assign to them the highest rank, that they may excel,*) for necessary uses, that they may not be unfruitful.
15 All who are with me salute thee. Salute those who love us in faith. Grace (be) with you all. Amen.

> It was written from Nicopolis of Macedonia, to Titus, who was ordained the first bishop of the Church of the Cretans.

[1] "Odieux, ou, hays." "Hateful or hated."

# A TRANSLATION OF CALVIN'S VERSION

OF THE

# EPISTLE OF PAUL TO PHILEMON.

1   PAUL, a prisoner of Jesus Christ, and Timothy a brother, to
2 Philemon our friend and fellow-labourer, and to Apphia the
  beloved, and to Archippus our fellow-soldier, and to the church
3 which is in thy house.   Grace (be) to you and peace from God
  our Father and the Lord Jesus Christ.
4   I give thanks to my God, making mention of thee always
5 in my prayers, hearing of thy love and faith, which thou hast
6 towards the Lord Jesus and towards all saints, that the communication of thy faith may be effectual, by the knowledge of
7 every good thing which is in thee towards Christ Jesus.   For
  we have much grace (*or, joy*) and consolation on account of thy
  love, because the bowels of the saints have been refreshed by
  thee, brother.
8   Wherefore, while I have great confidence in Christ to com-
9 mand thee what is proper, yet for love's sake I rather entreat
  thee; being such a one as Paul the aged (*or, elder,*) and now
10 also a prisoner of Jesus Christ.   I beseech thee for my son,
11 whom I have begotten in my bonds, Onesimus, who formerly
  was unprofitable to thee, but now is profitable both to thee and
12 to me; whom I have sent back; receive him therefore, that is,
13 my bowels; whom I was desirous to keep beside me, that he
  might minister to me instead of thee in the bonds of the gospel.
14   But without thy opinion I would do nothing, that thy benefit
15 might not be by constraint, but of free choice.   For perhaps
  for this reason he was separated for a time, that thou mightest
16 receive him for ever; not now as a slave, but above a slave,
  a beloved brother, especially to me, how much more to
17 thee, both in the flesh and in the Lord?   If therefore thou
18 holdest me to be thy associate, receive him as myself.   And if
  in anything he hath done thee injury, or oweth thee anything,
19 place it to my account.   I Paul have written it with my own
  hand, I will pay it; not to tell thee that thou owest me even
  thyself.

20 Yea, brother, let me enjoy thee[1] in the Lord; refresh my
21 bowels in the Lord. Being convinced of thy obedience, I have
written to thee, knowing that thou wilt do beyond what I write.
22 But at the same time prepare for me a lodging; for I hope
that through your prayers I shall be given to you.
23, 24 Epaphras, my fellow-prisoner in Christ Jesus, Marcus,
25 Aristarchus, Demas, Luke, my fellow-labourers, salute thee. The
grace of our Lord Jesus Christ (be) with your spirit. Amen.

It was sent from Rome to Philemon, by Onesimus a slave.

[1] "Ou, recoive ce plaisir de toy."  "Or, receive this pleasure from thee."

# TABLES AND INDEX

TO THE

COMMENTARIES ON THE EPISTLES

TO

TIMOTHY, TITUS, AND PHILEMON.

# TABLE I.

OF PASSAGES FROM THE HOLY SCRIPTURES WHICH ARE QUOTED, OR INCIDENTALLY ILLUSTRATED, IN THE COMMENTARIES ON THE EPISTLES TO TIMOTHY, TITUS, AND PHILEMON.

### GENESIS.

| Chap. | Ver. | Page |
|---|---|---|
| ii. | 21 | 69 |
|  | 24 | 78 |
| iii. | 16 | 68 |
|  | 22 | 70 |
| xix. | 24 | 206 |
| xxii. | 18 | 284 |
| xlv. | 5 | 356 |
| xlviii. | 16 | 228 |

### DEUTERONOMY.

| Chap. | Ver. | Page |
|---|---|---|
| viii. | 3 | 171 |
| xvii. | 6 | 140 |
| xxv. | 4 | 137 |
| xxx. | 11 | 86 |

### JUDGES.

| Chap. | Ver. | Page |
|---|---|---|
| iv. | 4 | 67 |

### 1 SAMUEL.

| Chap. | Ver. | Page |
|---|---|---|
| xvi. | 7 | 307 |

### 1 KINGS.

| Chap. | Ver. | Page |
|---|---|---|
| xxii. | 21-23 | 99 |

### 2 KINGS.

| Chap. | Ver. | Page |
|---|---|---|
| i. | 10 | 269 |

### PSALMS.

| Chap. | Ver. | Page |
|---|---|---|
| i. | 2 | 115 |
| ii. | 8, 10 | 55 |
|  | 12 | 53 |
| xviii. | 49 | 63 |
| xix. | 9 | 93 |
| xxxiv. | 5 | 168 |
|  | 10 | 158 |
| xxxvi. | 6 | 172 |
| li. | 5 | 93 |
|  | 6 | 144 |
| lxvii. | 5 | 63 |
| lxix. | 9 | 268 |
|  | 28 | 227 |
| civ. | 14 | 103 |
| cix. | 8 | 34 |
| cx. | 4 | 61 |
| cxvii. | 1 | 63 |
| cxxxix. | 1, 3 | 241 |

### ISAIAH.

| Chap. | Ver. | Page |
|---|---|---|
| iv. | 1 | 228 |
| xi. | 1 | 215 |
| xlii. | 1 | 280 |
| xlix. | 23 | 53 |
| lviii. | 7 | 349 |

### JEREMIAH.

| Chap. | Ver. | Page |
|---|---|---|
| v. | 3 | 307 |
| viii. | 7 | 122 |
| xxix. | 7 | 51 |

### EZEKIEL.

| Chap. | Ver. | Page |
|---|---|---|
| xxxiii. | 8 | 118 |
| xxxvi. | 25 | 231 |
|  | 25, 27 | 334 |

### DANIEL.

| Chap. | Ver. | Page |
|---|---|---|
| xii. | 3 | 150 |

## HAGGAI.

| Chap. | Ver. | Page |
|---|---|---|
| ii. | 11-14 | 307 |

## MALACHI.

| Chap. | Ver. | Page |
|---|---|---|
| i. | 11 | 64 |

## MATTHEW.

| Chap. | Ver. | Page |
|---|---|---|
| v. | 45 | 51, 103 |
| vi. | 11 | 105 |
|  | 20 | 172 |
| x. | 10 | 187 |
| xi. | 19 | 94 |
|  | 28 | 58 |
| xiii. | 25, 38 | 97 |
|  | 43 | 150 |
| xvi. | 18 | 199 |
| xviii. | 16 | 140 |
| xxiii. | 9 | 20 |
| xxv. | 15 | 173 |
|  | 18, 25 | 115 |
|  | 40 | 172 |

## LUKE.

| Chap. | Ver. | Page |
|---|---|---|
| i. | 74, 75 | 317 |
| ii. | 36 | 124 |
| vii. | 29 | 94 |
| ix. | 55 | 269 |
| xxi. | 19 | 210 |

## JOHN.

| Chap. | Ver. | Page |
|---|---|---|
| i. | 14 | 94 |
| v. | 22 | 148 |
| x. | 29 | 200 |
| xvi. | 13 | 282 |
| xvii. | 17 | 282 |

## ACTS.

| Chap. | Ver. | Page |
|---|---|---|
| i. | 8 | 198 |
| v. | 1 | 48 |
| vi. | 3 | 85 |
| ix. | 15 | 34 |
| xiii. | 6 | 48 |
| xv. | 9 | 27 |
| xvii. | 28 | 168 |
| xviii. | 18, 29 | 179 |
|  | 23 | 89 |
| xxiv. | 10 | 282 |
|  | 14 | 186 |

| Chap. | Ver. | Page |
|---|---|---|
| xxvi. | 1 | 282 |
|  | 6 | 183 |
|  |  | 186 |
| xxviii. | 20 | 186 |

## ROMANS.

| Chap. | Ver. | Page |
|---|---|---|
| i. | 3, 4 | 94 |
| iii. | 29 | 56 |
| iv. | 20, 21 | 201 |
| v. | 5 | 111 |
| vi. | 4 | 322 |
| vii. | 8 | 186 |
| viii. | 15 | 191 |
|  | 24 | 332 |
|  | 29 | 217 |
|  | 34 | 59 |
| ix. | 7 | 281 |
|  | 16 | 230 |
|  | 21 | 229 |
| x. | 17 | 60, 91, 354 |
| xi. | 33 | 42 |
| xii. | 7 | 296 |
| xv. | 9 | 63 |

## 1 CORINTHIANS.

| Chap. | Ver. | Page |
|---|---|---|
| i. | 2 | 64 |
| iii. | 6 | 284 |
| iv. | 7 | 330 |
|  | 15 | 20 |
| v. | 5 | 47 |
| vii. | 32 | 123 |
| ix. | 16, 17 | 286 |
|  | 24 | 211 |
|  | 25 | 213 |
| xii. | 3 | 99 |
|  | 28 | 47 |
| xiii. | 9-12 | 168 |
| xv. | 50 | 169 |

## 2 CORINTHIANS.

| Chap. | Ver. | Page |
|---|---|---|
| iii. | 5 | 75 |
| iv. | 10 | 218 |
| v. | 19 | 197 |
| ix. | 7 | 355 |

## GALATIANS.

| Chap. | Ver. | Page |
|---|---|---|
| iii. | 1 | 282 |
| iv. | 4 | 285 |
|  | 29 | 245 |

## EPHESIANS.

| Chap. | Ver. | Page |
|---|---|---|
| ii. | 2 | 235 |
|  | 3 | 144 |
| iii. | 18 | 92 |
| iv. | 2 | 152 |
|  | 11 | 118 |
| v. | 11 | 146 |

## PHILIPPIANS.

| Chap. | Ver. | Page |
|---|---|---|
| ii. | 7 | 93 |
|  | 12 | 118 |
| iii. | 6 | 40 |
|  | 12 | 162 |
|  | 16 | 342 |
| iv. | 8 | 227 |

## COLOSSIANS.

| Chap. | Ver. | Page |
|---|---|---|
| i. | 5 | 282 |
|  | 29 | 200 |
| ii. | 8 | 92 |
|  | 18 | 29, 58 |
|  | 21 | 109 |
| iv. | 17 | 848 |

## HEBREWS.

| Chap. | Ver. | Page |
|---|---|---|
| iv. | 15 | 57 |
| vii. | 17 | 61 |
| xii. | 9 | 20 |
| xiii. | 8 | 197 |

## 1 PETER.

| Chap. | Ver. | Page |
|---|---|---|
| iii. | 1 | 313 |

## 2 PETER.

| Chap. | Ver. | Page |
|---|---|---|
| ii. | 3 | 156 |
| iii. | 3 | 97 |

## 1 JOHN.

| Chap. | Ver. | Page |
|---|---|---|
| i. | 1, 2 | 286 |
| ii. | 19 | 227 |
| iii. | 2 | 169 |
|  |  | 197 |
| iv. | 1 | 99 |
| v. | 4 | 199 |

# TABLE II.

### OF GREEK WORDS EXPLAINED.

| | Page | | Page |
|---|---|---|---|
| ἀδιάλειπτον, | 185 | ἐπιταγή, | 323 |
| ἀδόκιμοι, | 308 | ἐπιφανείας, | 196, 321 |
| αἰών, | 284 | ἑτεροδιδασκαλεῖ, | 153 |
| αἰωνίων, | 284 | εὐσεβεῖν, | 122 |
| ἀνέγκλητον, | 76 | ἵνα, | 21 |
| ἀνεπίληπτον, | 76 | καλόν, | 73, 203 |
| ἀνόμους, | 31 | κάρκινος, | 224 |
| ἀντίλυτρον, | 60, 61 | κατά, | 289 |
| ἀντιπελαργία, | 122 | κοπιῶντα, | 212 |
| ἀνυποτακτοί, | 297 | κρῖμα, | 84 |
| ἀπειθεῖς, | 307, 327 | λογομαχεῖν, | 220 |
| ἀπέραντος, | 24 | λογομαχίας, | 155 |
| ἀστοχεῖν, | 28 | λύτρον, | 60, 61 |
| αὐθάδη, | 80 | ματαιολογία, | 28, 297 |
| ἀφιλάργυρον, | 81 | μελέτα, | 116 |
| ἀψευδής, | 285 | μῦθος, | 23 |
| βδελυκτοί, | 307 | νέκρωσις, | 224 |
| γάγγραινα, | 224 | νηφάλεος, | 78 |
| γυναικοκρατία, | 68 | ὀρεγόμενοι, | 160 |
| δεήσεις, | 50 | πάροινον, | 80 |
| διαβεβαιοῦσθαι, | 337 | παροίνῳ, | 81 |
| διαβόλου, | 84 | πᾶσιν, | 117 |
| διάκονοι, | 120 | περιεργίαν, | 161 |
| διδακτικός, | 233 | πόλις, | 289 |
| δύσκολα, | 73 | πραγματείαις, | 210 |
| εἰς, | 351 | πρεσβύτερος, | 137 |
| ἐμφατικώτερον, | 98 | προΐστασθαι, | 337 |
| ἐν, | 202 | προκρίμα, | 144 |
| ἐνθουσιασμούς, | 266 | προσευχαί, | 50 |
| ἐντεύξεις, | 50 | προσευχή, | 50 |
| ἐντρεφόμενος, | 107 | πρόσκλισιν, | 144 |
| ἐπανορθωτήν, | 289 | προφῆται, | 300 |
| ἐπί, | 283 | σεμνότης, | 311 |

# TABLE OF GREEK WORDS EXPLAINED.

| | Page | | Page |
|---|---|---|---|
| σοφιστικήν, | 156 | ὑπαλλαγή, | 195 |
| σπαταλῶσα, | 125 | ὑποτύπωσις, | 22, 202 |
| στοργαὶ φυσικαί, | 127 | φελόνη, | 265 |
| συμπάθειαν, | 326 | φιλάγαθον, | 295 |
| σφάκελος, | 224 | φιλαυτία, | 238 |
| σώφρονα, | 78 | φλυαρία, | 23 |
| σωφρονίζωσι, | 312 | χαράν, | 351 |
| σωφροσύνη, | 78, 319 | χάριν, | 351 |
| τὰ καλά, | 339 | χήρα, | 121 |
| τὸ ἀγαθόν, | 355 | χηραί, | 120 |
| ὑβριστήν, | 80 | χρήσιμον, | 221 |
| ὑδροποτεῖν, | 147 | | |

# INDEX.

**A**

AFFLICTIONS ought to be joyfully received, 218.
believers are not miserable in, 111.
mitigated by the prospect of their happy and joyful end, 243.
the gospel cannot be without, 193.
Aged men, the duties of, 310.
Aged women, the duties of, 311.
Alexander named along with Hymenæus, 47.
All, often denotes not all men, but all ranks and classes of men, 54, 57.
Ancestors, why Paul glories in following the religion of, 185.
Angels, why called elect, 143.
the sight of Christ drew the attention of, 94.
Apollonius, a fragment taken out of the writings of, 102.
Apostasy from the faith is a heinous crime, 98.
Appearing of Christ, the, and his kingdom mean the same thing, 252.
Apostle, why Paul affirms himself to be, 19.
how he confirms it, 20.
Apostles were made for the sake of publishing the gospel, 286.
the high honour of the office, 33.
Archippus, why called a fellow-soldier, 348.
Astray, metaphor taken from those who shoot with a bow, 28.
Austerity of life to be highly valued, 109.
Avarice is the root of all evils, 159.
is a destructive plague in teachers, 299.

**B**

BAPTISM, why it is called the washing of regeneration, 333.

Basil's discourse on the assistance to be derived from heathen authors, 301.
Believer, the house of a, ought to be like a little church, 83.
Believers should always have their eyes fixed on the future resurrection, 321.
are reminded of what they formerly were, 326.
should exercise themselves in good works, 338.
have a knowledge of sound doctrine, 104.
are not miserable in afflictions, 111.
pastors should be examples of, 113.
Believing men, so called on account of their pre-eminence in faith, 209.
Benedict Textor, a physician quoted by Calvin, 223.
Bishop, the meaning of the word, 75.
Bishop, the office of a, is excellent, and full of difficulty, 73, 74.
ought it to be desired? 74.
denotes the same office as the word pastor or elder, 75.
the weight and dignity of a, 89.
Bishops must be able to teach, 79.
this injunction disregarded by the Papists, 80.
must not be covetous, 81.
must rule their houses and children well, 82.
are enjoined to be hospitable, 79.
must be temperate, 80.
must lead a good and inoffensive life, 84.
ought to affirm strongly those things which edify godliness, 337.
ought to preach throughout their whole life, 313.
are elected principally for the sake of teaching, 295.

Bishops, what their children are required to be, 293.
    must be peaceable, 81.
    their families should be a model of honourable discipline, 292.
    should be blameless, 76.
Blasphemer, a, Paul had been, 35.
Blasphemy, how prevented by excommunication, 48.
Bondage of sin, the, Christ died to redeem us from, 322.
Brother, a, Christ held out to us the hand of, 57.
Bruno, the founder of the Carthusians, 148.

## C

CALL on the name of Christ, to, is to glory in his honourable title, 228.
Calling on the name of God, taken generally for worship, 232.
Calling of the gospel, the, is connected with the promise of eternal life, 183.
Cancer distinguished from gangrene, 224.
Captivity, the, of wicked men by the devil, is voluntary, 235.
Carthusians, so called from Chartreux, 148.
Celibacy, tyrannical law of the Papists concerning, 132.
    not to be enforced on pastors, 77.
    of nuns, produces monsters of crimes, 131.
Childbearing, how the woman shall be saved through, 71.
    how it is acceptable to God, 72.
Christ is the one Mediator between God and men, 56.
    is a man, but is also God, 57.
    was revealed at the appointed time, 61.
    why called our hope, 20.
    his sacrifice and intercession are the two parts of his priesthood, 60.
    distinction of the two natures of, 92.
    holds out to us the hand of a brother, 57.
    was received into glory, 95.
    died in order to redeem us from the bondage of sin, 322.
    the unity of the person of, 92.
    all who deny, are disowned by him, 219.
Christ, through him alone we are made partakers of the Spirit, 335.
    the attention of angels drawn by the sight of, 94.
    why eternal life is said to be in, 183.
    why grace is said to be in, 208.
    how was he justified? 93.
Christian doctrine, faith taken for the sum of, 107, 176.
Christian perfection, three parts included in, 311.
Church, the, is the pillar and foundation of truth, 89.
    defends and supports the truth, 90.
    is recognised by the lofty and conspicuous place which the truth of God holds in it, 91.
Committed, a thing, why the grace given to Paul is said to be, 173.
    sometimes denotes also the honour of the ministry, 203.
Condemnation of the devil, what is meant by the, 84.
Confession, a good, made not only in words but in actions, 163.
    testified by Christ, and why called good, 164.
Conscience, a good, consists of faith and truth, 63.
Conscience, a pure, cannot be separated from a hearty fear of God, 186.
Conscience, a bad, is the mother of all heresies, 46.
    is always accompanied by timidity, 88.
Contentment, reasons for, 158.
Cornelius Celsus, his distinction between cancer and gangrene, 224.
Cowardice, the spirit of, contrasted with the spirit of power, 191.

## D

DANGER of making holiness consist almost wholly in minute observances, 304.
    of making the smallest departure from sound doctrine, 299.
David, the seed of, denotes both the human nature of Christ, and his Messiahship, 214.
Deacons, a public office in the Church, 85.
    should be well instructed in the mystery of faith, 86.
    should be persons whose integrity has been tried, 87.

Deacons, among the Papists, immediately rise to the priesthood, 88.
Death of Christ, the, is one of the parts of his priesthood, 60.
Demas forsook Paul, and why? 264.
  mentioned with commendation in the Epistle to Philemon, 360.
Denial of Christ proceeds not only from weakness, but from unbelief, 218.
Devil, the, holds unconverted men captive, 235.
  what is meant by the condemnation of, 84.
  what is meant by the snare of, 85.
Devils, what are called doctrines of, 99.
Disobedient, why unbelievers are called, 307.
Distinction of the two natures of Christ, 92.
Doctrine, what is that which is according to godliness? 154.
  sound words contrasted with various kinds of, 202.
  exhortations and reproofs are merely aids to, 253.
  See *Sound Doctrine.*

E

EARNESTNESS recommended both to pastors and to the people, 253.
Edification consists in faith, 25.
  everything that does not tend to, is called idle talking, 28.
Edification of God, the, what is meant by, 24.
Elder synonymous with bishop and pastor, 75.
Elders, there are two kinds of, 138.
  must not be accused but by the testimony of two witnesses, 140.
  must not be harshly rebuked, 119.
Elect, the, are sometimes brought to God by a wonderful and unexpected method, 357.
Election, eternal, is the cause of faith, 280.
  metaphorically called the foundation of God, 226.
Encratites, an austere sect, 102.
Endless, why genealogies are called, 22.
Eternal life, was promised to men many ages ago, 284.
  the calling of the Apostle is connected with the promise of, 183.
  what it is to lay hold on, 162.
  why it is said to be in Christ, 183.
Eusebius quoted, 102.

Example of Paul, the, held out to Timothy, 243.
Excommunication, what are the intention and effect of, 48.
  how blasphemy is prevented by, 48.

F

FABLES, put for useless disputes, 23.
  for curious inquiries, 24.
  for subtleties that cannot edify, 108.
  for all trivial inventions, 304.
Faith contrasted with unbelief, 38.
  may be regarded as the mother of all the virtues, 40.
  the power of, exemplified, 200.
  taken for the sum of Christian doctrine, 107, 176.
  what is the actual trial of, 246.
  is the root of good works, 338.
  proved by its effects, 351.
  is the fruit of election, 280.
  what is meant by shipwreck of, 46.
  apostasy from, is a heinous crime, 98.
  why it is called knowledge, 282.
  love springs from, 27.
  put for fidelity, 316.
  connects the power of God with the word, 200.
  edification consists in, 25.
  the fight of, is good, and why? 161.
  deacons should be well instructed in the mystery of, 86.
Faithful, Paul had been accounted, 34.
Faithful saying, on what occasions Paul makes use of the phrase, 38, 337.
False apostles censured, 305.
Fanatics, who boast that public teaching is unnecessary for them, refuted, 251.
Fathers, in what sense Paul and other ministers of the Gospel are so called, 21.
Fear of God, the, a pure conscience cannot be separated from, 186.
  love is always accompanied by, 27.
Fellow-soldier, why Archippus was called, 348.
Fight of faith, the, is good, and why? 161.
Flesh, the, denotes that Christ was true man, 93.
Foolish, why unbelievers are called, 327.

Foolish, what questions are called, 339.
Foolish ornament, the teaching of the truth of God should be free from, 22.
Form of sound words, what is the, 201.
Foundation of God, the, a metaphorical term for eternal election, 226.
Free-will, warnings against the doctrine of, 208.
   refutation of the arguments in favour of, 230, 317.
Frivolous questions contrasted with sound doctrine, 32.

### G

GALEN, his definition of a cancer, 223.
Genealogies, why called endless, 24.
Gifts of God, the, should be diligently employed, 189.
Glory, Christ was received into, 95.
God, is the fountain of immortal life, 167.
   is called the Saviour, and why? 20.
   what is the edification of, 24.
Godliness, is profitable for both worlds, 108.
   what is the mystery of, 91.
   why the truth is said to be according to, 282.
   meditation is the beginning of the practice of, 283.
   put for the spiritual worship of God, 108.
   sound doctrine instructs men to, 309.
Good confession. See *Confession*.
Good works, faith is the root of, 338.
   believers should exercise themselves in, 338.
Goodness prompts God to love us, 330.
Gospel, the, is not opposed to the law, 32.
   is glorious, 33.
   had been promised in the Scriptures by the prophets, 285.
   all our hope lies in, 193.
   what are the chief things contained in, 286.
   was intrusted to Paul, 33.
   cannot be without afflictions, 193.
   why called the testimony of our Lord, 192.
   the apostles were made for the sake of publishing, 286.
   why Paul calls it "my gospel," 214.
Governor of the house of God, a bishop is a, 294.

Grace flows from mercy, 21, 184.
   the giving of, is nothing else than predestination, 195.
   two reasons why it is said to be in Christ Jesus, 208.
   was it given by the outward form of ordination? 190.
Grace put for joy, 351.
Grace of our Lord Jesus Christ, the, should be daily preached, 317.
Gratian, a Benedictine of the twelfth century, 142.

### H

HANDS, what is meant by the lifting up of the, 64.
Heathen authors, Basil's discourse on the assistance to be derived from, 301.
Herald, a, what is the duty of, 198.
Heretics should be avoided, 340.
Hermogenes and Phygellus were accounted infamous, 205.
Holy, why the calling is said to be, 194.
Holy Scriptures, the, are divinely inspired, 248.
   all our wisdom is contained in, 252.
   contain a perfect rule of a good and happy life, 249.
   should be read, not to gratify our fancies, but for edification, 250.
   should be perused with great diligence by pastors, 115, *note* 1.
Holy Spirit, the, through Christ alone we are made partakers of, 335.
Hope, why Christ is called our, 20.
Hospitality enjoined on bishops, 79.
House of God, the, women should conduct themselves with modesty in, 67.
Husbandmen do not gather the fruits till they have first toiled hard, 212.
Hymenæus had made shipwreck of faith, 47.
Hypocrisy, a word of very extensive meaning, 100.
Hypocrites, despise the chief part of religion, 307.
   deceive under a mask of piety, 238.

### I

IDLE talking contrasted with useful and solid doctrine, 297.
   put for everything that does not edify in godliness, 28.

Infidelity pollutes everything that the man touches, 307.
Infidels, they who do not support their families are worse than, 127.
Inspired, the Holy Scriptures are, 248.
Intercession of Christ, the, is one of the parts of his priesthood, 60.

## J

JANNES and Jambres appear to have been magicians, 240.
reasons why their history is brought forward, 241.
Joy, grace put for, 351.
Justification is the free gift of God, 336.
Justified, how Christ was, 93.

## K

KINGDOM of Christ, the, and his appearing, sometimes mean the same thing, 252.
Knowledge, faith in Christ is the most valuable, 250.
why faith is called, 282.

## L

LAST days, the, denote the universal condition of the Christian Church, 236.
the hardship of the times predicted in them consists in the depraved actions of men, 237.
yet these persons kept up some appearances of piety, 238.
Law of God, the, zealots are the greatest despisers of, 30.
the Gospel is not opposed to, 32.
Laying on of hands put for ordination, 145.
Living and the dead, the, who are meant by, 252.
Livy quoted, 23.
Logomachies forbidden, 155.
condemned on two grounds, 220.
Love springs from faith, 27.
relates to both tables of the law, 26.
is always accompanied by the fear of God, 27.
Love and soberness distinguish from the fury and rage of fanatics, 192.

## M

MAGISTRATES, the duty of subjection to, 324.

Manifested, the word shows that in Christ there are two natures, 93.
Marriage, the prohibition of, by Papists, 100.
Martyrs ought to be aided by every kind office, 355.
must all men be? 244.
Mediator between God and men, Christ is the only, 56.
foolish distinction between one Mediator and the only Mediator, 58.
Meditation is the beginning of true religion, 283.
Mercy, grace flows from, 21, 184.
Moderation is a necessary qualification for teaching, 234.
Monks, the Apostle gives a lively description of the order of, 239.
Mystery of faith, the, deacons should be well instructed in, 86.
Mystery of godliness, the, what is meant by, 91.

## N

NATURES of Christ, distinction of the two, 92.

## O

OBEDIENCE, the gospel presents us with the strongest motives to, 318, *note* 1.
Onesimus claimed by Paul as his own brother, 357.
Ordination, the laying on of hands put for, 145.
was grace given by the outward form of? 190.

## P

PAPISTS have no foundation for their prayers to dead men, and for the dead, 54.
do not acknowledge Christ to be the only Mediator, 58.
Papists, by making dead saints to be companions of Christ, transfer to them the glory of his priesthood, 61.
disregard the injunction that bishops shall be able to teach, 80.
the prohibition of marriage by, 100.

Pastors, meaning of the word, 75.
  ought to be well instructed in the knowledge of sound doctrine, 296.
  should be examples of believers, 113.
  should not give silent permission to wicked and dangerous doctrines, 298.
  ought to preach throughout their whole lives, 313.
  must fight as soldiers of Christ, 161.
  must avoid those things which are inconsistent with their office, 211.
  should be, not lazy disputants, but workmen, 222.
  why they are said to save the Church, 118.
  should laboriously peruse the word of God, 115, *note* 1.
  should zealously defend the doctrine of Christ, 255.
  should endeavour to draw disciples gently, 353.
  should diligently cultivate their talents, 117.
  should be careful to lead a holy and blameless life, 113.
  ought to have two voices, 296.
  should stand aloof from foolish contentions, 233.
Prayer should be offered for all men, 50.
  why it should be without wrath, 64.

## Q

Questions, uninstructive, must always be foolish, 232.
  and always produce quarrels, 233.
Questions of the scholastic divines not fitted to edify, 108.
Questions connected by the apostle with disputes about words, 155.
Quotation from Epimenides given in three languages, 300.

## R

Ransom, the name implies that the sufferings of Christ were vicarious, 61.
Regeneration is the beginning of salvation, 217.

Regeneration, meditation on the heavenly life begins with, 319.
  why baptism is called the washing of, 333.
Repentance is the gift and work of God, 234.
  begins with the knowledge of the truth, 235.
Reprobate, taken sometimes in an active signification, 308.
Reproofs are mere aids to doctrine, 253.
Resurrection of Christ, the, Satan labours to destroy this article of our faith, 213.
Resurrection of the dead, the, believers should always have their eyes fixed on, 321.
  declared by Hymenæus and Philetus to be already past, 225.
  the hope of, ought to render us active in doing good, 321.
Revelation of Christ, the, put for his second coming, 165.
  will be at the proper time, 166.
Rich, the, warned against proud and deceitful hope, 170.
  admonished to trust in the living God, 171.
Riches, what is the lawful use of, 172.

## S

Sadducees, the, confined their hope to this world, 283.
Salvation, begins with our regeneration, 217.
  proceeds from God alone, 118.
  already obtained by us, 332.
  completed by our perfect deliverance, 217.
Sanctification of all good things, what is meant by, 105.
Satan persecutes in various ways the servants of Christ, 244.
  never has any lack of the means of deceiving men, 256.
  to turn aside from Christ is to follow, 136.
  what is meant by being delivered to, 47.
Saviour, why God is called, 20, 111, 287.
Scholastic theology contains nothing but contentious or idle speculations, 24.
Science falsely so called, what is meant by, 175.

Scriptures. See *Holy Scriptures.*
Self-love is the source of many vices, 238.
Servant of God, the, should stand aloof from foolish contentions, 233.
 is ill qualified for teaching, if he have not moderation, 234.
Servants, the duties of, 315.
Shipwreck of faith, what is meant by, 46.
 Hymenæus and Alexander had made, 47.
Sinners denote trangressors of the second table, 32.
Slander, the propensity to, condemned, 325.
 a Christian man should give no occasion for, 315.
Slaves, their duties to their masters, 150.
 must not disobey their masters because they are brethren, 152.
Slothfulness, talkativeness produced by, 133.
Snare of the devil, the, what is meant by, 85.
Soldiers of Christ, pastors must fight as, 161.
Sophistry ought to be detested, 156.
Sophistical arguments of the Papists, about forbidding the eating of flesh, refuted, 305.
Sorbonne, the schools of, their pride and haughtiness, 29.
Sound doctrine, contrasted with frivolous questions, 32.
 can be maintained only by a good conscience, 45.
 all believers have a knowledge of, 104.
 instructs men to godliness, 309.
 all vices are contrary to, 32.
 means that which actually edifies souls, 309.
 consists of two parts, 310.
 pastors should be well instructed in the knowledge of, 296.
 the danger of making the smallest departure from, 299.
Sound words, what is the form of, 201.
 contrasted with various kinds of doctrine, 202.
Spirit sometimes denotes the Divine nature of Christ, 94.
Spirit of power, the, contrasted with the spirit of cowardice, 191.
Spiritual riches, the value of, 172.
Suetonius quoted, 23.

Sum of Christian doctrine, the, faith taken for, 107, 176.

T

TALKATIVENESS is produced by slothfulness, 133.
Tatian the founder of an austere sect, 101.
Teaching of the truth of God, the, should be free from foolish ornament, 22.
Temperance enjoined on bishops, 80.
 includes patience under it, 319.
Testimony of our Lord, the, why the gospel is called, 192.
Thanksgiving due to God for his benefits, 103.
That day, a lively description of Christ's second coming, 206.
Time, the appointed, for revealing the grace of Christ, 61.
Timidity, a bad conscience is always accompanied by, 88.
Timothy had enjoyed a godly education from his infancy, 187.
 what were the prophecies concerning, 43.
 the example of Paul held out to, 243.
 were his mother and grandmother Christians ? 187.
 why called by Paul his son, 20, 43.
Titus, the occasion of writing the Epistle to, 277.
 the care of organizing the Church was committed to, 288.
 why he is charged that no man shall despise him, 323.
Truth, the, the Church defends and supports, 90.
 a name often given to the heavenly doctrine, 282.
 repentance begins with the knowledge of, 235.
 why said to be according to godliness, 282.

U

UNBELIEF, faith contrasted with, 38.
Unbelievers, why called disobedient, 307.
Ungodliness, what is included in, 318.
Ungodly denotes trangressors of the first table, 32.
Uninstructive questions must always be foolish, 232.
Union of the Church, inconsistent with heresies and sects, 342.

## V

Vain talking condemned, 297.
Various, why sinful desires are called, 328.
Vessel sanctified for honour, what is meant by, 321.

## W

Warfare applies universally to all believers, but especially to Christian teachers, 44.
   why it is called good, 45.
   profane, compared with spiritual and Christian, 210.
Warriors, all who serve Christ are, 210.
Water forbidden to Timothy as an ordinary beverage, 147.
Weariness in the right course prevented by fixing the eyes on the future resurrection, 321.
Wicked men not excused by the captivity in which Satan holds them, 235.
Widows, rules for receiving, 121.
   ought to be honoured, 120.
Widows, not to be received under sixty years of age, 128.
   must have a good character for kindness and hospitality, 129.
Wives, reasons why they should be subject to their husbands, 68.
   of bishops and deacons, the duties of, 87.
Women must not teach publicly, 67.
   their dress should be regulated by modesty and sobriety, 66.
   should conduct themselves with modesty in the holy assembly, 67.
Word of God, the, remarkable applause bestowed on, 296.
   faith connects the power of God with, 200.
   all lawful enjoyments are connected with, 105.
   See *Holy Scriptures*.
World, the, Christ was believed by, 95.
Wrath, why prayer should be without, 64.

## Y

Youthful desires, what are meant by, 232.

www.ingramcontent.com/pod-product-compliance
Lightning Source LLC
Chambersburg PA
CBHW050611300426
44112CB00012B/1453